Beatriz Eisenhour

D1074135

Second Edition

Women's Basketball

Mildred J. Barnes

Central Missouri State University

ALLYN AND BACON, INC.
BOSTON • LONDON • SYDNEY • TORONTO

To Gretchen Schuyler and Helen McNaughton
who typify the quality of leadership needed by youth today

Library of Congress Cataloging in Publication Data

Barnes, Mildred J
    Women's basketball.

    (Allyn and Bacon sports education series)
    Bibliography
    Includes index.
    1. Basketball for women—Coaching.   I. Title.
GV886.B32 1980   796.32'38   79-15282
ISBN 0-205-06604-6

Printed in the United States of America.

Contents

Foreword

The Allyn and Bacon Sports Education Series

Arthur G. Miller, Consulting Editor

Chairman, Department of Movement, Health & Leisure, Boston University

Sports play a major role in the lives of almost everyone — players, coaches, officials, and spectators! Interest in sports is the result of several factors, including more time for leisure because of fewer working hours per week and more vacation periods.

There is an increased emphasis on *physical fitness,* demonstrated through greater participation in jogging, tennis, golf, skiing, and other lifetime sports. Through sports participation, children and adults not only improve and maintain fitness, but also develop skills, group and personal satisfactions, and enjoyment.

Another factor in the growing interest in sports is the increase in television and radio broadcasts of sporting events. Team sports, such as baseball, football, basketball, soccer, and hockey, are seasonally covered by major networks. Lifetime sports are also receiving more air time. Activities such as gymnastics, swimming, and other aquatic sports continue to receive expanded coverage. Analysis of the skills and strategies of each sport by knowledgeable commentators using instant video replay and stop-action techniques make a game or activity more interesting to the viewer.

The Allyn and Bacon Sports Education Series has been developed to meet the need for players, coaches, and spectators to be informed about the basic and advanced skills, techniques, tactics, and strategies of sports. Each book in the series is designed to provide an in-depth treatment of a selected sport or activity. Players find the individual skills and accompanying picture sequences very valuable. Coaches gain basic and advanced knowledge of individual and team play, along with tech-

niques of coaching. Sports fans are provided information about the activities and are thus able to become more knowledgeable about and appreciative of the basic and finer aspects of sports.

The authors of the Sports Education Series have been carefully selected. They include experienced teachers, coaches, and managers of college and professional teams. Some books represent the combined effort of two or more authors, each with a different background and each contributing particular strengths to the text. For other books, a single author has been selected whose background offers a breadth of knowledge and experience in the sport being covered.

The Sports Education Series was initiated in 1970, and since that time, sixteen different sports have been covered, with more to be added. A number of the books have now gone into their second edition, bringing them up to date with changes in tactics, strategies, and new pictures.

Among the authors and titles of some of the individual sports books in the series are: *Dynamic Track and Field* by the well-known Jim Bush of UCLA with Don Weiskopf; *Advantage Tennis* (revised) by Jack Barnaby of Harvard; and *Women's Gymnastics* by Mimi Murray of Springfield College.

In the team sports area, Mildred J. Barnes of Central Missouri State University has recently revised *Women's Basketball.* Richard Kentwell, coach of the field hockey team at Yale collaborated with Dr. Barnes in the revision of the book *Field Hockey. Winning Volleyball* by Allen E. Scates of UCLA is in preparation for its third edition.

Other team sport books include *Handbook of Winning Football* by George Allen of the Los Angeles Rams with Don Weiskopf; *The Complete Baseball Handbook* by Walter Alston, formerly coach of the Dodgers; and *Basketball: Concepts and Techniques* by Bob Cousy and Frank Power.

Psychology of Coaching by Tom Tutko and Jack Richards offers beginning and experienced coaches in either individual or team sports many suggestions and techniques for improving their coaching.

The Sports Series enables readers to experience the thrills of the sport from the point of view of participants and coaches, to learn some of the reasons for success and causes of failure, and to receive basic information about teaching and coaching techniques.

Each volume in the series reflects the philosophy of the authors, but a common theme runs through all: the desire to instill in the reader a knowledge and appreciation of sports and physical activity which will carry over throughout his or her life as a participant or a spectator. Pictures, drawings, and diagrams are used throughout each book to clarify and illustrate the discussion.

The reader, whether a beginner or one experienced in sports, will gain much from each book in the Allyn and Bacon Sports Education Series.

Preface

The primary purpose for writing this text is to provide teachers, coaches, and players alike with basic fundamentals for the five-player game of basketball. Consideration was given to the knowledges needed by the beginning teacher, coach, and player as well as to those who are more experienced. An effort was made to provide information for the player and teacher in the physical education class situation, as well as information for players and coaches in the competitive situation.

The book is divided into five parts.

Part I *Individual Skills* deals with the development of individual offensive and defensive skills. Considerable attention is devoted to passing, dribbling, shooting, feinting, and cutting. Fundamental defensive skills related to body position and methods of guarding a player with and without the ball are discussed. Attention is also given to guarding a post player. Both offensive and defensive rebounding are discussed.

Part II *Two-, Three-, and Four-Player Tactics.* The basic elements of team play are developed in this section. The author addresses pass and cut tactics, various kinds of screens, and scissor maneuvers. Each is discussed in terms of use, development, and defensive moves to employ against these tactics. Counteraction by the offense is suggested.

Part III *Team Offense and Defense* deals with the start and development of the fast break and the means by which the defense plays against a player advantage. Basic offensive and defensive principles are discussed. Man-to-man and zone defenses are given considerable attention. Several continuity offenses based on a single post, double post, triple post and motion are developed to counteract the defense encountered. Half court and full court pressure defenses and offensive tactics to use against them are reviewed.

Part IV *Special Situations* identifies stall-type offenses and defensive tactics to use against them. Also discussed are offensive and defensive positioning and strategy involved in jump ball, out-of-bounds, free throw, and end-of-period tactics.

Part V *Teaching and Coaching* is designed to provide the physical education class instructor with suggestions for class organization, teaching aids, and progressions. It also provides the coach with suggestions for preparations for the season, selecting a team, team tactics based on a team's own personnel and that of the opponent's, and team statistics.

Scattered throughout the book are over 375 drills which provide the instructor or player with ideas for developing individual skills or team play. Sufficient time should be provided for beginning players to acquire some mastery in a few fundamentals rather than a cursory competency in a greater number of skills. In this way a solid foundation can be built, and each year additional skills can be mastered. While fundamental skills are acquired, fundamental strategy can be introduced. The reader will note that in most instances the drills call for players to be positioned in their normal playing positions. Use of circles, double-line formations, and so forth, seems antiquated unless the primary purpose of the drill is the improvement of peripheral vision, speed of passing, and so forth. It appears far more sensible when developing passing skills, for example, to teach pass-and-cut or screening techniques simultaneously. By using this method the student can see the need for accuracy, acquire the timing necessary, and develop the correct speed and distance for the pass. At the same time, she is learning a tactic that can be used while playing. When defense players are added, she can understand the need for learning to pivot, to fake well, and to release the ball at varying levels so that a natural teaching progression is based on the students needs and is self-motivating.

Most skills should be learned individually and then attempted against an opponent. Other skills, passing, for example, must be practiced with a partner and later with opponents. Additional players are added to the small groups until players are practicing in a five-on-five situation. Small groups provide considerably more practice and promote better learning than playing a full court game.

Throughout the book the reader will find close

vii

to 500 photographs depicting individual and team play. Many of the illustrations demonstrate sequential action to provide both player and reader with a better view of the action described.

Another feature of the text is the Glossary. Included are common terms that player, teacher, and coach should know.

Acknowledgments

The author wishes to express her gratitude to the players, coaches, umpires, and friends who have made the game of basketball so enjoyable over the years. Particular gratitude is expressed to her former players who have provided her with considerable satisfaction and reward.

Special thanks is extended to the Association for Intercollegiate Athletics for Women (AIAW) and to the Amateur Basketball Association of the United States of America (ABAUSA) and to Bill Wall in particular for the opportunities and involvement in national and international competition. The experiences and memories will long be remembered. Thanks is extended also to all those coaches who have discussed tactics and offered suggestions for the book. Appreciation is extended to players who have provided insight into learning progressions.

The author is particularly indebted to Gil D. Haynes, H. Gordon Gray, and to the Tom Broderick Company, Inc. for providing the uniforms worn by players in some of the photographs. Numbers one and two are used on the uniforms for illustrative purposes in some of the photographs, although it is recognized that these single digits are illegal during competitive play. Olympic players are wearing their Olympic uniforms with international numbers which are not all legal numbers by United States standards.

The author is especially grateful to Steve Schoen, Manager, Photographic Services at Central Missouri State University and to Stanley Dressen, Robert Hammermeister, and Kem McDaniels for the photographs that appear throughout the book.

Thanks is also extended to the players who participated in the filming: Laurie Arrants, Deborah Brown, Kay Byers, Diana Burrell, Mary Kaye Dooley, Ronda Miles, Margaret Propst, Debbie Schooling, Gay Steenbergen, Robin Turley, and Deborah Watson. Thanks is also expressed to members of the 1977–78 Central Missouri State University team who were filmed: Kathy Anderson, Laura Clark, Debbie Easley, Christy Lewis, Reta McCartney, Patty Pink, Mary Jo Post, Candy Rangler, and Theresa Rankin. Appreciation is also expressed to Jorja Hoehn and Mary Rietbrock for their assistance. Special thanks is also extended to members of the 1976 United States Olympic team who were filmed while training on the Central Missouri State Campus: Pat Head, Charlotte Lewis, Nancy Lieberman, Gail Marquis, Ann Meyers, Mary Ann O'Connor and Sue Rojcewicz.

The author would also like to express her appreciation to Dean Martin for her suggestions in the preparation of the original manuscript, to Sue Boyd who typed the manuscript, to Brenda Smith who so capably typed the revision, to Kathy Anderson who helped with the diagrams, and to Marion Broer who granted permission to adapt diagrams from her book.

Symbols

Key to Diagrams

●	ball
– – – →	pass
⟶	path of player
～～～	dribble
)	screen
═══	hand-off

1, 2,
3, 4,
5 — players on the offensive team (players 1 and 2 are guards, 3 is the pivot, and 4 and 5 are forwards or wings)

$X_1, X_2,$
$X_3, X_4,$
X_5 — players on the defensive team (players X_1 and X_2 are guards, X_3 is the pivot, and X_4 and X_5 are forwards or wings)

Formations for drills

pairs — two opponents

partners — two teammates

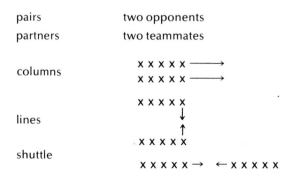

columns

lines

shuttle

1

Individual Skills

1

Offensive Skills

The primary purpose of the game of basketball is to score points and to score more of them than the opponents. Basic to the development of scoring opportunities is the ability to perform fundamental skills to get the ball into a position where shooting percentages are highest. In order to advance the ball to the scoring area, players must be skillful in rebounding, passing, receiving, cutting, feinting, pivoting, dribbling, and setting screens. All of these must be performed with the body under control.

Important to the development of any offensive system is the knowledge that most of the time players are performing without the ball. Since only one of five players may have the ball at any one time, the rest of the players must assist the offense by executing basic techniques to get free, assist a teammate in getting free, or simply keeping an opponent occupied. To get free, a player must know how to fake, pivot, cut, and use screens to her advantage. A player may also cut, without the primary intent of receiving a pass, to free a passing lane for her teammate or to set a screen to free her teammate. If a player is not involved in a particular offensive thrust, she must keep her opponent occupied so that she is less able to help her teammates. This is done by faking and cutting away from the desired passing lanes or exchanging positions with a teammate. In addition, a player must be alert to change from offense to defense, to adjust and react to any type of defense the opponents employ, to play her part in any fast break attempt, and to contribute to offensive rebounding.

The player with the ball must be skilled in passing, dribbling, shooting, and using screens. She must be able to adapt her style of play to that of the team offense. In so doing she must be able to find a free player in a more advantageous position as well as be able to work one-on-one when the situation arises.

PASSING AND RECEIVING

In order for any offense to be effective, there must be a combination of accurate and crisp passes that can be received easily. Two of the greatest nemeses to any offense are fumbled catches and inadvertent passes. They throw off the timing of a teammate's moves, allow time for the defense to adjust, and result in many turnovers. Players should have the same feeling when they throw the ball away as when they miss an easy layup.

Accuracy in passing is probably more important than speed, although soft and slow passes give the defense time to intercept or adjust their positions. The responsibility for a successful pass must rest with the passer. She must recognize her teammates' weaknesses in receiving passes and must pass the ball so they *can* catch it. Passing accuracy improves when a player starts in a balanced position. Beginners should step or turn in the direction of the pass, but advanced players may use more deceptive techniques.

The ball should be thrown with little spin. This is particularly true of the long overarm, full court pass. The ball has a relatively large cross section and air resistance will act more noticeably on it if there is sidespin. On some bounce passes, backspin and

3

topspin are desirable. These will be discussed under the description for bounce passes.

Passes should be snappy, crisp, and thrown to the side away from the opponent. Potential receivers who are closely guarded should extend an arm for a target away from the defender. Passes to loosely guarded teammates may be made directly to them. Passes should be received between waist and shoulder level, with the exception of bounce passes which should be received at waist level. Although generally the pass should be crisp, the speed and type should be adjusted according to the situation.

Passing in a skilled game should be fast and continuous. A deliberate type of passing attack gives the defense time to adjust their positions. Players should learn to catch and pass in one continuous motion and in the same plane. Before releasing the ball, however, the passer must exercise judgment in determining whether the receiver is free. Automatic passing to a predetermined receiver will result in numerous turnovers.

A passer will learn that her defender may take any of three defensive positions (or modifications of these) while guarding her — normal, sagging, or pressing. She should recognize that problems in passing differ according to whether the defender is guarding closely or loosely. In the former situation when an opponent is pressing or when she moves closer following the pickup of a dribble, the passer (if she has poise and body control) should find the passing lanes open. It becomes a matter of faking her opponent out of position before releasing the pass, so that the defender cannot deflect the pass or force a poorly thrown pass. She must not allow the defender to intimidate her or force her to turn her back on most of her teammates. Passes are then telegraphed and easily intercepted.

If an opponent guards loosely or sags after a dribbler picks up the ball, the ball handler finds it easy to pass well; but, she finds that the passing lanes are not as open. By dropping back, the defender places herself in a passing lane 6–8 ft. from the passer, which allows her more time to react and intercept the pass. Against a sagging defender it is important then for a player who dribbles to pass immediately after she catches her dribble. This does not allow the defender time to drop back and intercept. On the other hand if the defender plays loosely most of the time the ball handler may dribble toward the defensive player so that she can pass around her more easily. If this does not seem desirable at the time, the ball handler should use some means of deception in order to insure that the passing lane is open. She may fake one kind of pass and

alter the plane and/or the type of pass before releasing the ball. A player with good peripheral vision also can look in one direction and pass accurately in another. Whatever technique she uses, she must not telegraph her pass.

If a passer is confronted by a taller opponent, she should not try to pass over her; similarly, a passer should not use bounce passes against a short player. Overhead passes should be used if the passer is taller than her opponent. If the opponent guards with a wide side stride, passes can be made between her legs; if she has a forward-backward stride with one arm up and one arm out, the pass should be made under the high arm or over the shoulder and by the ear on the side of the lower arm; and, if both arms are low and to the side, the pass should be made over either shoulder or above the head.

There is a suitable pass for every situation. This is the reason for learning a variety of passes. Two-hand passes should be used for relatively short distances, and only one-hand passes should be used for long passes, i.e., distances greater than 20 ft. Passes intended for a cutter should lead the player so that she does not have to slow down to make the reception. A player should always attempt to use simple passes rather than gain recognition as a "fancy Nan." Use of the cross-court pass in both backcourt and frontcourt is extremely dangerous and should be exercized with caution.

RECEIVING

To eliminate or reduce interceptions, a player should go to meet each pass. This may be done by cutting toward the ball against a pressing defense or by taking a step and reaching for the ball against a sagging defense. The receiver should concentrate on watching the ball until it is in her hands. Too many fumbles occur when a player concentrates on her next move before she actually has caught the ball. As the ball approaches, arms relax and reach for the ball. Fingers and thumbs are relaxed and cupped with fingers pointing up or down, depending upon the height of the ball. (Fingers never point toward the ball, as the ball may strike the tips and result in a jammed finger.) The ball is caught by the pads on the fingers. The ball's kinetic energy is reduced with the giving of hands and arms toward the body.

The ball should be caught with both hands whenever possible. In advanced play this may not be desirable. If the ball is thrown to a spot away from a closely guarding defender, the catch may be

a   b   c

Fig. 1.1 *Receiving. The player cuts and indicates that the pass should be made to the off-guard side (a). The catch is made with one hand, and the player guides the ball to the other hand as quickly as possible (b). Note that the right knee is well flexed to allow the weight to be lowered and remain over the base (c). The pivot is made so that the player is a threat to drive, shoot, or pass.*

made by raising one hand and letting the ball fall to rest against it. Then it should be covered or secured with the other hand, much like a first baseman in softball catches the ball (Fig. 1.1). This same technique may be used when catching a lob pass or a long, overarm downcourt pass.

Players must make every attempt to catch a pass regardless of how poorly it is thrown. Turnovers are demoralizing and possession is too important to give the ball away without effort to retrieve it. Once the ball is caught, the fingers should remain spread along the sides of the ball in a cupped position so that the palms of the hands do not touch the ball. If a pass is not made immediately, the ball should be held at chest level so that the player is a threat to pass, dribble, or shoot. The ball is held securely. Feet are comfortably spread, preferably in a side stride position, trunk and elbows slightly flexed to protect the ball (Fig. 1.2).

PASSING

In all types of passing, there is little time to increase the ball's acceleration. It must be practically instan-

Fig. 1.2 *Holding the Ball. The ball is held close to the body at chest level to protect the ball before passing, dribbling, or shooting.*

taneous. The extension of the arm(s), and the fast wrist snap are used almost exclusively for imparting force to the ball. Rotation of hips, trunk, and shoulders is all but eliminated except in the long, full court pass.

Chest Pass

If the ball is held properly, it is already in position for the pass. Force is given to the ball by a fast extension of the elbows followed by radial abduction and wrist and finger extension at release. The wrist snap thus derived will produce some backspin on the ball. A follow-through with the backs of the hands facing each other and palms outward will assist the beginner in attaining the desired results. Beginners often have difficulty in keeping their elbows in and applying wrist snap. They derive most of their force from elbow extension only. This position of the back of the hands facing one another on the follow-through will insure the acquisition of proper wrist snap (Fig. 1.3).

Beginners also often start with the ball 10–12 in.

or more from their chest. As a result, they have relatively little distance over which to apply force. If the ball is brought back close to the chest on the "backswing," there is greater distance over which force can be applied.

Bounce Pass

The bounce is an effective pass because defenders seem to try instinctively to prevent the ball from going over their head. While an opponent has her arms up, the ball may be bounced under them. But players must recognize that the bounce is one of the slowest of all passes since it must travel a long path to cover a given distance. It is executed similar to the chest pass, except the force is exerted downward rather than forward (Fig. 1.5). The ball should strike the floor about two-thirds of the way to the receiver so that she may catch it at waist level. It is useful when attacking a zone defense, feeding a pivot, and climaxing a fast break.

Often the bounce pass needs to be preceded by a fake shot or high pass to raise the arms of the op-

a   b

Fig. 1.3 Chest Pass. The player holds the ball close to her chest with fingers well spread on the ball and elbows close to the side; hands are radially flexed to provide additional force to the pass. (a) Weight is transferred, arms extended and wrist snap provided by rotating palms outward (b).

Drills for Chest Pass

1. Partners stand about 15 ft. apart with one ball between them. Pass ball back and forth. Emphasis should be on quick and crisp passes. Later, move players further apart.

2. Each player has a ball and stands about 6 ft. from a clear wall space. Players attempt to execute as many passes as possible in a short period. Emphasis is on passing quickly and sharply. Later, add a competitive flavor by providing a 30-second time period. Who can execute the greatest number of passes during the time? This is an excellent drill for developing the desired wrist snap.

3. Partners position themselves as either two guards or as guard and wing. Players face the basket in their positions and fake before passing to their teammate. Continue to pass the ball back and forth. Caution must be exercised so that players do not start to face one another. Before passing they must be facing the basket, but may take a step toward the receiver as the ball is released.

4. Same as drill 3 above, only add two defensive players.

5. Partners position themselves as either two guards or as guard and wing. Using the chest pass, players use the give-and-go play. Player 2 passes to 5, and 5 returns the pass to 2 as she cuts for the basket. Continue from the other side (Fig. 1.4). Later, add defensive players.

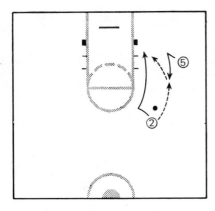

Fig. 1.4 *A guard and wing practice the chest pass while using a give-and-go pattern.*

ponent. When a bounce pass is used for a "lead" pass, it may be desirable to use backspin to cause the ball to bounce higher and slower on the rebound. If the defense is playing "tight" and there is little opening through which the ball may be passed, topspin can be used to cause the ball to rebound lower and faster. This also makes it more difficult to receive, however. Backspin can be applied by rolling the thumbs sharply downward under the ball at release, and topspin is applied by rolling the thumbs over the top of the ball at release. Bounce passes with topspin should bounce further from the receiver than normal and those with backspin closer to the receiver. Use of spins probably should be delayed for advanced play.

One-Hand Bounce Pass

This pass is more difficult to disguise than the two-hand bounce pass and once started is difficult to stop. Generally it requires a longer backswing, but it can be protected by using a crossover step prior to release. When the crossover step is not used, a short backswing should accompany the pass so as not to telegraph it. The pass can also be made while dribbling. (Fig. 1.6)

Two-Hand Overhead Pass

This pass is used extensively to feed the post player and in feeding cutters. The ball is raised overhead with elbows slightly flexed and the ball held slightly behind the head, wrists radially flexed. (This often causes a defensive player to move in closer to the ball handler and permits her to drive around the defender.) The pass is executed by a forceful extension of the arms, accompanied by radial abduction

a   b

Fig. 1.5 *Two-Hand Bounce Pass. It is executed similarly to the chest pass. The ball is at chest level (a) and the arms forcefully extend (b). Note the transfer of weight from the rear foot (a) to the forward foot (b).*

a   b   c

Fig. 1.6 *One-Hand Bounce Pass. The player is dribbling at full speed (a). She raises her trunk to slow her forward speed (b). The left foot moves forward to give added protection, and the ball is allowed to bounce higher than normal so that the force can be applied over a longer distance (c). The right hand is used to pass to the left so that the ball can be better protected against a defender on the dribbler's left.*

Drills for Bounce Pass

1. Partners stand about 8 ft. apart. Bounce pass back and forth. Emphasis should be on the crispness of the pass and it should be received at waist level.

2. Partners position themselves as two guards or as guard and wing. Practice the give-and-go play with the second pass as a bounce pass. Player 1 passes to 2, and 2 gives a bounce pass to 1 as she cuts for the basket. Repeat from the other side. Later add two defensive players.

3. Groups of three — the pivot player in a high post position (or a wing in her position), a guard, and her opponent. The guard fakes her opponent out of position and bounce passes into the post player. Repeat from various positions on the floor.

4. Partners position themselves as guard and wing. The guard has the ball and dribbles toward the edge of the circle. The wing cuts for the basket and receives a bounce pass.

5. Same as drill 4 above, only add defensive players. Let the wing try a reverse cut if the defender presses (Fig. 1.7).

6. Partners position themselves as guard and pivot player in a high post position. The guard dribbles toward the top of the circle but bounce passes to the pivot without first catching the ball. Later, add defensive players.

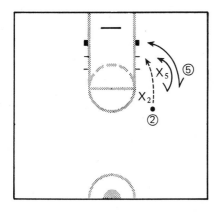

Fig. 1.7 *Player 5 is closely guarded by player X_5. 5 fakes toward 2 and uses a reverse cut to become free and receives a bounce pass from 2.*

(turning backs of hands toward one another). The ball is released while it is still above the head. If released lower, the ball will be directed downward, making it difficult to catch. Beginners may use a transfer of weight to give more force to the pass, but advanced players should rely on wrist snap for force. This is a pass that should be used extensively by a player who is taller than her opponent, and should be used infrequently by one who is shorter than her opponent. (Fig. 1.8). Since it is released so quickly, it is an extremely valuable pass. The chest pass, bounce pass, and overhead passes are the most frequently used passes.

Overarm or Baseball Pass

This pass is difficult to control and is unnecessary for beginners to learn. It is used when both speed and distance are desirable, on a fast break attempt, or on any half- or full-court throw. Its execution is accomplished in the same manner as any overarm throw. A forward-backward stride is taken, hips and trunk rotate, and the throwing arm is abducted and laterally rotated during the backswing, fingers spread behind the ball. As the arm is brought forward, it abducts and medially rotates while the elbow extends and wrist and fingers flex to give final force to the ball. During the release the weight is transferred to the forward foot. Because the preparatory movements are relatively slow due to the long backswing and because the ball is vulnerable behind the body on the backswing, this pass can be used only when the player is wide open.

Controlling the pass is difficult, particularly for players with relatively small hands. Frequently during the release the ball is rotated slightly so that the fingers are to the side of the ball, thus applying

a   b   c   d

Fig. 1.8 *Two-Hand Overhand Pass. The player prepares for an overhead pass (a), brings the ball forward (b), releases it (c), and follows through (d).*

Drills for Overhead Pass

1. Partners stand about 10 ft. apart. Pass ball back and forth, emphasizing snappy passes and receptions at shoulder level or higher.

2. Each player stands about 6 ft. from the wall and passes against the wall. Emphasis is on proper release.

3. Partners position themselves as pivot player in a high post position and guard. The guard uses an overhead pass to the pivot, who turns to face the basket and gives an overhead pass to the cutting guard.

4. Same as drill 3 above, but add defensive players.

5. Partners position themselves as wing and guard. The guard gives an overhead pass to the wing who returns a bounce pass to the guard as she cuts for the basket.

6. Same as drill 5 above, only add defenders.

7. Groups of three — one pivot player in a high post position and two guards (or one guard and one wing). One guard gives an overhead pass to the pivot who turns and gives an overhead pass to the other cutting guard (or wing) (Fig. 1.9).

8. Same as drill 7 above, only add defenders.

9. Partners position themselves as rebounder and outlet. Post player rebounds, keeps the ball high, pivots and gives an overhead pass to the outlet as a leadup to a fast break drill.

a

b

c

d

Fig. 1.9 *Blast with an Overhead Pass to the Cutter. An outside player passes in to high post (a); the outside defenders anticipate a scissor maneuver (b); the far side dark player fakes to the outside and blasts down the lane and receives an overhead pass (c) for an easy layup (d).*

Drills for Overarm Pass

1. Partners stand about 25 ft. apart. Using the overarm pass, throw back and forth, emphasizing as rapid release as possible.

2. Partners position themselves as guard and forward in the back court. The guard cuts downcourt, looking over her shoulder for the overarm pass. Emphasize accuracy of the pass and correct release so that excessive spin is not produced. (Fig. 1.10).

3. Partners position themselves as guard and forward. The forward starts under the basket as though she had rebounded, dribbles toward the sideline, and gives a pass downcourt to the guard as she cuts. Repeat, with the forward tossing the ball against the backboard and rebounding before moving toward the sideline. (Fig. 1.11).

4. Partners. Rebounder under the basket who tosses the ball against the backboard, rebounds, and gives overarm pass to teammate cutting at sideline.

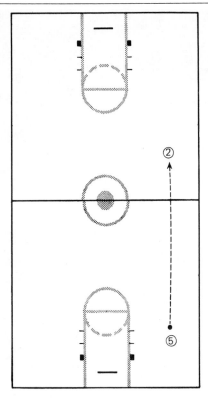

Fig. 1.10 *Player 5 throws an overarm pass to player 2.*

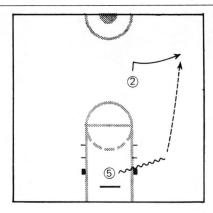

Fig. 1.11 *Player 5 starts under the basket, dribbles toward the side, and gives an overarm pass to 2.*

force off-center and resulting in sidespin as the ball is released. Over a long distance this sidespin is magnified and the ball may curve completely out of range of the receiver. With correct execution backspin is applied which prevents the ball from drifting.

Handoff Pass

This pass may be used any time a player cuts closely by a teammate with the ball. It is commonly used by the post player on scissoring maneuvers and by other players on screen plays. As its title implies, the ball is simply handed to a teammate, although most coaches recommend that there be a slight flexion of the fingers at release so that the ball is

---

Drills for Handoff Pass

1. Partners. Player 3 stands with her back to the basket at the free throw line and player 2 has a ball and stands about 12–15 ft. from her and facing her. Player 2 passes the ball to 3, fakes outside, and cuts close by 3 who hands off to 2. 2 drives in for a layup. Work from both sides. Exchange places. Later, add a defensive player against 3.

2. Groups of three. One ball per group. Players 3 and 2 take the same positions as in drill 1 above, and player 1 takes a position about 10 ft. to the side of 2. Player 2 starts with the ball, which is passed to 3. Player 2 cuts first by 3, followed closely by 1 around the other side of 3. Player 3 may hand off to either player. Let 1 and 2 alternate starting the play. Rotate positions. Later, add defensive players. (Fig. 1.13).

3. Repeat drill 2 above, except replace 1 with a corner player. Execute with either player starting the pass and practice from both sides of the basket (Fig. 1.14).

a   b

Fig. 1.12 *Handoff. A point player passes to the wing (a) and cuts behind her teammate for the handoff (b).*

slightly elevated from the hand. The release should be so timed that the receiver can catch the ball at waist level (Fig. 1.12).

OTHER PASSES

The passes already discussed are the basic passes used in a game by skilled players. Underhand passes tend to be too slow and telegraphic for to-day's fast moving play. The flip pass, hook, and behind the back passes are useful passes under the proper circumstances but, because control is more difficult, should be used only when necessary.

Lob Pass

A lob pass is a modified chest pass used to lead a player on a cut or to pass the ball to a teammate

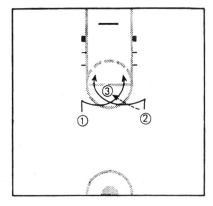

Fig. 1.13 *Player 2 passes to 3 and cuts close to 3. Player 1 follows and cuts to the other side of 3. 3 may hand off to either 1 or 2.*

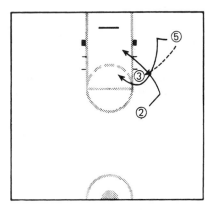

Fig. 1.14 *Player 5 passes in to player 3 and cuts around her. Player 2 cuts to the other side of 3. 3 hands off to either player.*

whose opponent is playing in front of her. Typical is the lob pass given to the pivot player when her opponent is guarding her from the front. When the opposing team is using a pressing defense and face guarding, the lob pass is often used in the backcourt by the player trying to in-bound the ball from the end line. Its execution is identical to the chest pass except that it is released higher and more softly. It can be a dangerous pass to use in the backcourt, as the opponents may divert a player to cover the area into which the pass would go. Therefore, it should be used with great caution.

A common use of the pass is to give the post player a lob when she is fronted. Good execution provides layup opportunities (Fig. 1.15).

Flip Pass

This is a backward pass most commonly executed over the shoulder. The backward flip also can be done underhand from hip level, bounced, or behind the back in a modified hook. It may be used by a pivot player after faking an opponent to a lower level or may be passed to a trailer on a fast break or a back screen.

For the shoulder level pass the ball is rotated so

Drills for Lob Pass

1. Partners. Player 1 plays in a medium pivot position outside the lane and player 2 plays about 10 ft. from 1. Player 1 pivots and extends one arm into the air. Player 2 gives 1 a lob pass and 1 shoots. Later, player 1 should try to shoot before returning to the floor following the reception. Exchange places, if desirable. Practice from both sides of the court.

2. Same as drill 1 above, only add two defensive players; the player guards the pivot fronting her.

3. Groups of four players — two attack and two defense. The attack player has the ball out of bounds at the end line and is guarded by an opponent. The other attack player starts close to the end line. She is guarded closely by a defensive player who is face guarding and between her opponent and the ball. The attack player fakes a cut toward the end line and then cuts back with arm raised. A lob pass is made over the defensive player's head. Rotate positions. Practice from both sides.

a

b

Fig. 1.15 *Lob Pass. The low post is fronted. The ball handler sees that there is no weak side help and gives a lob pass (a) and the post is free for a shot (b).*

that the passing hand is in front of the ball. The lower arm flexes followed by finger flexion to give the final impetus. It is a short pass and is received just behind the passer (Fig. 1.16). For the underhand pass the arm is extended at the side, the ball is cupped in the passing hand, the arm is extended backward, and finger flexion gives the final force. Rather than the underhand pass, the ball may be bounced. The passing hand is on the front side (height depending on angle desired for bounce — higher for a short pass, lower for a longer pass). The arm extends downward and fingers flex at release to cause the bounce.

The ball is flipped behind the back in a modified hook when a player is guarded closely on one side and a teammate is free on the other side. It is also useful for the middle man on a fast break. In the latter instance it is executed following a dribble. The ball is brought up close to shoulder level with two hands, at which time one hand is removed and the other is in front but to the side of the ball. For this pass the ball is out to the side of the body rather than in front during the preparation. The lower arm is then flexed, followed by finger flexion to give the impetus to the ball over the shoulder and behind the head (Fig. 1.17).

a

Fig. 1.16 *Flip Pass. A fast break has developed, but three defenders have recovered (a); the point flips the ball backward to a trailer (b) who is free for a jump shot (c).*

b

c

Drills for Flip Pass

1. Partners. One ball per pair. Use the same series of drills as explained under handoff (page 12), except fake a handoff and use a flip shoulder pass.

2. Partners. Any position on the floor about 10 ft. apart, even with one another and both facing the basket; one ball per pair. Player 1 passes the ball to 2 and runs behind her (back screen) to receive a shoulder flip pass. Player 1 then may shoot or drive for the basket. Alternate passers and start from different positions on the floor. Later, add defensive players.

3. Partners. One ball per group. Player 1 dribbles (3 or 4 times) and then uses a shoulder flip pass back to 2 who is trailing. Exchange places. Also try the underhand and bounce passes.

4. Same as drill 3 above, only add a defensive player who moves out to force player 1 to pass off.

5. Partners. Player 2 starts at the center line with the ball; 1 is on her left. 2 starts dribbling with 1 cutting downcourt in the left lane. At the free throw line, 2 gives a back flip pass to 1 who drives in for the layup. Exchange places; place 2 to the right of 1. Trailer should call, "trailer left" or "trailer right."

6. Groups of three. One ball per group. Player 1 is flanked by players 2 and 3. 1 dribbles downcourt as 2 and 3 cut in their lanes. 1 has a choice of passing to 2 or 3.

7. Same as drill 6 above, only add two defensive players who are stationed between the free throw line and the basket. Let the defensive players defend in any manner they wish and force 1 to find the open player. Exchange positions.

a   b

Fig. 1.17 *Flip Pass—Behind the Back. The opponent moves into good defensive position, preventing a chest or bounce pass to the dribbler's left (a). Fingers are well spread on the ball, and flexion of the lower arm has*

c   d

Fig. 1.17 *continued*
started (b). Fingers are flexed at release and during the follow-through (c). Notice the perfectly placed pass to the teammate running at full speed and the receiver's widespread fingers.

Hook Pass

A hook pass is used only when a player is closely guarded and when a pass in front of the body is impossible. The pass is made to a teammate who is either beside or behind the passer. To execute a pass to the left, the player steps with her left foot, rotates her trunk so that her shoulders are aligned with the direction of the pass, and looks over her left shoulder. Her throwing hand is under the ball and the ball rests on the forearm. With arm extended laterally, the ball is pulled overhead and released with a final flick of the fingers. The arm follows through overhead (Fig. 1.18). As the pass is started, most players find it helpful to jump off the forward foot (left foot for a right-handed player) and return to the floor in the direction the player was originally facing.

Behind the Back Pass

When a player is closely guarded, and wishes to pass to a player ahead of her, this pass is a valuable tool if the passing lane for other passes is obstructed. Accuracy is difficult to attain because of its sidearm nature. The ball is cupped in the throwing hand and the arm is extended and swung in a circular path to the side of the body and then behind the back. Final force is given by finger flexion. This pass may be modified by a player who bounce passes behind her back.

Tip Pass

This pass is executed much like a volley in the game of volleyball. As the ball is received, it is not caught but flicked or volleyed to the intended receiver.

a   b

Fig. 1.18 *Hook Pass. The defensive player is well positioned to force the hook pass (a). Note the cupped position of the ball as the fully extended arm is raised overhead (b).*

Drills for Hook Pass

1. Partners face each other about 12 ft. apart; each pair has a ball. The player with the ball pivots away from her partner and hooks to her. Player 2 pivots away and returns a hook pass to her partner. Continue. Later, add a dribble and pass.

2. Circle of five or six players with one ball per circle. Players form a wide circle and are well spaced. All players start trotting counterclockwise around the circle. The player with the ball dribbles and executes a hook pass to the player behind her. That player dribbles and hooks to the player behind her. Continue. Watch for traveling. Later, eliminate the dribble.

3. Columns. Players hook pass to each other down the court and return, thereby hooking both left and right.

More Passing Drills

The following drills are included to help players needing improvement in attributes necessary for good passing. Drills 1–4 are devised for improving finger and wrist strength. Drills 5–9 will help players to release the ball more quickly and will improve their peripheral vision. Drill 10 may be used for both purposes.

1. One ball per player. Each player stands about 8 ft. from a smooth surfaced wall. Using a chest pass, players throw the ball as hard against the wall as possible. Later, give them a 30-sec. time period and have them count the number of passes during that period. Keep a daily record to show improvement. Increase distance from the wall.

2. Individually and informally suggest to players with weak wrists and fingers that they obtain an old tennis ball and squeeze it at their convenience.

3. Same as drill 1 above, but use a weighted basketball. Take an old basketball and fill it with rags, newspaper, or sand.

4. Partners are 12 ft. apart and move down the court while receiving a pass with one hand and passing with the same hand. Alternate right and left hand.

5. Partners stand about 10–12 ft. apart and face each other; one ball per couple. Players pass the ball back and forth as though it were a hot potato — catch and pass, catch and pass, etc. Later, each player should vary the level at which the receiver must catch the ball and return the ball by using a pass suitable for that level, i.e., the ball must be released at the same height at which it is caught.

6. Circle of six players with a leader in the center. The leader passes the ball to each player who immediately returns it to her.

7. Same as drill 6 above, except a second ball is added. The leader, 1, and a player in the outside circle, 2, have a ball. 1 and 2 pass at the same time — 1 to 3 and 2 to 1. The passing should continue twice around the circle; then someone replaces 1. Players in the circle always return the pass to 1, and 1 always passes to the next player in the circle. The purpose of this drill is to improve reaction time, to increase peripheral vision, and to improve accuracy in passing. Therefore, all players should return the ball to 1 as soon as they have caught it. Keep 1 moving quickly.

8. Same description as drill 7 above, except players are in a semicircle and 1 passes to any player rather than always to the next player in the semicircle.

9. Groups of three in a triangle. Two players with a ball pass alternately to the player without the ball. Pass quickly. Increase the pace. Change positions.

10. Individually players may use the Toss Back in any drills described for that apparatus.

More often the tip pass may be used by a rebounder who cannot control a rebound and who tips the ball away from the basket.

DRIBBLING

Unquestionably dribbling is a highly important skill for every player to learn, although sometimes it appears that teachers/coaches should spend more time on *when* to dribble rather than *how* to dribble. Nevertheless, players at an advanced level must be able to control the ball while dribbling with a variety of moves.

Dribbling is used by a player

- to move away from a congested area when no teammate is free for a pass

- to initiate and continue a fast break situation
- to advance the ball from the backcourt to the frontcourt
- to advance the ball against a pressing defense
- to move the ball closer to a teammate for a shorter pass
- to drive for a goal

Players must be reminded constantly that passing promotes a faster game than does dribbling. Dribbling serves a very real purpose, but beginners must be taught early that the only time they should dribble is when it meets one of the criteria stated above. Emphasis should be placed on covering distance (under control) with each dribble. When a player is in the open one bounce is ample to cover 15–20 ft. A player should not be allowed to take one bounce or dribble every time she receives the ball. Once developed, this bad habit is difficult to eliminate. Another common error is a player's catching the dribble as soon as an opponent moves in to guard closely. This eliminates the future possibility of driving; the defender then needs to be concerned only with defending against a pass or shot. Players must have sufficient confidence in their dribbling ability so that the approach of an opponent is not intimidating.

In executing any type of dribble, the hand is cupped and fingers are spread. The ball is pushed against the floor by flexion of the fingers. Little force is necessary. As the ball rebounds from the floor, fingers meet it, the hand rides up slightly with the ball in contact before the next push, and the dribble is continued.

When starting any dribbling maneuver, the ball should be held at waist level or lower, and the push should be initiated from there. If the ball is started any higher, as beginners often do, there is a tendency to "carry" the ball before releasing it. When players are first learning the technique of dribbling, teachers/coaches must carefully watch the pivot foot to see that it is not dragging along the floor, or that a step is not taken with the pivot foot befor the ball is released. Starting the ball low on the dribble should eliminate both of these problems.

While dribbling, the player should keep her head up so that she can pass to a teammate as soon as she is free. Although eyes are focused ahead, some visual contact with the ball is afforded. The trunk is flexed but the back is relatively straight. The right hand should be used when dribbling to the right and the left hand when dribbling to the left while a player is being guarded. Failure to do so leaves the ball open for a defensive steal. If a player is wide open there is no reason why she cannot use her preferred hand, however. Considerable attention must be devoted to dribbling with the correct hand.

The distance that a player wishes to cover will determine where the fingers will contact the ball and, therefore, the angle of the bounce. When a player is open, she can angle the ball further forward and cover greater distance with fewer dribbles. To do this the fingers contact behind the ball. If a more controlled dribble is necessary, contact will be made closer to the top of the ball. If a change in direction is desirable, contact on the left side will push the ball to the right side and vice versa; contact on the front side of the ball will pull the ball back toward the dribbler. Just prior to shooting, bounce the ball hard and it will rise higher on its own and the shot can be released quicker.

Teachers/coaches should spend considerable time allowing players to develop various dribbling moves. The abilities to pull the ball left and right, forward and back with each hand are valuable in themselves but are also lead-up skills to the reverse, behind the back, and between the leg dribble.

Speed or High Dribble

This dribble is used only when a player is wide open. It is the common means for advancing the ball on a fast break until an opponent is approached. The player is only slightly crouched and pushes the ball further forward so that fewer bounces are necessary to reach the desired objective at maximum speed. Each dribble is made approximately from hip level. The ball is dribbled in front of the body. Shoulders can remain square and the nondribbling hand should remain at the side since there is no need to protect the ball.

Control or Low Dribble

This dribble is used when a player is being closely guarded, when in a congested area, or while waiting for teammates to regain offensive balance after an unsuccessful scoring attempt. Because of the possibility of an opponent's stealing the ball, it must be dribbled lower with frequent contacts for control and change of direction. The ball is contacted at knee level, which forces the trunk to flex; knees are well flexed so that the body is low. The nondribbling (free) arm is flexed with the shoulder forward to help protect the ball.

Change of Direction

When a player is advancing the ball and being guarded loosely, it is wise for her to change the direction of her dribble frequently to cause her opponent to adjust and possibly force her off balance. The directional change is also wise to prevent a defensive player from approaching from the rear and tapping the ball away. Such a tactic is much easier when a dribbler is moving in a straight path. As the dribbler only wants to zigzag downcourt, a sharp lateral movement is not necessary. The ball is contacted high behind the ball but only slightly off center. The rebound is then received by the other hand, which continues to dribble until another change is desired.

Crossover

A sharp directional change is accomplished by this technique. It is used when a player wishes to evade her opponent and the opponent's distance is sufficient to allow the ball to be crossed in front of the player. It is also effective when the dribbler is being overplayed. If dribbling to the right, the change of direction is started when the right foot is forward. The dribbler reaches down to contact the ball sooner than usual — to get the ball on a short hop, so to speak. The ball is contacted on the right side so that very little forward momentum is given. As the ball is pushed across the body, the right foot pushes off and a step is taken with the left foot as the left hand resumes the dribble. The right shoulder is lowered and brought forward to protect the ball. It is important that the lateral movement of the ball be accomplished with one bounce only and that the ball be protected immediately after it crosses the body (Fig. 1.19).

Change of Pace

This technique is designed to make the opponent believe the dribbler is slowing or will stop, thus slowing her reaction to backward pursuit. The dribbler decreases her forward speed by raising her trunk to a more erect position and contacting the ball closer to the top. When it appears as though the defender is lulled into a sense of security, a hard push-off is made by the right foot (when dribbling with the right hand), the ball is contacted further to the rear, and the left foot moves forward to aid in protecting the ball. It should be noted that in this technique the player continues to dribble with the same hand and in the same direction as before the hesitation (Fig. 1.20), although the change of pace

may be combined with the crossover dribble. Because the change of pace involves a temporary decrease in acceleration, it should be used only when a player is relatively free, certainly not when the opponents are pressing, double teaming or approaching from the rear. It is used most often when advancing the ball into the frontcourt or in one-on-one techniques. A stutter step may also be used to make the change of pace more effective. The dribbler moves just beyond the reach of the defensive player. She takes several steps in place quickly and then accelerates by her opponent. The stutter step may be done in combination with the crossover dribble.

Behind the Back

Advanced players may find this technique a valuable tool to add to their dribbling repertoire. Although a player should never dribble behind her back when the crossover dribble can be used, it is useful when a dribbler is closely guarded and being overplayed. It can also be used occasionally for the psychological advantage that is gained against a less experienced player.

To start the behind the back dribble, the player must be ahead of the ball. She may attain this position by overrunning the ball slightly or by deliberately pulling the ball back into the desired position. If the player is dribbling with her right hand, this is accomplished by bouncing the ball backward once and then contacting the outside rear portion of the ball to direct it diagonally forward to the left side. The backward bounce is taken when the right foot is forward. The dribble behind the back and diagonally forward is taken when the left foot moves forward so that the leg is out of the way. The left hand then controls the ball as the dribble is continued. The entire dribble should be executed so that control is retained over the ball and speed down the court is not lessened (Fig. 1.21).

This dribble is effective when a player has an awareness of opponents who are behind her. It can be utilized when advancing the ball downcourt in a one-on-one situation or on a drive from the corner. It can be utilized in the lane to a lesser degree because of collapsing defenses and little protection of the ball while it is behind the player's back.

Reverse (Spin) Dribble

The reverse or spin dribble is another means of changing direction when being overplayed and when the crossover dribble is too dangerous to attempt. Because of its nature, this technique is the

a

b

c

d

Fig. 1.19 *Crossover Dribble. The dribbler approaches the defender at an angle (a). As her right foot is forward, the dribbler contacts the ball on its right side and bounces it across her body (b and c). The ball is then dribbled with the left hand forward (d).*

a   b   c

d   e   f

Fig. 1.20 *Change-of-Pace Dribble. The dribbler is moving at full speed (a). She is slowed down (b) and pulls her trunk erect to give the appearance of stopping, and has caused the defender to raise her arms (c). She flexes her trunk to proceed forward (d) and has beaten her opponent (e and f).*

a b c

Fig. 1.21 *Behind-the-Back Dribble. The defender takes away the sideline (a). The ball handler does behind-the-back dribble (b) and is free to continue her drive. (c).*

slowest means of changing direction. The advantage of this dribble is that a player may maintain visual contact with the ball throughout the maneuver. Its disadvantages are that the player must turn her back to the basket and lose visual contact with the basket and teammates ahead, and be susceptible to a double team effort from her blind side.

During the execution, a player reverses her direction and therefore must overcome her forward momentum prior to the reverse motion. To do this while dribbling with her right hand, she firmly plants her left foot while keeping the trunk flexed. The pivot or spin is made on the left foot while the right hand controls the underneath-outside portion of the ball. The spin must be made rapidly so that the ball is not carried. The head rotates quickly to the right. The right foot steps opposite the opponent's foot so that the opponent is put on the dribbler's hip. The left foot steps forward as the dribble is continued with the left hand. (Fig. 1.22).

It should be noted that only one bounce is required while the body turns. The subsequent bounce should be forward. Too often beginners do not turn quickly enough and require several bounces before they can proceed in a forward direction. The turn can be made rapidly, provided the dribbler swings in a 180-degree turn and places her foot opposite that of the defender. If more than once bounce is required before the dribbler is

turned, the opponent has time to adjust and can assume an overplaying position in the other direction.

Teachers/coaches should also watch the trunk of the dribbler as the foot is planted. If the trunk inclines backward, the spin is telegraphed to the defender.

Backward Dribble

Although this dribble is not often used in the normal course of the game, it does have value. At least the team's playmaker should know its usefulness. If she dribbles into the scoring area and all passing lanes are cut off by the defenders, she can use the backward dribble to back out to the top of the key to start another offensive thrust. This enables her to keep the ball alive while her teammates reposition. The fingers contact the front of the ball and the player can slide backward while looking for a free player. Another use of this dribble occurs when there is a loose ball in front of the player and she can simply pull it back to control it.

Between the Legs (Forward)

This dribble accomplishes the same purpose as the crossover, spin, or behind the back dribble. It is

a

b

c

d

Fig. 1.22 *Reverse Dribble. The dribbler approaches the defender (a), plants her left foot (b) and spins by her as she hooks her right foot past dark 20's hip (c) and is free (d).*

used when an opponent is guarding too closely for the crossover. It has an advantage over the spin dribble in that the player faces the direction she is going throughout the movement. Because the ball does not travel as far laterally as with the behind the back dribble, it is quicker and the body protects the ball.

The execution is similar to the behind the back except the ball is contacted so it moves forward between the legs. When dribbling with the right hand the weight is on the right foot as the ball is bounced forward between the legs.

Between the Legs (Backward)

Rather than changing direction laterally, the dribbler wishes to move in a backward direction quickly. She plants her right foot when dribbling to the right, pulls the ball backward between her legs and continues to dribble with her left hand or picks the ball up for a shot or pass.

The technique is used to free a player for a shot and its use protects the ball throughout the maneuver. It is a worthwhile technique for the good ball handler to develop.

Dribbling Drills

1. Columns at one end of the court. The first person in each column speed dribbles downcourt with the right hand and back with the left hand. Give the ball to the next person and go to the end of the same column. Repeat.

2. Same as drill 1 above, except speed dribble halfway down, control dribble the rest of the way. Repeat and return to place.

3. Same as drill 1 above, except players change hands and direction on signal. Therefore, dribbling will be in a zigzag manner.

4. All players hold a ball of some type. All dribble simultaneously and in any direction, avoiding collisions. Make sure all change hands and direction during the dribbling activity. Avoid letting players move in a circle. They have fun maneuvering in and out and, to one's amazement, avoid collisions. This is a control dribble and the ball must be kept low for changing direction. Regulate the size of the area to make the dribble challenging.

5. Columns of six or seven players are spaced about 6 ft. apart. The last player in the column has the ball and dribbles to the left of the first player, to the right of the second, and so on, until she has gone down and returned to her starting position. She gives the ball to the next player, who continues. Repeat until all have participated. When a dribbler goes around a player to the left, she dribbles with her left hand; when she goes around the player to the right, she dribbles with her right hand.

6. One column is in the middle behind the end line with chairs spaced as shown in Fig. 1.23. The first player dribbles as shown, always going to the inside of the chair, around it to the outside, and continuing. Dribblers stay at the opposite end in a column. The next dribbler may start as soon as the preceding one is around the first chair. Emphasize use of correct dribbling hand.

7. Each player with a ball. Dribble in place, moving the ball to the left, right, across in front and in back, in any sequence.

8. Each player with a ball. Dribble the ball forward and back with the right hand on the right side of the body. Repeat with the left hand on the left side.

9. Each player with a ball. Dribble the ball in front of the body from the right side to the left side with the right hand only. Repeat with the left hand.

10. Each player with a ball. Dribble the ball in a square around the body. Start on the right side with the right hand. Bounce the ball backward and behind the back to the left side, with the left hand bounce the ball forward and across to the right side. Take four bounces to complete square. Continue. Change direction.

11. Each player with a ball. Make a figure 8. With the right hand on the right side bounce the ball back, then forward between the legs; with the left hand bounce the ball back and forward between the legs to the right side. Continue. Change direction. Beginners may need eight bounces but this should be reduced to four bounces as soon as possible.

12. Each player with a ball. Walk forward bouncing the ball between the legs on each step. Repeat walking backwards. Increase to a jog and full speed.

13. Each player with a ball. Holding the ball with both hands bounce it back between the legs (side stride). Catch the ball behind the back and bounce the ball forward between the legs. Continue.

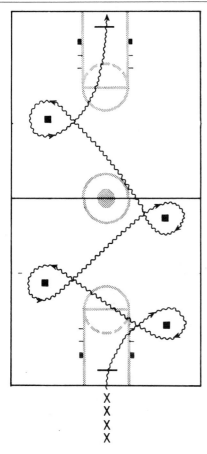

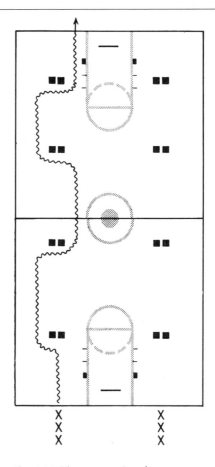

Fig. 1.23 *Players dribble to the inside of the chair, around it to the outside, and on to the next chair.*

Fig. 1.24 *Players practice the crossover dribble as the chairs are approached.*

14. Ike-Mike Drill. Separate players into groups of eight or ten players with a leader. The leader facing the group dribbles in any direction but changes direction frequently, moving left, right, forward, and back. The players in the group mimic her and move in the same direction of progress, that is, if the leader moves forward, the group moves backward. Change leaders.

15. Same as drill 14 above, only play tag. The leader tries to touch anyone while continuing to control her dribble. When a player is touched, places are exchanged. Caution the players that they must follow only the directional changes of the leader to escape a tag.

16. Paris. The dribbler utilizes a zigzag dribble to the opposite end. Her opponent starts two steps behind the dribbler. Without fouling, the opponent tries from the rear to slap the ball away from the dribbler. Emphasize an upward, underhand motion to send the ball forward. (In a game a teammate would be ready to recover the ball for the de-

fender.) Remind the dribblers that they are trying to advance to the opposite end as fast as possible; therefore, the zigs and zags should be as short as possible so that their forward direction is little delayed. Be certain to give all players an opportunity to dribble under stress and to be a chaser.

17. Columns. Place eight chairs in front of each column as shown in Fig. 1.24. The first player starts dribbling with her right hand and approaches the chair on the right in the first group of chairs. As she reaches the chair, she does a crossover dribble and continues dribbling with her left hand past the chairs. At the next group of chairs she approaches the chair on the left and uses the left-to-right crossover. She continues to the other end. Insist that players dribble up to the chairs before starting the crossover; otherwise the desirable lateral movement of the ball will not be acquired.

18. Columns at one end of the court. The first player becomes the dribbler and the second player becomes the opponent who takes her position about 6–8 ft. in front of the drib-

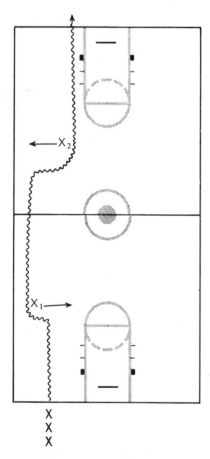

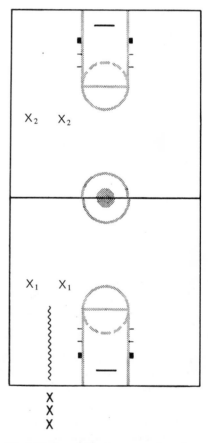

Fig. 1.25 As opponents X_1 and X_2 move to defend, the dribbler uses a crossover dribble toward the direction from which the defender comes.

Fig. 1.26 As a defender approaches, the dribbler uses a crossover dribble toward the direction from which she came.

bler. The purpose of this drill is for the dribbler to use the crossover dribble frequently while progressing downcourt and for the defender to make a stab at the ball only if she is certain she can gain possession of it.

19. Shuttle formation with no more than two groups at each end of the court, and two players spaced as shown in Fig. 1.25. The player with the ball dribbles toward the opposite end. As the dribbler approaches, player X_1 moves laterally to try to defend. The dribbler uses a crossover dribble to continue in the direction *from* which the defender came. As X_2 is approached, another crossover is executed and the dribbler continues to the end of the court. Continue.

20. Same as drill 19 above, only four defenders are on the court as shown in Fig. 1.26. As the dribbler approaches each set of defenders, one of them (designated ahead of time) approaches the dribbler. In this drill the dribbler cannot predetermine to which direction she will cross over; it depends on the direction from which the defender comes, which is more gamelike.

21. Shuttle formation with groups at each end of the court. The first dribbler progresses downcourt using a change of pace maneuver. Use the right hand going downcourt and the left hand when returning. Later, alternate hands during each trip and add a defender.

22. Same as drill 21 above, only try the behind the back or reverse dribble.

23. Shuttle formation with no more than two groups at each end of the court. The first player in each column is the dribbler; the second, the defender. The dribbler tries to progress to the opposite end by using any dribbling maneuver. During each trip, try several maneuvers. Repeat.

24. Pairs at each restraining circle. One player dribbles while her opponent tries to obtain possession of the ball. Both players must stay within the boundaries of the circle. Exchange places. Use all types of dribbles.

SHOOTING

Usually there is little difficulty in motivating students to learn to shoot. Most students want to learn and perfect this skill. After ball handling (passing, catching, and dribbling), shooting probably ranks next in importance. All players must develop some degree of proficiency in shooting. If a player is recognized as one who takes few shots and is relatively inaccurate in those that she does take, an opponent does not have to be very concerned about this player's scoring ability. Instead, she can focus her attention on assisting teammates who have more difficult opponents to guard. By being able to sag off her own opponent, a defender can help immensely in developing a better team defense. A good player must develop a jump shot, set shot, and ability to drive. With these three shots she is a threat from almost any position on the floor and will demand a great deal of attention from the opponents.

In developing shooting technique, attention should be devoted to correct shooting principles. Accuracy is dependent upon balance, concentration, confidence, and correct release. Balance can be achieved by keeping the center of gravity over the base. The head should be turned toward the basket, and shoulders, hips, and feet should be squared to the basket. This brings the body in line with the target.

Shooters should concentrate on the target while taking aim, during the shot, and after the ball has been released. Shooters should not watch the arc of the flight, for they tend to raise their head slightly early causing the shoulders and trunk to be elevated which, in turn, may cause inaccuracy.

Confidence develops after players become aware that they are successful within a certain range of the basket. This confidence increases with additional game experience against various types of defenses. To be a successful shooter a player must believe that every attempt she makes will result in a score. Individual defense or team defense against an opposing team may be geared to break down the confidence of good scorers. After being intimidated several times, a shooter's confidence is jeopardized and she tends to begin to pass off to other players without taking her normal number of shots. The psychological advantage of a Charlotte Lewis or a Lusia Harris blocking shots cannot be underestimated. Even in beginning play a good defensive player can intimidate an offensive player to the extent that she rarely takes a shot; or even to the point where she may receive passes infrequently. Shooters can gain confidence by practicing against different defensive players and acquiring moves to place the opponent at a disadvantage.

There are three important aspects of the shooting process: correct grip on the basketball, body alignment with the target, and alignment of the shooting hand and arm to the target. The body will be correctly aligned if the shooting foot (right foot for right-hand shooter) faces the target. This tends to square the hips and shoulder to the target.

For proper grip of the ball the pads of all of the fingers and the pads at the base of all of the fingers contact the ball. The more distal pad of the thumb also contacts the ball. Contact with the ball by the pad at the base of the thumb is optional, although preferred (Fig. 1.27). Contact with the ball only by the most distal pads of the fingers provides too little control and is highly undesirable. At no time should the very center portion of the hand contact the ball (Fig. 1.28).

The guiding or balance hand is placed on the side of the ball or on the underneath and front side of the ball. In both instances the fingers point upward. The pads of the fingers contact the ball similarly as the shooting hand, although as much of the little finger may not be in contact with the ball.

When a player receives a pass or picks up her dribble, her shooting hand should be in correct position on the ball. The thumb is at a 45 degree angle with the index finger and the other fingers are comfortably spread. The player simply rotates the ball and allows the ball to slide through her guiding hand to adjust the grip for shooting. As a player starts to shoot, she moves the ball to the center of her body and straight up the midline of the body in front of her face before she releases the shot (Fig. 1.29). Emphasis should be placed on the raising of the ball in this manner. Players should be corrected when the ball is received to the side of the body and the ball is raised from that position as shown in Figure 1.30.

The elbow, hand, and index finger point toward the target and are in line with the shooting foot. The index finger is in line with the shooting eye. The knees are flexed comfortably. The eyes are on the target. The force for the shot is derived from the extension of the legs and the flexion of the wrist. The arm extends naturally from the hinge action at the elbow joint and the forward force comes from the hand flexion. Too much emphasis on "straightening" the arm often causes players to cock their wrist more, getting their fingers further under the ball, which in turn prevents their fingers from af-

Fig. 1.27 *Grip. Correct position of the hand on the ball.*

Fig. 1.28 *Incorrect Grip. The palm is in contact with the ball, and the wrist is not cocked.*

a   b

c   d

Fig. 1.29 *Elevation of the Ball to Shooting Position. The ball is received to the side of the body (a), brought in to the midline of the body (b), and raised overhead (c).*

a

b

c

d

Fig. 1.30 *Poor Elevation of the Ball to Shooting Position. The ball is received to the side of the body (a); is raised overhead to the side of the midline (b–d).*

fording the proper flexion. With the proper thrust of the fingers the ball will go off the finger tips of the index and middle fingers last. Those two fingers are the guide for accuracy. The thrust of the fingers at release causes the proper follow through with the palm of the hand facing the floor (Fig. 1.31). Backspin on the ball is produced which prevents the ball from floating (due to air resistance) and also causes the desirable rebound action when the ball hits the backboard. The guide arm also ends high with fingers pointing upward.

During the shot the head, back, and hips are in vertical alignment. When the player jumps to shoot, she should land in the same place from which she took off.

A few other comments should be addressed to the alignment of the body to the target. Unquestionably, footwork is the key to this alignment. When a player catches the ball she can land in a jump stop with both feet contacting the floor simultaneously or she can land with her inside foot first followed by the outside foot. Both techniques have advantages and in both instances the feet may be parallel or one foot slightly in front of the other.

In utilizing the jump stop, the shot can be executed quicker as the player already has both feet on

Fig. 1.31 *Proper Follow-through on a Shot. The guiding hand is still high, and the palm of the shooting hand faces the floor.*

the ground and is ready to extend the legs to start the shot. However, if the shooting foot does not land facing the target, the player must "square" her body in the air or she will not be square at release. When catching the ball and planting the inside foot first, a slight adjustment can be made in its position as the outside foot contacts the floor. It probably is easier for many players to square in this fashion although it takes somewhat longer to get the shot off.

After practicing for any length of time, players become aware of their shooting range and the types of shots with which they are most proficient. They also know the places on the court from which they are most successful. They should continue to maintain their proficiency from these areas but also work to develop other shots and from a greater range. However, during a game, players should only attempt shots in which they have great confidence and only if they have balance and time to take an unhurried shot.

Another important factor for all players to remember is the desirability of taking high percentage shots. The closer a player is to the basket, the greater chance she has of making the shot. Therefore, for beginning players it is highly desirable that most scoring efforts be limited to layup shots or other shots within 6–8 ft. of the basket. More highly skilled players will be forced to take longer shots because of the better defense against which they will be playing. Nevertheless most of their shots should be taken within a 15-to-20-ft. radius of the basket. Beyond the 20-ft. radius the percentage of successful shots decreases rapidly. This point should be made very clear to all players so that they can maintain their poise and patience until they can move the ball into good shooting territory. Team offenses should be dedicated to maneuvering the ball for as many layups and shots within a 10-ft. radius of the basket as possible.

When practicing shooting, drills should be presented and players should be encouraged to practice the aforementioned types of shots that are so important for each player to develop — mainly, the set shot, jump shot, and driving layup shot. Practice should be devoted to drills utilizing the various kinds of shots from appropriate places on the court. Increased maneuverability in driving shots, greater accuracy in executing all types of shots, and increased range for these attempts are of great consequence.

Some players develop a favorite spot on the court from which they like to shoot. Once the defense is aware of this, they can overplay the opponent in this area and prevent her from shooting, or at least impose considerable harassment. If the shooter lacks confidence from other areas on the court, the defense can render her practically useless as a scoring threat.

Although there is a need for players to learn to shoot with confidence from various places on the court, it is important for players to practice from those places where they will most likely take their shots. It is from these spots that they must learn to receive a pass, pivot (if necessary), shoot immediately, or drive for the goal. Much practice time should be devoted to perfecting these moves. *All* players therefore need not practice shooting from the same spots unless the offensive pattern requires rotation of players to all positions. If this is not the case, it is more beneficial for each player to practice the type of shots she is likely to use in the game plan.

It is also important for players to learn to release the ball as rapidly as possible. The principle in softball where the catch becomes part of the throw should be followed in basketball. When a player is open and in scoring range the shot should be taken immediately. Often in practice players receive a pass from a rebounder, bounce the ball a few times, and then take a shot. This is not very gamelike. It would be much better practice to receive the pass and take the shot immediately or practice whatever feinting techniques are desirable before the attempted shot. In highly competitive play, the opening rarely exists for more than a split second. This is not to say that a player should rush a shot. Far from this. The faster a player can release the ball though, the fewer times she will be rushed; consequently, the more times she will be able to shoot in the game.

Another point should be made very clear and emphasized repeatedly. Even though a player is in good shooting position and well within her range, it is far better to pass off to a teammate who is open and closer to the basket for a shorter shot. A layup is more likely to score than even a 10-footer! It is important to instill players with the concept that an assist for a field goal is as important as the scoring of the field goal itself. Development of this belief was one of the reasons for the Boston Celtic dynasty for so many years. This was particularly evident in the playoffs of 1969 when they were opposed by the Los Angeles Lakers. At the conclusion of the playoffs won by the Celtics, one of the Lakers admitted that they had far better personnel but that the Celtics were a far better team! The same thing might be said of the Portland victory over Philadelphia in 1977. Teamwork and unselfishness does a great deal to overcome individual weaknesses.

Arc of Flight

As is the case of any projectile, a shot follows the path of a parabola; but since the ball does not drop to the same height from which it was released, the height of its arc will occur closer to the basket than to the shooter. This trajectory of the ball's flight is dependent upon its velocity and angle of release. Since excessive distance is not involved in shooting, velocity is not the greatest concern. The angle of release becomes the primary matter of interest.

Since the basket is supported 10 ft. above the floor, the ball must descend from above through the net. One can easily visualize that if the ball could drop vertically at a 90 degree angle with the floor, it has the greatest chance of passing through the basket. As that angle is reduced from 90 degrees, the opening to the basket reduces sharply. As the angle diminishes, there is a greater chance of the ball hitting the front or back rim and rebounding away from the basket. Therefore, the higher the arc, the greater the chance of the ball dropping through the basket. The lower the arc (flatter the trajectory), the less chance of the ball entering the target — or, said in another way, the greater the accuracy that is needed. However, the higher the arc the greater the ball's velocity. Therefore, the greater the rebound when the ball strikes the backboard or rim of the basket. A high arc also requires greater strength than a low arc because the ball must travel further. All factors considered, it appears as though it is best to encourage shooters to release the ball at a 45 degree angle. However, if this desirable release cannot be achieved it is better to err in shooting at a greater angle rather than a smaller angle.

Point of Aim

There seems to be a growing trend toward the use of the backboard on all shots except those directly in front of the basket or along the baseline. The point of aim on the backboard will vary and will be discussed in the next section.

Considerable attention has been given by numerous authorities to exactly what part of the basket a player should aim for in order to be successful. Among those suggestions advanced are: over the front rim, the rear rim, the hooks that hold the basket to the back rim, the space between the rim, and there are probably others. If one considers that a shot is nothing more than an accurate pass, it seems wise to aim where a player wants the ball to go — the center of the basket. If a player is capable of developing a high degree of accuracy, then the player will hit what she aims for. There is no need to hit the rim, if a player can hit the center of the basket. There is greater margin for error in the center of the basket than there is on the rim or hooks. If a player does aim for the center of the basket and is consistently short or long, then a modification of her point of aim would be necessary.

Regardless of the target a player aims for, her eyes should remain focused on it throughout the shot. Her eyes should never be raised to follow the flight of the ball.

Use of the Backboard

Since players do not shoot with the same arc and force, it is erroneous to identify a point of aim for all shooters. For any specified shot there is probably no one spot that all shooters could use with ease and obtain similar success. The layup shot probably comes closest, but there still would be some variations.

When the backboard is used, the point of aim moves further from the basket or closer to the edge of the backboard as a player moves closer to the sideline. Her point of aim moves closer to the basket as she moves closer to the center of the floor.

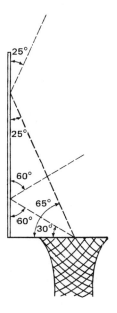

Fig. 1.32 *The ball approaches the basket at these angles when rebounded from different spots (gravity and spin neglected).*[1]

The height of the shot against the backboard depends on the arc and force of the shot and the distance from the basket that the ball strikes the backboard. The greater the arc, the higher the ball should strike the backboard; the flatter the arc, the lower it must hit. It can be seen in Fig. 1.32 that the ball striking higher on the backboard approaches the basket at a greater angle than the one hitting lower on the backboard. The ball that approaches the backboard at a 25 degree angle approaches the basket at a 65 degree angle whereas the ball that approaches the backboard at a 60 degree angle approaches the basket at a 30 degree angle. This means that the ball striking higher on the backboard has a better chance of entering the basket because it approaches the basket more nearly at a right angle and, therefore, requires less accuracy to score.

A ball shot with much force must hit lower on the backboard than a ball shot with a lighter touch; otherwise the force causes the ball to rebound away from the basket before it has time to drop through. A ball shot closer to the sideline must hit higher on the backboard than a ball shot closer to the basket with the same arc because the ball must hit out further from the basket (Fig. 1.33). Since it has a longer distance to rebound, it will take more time to reach the basket, and gravity has a longer time to act on it. Side shots must also be shot with somewhat greater force, because the ball has further to carry after it strikes the backboard. A player who shoots at the same angle from the basket but at varying distances can use the same point of aim against the backboard, provided that arc and force are relatively the same. This is shown in Fig. 1.33. Some variation is possible because the ball need not enter the center of the basket.

Backspin on the ball will decrease the angle of the rebound and so increase the angle of approach to the basket. This occurs because a ball with backspin pushes upward against the backboard on contact and consequently is pushed downward. Since it will drop closer to the backboard and fall more quickly (because of the downward push rendered by the backboard and the force of gravity), backspin helps to compensate for the effects of a ball hitting too hard against the backboard.

TYPES OF SHOTS

Layup Shot

The layup is probably the most important of all shots. It is a shot that skilled players can ill afford to

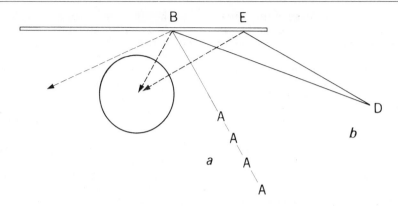

Fig. 1.33 *(a) Use of the same spot on the backboard when shots are taken from the same angle (A–B) but at varying distances from the basket; (b) a shot taken from closer to the sideline must strike the backboard further from the basket (D–E) in order to be successful. If a shot is taken from D and hits the backboard at B, it will miss the basket entirely.*[2]

miss and one with which beginning players can achieve reasonable success. It is the shot used when a player is close to the basket and often is used to culminate a fast break. Because it is taken close to the basket, a layup shot must descend into the basket quickly. Therefore, it must be shot softly against the backboard or it will rebound past the basket.

In executing the shot from the right side of the basket the player catches the ball as she steps on her right foot. She then steps left and jumps high into the air (like a high jump, not a long jump) while carrying the ball high overhead. The ball is laid gently against the backboard as the player follows through toward the point of aim which is slightly higher and to the right of the basket. A soft shot will result if the player carries the ball high above her head before the release and lets the ball roll off her fingertips (Fig. 1.34). Very little spin is desired. The follow-through is completed as the player lands with ankles and knees flexed and is ready to rebound or go on defense.

Beginners have difficulty with the shot

- when they approach from a poor angle (either too acute or too wide)
- when they start to release the ball at chest, shoulder, or head level
- when they attempt to use two hands (tried more often on the side of the nonpreferred hand)
- when the shooting hand is under the ball so that after the ball hits the backboard it is still traveling in an upward flight.

Elimination of any of these problems should bring better results. Greatest emphasis should probably be placed on raising the ball high overhead. This tends to allow the ball to roll off the fingertips and reduces the force.

When shooting from the left side the ball should be caught with the step on the left foot and the shot should be taken with the jump from the right foot. The ball should be shot from the left hand. Beginners or less skilled players may be permitted to shoot with the preferred hand at all times. Takeoff should be from the appropriate foot (left foot for right-handed shooters). When the approach is down the middle the ball can be shot with either hand (the one away from the defender) and the takeoff should be made from the appropriate foot. The point of aim is just over the front rim of the basket, not the backboard. The approach down the center should be used only when there is no alternative. Anytime it is possible, the player should veer to one side or the other and shoot with the preferred hand. After the shot, the player should be ready to rebound if the shot is missed or to hurry back on defense if the attempt is successful.

When shooting layups it is generally accepted that the right hand is used from the right side and the left hand from the left side. Players must be encouraged to shoot with either hand near the basket, but there are occasions when a left hand layup from the right side is desirable and the same can be said about the right hand layup from the left side.

If a defender has taken away the baseline on a drive, the inside hand is the freer hand for shooting

a

b

c

d

Fig. 1.34 *Layup Shot. The player catches the ball on her right foot (a), steps left (b), and shoots (c). Note the follow-through. The left hand layup is released as the player jumps off her right foot (d).*

purposes. On a baseline drive from the corner it is easier and quicker to shoot with the inside hand since the shoulders and hips need not be turned as far to become square to the target (point of aim).

Variations of this shot take place when a player "floats" on a drive. This technique is shown in Fig. 1.35. The number of fakes or "pumps" used will vary according to the situation.

Power Layup

This layup may be executed from a dribble or after receiving a pass. The player lands with both feet simultaneously and jumps high and toward the basket releasing the ball on her upward flight (Fig. 1.36.) It is a power move taking the player toward the basket and placing her in good rebounding position.

Set Shot

The set shot is generally limited to shooting from those areas that are considered long shots. This distance will vary depending upon the skill of the players. For experienced teams, however, the set shot should probably be used in the range of 20–25 ft. from the basket. For beginning players a "long shot" may be a distance of only 10–15 ft. Regardless of the players' potential, they should only attempt shots for which they do not have to strain. Therefore, the type of shot and range must depend on the ability of the individual player. In advanced play, teams will have difficulty in penetrating the defense for close shots if they do not have a potential outside shooter. Without an outside scoring threat the defense can sag and wait for the offense to try to penetrate.

There are two types of set shots — namely, the two-hand set (chest shot) and the one-hand set (push shot). The two-hand shot has gone out of favor in this country although still used most effectively in the Asiatic countries. It will not be discussed in this text.

The one-hand shot has become preferable because its release is quicker, its execution is similar to a jump shot and, actually, is a leadup to the jump shot.

This shot may be attempted while stationary or while moving. When stationary it is usually used when a player is beyond her range for a jump shot. When on the move, it is used when the player desires to continue her forward progress. Actually the layup is a one-hand set done on the move.

The player takes her usual stride position with feet pointing toward the target. The ball is held at chest level. Knees are flexed as the wrist cocks near chin level with the index finger in line with the outside portion of the cheek and the elbow in line with the shooting foot. The knees extend as the ball is pushed up and forward. The player should land at the same spot from which she took off. (Fig. 1.37 a–c).

When the shot is done on the move the player has additional momentum. She may choose to allow her forward momentum to continue if there is an opening so that she can release the ball closer to the basket. The release of the ball is the same as while stationary, but the player must square her body to the target to release (Fig. 1.37 d–h). Emphasis should be placed on the inside foot facing the target on takeoff.

Another use of the shot occurs when a player fakes a shot, causes the opponent to go up in the air, and moves her shooting foot to the inside of the defender for a relatively unobstructed shot. This technique is valuable when a player has completed her dribble; otherwise she would drive by her opponent. The shot can be taken even when the opponent is overplaying the baseline side and gives away the inside move (Fig. 1.38).

To help students acquire the kinesthetic sense of the proper release for the one-hand set, players may be spaced informally around the gymnasium, each with a ball. Each player raises the ball overhead properly and attempts to gain the feeling of the ball rolling off her fingertips as she releases it straight up into the air so that she may catch it without moving. Little force is necessary at the start and then the ball may be "shot" higher with more force, still allowing the player to catch her "shot" without moving. This is an excellent technique for beginning players to use if they tend to release the ball too low or from the palm of the hand or the greater portion of all of the fingers at the same time.

Jump Shot

The jump shot has revolutionized the game of basketball. Every good player should have this shot in her repertoire. It is a shot that can be used from all ranges — short, medium, or long. Because this shot is released at the peak of the jump, all the force must be exerted from the shooting hand; thus, greater strength is necessary for shooting this shot in contrast to others from comparable distances.

In order to block this shot a defensive player of the same height must jump as soon as the shooter. Any type of feint should delay the defender's jump and, therefore, prevent her from blocking the shot. The shooter should have difficulty in getting

a b

c d

Fig. 1.35 *Layout Dribble. The player dribbles (a), catches the ball on her right foot (b), steps left (c) and reaches for the layup (d).*

Fig. 1.36 *Power Layup. The medium post maneuvers for a pass (a and b), fakes right (c), dribbles (with the wrong hand) (d), lands on both feet as she catches the ball (e), and does a power layup (f).*

a

b

c

d

Fig. 1.37 *One-Hand Set (a–c). The player eyes the basket and moves toward a forward-backward stride (a). Her knees are flexed and the ball is raised overhead (b). Legs are extended and she follows through (c). Moving One-Hand Set (d–h).*

e

f

g

h

Fig. 1.37 (Continued) The player fakes to her left (d and e). Note the good position of the ball. She pushes off from her right foot (f), steps across with her left foot (g), and releases the shot (h).

a b c

d e

Fig. 1.38 *Step Past the Defender. The ball handler drives (a), and the defender takes the baseline (b). The offensive player uses her left foot as her pivot foot (c), steps past the defender (d), and is free for a shot (e). (Note: the distance covered from the time the offensive player catches the ball.)*

the shot off only against a much taller opponent. The jump shot may be executed by a player facing in any direction, although the release is always made when the player has turned to square her shoulders with the basket. The player may start with her back to the basket, in which case she generally does a fall away jump shot. She may be facing the endline on either side of the court or facing the sideline prior to her shot. In either case, as she makes her jump into the air she also turns to face the basket before the release.

The shot may be made while a player is stationary, following the reception of a pass on a cut (Fig. 1.39), or following a dribble (Fig. 1.40 and 1.41). In

Fig. 1.39 *Jump Shot. Following a drive, the player eyes her target as she prepares for her jump (a), shot (b), and follow-through (c). The hand is hyperextended with the index finger in line with the outside portion on the cheek and the elbow pointing toward the target (d).*

a b c

Fig. 1.40 *Jump Shot. Another player drives around her opponent (a), lands with a two-foot stop with both knees well flexed (b), and extends for the shot (c). Note how the player in (b and c) did not plant either foot facing the target and therefore is not square. In (c) the head is turned to eye the target and the trunk is turned to allow the elbow to point toward the target. This is a common error.*

the first instance the shot must be preceded by some kind of a fake to give the shooter a split-second advantage if she is guarded rather closely. If not, a fake is undesirable. In either of the other two instances, if the player gains a slight advantage over her defender, the shot can be made immediately; otherwise it, too, should be preceded by a feint of some sort. When a player is on the move, either dribbling or receiving a pass while cutting, the shot (if made immediately) may be made from a greater distance from the basket because of the added momentum that the body has gained. When shooting from a stationary position, greater success will be achieved when the player is closer to the basket. If a player drives, stops, and fakes and then goes up for her shot, she has lost some of her forward momentum and her shooting range will diminish. Players should be made aware of these factors and encouraged to shoot from varying ranges accordingly.

Players generally need the force from a 2-ft. takeoff regardless of what movement has preceded the start of the shot. Stronger players may be able to use the 1-ft. takeoff if they are on the move. If this is the case, the takeoff should be from the foot opposite

the shooting hand. If the 2-ft. takeoff is used, it may be from either a side stride or forward-backward stride — the latter most commonly used when a player is on the move, since it provides better balance stopping the forward movement. As the shot is started, ankles, knees, and hips flex to provide a powerful extension directly upward. Arms raise so that upper arms are parallel to the floor and the shooting elbow points toward the basket. As the player jumps in the air, hands turn the ball so that the shooting hand is behind and under the ball and the other hand steadies the ball until the shot is released. This occurs at the peak of the jump. The player literally tries to "hang" in the air before releasing the ball. Shooting on the way up (a common mistake) or on the way down defeats the purpose of the jump shot. Timing the release is critical. When the ball is overhead, the hand is cocked parallel to the floor with the index finger in line with the eyebrow as shown in Fig. 1.39 d. The ball is released by extension of the arm and hand and finger flexion. Follow-through is high and toward the basket. The guide arm also ends high.

The greatest problem for beginners seems to be

a   b

c   d   e

Fig. 1.41 *Getting Square. The player cuts toward the ball (a), lands with both feet at the same time to get square (b), and shoots (c). The player also may catch the ball as the inside foot lands (d) and square to the hoop with the subsequent (e).*

in acquiring the feeling of releasing the ball at the apex of the jump. Some preliminary techniques may help them acquire this kinesthetic sense. Players (each with a ball) can be positioned informally around the gym, or they may imagine they are holding a ball. On signal, they jump into the air, raise their arms overhead so that upper arms are parallel to the floor (particularly the shooting arm), the elbow of the shooting arm points toward the basket, and the hand is overhead and parallel to the floor. They return to the floor with the ball still in their hands. Repeat a few times. After making any general corrections, let them continue jumping at their own speed. Next, let them find a partner and stand about 6 ft. apart. Each twosome should have a ball. Let them practice jump passing to each other, emphasizing a high arc as for a shot. Once they seem to acquire the correct technique, let them try the shot at a basket. Encourage them to stay close to the basket — up to 6 ft. from it. As they become proficient at this distance, they may move further from the basket.

Hook Shot

The hook shot is used most extensively by pivot players, although other players also find it useful. Its use is generally limited to short ranges when a player is closely guarded. The shot may be executed either while a player is stationary or following a dribble. This shot is made with the back to the basket while stepping away from the basket so that the shooter is in poor rebounding position.

For a right-hand hook shot the player steps to her right with her left foot and, at the same time, rotates her trunk slightly left and looks over her left shoulder for her point of aim. The ball is held in the right hand, supported by the forearm. The shooting arm extends in a horizontal plane and the arm is brought up overhead while remaining in an extended position. The ball is released by hand and finger flexion when the ball is almost directly overhead. The arm follows through overhead and toward the basket, and the body turns to face the basket on landing (Fig. 1.42). Beginners tend to flex the

a   b   c

Fig. 1.42 *Hook Shot. Preparation (a), release (b), and follow-through (c).*

arm while raising it overhead and/or bring the arm in front of the face for the release rather than overhead. These points must be emphasized.

This shot is impossible to defend by an opponent between the shooter and the basket, which is why it is so effective when close to the basket. However, the shooter does need several feet of space to the side of her shooting arm because her arm is extended throughout the shot and it takes a relatively long time to raise the arm overhead in this position. A teammate's defender may try to block the shot from the rear or side.

The shot can be used following a rebound if there is sufficient space. It is also effective following a drive. In this instance, the player has some momentum from moving, so the shot must be made with greater fingertip control. Pivot players, in particular, should learn to execute this shot well, going in either direction and using either hand.

Layback Shot

When a player is guarded closely near the basket on her nonpreferred shooting hand side (left side for right-handed shooter), the layback shot may be used in preference to a hook. The player may have recovered a loose ball or a rebound on that side of the basket, or she may have been dribbling in on the right side of the basket, forced under the basket and around to the left side. In any case the shot is started when the player has her back to the basket (pivoting if necessary to get into this position). She looks back toward the basket, takes a step with the foot opposite her shooting hand, raises her shooting hand, and releases the ball as high as possible (Fig. 1.43).

Stab Shot

This shot is executed close to the basket, generally in the lane, and is valuable because it takes the shooter toward the basket for rebounding opportunities. The shot is usually taken following a dribble. The player lands with her feet facing the sideline that allows her to protect the ball with her body. She jumps off both feet toward the basket. The ball is released upward. A three-point play often results as the defensive player bellies up on the shot (Fig. 1.44).

a b c

Fig. 1.43 *Layback Shot. Note that the eyes are on the point of aim throughout the shot.*

Pump or Double Pump Moves

The pump and double pump moves have been popularized by many of the top collegiate and men's professional players. A pump is a faking maneuver in which a shooter fakes one kind of a shot and shoots another one. A double pump refers to two such fakes. Examples of a pump are: fake a normal layup and shoot it underhand; fake the underhand shot and shoot the normal layup; fake the left-hand layup and shoot the right-hand layup; and fake the right-hand layup and shoot it left-handed.

Tip-In

The tip-in is an excellent tactic used to score from a rebound when the player can control the ball.

To execute the shot the player must have previously acquired good rebounding position in front of her defensive player and within a few feet of the basket. Her hips, knees, and ankles are flexed; hands are up, elbows about shoulder high. (Although more height can be gained by starting with the arms in a lower position, in the congested rebounding area a player may not have enough space

Fig. 1.44 *Stab Shot. The defensive player takes away the baseline (a). The offensive player drives inside (b), lands with her feet facing the sideline (c), and leans toward the hoop for the layup (d).*

to raise her arms when desired.) As a missed shot rebounds off the backboard the player must judge the angle at which it is descending and time her jump so that she can tap the ball at the peak of her jump. In essence, as she contacts the ball she controls it with her fingertips instantaneously and then pushes it upward just as she would in executing a layup shot. She lands with ankles, knees, and hips flexed ready to make another attempt if the shot is missed (Fig. 1.45).

Offensive Rebound Shot

When the offensive player has rebound position on the defender but is too far from the basket or cannot control the ball to tip it, she should catch the rebound and then go back up for her shot. It is advisable for her to move toward the basket in this maneuver. In other words, some type of layup is preferable to a jump or hook shot. It takes her closer to the basket for the shot and also may cause the defender to foul her.

Once the player has rebounded the ball, she tries to fake her opponent into the air, thus allowing the shooter to take a step toward the basket. She carries the ball high overhead before releasing it. The follow-through is similar to any other one-hand shot.

The power layup is also appropriate. If a player near the basket can not tip-in the ball, she should rebound the ball, land, and go back up with the power layup.

Free Throw

The importance of free throw shooting should not be underestimated. It is one of the most vital scoring opportunities in any game. Looking over statistics from previous years it can be seen that in roughly 20 to 30 percent of all games the winning team makes more free throws than the losing team. This may mean the difference in winning several games during the season. It may also mean the difference between a winning season and a losing season.

Free throw practice should be incorporated into every practice session. For best results, practice should be held at various times in the daily schedule during the season. Shooting early in the practice session when players are fresh is common early in the season as shooting form is perfected or while beginners are learning. After the shot is learned, practice should be made when players are somewhat fatigued under more gamelike conditions. At this stage players should take no more than two

shots at a time to simulate game conditions. Shooting ten in a row is of little value beyond the early learning stage.

Players should be encouraged to use the same type of shot for free throws that they use successfully on other 15-ft. shots. For some, it will be a one-hand set and, possibly for a few, it will be a jump shot.

Regardless of the style of the shot, a player should establish a certain routine that is followed automatically under game conditions. Of course, these must be learned in practice sessions so that their use becomes automatic.

1. Once in the free throw area the player should check the positioning of her teammates and that of the opponents.
2. She should then approach the free throw line, accept the ball from the official, and place her feet behind the line. (When players are learning, particular attention should be given to their foot position to assure that they do not touch or go over the line during the shot or on the follow-through.)
3. The player should bounce the ball a few times to get the feel of the ball and also to relax shoulders, arms, and fingers.
4. The shooter should then place her hands on the ball in the position she desires and sight her target.
5. She should take a deep breath for further relaxation and then shoot.

The free throw is deserving of extensive practice. Approximately 25 percent of all points made in a game are scored by this means. Is ample time spent on this technique in practice sessions? In practice all players should be able to shoot between 70 and 80 percent of their attempts. This may be somewhat reduced under game conditions.

DRILLS

When players are learning a particular shot, they should practice without opposition and within 3–5 ft. of the basket. They should concentrate on body alignment, grip, raising the ball properly, the cocking of the wrist, flexion of the wrist at release and follow-through of both arms. Once they learn the technique of the shot and become somewhat proficient in its use, more gamelike conditions should be added in a progressive sequence.

Depending upon the type of shot, the next progression would permit the shooter to dribble or receive a pass prior to the shot. Since the player has

a

b

c

d

Fig. 1.45 *Tip-in Shot. Fingers control the ball as it is pushed upward.*

control of the ball, the addition of the dribble is easiest. This can be done while learning the layup, jump, and hook shots. Following the dribble sequence, the player should then receive a pass and execute the shot directly; later, a dribble can follow the reception of the pass if court position permits. It is better not to precede set shots with a dribble. The player should shoot immediately after receiving a pass.

An opponent should then be added. At first the defender should remain stationary, putting a hand up to block the shot and offering only token resistance. Next, the defender should be permitted to move just one foot and finally she is free to try to oppose the shooter under gamelike conditions.

The shooter then should add a feint to the sequence to gain an advantage over the defender.

Throughout this progression the instructor can assure that the shooter is able to get her shot off by designating where the defender may take her position. For example, if set shots are being attempted, the defensive player should be instructed to guard loosely. If driving shots are being practiced, the defender should move in closer to the shooter. As the shooter gains confidence and improves in marksmanship, the defensive player should be permitted to defend in any manner she wishes so that the shooter can learn to adjust to the defender's position — that is, to drive if she is close and to set if she is loose.

Layup Drills

1. Five or six players at each basket with two or three balls. Two or three players shoot while positioned to the side or in front of the basket. Each player shoots four or five shots and gives the ball to another player.

2. Two columns, one on each side of the basket at a 45 degree angle (Fig. 1.46). The first player in each column stands at the edge of the free throw line. More advanced players should start from the top of the restraining circle. For beginners, lines can be placed on the floor at a 45 degree angle to the basket so that they can approach the basket from a good angle. (Beginners have a tendency to increase this angle — move closer to the sideline — which makes the shot more difficult.) The right line is the shooting line and the left is the rebounding line. The first player in the shooting line dribbles in, takes her layup, continues running under the basket while watching to see if her shot is successful, and then goes to the outside and end of the line on the left. The first player from the line on the left runs in, obtains the rebound, pivots to face the next shooter, passes to her, and runs to the inside and end of the right-hand line. Continue. Shoot also from the left and down the center. With beginners, several items must be stressed. They tend to rebound their own shot and get in the way of the proper rebounder. If this is a problem, they may be instructed to continue under the basket and touch the wall before continuing to the end of the line on the left. Rebounders must be encouraged to jump for the rebound and not permit any ball to hit the floor. If the shot should bounce off the rim away from the rebounder, she should hustle to retrieve it, pivot from that position to face the shooter, and pass to her. The rebounder should not retrieve the ball and walk back under the basket before passing it to the shooter. As players improve they should be encouraged to use one bounce only; perhaps two from the top of the circle.

3. Same as drill 2 above, only the shooters do not dribble in for the layup. As the rebounder gets the ball in her hands, the shooter cuts in to receive a pass from the rebounder and then shoots without benefit of a dribble. Emphasis must be placed on the two-step takeoff for the shot. Rebounders must be instructed *not* to pass until the shooter is cutting. Shooters must not start their cut until the rebounder has retrieved the ball.

4. Partners with a ball. One player dribbles in and shoots, her opponent follows, rebounds, and both go to the opposite side; continue.

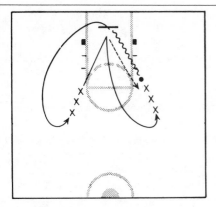

Fig. 1.46 *Two lines for layup drill: shooting from the right and rebounding from the left.*

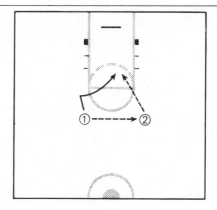

Fig. 1.47 *Give-and-Go Play. 1 passes to 2 and receives a return pass as she cuts for goal.*

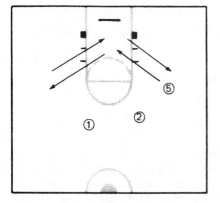

Fig. 1.48 *Shooting Layups on the Move. Player 5 receives passes alternately from 1 and 2.*

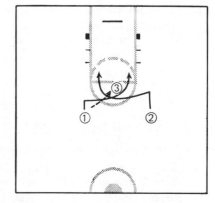

Fig. 1.49 *Practice of a Scissor Maneuver. Two guards practice cutting techniques and the pivot hands off to either one.*

5. Give and go. Players are lined up at each basket (Fig. 1.47). Player 1 passes to 2 and cuts for the basket; 2 passes to 1 for a layup. Player "gives" a pass and "goes" for the basket. Practice from both sides.

6. Threes or in three columns; Player 5 opposite the foul line on the right side; Players 1 and 2 at top of the key, each with a ball (Fig. 1.48). 5 cuts, receives a pass from 1, shoots, rebounds, passes to 1, moves to the left side, cuts to basket, receives a pass from 2, shoots, rebounds, passes to 2. Continue for 30 seconds. Rotate.

7. Players line up as shown (Fig. 1.49). 1 passes to 3 and cuts close to and around her; 2 cuts after 1 and goes to the other side of 3; 3 hands off to either player for a layup. While players 1 and 2 recover the rebound, the next player in line on the left passes in to 5 with a second ball. Continue. Start the ball with the line on the right. Move the two lines

to another angle. Occasionally, let player 3 fake to 1 or 2 and then go up with a hook or jump shot herself.

8. Post players make 100 shots within 6 feet of the basket while other players make 50 shots from 18 feet.

9. Columns (Fig. 1.50). It can be seen that player 1 has a two-step advantage on player X_1. Player 1 drives for goal while X_1 tries to defend. Players 1 and X_1 rebound while the next players in line start with another ball.

10. Columns at each side of the basket starting near the free throw line. First player in each line with a ball. The shooter drives toward the baseline, stops with her outside foot forward (right foot on the right side), pivots toward the basket, and shoots (Fig. 1.38). She recovers her own rebound, passes it back to the line from which she shot, and goes to the end of the other line. Lines alternate shooting.

11. Four players and three balls positioned as shown in Figure 1.51. Player 4 starts at 1, picks up ball, shoots; goes to 2, 3, 2, 1, etc. All shots should be layups achieved by taking step to basket; players at spots 1, 2, 3 recover rebounds and replace the ball on the spot. Continue for 30 seconds. Rotate.

12. Column to the right of the basket. Each player with a ball. In succession each player dribbles in to the basket and shoots a right-hand layup. Only the right hand is used; the left hand never touches the ball. Repeat from the other side.

Set Shot Drills

1. Partners. Shoot to partner; shoot to target on wall.

2. Five or six players stand at each basket with two or three balls. Two or three players shoot from a range within their ability, rebound, and pass to another player. After the player rebounds she takes a layup, if desired. If preferred, one or two players may rebound all shots and pass out to the shooters who take only the set shot. Places are exchanged. Another variation allows players to shoot and rebound for a few minutes while the others await their turn. Exchange places.

3. Competitive shooting. A column is formed at each basket behind a designated spot. Two or more balls at each basket. Each player in turn shoots from the spot, recovers her rebound, and passes to the next shooter. Each shot that is made is counted, and the group that reaches 25 (50, 75, 100, 200, 300) first wins.

4. *"21."* Four or five players at each basket (one ball). Each player in turn takes a long shot from behind a designated spot and follows her shot with a layup. If made, the long shot counts 2 points; the layup counts 1 point. If both shots are made, the player has another turn. The first player to reach 21 points wins.

5. *"Ghost."* Four or five players stand at each basket (one ball). The first player shoots any type of shot from any place on the court. If the shot is made, the next player must attempt and make the same shot; if she does not, she becomes a "G". For every miss, another letter is added until GHOST is spelled, and that player is eliminated from competition. The last player to remain is the winner.

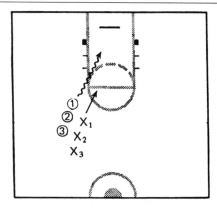

Fig. 1.50 *Player X_1 attempts to overcome a two-step advantage as 1 drives for goal.*

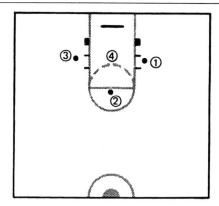

Fig. 1.51 *Recovering the Ball and Shooting a Layup.*

6. Eight players at each basket (two balls). Each player has a partner. One player with a ball stands near the baseline and passes out to her partner who shoots. The passer moves out to try to block the shot. Exchange places. Repeat. Alternate with other couples. Shoot from different places on the court.

7. Pairs informally at each basket. The shooter has the ball and is guarded closely. The shooter fakes a drive for the basket, forcing her opponent to drop back. She then takes a long shot. Exchange places. Attempt from different places on the court.

8. Pairs at each basket. The shooter is guarded loosely. She fakes a shot, drawing her opponent, and then drives around her. Exchange places.

9. Pairs at each basket. The shooter immediately takes the shot the defense allows: if guarded closely, she drives; if guarded loosely, she shoots long.

10. One-on-one. Allow the defense to guard loosely or tight with the shooter using the option given. Play a designated number of points.

Jump Shot Drills

Any of the drills described for set shots may be used to practice jump shots from a stationary position. For the drills described below a layup shot can be substituted for the jump shot if the player is close to the basket.

1. Five or six players at each basket (two or three balls). Player with the ball drives, stops, and executes a jump shot. She rebounds her own shot and passes to another player. As she gains confidence in this shot, she should try adding a feint prior to her shot.

2. Two columns at each basket (Fig. 1.52). The first player drives and executes a jump shot. Both players rebound and pass to the next player.

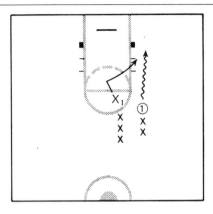

Fig. 1.52 *Player 1 drives for a shot as X_1 tries to prevent it. Both rebound.*

3. Pairs informally at each basket. The shooter is guarded closely. She fakes in one direction, drives to another, and shoots a jump shot. If the guard is able to remain with her, the shooter fakes before shooting her jump shot. Exchanges places.

4. Pairs informally at each basket. The shooter is guarded closely. She fakes a shot and drives around her opponent for a jump shot. Rebound and exchange places.

5. Pairs informally at each basket. The shooter is guarded closely. She uses a rocker step to fake the guard out of position (fake a drive, fake a shot, and drive) and does her jump shot. Exchange places.

6. Post player in a medium or low post position and her opponent. The pivot player fakes to the inside (toward the lane), steps toward the outside, and shoots (Fig. 1.53). Add a fake to the baseline and move opposite. Work with a dribble and without.

7. Pairs informally at each basket. The shooter starts on the left side of the basket, drives across the lane, stops, fakes a shot drawing her opponent in the air, steps to the left with her right foot, and executes a jump shot.

8. Partners: one shooter, one passer. The shooter starts to the side of the basket, receives a pass, and shoots; moves to receive the next pass, shoots. Move to get five shots going left and five shots going right. Exchange places. Use two balls.

Hook Shot Drills

1. One player with the ball near the baseline at each basket; others waiting their turn. From a position under the basket, step to the side and shoot the hook. Try several times and pass to another player.

2. Same as drill 1 above, except start to the left of the basket, dribble across and shoot a hook. Later, move further from the basket. Start on the right and move for a left-hand hook.

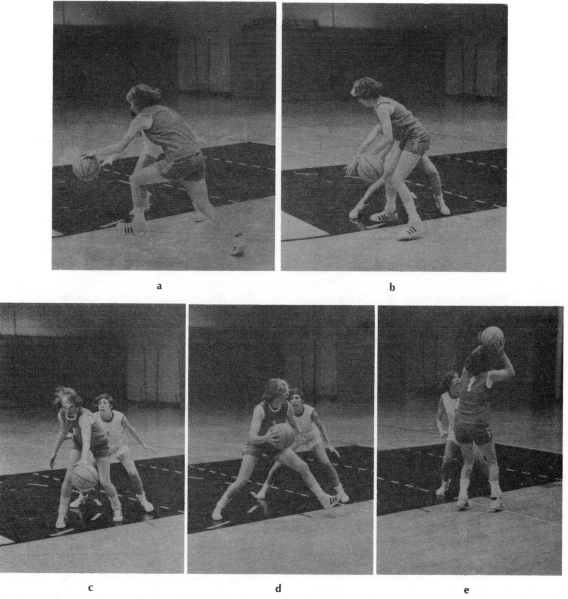

a   b

c   d   e

Fig. 1.53 *Pivot Fake. The pivot player fakes a drive into the lane (a), reverses direction (b and c), and prepares for a jump shot (d and e).*

3. Any layup drill. Use the hook shot instead of the layup.

4. Pivot player practice. Have the pivot player position herself anywhere along the key. A teammate passes into her and she drives and hooks or turns and hooks. Add an opponent against her.

Tip-In Drills

1. Two or three players at each basket with a ball; other players waiting their turn. One player tosses the ball against the backboard so that it will rebound without hitting the rim; the other player attempts a tip-in. Repeat and exchange places. Attempt from both sides of the basket.

2. Groups of five; two on one side of the basket and three on the other (Fig. 1.54). 1 tosses ball against the board; 2 tips it across. Players go to end of opposite lines. Continue. On fifth consecutive tip the player scores, change sides. Try with three players.

Rebound Shot Drill

Pairs stand informally at each basket (one ball). One player with the ball goes under the basket and tosses the ball against the backboard so that the ball rebounds out 5–6 ft. from the basket. She then becomes the defensive player. The other player rebounds and does a power layup. Exchange places and alternate with the others in the group. Attempt from both sides.

Free Throw Drills

Rarely should more than two players be involved with free throw shooting at any one basket. One player can shoot, the other one can rebound; any additional players are unnecessary and could better use the time by practicing other techniques until a basket is free at which time they can practice their free throw shooting.

1. Pairs. One player shoots two free throws and the other player rebounds. Rotate.

2. Pairs at each basket. Competitive shooting; each player shoots two and rotates; first team to make 25 (50, 100) shots wins.

3. Pairs. Shoot two and rotate; shoot a total of 50 free throws; record number made.

4. Pairs. Each player shoots one free throw at a basket and rotates clockwise to next basket; first group to make 25 (50, 100) free throws wins. (Leave the ball at the basket.)

5. For any of the above drills, at the proper stage in the learning process, the player may be instructed to run a lap for every missed free throw.

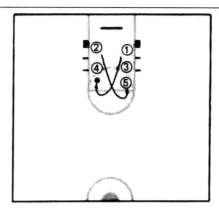

Fig. 1.54 *Five Player Tip Drill.*

6. At the end of a practice session, each player must shoot three (four, five) consecutive free throws before leaving. Place a time limit.

7. At the end of practice each team must shoot five (10, 15, 20) consecutive free throws before leaving. Alternate players. Place a time limit.

8. At the end of practice each player must make 20 (21, 22, 23) free throws out of 25 before leaving.

9. Take two shots; miss the first, run two suicides; miss the second, run one additional suicide.

10. Call player's name; if she misses the free throw everyone else runs one suicide.

11. Call player's name; if she makes it, all debts are canceled.

12. Whole team shoots one free throw; for each free throw missed, whole team runs one suicide.

13. Team — each player shoots until misses (maximum 3); rotates.

14. Team — each player shoots one; makes it, shoots another; rotates.

FOOTWORK

Without question, footwork must be considered one of the most important elements of the game. Footwork is basic to body control and balance, and without it very few other fundamentals may be learned effectively. Good footwork refers to the ability to start and stop quickly, change direction, pivot, and employ various feinting techniques requiring footwork for their success.

Speed is another important factor. Players with exceptional speed can be a great asset to a team. Numerous instances can be documented in which a faster team literally "ran circles" around a slower team with otherwise superior personnel. If a team possesses speedy individuals, its assets should be used to the best advantage in both the offensive and defensive aspects of the game.

Starts

Many players automatically start a move in the correct manner. For those few who do not, the following directions may be of help. The player should lower her shoulder and lean with her head and shoulder in the direction she wishes to go. At the same time, she plants her opposite foot hard against the floor, pushes off, and takes short quick steps until momentum is gained (Fig. 1.55).

a   b

Fig. 1.55 *Start. The player fakes to her left (a) and pushes hard off her right foot (b).*

Stops

Players must move at a pace whereby they can stop efficiently without loss of balance. Beginning players with poor body control may be forced to move at a pace considerably less than full speed in order to stop and change direction to avoid fouls and/or violations.

Basically, there are two ways in which a player can come to a stop — the two-step stop and jump stop. Beginners should concentrate on the two-step stop which is made in a forward-backward stride in the direction of movement. Because of this, balance is easier to maintain than with the two-foot jump stop. Advanced players should be adept at either one.

Whichever stop is used, it is important that hips are low, knees are flexed, back is straight, and trunk is leaning slightly forward with the head over the midline of the body. Arms should be flexed. If the stop follows a reception of a pass, elbows are brought close to the body to protect the ball.

Two-Step Stop

The player lands in a two-step stop with one foot landing first, followed by the other foot in a for-

ward-backward stride with the feet 2–3 ft. apart (Fig. 1.56). The rear foot must become the pivot foot. This stop is more suitable when the defense is not harassing the offense and when a player is in scoring territory. With a quick pivot after receiving the ball, the player may drive for the basket or shoot immediately. Most coaches recommend that players on the right side of the court use the right foot as their pivot foot and that players on the left side of the court use the left foot as their pivot foot. Other coaches recommend that a right-handed player use the left foot as a pivot foot and that a left-handed player use the right foot as the pivot foot regardless of which side of the court the individual is playing on.

Jump Stop

The entire surfaces of both feet contact the floor simultaneously in a side stride about shoulder width apart or slightly wider. Balance is hazardous with a much narrower stride. This stop is often used when a defensive player is pressuring a dribbler. By using this stop, a pivot can be executed quickly away from an opponent, followed immediately by a pass to a teammate (Fig. 1.57). It is also used fre-

a   b

Fig. 1.56 *Two-Step Stop. The player catches the ball on her right foot (a). The second step is taken on the left foot as the right knee flexes to allow the center of gravity to fall over her feet (b).*

a   b   c   d

Fig. 1.57 *Two-Step Jump Stop. The dribbler moves toward the sideline (a). She comes to a jump stop (b and c), and pivots and prepares to pass (d).*

quently prior to a jump shot. Either foot may be used as the pivot foot.

When a player lands in a jump stop either foot may be the pivot so that she can turn to face the opposite direction. The post player uses this technique to face the basket, and any other player may use it to protect the ball against an opponent.

Change of Direction

A change of direction is often necessary to fake a defender out of position and to beat her to a passing lane. Any change of direction for this purpose should be angular rather than in a curved or rounded path.

Drills for Stops and Starts

1. Informally, all players face the same direction. All run forward; on signal, all stop. Continue. Designate which stop should be used.

2. Each player with a ball dribbles anywhere on the court and comes to a two-step stop on signal.

3. Each player with a ball dribbles and uses a jump stop.

4. Two columns on each side of every basket with a ball, one column in the guard position, and one in a low post position. A player in the guard position passes to a pivot player moving from a low to a high post position. The pivot player uses a jump stop. The pivot player passes to the next player in the guard position. Continue. Exchange places, if desired.

5. Same as drill 4 above, except move the column from the low post position to the wing position. The wing cuts up to receive a pass in a stride position. Continue.

Drills for Change of Direction

1. Columns at one end of the court. On signal, the first person in each column starts to her left, takes three steps in that direction, three steps in the other direction, and continues downcourt. Each successive player starts when there is sufficient space for her speed.

2. Columns. Designate spots on the floor. Each person in turn runs to that spot, changes direction, and runs to the next spot, etc. Emphasize quick changes on the spot.

3. Players in their normal playing positions are spaced at each basket. Wings take a few steps toward the basket and then cut out for an imaginary pass from a guard; post players cut toward the sideline and then up toward a player with an imaginary ball; guards cut toward the sideline or toward the basket and back for an imaginary pass from the other guard. Later, add a passer for each group.

4. Two columns — one offensive and one defensive at each basket. An offensive player starts in a guard position with an opponent defending against her. An extra player in a forward position has the ball. The guard uses zigzag cuts to free herself of her opponent for a pass from the forward and a layup. Rotate positions and start from different places on the floor.

5. Pairs. The attack player tries to evade the defensive player by stops, starts, and changes of direction.

To change direction when running, the movement should be quick and abrupt. When a player wishes to cut to the right, she plants her left foot, pushes off sharply from it, lowers her right shoulder, faces to the right, and starts in that direction with her right foot. The action is similar to a start. A crossover step is not recommended because the directional change cannot be as sharp or quick. The change of direction to the left is made in the opposite manner.

To change direction when a player is running forward the player stops in a forward-backward stride position. Body weight is thrown back over the rear foot as the pivot is made on that foot. The forward foot during the stop takes the first step in the opposite direction as the shoulder on that side is lowered and the push-off is given by the other foot.

Pivots or Turns

There seems to be little agreement on the difference between a pivot and a turn. For the purposes of this book, the terms will be used interchangeably. During any turn the ball must be protected. Keep it close to the body.

Simple Pivot

A simple turn is made by pivoting on the balls of both feet. Feet may be in any position, but the turn is made without lifting either foot. Beginning players need to practice this technique to avoid throwing poor passes, because their legs become tangled. When passing, beginning players should face the direction of the pass; this can be accomplished

Fig. 1.58 *Reverse Pivot to Get Free. Against a tight-playing man-to-man defense, a point player passes to a wing (a); does a reverse pivot against her opponent (b), and is free for a pass (c and d).*

by using the simple turn. If a foot fake or a two-step stop has been executed, a pivot is made on the ball of the pivot foot while the other foot steps toward the direction of the pass.

Reverse Pivot

The reverse pivot is used when a player does not have the ball or while she is dribbling. It normally cannot be used after a player with the ball has stopped because the forward foot must be used as the pivot foot.

To start the pivot the player plants one foot in between her opponent's feet. The head is turned and opposite shoulder lowered as the pivot is made. The opponent should be kept on the hip so that as the free leg is swung around, the opponent will be beaten. The free leg swings 180 degrees and the player continues to move in the desired direction (Fig. 1.58).

This pivot can also be used to "post up" or to free a player to receive a pass against an overplaying defender (Fig. 1.59).

Drills for Pivots or Turns

(Use the same drills described for stops followed by one of the turns described.)

FAKING (FEINTING)

Faking is a technique used to deceive an opponent. It is a move made usually opposite to the intended direction. Although generally considered an offensive technique, it can be used with equal success by defensive players.

Offensively, feints or fakes are used either when a player has the ball or when she is trying to free herself to receive a pass. One sees players practicing fakes with the ball, but often they give little attention to fakes without the ball. Perhaps more time could be spent wisely on these maneuvers. It is often because players are unable to get free that one sees a passer under stress throw the ball away. This is evident not only in beginning play, but also by some advanced players when they encounter a pressing defense.

Fakes normally are done with the head, eyes, shoulder, body, arms, and feet. Ball fakes can be used, but elbows should be kept in contact with the body so that the ball stays within the lines of the body. Extending the ball beyond the lines of the body is an invitation for an opponent to slap at the ball and tends to send the center of gravity beyond

the base. It is important to keep the center of gravity over the base when executing any of the fakes. If the center of gravity is forced outside the base or near the edge of the base, time is required to move the center of gravity back over the base, thus limiting the quickness with which an alternate move may be made. While time is being consumed during this action, the defensive player is also given time to recover to make a new move. On all feints, it is also important that the head moves in the direction of the feint and that eyes focus in that direction.

Feints Without the Ball

Fakes of this nature are made to free a player or to take an opponent away from the play. When a fast directional change is required, the player takes a step with one foot, pushes hard off it, and takes a step in the opposite direction with the other foot (refer to Fig. 1.55). (When the initial step is taken, the opposite knee flexes to keep the center of gravity over the base.) This technique is used when working a give and go, splitting the pivot, or simply getting open for a pass. A simple head and shoulder fake may accomplish the same purpose.

A player may also cut in one direction followed by a quick change of direction. This is a slow means, since several steps are taken before the change in direction is made. This method is used more often when an opponent is being lured out of the play or when she is not involved with the ball immediately before she is to receive a pass. This type of cut is most commonly made in a V (Fig. 1.60) or a buttonhook pattern (Fig. 1.61).

If a defensive player is guarding closely, a player may cut toward the ball, do a reverse pivot, and cut behind the defensive player for the basket simulating a backdoor play (Fig. 1.62).

A change of pace is another means of deceiving an opponent. It is usually accomplished by a player running at normal speed, slowing down, and then speeding up. It is accomplished by placing one foot in advance of the center of gravity and extending (straightening) the trunk which causes a decreased speed. To speed up, the trunk flexes, causing the center of gravity to fall outside the base; the front foot pushes off as the leg extends.

Another technique that can be used on occasion by advanced players is one in which the opponent is lulled into a belief that her opponent will not become involved in the action. This is accomplished by standing in a relaxed manner, arms at sides, weight on one foot, and generally giving the appearance of watching the play. As soon as the opponent has been duped, the player cuts hard for a

a   b

c   d   e

Fig. 1.59 *Posting Up. A weakside wing cuts toward her sagging defender (a). She starts her reverse pivot (b), is free for the pass (c), and maneuvers for an easy shot (d and e).*

Feinting Drills Without the Ball

1. Fake left, cut right; fake right, cut left; fake forward, cut left; fake forward, cut right; fake forward, cut back. Repeat.

2. Place the players at each basket in their normal playing positions. Let each player try the fakes she will most likely use from her position: *guards* — fake left or right and cut in the opposite direction, or fake left or right and cut toward the basket; *wings* — fake toward the basket and cut toward a guard; fake toward the guard and cut toward the basket; *post* — fake left or right and cut opposite; fake left or right and cut toward a guard; fake toward a guard and cut to the opposite side of the key.

3. Same as drill 2 above, but add an opponent against each player. In turn, let each player try to get free from her opponent.

4. Two players (two guards, a guard and a wing on the same side of the court, or a wing and post) in their normal playing positions and their opponents. Start the ball with either attack player. Her teammate uses some feint to free herself for a pass. Repeat.

5. Players execute a change of pace. Add an opponent. Alternate.

6. Place players and their opponents on the court in their normal playing positions. Any offensive player may start with the ball (preferably a guard) and the other players try to get free only by using a change of pace or by lulling their opponent to sleep. Each player should watch closely to see if her opponent turns her head. If she does, a sharp cut should be made toward the ball or the basket depending upon the situation.

7. Same as drill 6 above, except offensive players should vary their fakes.

8. Same as drill 6 above, but request the defense to play tight or press their opponent. Offensive players should use the backdoor cut when the opportunity presents itself.

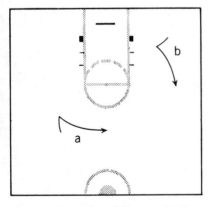

Fig. 1.60 *Examples of V cuts:* (a) *by a guard,* (b) *by a forward.*

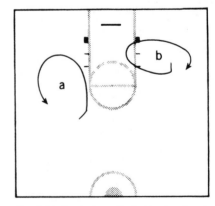

Fig. 1.61 *Examples of a buttonhook cut:* (a) *by a guard,* (b) *by a forward.*

pass. If an opponent does not watch the ball, a player may stand innocently with her arms at her sides and, at the last instant, reach up for a pass. Similarly, a player can fake a reception to draw her opponent closer before cutting on her.

Feints with the Ball

Feints with the ball are designed to open passing lanes, to free oneself for a shot, or to drive toward the basket. Feinting with the ball is much easier than

a b

c d e

Fig. 1.62 *Reverse Pivot. The player cuts toward the ball (a). She raises her trunk and prepares to reverse as her inside foot (left) strikes the floor (b). She pushes off from her left foot (c). Her step with the right foot takes her beyond her opponent (d), and she is free for a pass (e).*

without it because the defensive player must try to defend against a pass, shot, or a drive. To defend against a shot, the opponent must draw close; to defend against the drive, she must play looser. Because of the dilemma this places the defensive player in, it is imperative that offensive players use the dribble wisely. Simply bouncing the ball in place or taking an automatic bounce whenever the ball is received plays right into the defensive player's hands because one of the options has been used and the defender need be concerned only with the shot or

pass. Regardless of the type of feint used, the ball always stays close to the body and the center of gravity over the base. Otherwise no advantage is gained by the ball handler following her feint.

Feints to Open Passing Lanes

Use of the head, eyes, shoulders, arms, and feet can be used for this purpose. Ball fakes can also be used if the ball stays near the midline of the body. Regardless of the type of fake used, it should involve

Fig. 1.63 *Jab Step. The ball handler is in a side stride position (a), jabs with her right foot (b), and drives for the hoop (c and d).*

a

b

c

d

the use of the head and eyes. Following a fake in one direction, the player should pass in another. A player may fake left and pass right, or she may fake a pass at one level and pass at another. For example, a player may fake a shot or an overhead pass and follow it with a bounce pass. Whichever technique is used, the ball must be passed immediately after the defender takes the fake so that the opponent does not have time to readjust her position. Following a fake there is not time for a long backswing, so players must develop arm and hand strength to produce the required force for a pass primarily with wrist action. During the fake and subsequent ac-

tion, beginners tend to throw their body too close to the edge of the base or take too long to release the pass. These problems must be overcome.

Feints for a Shot or a Drive

Generally, the purpose of these feints is twofold: to fake a shot and draw an opponent close so that a player can drive around her; or to fake a drive, forcing the opponent to give ground, and then shoot. Players may also fake in one direction and move in the opposite. Players should recognize that a defensive player is more vulnerable when a drive is

Fig. 1.64 *Crossover. The player fakes to the left with the left foot. Note the extreme flexion of the right knee to keep the player's weight within her base (a). She crosses over with her left foot as she starts her drive to the right (b). Drive for the layup (c–e).*

made in the direction of her front foot. Greater advantage should be made of this fact, particularly against teams that do not sag or float to help teammates. Whenever a ball handler is contemplating a drive or shot, she should focus her attention on her defender's feet. In this way she can observe the weight shift of the defensive player and/or a foot being lifted from the floor. This indicates to the ball handler when and in what direction she is free to move. There are several fakes that may be used to achieve the purposes stated above. All feints can be done in either direction, but a description is given to one side only.

Jab Step

The player with the ball takes a side stride position. She takes a quick, short step in any direction and

a

b

c

d

Fig. 1.65 *Double Fake. The ball handler fakes right (a), fakes left (b), pushes off hard from the right foot (c), and makes a strong move right to the basket (d).*

returns to the starting position. Several steps taken in this manner should drive an opponent off balance (Fig. 1.63). A sequence such as forward, return, left, return, followed by a drive to the right may be successful.

Crossover

The player fakes a drive to the left with the left foot while keeping the right knee flexed to keep her center of gravity over her base. The left foot crosses over to the right side, placing the left shoulder between the opponent and the ball. The drive is started to the right as the ball is dribbled with the right hand. In order to profit from a successful feint, the crossover step should be outside the opponent's foot on that side so that the head and shoulders are immediately ahead of the defensive player (Fig. 1.64).

Double Fake

A player fakes in one direction, fakes in the opposite direction, and drives in the direction of the first fake. Usually the drive is taken to the side where the crossover step can be utilized to protect the ball with the body. Therefore, the first fake is made with a crossover step. The player crosses over with the left foot while keeping the right knee flexed, and then pushes hard off the left foot to push the body

back to the left. The stride is long enough to show the intent of driving in that direction and then a hard push is given once more as the left leg crosses over and the drive is made to the right as described previously (Fig. 1.65).

Fake and Drive in the Same Direction

By using a hesitation rather than a double fake, a player can drive in the direction of her original fake. The player uses a crossover step with the left foot and then extends her trunk by pulling her head and shoulders up and back. The trunk is flexed immediately afterward, placing gravity outside the base again; the right leg extends, giving the initial push-off. A forceful extension of the left leg is also necessary to gather momentum (Fig. 1.66).

Rocker Step

In this move the player fakes a drive, pulls back to fake a shot, and then drives in the direction of the original fake. For example, the player fakes left with her left foot, keeping her right leg flexed and hips low and over the base. Then she draws her left foot back behind the right, keeping the trunk flexed and gravity near the front edge of the base. At the same time a shot is faked to draw the opponent close, at which time the right leg extends as a step is taken to

a   b   c

Fig. 1.66 *Fake and Drive in the Same Direction. The ball handler fakes right (a), fakes a shot (b), and drives hard to the right (c).*

a b c d e f

Fig. 1.67 *Rocker Step. The player fakes to her right (a) and brings her left foot back and fakes a shot which brings the defender close to her (b). She pushes off hard from the right foot (c) and drives for the layup (d–f). Note the height of the ball before release.*

Feinting Drills with the Ball

1. Groups of three — two offensive and one defensive player guarding the player with the ball. The offensive players must remain stationary and attempt to pass the ball back and forth. The defensive player guards the player with the ball and a pass may not be attempted until she is in position to guard. All types of fakes should be attempted, and various passes at different levels should be used. Rotate players and repeat.

2. Each player has a ball. All try two or three of the fakes described.

3. Pairs position themselves as one offensive and one defensive player in their normal playing position. The offensive player tries any of the fakes she knows against her opponent. The defender is instructed to "take" the fake (if it is well executed); later the defender is instructed not to take the fake forcing the offensive player to react properly; still later, allow the defender to use either alternative. Exchange places. Emphasize correct reaction to the defender's move.

the left and the drive is started. The ball is dribbled with the left hand (Fig. 1.67).

Fake a Shot and Drive (up and under)

The player fakes a shot by using her head, eyes, arms, and hands in the same manner that she normally does for a shot from that position on the floor. As the defensive player moves in to defend against the shot, the offensive player may drive in either direction but preferably toward the defender's forward foot and arm.

No Feint

Sometimes an opponent can be caught off balance if a player starts a drive as soon as she catches the ball without any preliminary feint. Since the defensive player is usually playing ball side of her opponent, the drive is made to the other side. If a player receives the ball from the right, she immediately steps left with her left foot and starts her drive in that direction.

CUTTING

To participate in any offensive action, a player must be able to cut. Cutting means running to get free to receive a pass or running away from the possible pass area to clear it for a teammate. Usually a cut is preceded by some type of fake to cause the defensive player to start in the wrong direction and enable the offensive player to get at least a half a step

advantage on her opponent. This means that in order to cut a player must be adept at starting, stopping, faking, and changing direction quickly. One of the greatest faults of beginning players is the inability to cut. Rather than running, beginning players often attempt to get free by sliding three or four steps in one direction and then an equal number of steps in the opposite direction. In essence, they are sliding back and forth in one place and this type of tactic is very easy to defend against. Beginners must learn that on offense all movement patterns are made by running, not sliding.

Most cuts should be made sharply and angularly. A cut performed in this manner is much more difficult to defend against than is a cut in an arc or circle (Fig. 1.68a). When an offensive player chooses to move in an arc, the defensive player can follow a straight path and beat her opponent to her desired position (Fig. 1.68b).

It is important to know not only how to cut but also when and where to cut. Where the cut is made depends on the position of the offensive player's opponent and the team offensive system being played. Basically, only one cutter should be moving at a time. If two players have cut simultaneously, only the player in the better position for receiving a pass should continue her cut into the receiving area. The other player should move away from the primary receiver so that the passing lane remains open.

The timing of the cut is equally important. The cutter must reach the desired receiving area when that area is cleared of other players. Secondary receivers must be ready to make their cuts if the passer finds that the primary cutter is not free. Generally, one cut follows another in a sequential pattern. No two people are cutting into the same area at the same time, but someone is cutting all of the time. On offense there should be extensive movement. A team that stands around will not have much success. But it must be recognized early that everyone cannot be moving into the same area. This is what makes offensive play so difficult to coordinate. Each player must adjust her moves according to what her teammates are doing. One player should cut into the passing lane, followed by another and another. If the initial cutter does not receive a pass she must clear the area for a second cutter. In this way a passing lane should remain open at all times.

There are three types of cuts that can be used, each with their own modifications. All of these cuts are effective both when advancing the ball from the backcourt to the frontcourt and for offensive maneuvers in the frontcourt for scoring possibilities.

Front Cut

The front cut is preceded by a fake in the opposite direction followed by a quick change of direction. The player should move in front of and ball side of the opponent. This move is effective when the defensive player is not overplaying her opponent to the ball side. If the player is successful in making her front cut, she should be free for a pass (Fig. 1.69).

Reverse Cut

When the defensive player is overplaying and pressing her opponent, the offensive player finds the reverse cut (also called the back or backdoor cut)

more suitable. Because of the defensive player's position, she is unable to cut in front of her to open a passing lane; the open lane is behind the defensive player. The offensive player fakes toward the ball and, with a quick change of direction, cuts behind the defensive player. If executed quickly, the cutter should be free for a pass (Fig. 1.70). A more subtle use of this maneuver can be executed by a player on the weak side, usually a forward. With good acting the offensive player can give the appearance of being uninvolved in the play pattern and may cause her opponent to relax slightly. As that occurs, the offensive player can cut behind the defensive player to receive a pass. In this instance the preliminary fake prior to the cut is unnecessary and only alerts the defender to the move.

V Cut

A third method of cutting is known as a V cut. It differs from the front and reverse cuts only in that the intended cut is preceded by several steps in a different direction rather than the simple fake. Because of this, it takes longer to execute and therefore must be started sooner than the front or reverse cut in order to reach the passing area at the proper time. Use of this cut may be necessary if the opponent is exceptionally good defensively, or it may be used in order to clear the space into which the cutter wishes to move. By cutting in another direction and taking the defensive player with her, the offensive player can cut back into the space just vacated. This type of cut is also used to drive an opponent into a screen (Fig. 1.71).

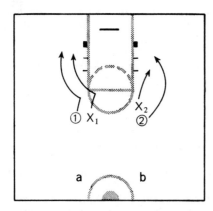

Fig. 1.68 Player 1 makes an angular cut, and 2 makes a cut in an arc. A defense player can guard against this cut to an easier degree.

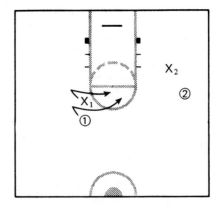

Fig. 1.69 Front cut made by player 1 and the accompanying move made by X_1.

a

b

c

d

Fig. 1.70 *Reverse Cut. Dark 6 is overplaying her opponent (a). The offensive player cuts backdoor (b), receives the pass (c), and moves in to score (d).*

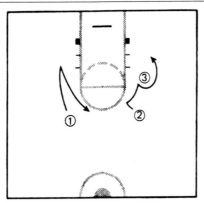

Fig. 1.71 *V cut made by player 1 to free a space to receive a pass; player 2 makes a V cut as she uses player 3 as a screen.*

OFFENSIVE REBOUNDING

Rebounding is probably one of the most overlooked aspects of all offensive tactics. For some reason, teachers and coaches seem to attach little importance to offensive rebounding. At least from the time spent in practicing offensive rebounding it appears that the importance of this technique is underestimated. When one considers that few teams can boast a shooting percentage higher than 45 percent and for many the percentage is considerably less, one can better understand the importance of good rebounding techniques. If one does not develop offensive rebounders, a team is permitting its opponents to obtain the rebound at least 50 percent of the time. This seems rather futile when generally the team that gains the greatest number of rebounds wins.

It is generally conceded that offensive rebounding is the responsibility primarily of the pivot player and two forwards. Often they are in a position closer to the basket than are the guards and therefore are in better rebounding position. It is also important to recognize that on any attempted field goal a team must maintain defensive court balance so that the opponents cannot gain a fast break opportunity. This means generally that a team deploys two players — one at the free throw line and the other back near the top of the circle, for this purpose. If a guard has been used in a cutting maneuver, a forward must move back to the free throw line to maintain this proper defensive alignment.

Whichever players happen to be involved in rebounding assignments, they must be aggressive in order to gain good position for rebounding. There is no question but that the defensive team has a distinct advantage in any rebounding situation. If they have been in proper position, they are closer to the basket than any of the offensive players and therefore should be in a position to block off the offensive rebounders. This means then that the offensive players must anticipate the shooting attempts of their teammates. They have the advantage of knowing the habits of their teammates, and when they are likely to shoot. Beginning players, especially, must be reminded immediately to rebound any shot rather than to stand and admire the beauty of its flight. Of course, if they have defensive responsibilities, this suggestion does not apply.

Offensive rebounders must find a way to get to the boards. Against a zone defense they may find it easier because defensive players often block out areas under the basket rather than players. Even against a man-to-man defense the weak side forward or wing is often free to move to the boards. Even if defensive players are well instructed in blocking-out techniques offensive players must be aggressive and find a way to regain possession if the field goal attempt is unsuccessful (Fig. 1.72).

The fastest path to the boards is usually to the inside, but generally this path is better protected by the defender. Before the defender pivots for the block out, the offensive player can fake in one direction and go in the opposite. This may cause a poor block out and allow the offensive rebounder to go to the basket (Fig. 1.73). A double fake may also be used or standing idly may cause the defender to turn her head allowing the offensive player to cut in the opposite direction.

If none of these techniques is successful, once blocked out the offensive player must still make an effort to rebound. Depending upon which path is most open, the player can step left with her left foot or right with her right foot to get around the defensive player. She may also fake the step left and crossover with her left foot and go around the defense player on the right side. And finally she can use a reverse pivot previously described.

Once the offensive player starts to the boards she must find a free space into which she can maneuver. Moving directly behind a defensive player is poor positioning and results in numerous fouls. The offensive player must gain inside position, if possible. Cutting to the baseline side and sliding in front of a defensive player is a useful technique. When it is impossible to gain the inside position, the offensive rebounder should try to get even with the defensive player. Once even, a step is taken slightly forward and sideward so that the defensive player is literally behind the offensive player.

a　　　　　　　　　　b　　　　　　　　　　c

Fig. 1.72 *Offensive Rebounding. A shot is taken and the high post uses a reverse pivot to move past a poor block-out by the defender (a–c).*

Rebound Drills

1. Groups of three. One player tosses the ball against the backboard. Another player times the jump, catches it, pulls it into her chest, pivots, and passes to a teammate near the sideline.

2. Pairs. One offensive player with the ball and one defensive player playing 4–5 ft. away from the offensive player. The offensive player shoots and attempts to outmaneuver the defensive player who tries to block her out.

3. Pairs — offensive player with the ball and a defensive player guarding her. The offensive player works one-on-one against the opponent and shoots when the opportunity arises. She immediately attempts to follow in her shot for a rebound; meanwhile, the defensive player attempts to block her out.

4. Four players — two offensive and two defensive players. They play two-on-two and shoot when the opportunity arises. Both defensive players try to block out their opponents while the offensive players try to get in position for the rebound. Add two more players and play three-on-three.

5. Six players as shown in Fig. 1.74. One player shoots and the coach designates which tactic the offensive players will use to gain rebound position (step around, fake and crossover, reverse pivot). Change tactics. Change offensive and defensive players.

6. Play five against five, emphasizing defensive balance. Two players stay back at the top of the key and the others work for offensive rebounds.

a   b   c

d   e

Fig. 1.73 *Offensive Rebounding. The offensive player shoots (a), moves around the poor block (b and c) to beat her defender to the boards (d) for the rebound (e).*

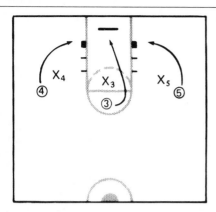

Fig. 1.74 *Offensive Rebounding.*

Once in position the rebounder should take a wide stance to give her a firm base in case contact occurs under the basket. Her knees and ankles should be flexed, her elbows should be at shoulder level, and her forearms and hands should be extended. This places her in a good jumping position and also makes her wide so that she cannot be easily nudged out of position. Of course, the timing of the jump is important and this timing can be learned only through considerable practice. Often a player with good timing is a better rebounder than a "good jumper."

As the ball rebounds, the offensive players must make every effort to gain possession without fouling. They must keep moving and readjusting their positions, on subsequent rebounds. If the offensive rebounder can get to the ball, she has three options: tip the ball into the hoop; catch the ball and go back up with a shot or pass it out of the lane; or tap the ball back to a teammate. If the player is in good position, the most desirable choice would be to tip the ball into the hoop. If her position is not that good, she should catch the ball and go back up with a shot. Too often a player attempts a tip-in when the catch and subsequent shot is the better choice. If her position does not warrant the shot or if she is short and among giants she may find it more effective to pass or dribble the ball out of the key and start a new offensive thrust. If she cannot tip the ball into the hoop or cannot catch it, she then must make every effort to keep the ball alive by tapping the ball back to a teammate.

The effectiveness of a team's offensive rebounding can be measured in several ways: (1) the number of extra shots the offensive team gains; (2) the number of times the team gains two, three, or four shots at the basket in one offensive effort; (3) the offensive rebounds totaling 40 percent of all rebounds gained; (4) the number of times the opponents gain fast break opportunities, often caused by a lack of pressure on the defensive rebounder, and (5) the number of points scored in relation to the number of possessions.

REFERENCES

1. Adapted with permission from Broer, Marion, *Efficiency of Human Motion*, Philadelphia, Pa.: W. B. Saunders Co., 1973, p. 326.
2. *Ibid.* pp. 328, 329.

2

Defensive Skills

High scoring games provide great interest and entertainment, and most players and fans enjoy a fast-moving contest with many goals scored. Most spectators focus their attention on the ball and the offensive players in the immediate area; only a few focus their attention on the defensive players. Because of this, youngsters learn very early in life that offensive skills attract the attention of teammates and adults as well, and therefore concentrate their attention on learning those skills. If one watches children playing without supervision, one observes that they practice shooting skills and other offensive techniques such as dribbling and faking. One can hardly blame them when sports writers and fans give the greatest acclaim to the fancy ball handlers and high scorers. Sports writers and fans rarely pay tribute to the defensive wizard.

The teacher/coach, however, is extremely aware of the vital role that defense plays for any team's success. The teacher/coach often must sell players on the importance of defense because players frequently have directed most of their attention to offensive skills. During this process the teacher must help players develop a keen sense of pride in their defensive ability. They must learn to be so determined, so unrelenting, and so motivated in their efforts that they want to prevent their opponent from ever receiving the ball. Should the opponent receive a pass, they are keen to prevent her from penetrating the defense. This defensive attitude must be inculcated so that players like to play defense as well as they like to play offense.

Techniques to be learned include: combat fakes; guard the dribbler; guard the shooter; over-

play the strong side; provide weak side help; defend against cutters and a flash post; use of the body, arms, and voice; defend against screens and picks; and blocking out.

A teacher will probably find that students learn defensive skills quicker and easier than they learn offensive skills, because timing of moves with the ball is not as difficult. This does not indicate that less time should be spent on defense. To build a sound team, an equal amount of time probably needs to be devoted to both aspects of the game.

The concepts of aggressiveness, concentration, determination, anticipation, and prevention must be developed by defensive players. At all times, they must be positioned to help a teammate or positioned so that their opponent cannot get possession of the ball. If she does, great pressure must be exerted to make any maneuvering by her most difficult. There is a difference between a defensive player who is in the proper place at the proper time and one who is there and also displays tenacity in her movements.

It is the task of the defense to force the offense to work hard to get the ball into scoring position and to force them to make their movements to places other than where they would like to cut. The teacher must assist *all* players in developing the attitude and skills necessary for defensive success. If one player is weak or loses alertness, the whole defensive structure is weakened. A strong defense places an immediate burden on the opposing team and forces them to make certain adjustments. Any time they are forced to alter their usual strategy, their efforts are weakened.

A well-coached defensive team will always be more consistent than a team that concentrates on offense. "Off nights" seldom occur on defense, although players do have off nights in shooting. These usually occur because of tension. This may be due to the importance of the game or the pressure defense played by the opponents. It may also be due to:

1. lighting in the facility
2. backboard structure or rim stability which causes the ball to rebound differently
3. size of the court surface
4. a difference in space between the edge of the court surface and spectators
5. the size of the facility itself

All of these factors may interfere with offensive capacity, whereas none of them should interfere with the defense. As a result, a well-coached team should always maintain stability in their defense.

When teaching defense to players, the principles of man-to-man defense are basic regardless of the defensive system that ultimately will be played. Each player must learn the techniques of guarding a player either with or without the ball and must learn how to guard a dribbler. These situations will be encountered and must be counteracted whether a team is playing man-to-man defense, any of the numerous zones, a combination, or matchup defense.

Once the basic principles of man-to-man defense are acquired, players may increase their defensive vocabulary by learning to press or employ one or more of the zone defenses to further frustrate the opposition. A variety of defenses, however, does not automatically insure success. A team's ability to apply the principles involved in each is the real test. The number and type of defenses that players can perform well are dependent upon their individual abilities, experience, and practice time available. It is far better for a team to master one defense than to attempt several with little degree of proficiency in any.

BODY POSITION

Proper body position is the most important fundamental in learning defense. This is basic to all other defensive techniques. Without proper body position, a player is subject to fakes, changes of direction, and other evasive techniques employed by an opponent.

Conditioning is an important factor in defensive body position for it is when a player tires that she straightens up. "Stay low" is a common phrase used by good defensive coaches. Any player can learn correct body position and must practice it to the extent that she can maintain the correct position throughout a game.

Foot Position

Feet should be comfortably spread but greater than shoulder width and in a forward-backward stride. The inside foot (the one closer to the midline of the court) should be forward. The foot closer to the sideline becomes the rear foot. A defensive player playing to her left of the defensive goal should have her right foot forward and left foot back. The staggered position of the feet should never be closer than approximately one and one-half feet. Weight should be divided evenly between the two feet, never on the forward foot. If weight is not evenly distributed, it should be closer to the rear foot to enable the player to retreat to the basket more quickly.

Some coaches prefer the foot position reversed — outside foot forward and inside foot to the rear. The choice of the staggered foot position is dependent upon the coach's philosophy of whether she wants to force the opponents toward the inside (middle) of the court or toward the sideline. When forward, the inside foot tends to force the opponents toward the middle. If this seems desirable, then a coach should adopt this technique. The coach who prefers to force the opponents away from the middle or toward the sideline should encourage the outside foot forward. Proponents of the method described initially subscribe to the theory that it is better to force the opponents toward the middle where other defensive players can help. Advocates of the other theory believe that opponents should be forced away from the middle and toward the outside of the court where shooting angles are poorer.

Position of the Knees

Knees should always be flexed so that the thighs are parallel to the floor. During the early learning stages, the proper degree of flexion should be checked frequently by this method. Players tend to extend their knees and assume a more upright position. This must be checked early, and drills should be used frequently to help players attain the leg strength necessary for maintaining this position over a prolonged period of time.

Hips and Back

If a player has assumed the correct foot and knee position, her hips and back should automatically be in proper position. Hips should be flexed and the back should be relatively straight. Sometimes in an effort to stay low with knees almost straight a player will flex her back so that it is nearly parallel to the floor. This forces the head and weight to move forward so that the player cannot retreat quickly. As long as proper knee position is maintained, the back and hips should be in proper alignment.

Arms and Hands

The forearms are flexed to approximately 80 degrees, and the hands are almost fully extended, fingers only slightly flexed. Arms and hands are supinated (palms up). This position tends to keep the body in better balance than the technique in which one arm is raised overhead and the other arm is to the side. This latter technique tends to raise the center of gravity and makes the player more susceptible to fakes by the opponent. With arms and hands low, the center of gravity is lowered and the player can maintain balance to a better degree and therefore react more quickly to her opponent's moves. Any movement made by the hands to harass an opponent should be in an upward rather than downward direction. Hitting or tapping downward often produces unnecessary fouls.

Head and Eyes

The head is held with chin up; eyes are focused on the waistline or hips of the opponent if she has the ball. Eyes should never focus on the ball itself nor on the opponent's eyes or head because they are used to fake the defensive player out of position. Since the hips move only when a player moves, a defensive player is more likely to maintain a good defensive position if she watches this area.

If the opponent does not have the ball, the defensive player should position herself so that she can see both the ball and her opponent without turning her head. This means that as an opponent moves further from the ball, the defensive player moves further from her opponent so that the correct position can be maintained.

Voice

It is strange that many players become "voiceless" on the court when it is normally hard to keep them quiet! On defense, players must communicate with their teammates. Among other things, they must call "help," "tight," "stop the ball," "pick," "got her," "cutter coming," "high post," and not the least of all, "thanks." Telling teammates the position of opponents and declaring who has whom are necessary elements for good defensive play.

In summary, the defensive body position places the feet in a forward stride position; knees are flexed; back is straight; arms are flexed; fingers are almost extended; arms and hands are supinated; head is in a comfortable position; eyes are focused on the hips if the opponent has the ball; eyes focus on both ball and opponent if she does not have the ball. By assuming and maintaining this position, the defensive player will be well balanced and ready to react to any movement by her opponent (Fig. 2.1). This should be the observable position any time a player is on defense.

Foot Movement on Defense

There are few occasions when a defensive player is stationary. If either her opponent or the ball moves, it is likely that the defensive player will have to readjust her position. A defensive player should never run in making these adjustments. She always slides. To move laterally across the court, a player simply uses a side step. To move to her left she steps left with her left foot, sliding her right foot toward it, stepping left with the left foot again, then sliding the right foot toward it. This procedure continues until the player wishes to change direction (Fig. 2.2). Movement in a forward or backward direction is done in basically the same fashion. To move forward, the front foot steps forward as the back foot slides toward it. To move in a backward direction, the back foot steps first with the forward foot sliding toward it. At no time should the feet be crossed. When moving forward, care must be taken to insure that the player does not retain her weight for any length of time on her forward foot. The balanced position with weight distributed evenly over the base must be maintained most of the time.

In all cases, sliding steps are made with as long a stride as can be comfortably managed. Feet should never come together as seen in Fig. 2.2b because the stance is so narrow that it is easy for an offensive player to move past the defender. The slides must be made quickly with the feet as close to the floor as possible. This is necessary for a rapid change of direction.

Defensive players should rarely be in a position where they are forced to run to stay with their opponent. It is a clear indication that the defensive

a   b

Fig. 2.1 *Basic Defensive Position. Light No. 5 has her hips and knees flexed and her weight is centered over her base, allowing her to move in any direction (a). She makes an upward jabbing motion at the ball while keeping her weight low (b). This motion should never be made downward.*

a   b

c   d

Fig. 2.2 *Defensive Footwork. As light No. 5 cuts, dark No. 3 slides to keep in good defensive position.*

player has been beaten by her opponent. It also indicates that further attention should be devoted to proper footwork by that particular player. However, during the course of a game such a situation may arise and a defensive player must have some means of guarding her opponent as she is cutting free toward the basket. When this occurs, the defensive player pivots and runs toward her opponent with the arm closer to the basket raised overhead and the other one extended to the side. In this position the defensive player has a chance to deflect either a lob or bounce pass. She watches her opponent's eyes, which may indicate the direction from which the pass is coming (Fig. 2.3).

Fig. 2.3 *Guarding a Free Player Cutting Through the Lane. Dark No. 5 has allowed her opponent to become free. The defender must turn and run toward her opponent with one arm extended and the other one to the side to deflect a pass to her opponent. After light No. 5 clears the lane, dark No. 5 can move to regain proper defensive position.*

Drills for Basic Defensive Body Position and Foot Movement

1. Individually; all players use the stutter step moving their feet as rapidly as possible for 30 seconds. Feet barely leave the floor. Repeat.

2. All players stand with their backs to one basket. They assume the basic defensive position while the teacher/coach checks the position of the feet, knee flexion, and arm position. During the early stages of learning, the teacher may place tape down the midline of the court to distinguish the left side from the right side of the court. This will assist the players in determining which foot should be forward.

3. Same as drill 2 above, except the players move forward and back, to their left and right. For ease in observing correct footwork, the teacher may request that the group on each side of the midline stay on their half of the court. Later, the groups should move across the dividing line so that the players must change the forward foot. Still later, the tape should be removed so that the visual cue is eliminated and players must recognize by other means when they have crossed the midline of the court.

4. All players with their backs to one basket move left, right, forward, and back down the court on command from the teacher. One of the purposes of this drill is to gain endurance and leg strength so that players can continue this drill up to fifteen or twenty times without coming to a standing or resting position.

5. Same as drill 4 but alternate 30 seconds of foot work with 30 seconds rest. Repeat up to ten times.

6. All players have their backs to one basket and a leader faces them, serving as a common opponent for all. The leader moves forward, backward, left, and right with changes of pace and the defensive players react to her by moving in the corresponding direction. Emphasis should be placed on the basic defensive body position and sliding step. No player should use a crossover step.

7. One attack player and one defensive player. No ball. The attack player moves downcourt by changing direction frequently, and the defensive player tries to maintain a good defensive position. Players should remain at the opposite end of the court until all individuals have reached that end. Alternate positions.

8. One attack and one defensive player, with the defensive player tied to the attack player with a 5-ft. string (not a rope). The string is tied to a pinnie or belt worn by each player. The offensive player moves downcourt, using stops, starts, and changes of direction. The defensive player must move correspondingly so that the string is not broken. As soon as defensive players maintain good body position the length of the string can be decreased to 4 ft. and then 3 ft., if desired.

DEFENSIVE PRINCIPLES

As soon as players lose possession of the ball in their offensive court or following a field goal, they must return as rapidly as possible to their own backcourt unless, of course, they are utilizing a full court press. As the defensive players retreat, it is desirable for them to run downcourt as fast as possible and beat their opponent to the other end of the court. They should not be satisfied in running beside their opponent, because a lead pass will beat them. Never should a defender run beside her opponent when the ball is ahead of her. She must hustle downcourt and be in position to help a teammate. Having beaten her opponent and the ball downcourt, the defensive player should turn as she approaches the center line and run backward downcourt the remaining distance so that she can eye the ball and help teammates locate their opponents. The major objective of the defense is to be waiting in their backcourt as the offensive players approach the center line.

Once players reach their back court area, there are certain principles that each player should follow under normal circumstances. These principles apply to any style of defense that a team is playing — man-to-man or zone.

1. At all times, the defensive player must maintain the proper defensive body position previously described.
2. The defensive player must always be in position so that she can see both the ball and her opponent. Players should try to improve their peripheral vision.
3. The defensive player must never cross her feet when she moves in any direction. A sliding step must always be used.
4. The defensive player must force the ball toward the middle of the court. She must take a position that will cause this action by the offense.
5. The defensive player should always stay ball side of her opponent and generally basket side as well. This simply means that the player is closer to the ball than her opponent. If the ball is to the left of her opponent, the defensive player is also to the left of her opponent. She should overplay her opponent to the best of her ability.

6. The defensive player should face the ball; she should rarely turn her back to the ball.
7. The defensive player should position herself so that her opponent can never drive by her toward the sideline and more importantly that she cannot drive by her on the baseline.
8. The defensive player should front an opponent who cuts across the lane within nine to ten feet of the basket. She should never permit the offensive player to be between her and the ball in this dangerous area (Fig. 2.4).
9. The defensive player should be ready to assist any teammate if necessary when her opponent does not have the ball. She should be ready to help defend against a dribbler who is free or a cutter who has evaded her opponent.
10. The defensive player on the weak side is primarily responsible for helping a teammate against lob passes and backdoor cutters.

GUARDING A PLAYER WITHOUT THE BALL

Once players have retreated to their defensive end, they can wait for the opponents to bring the ball downcourt where they can meet them as they move into scoring territory (within 20–25 ft. of the basket). Pressure should be exerted against the ball handler at this time. Other players should obtain proper defensive position against their opponent, who may maneuver for a pass or attempt to keep the defender away from the scoring thrust so that she cannot assist her teammates in the prevention of a score.

Defending against a player without the ball is difficult and demands a great deal of attention. This is *not* the time for a player to rest either physically or mentally. For some reason defensive players guarding an opponent without the ball tend to lose alertness both physically and mentally. A good defensive team, however, does not allow this to happen. Much attention must be given to the position of these players in practice. They must understand that their position and actions are equally important as those of the defender guarding the player with the ball. No defense can be sound unless all players are "with it." They must recognize that the responsibility for team defense lies with each and every player, regardless of the position of the ball or the type of defense being played. On every ball movement (dribble, pass, or shot), each defensive player must readjust her position in relation to the new position of the ball. This must be done quickly so that passing lanes are blocked to the nearest receivers.

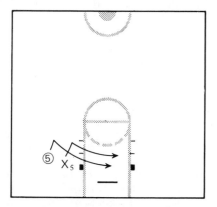

Fig. 2.4 *Defensive Positioning When a Player Cuts Across the Lane Near the Basket. The defender fronts her as she moves across the lane, making it more difficult for her to receive a pass. She does not allow the attack player to cut in front of her this close to the basket.*

Players guarding opponents some distance from the ball can move further from them to be of assistance to teammates if needed.

Defensive players should be alert for possible screen situations. When a screening player is approaching, the defender must assist her teammate by calling "screen" or "pick" so that the defensive player can make the proper adjustment and not be surprised by the screen. When playing man-to-man it is important that players do not rely on switching whenever screens are set. Nevertheless, during the course of the game it is likely that a switch in defensive assignments will be necessary. When this occurs it is the responsibility of the back player to call the switch — not the defensive player being screened. Following the switch in defensive assignments the defensive players involved should stay with their new opponent until they can return safely to their original opponent. If the offensive team gains a distinct height or speed advantage, this should be done at the earliest possible time. If no height or speed advantage is gained by the offense, there is no need in hurrying the change in respective defensive assignments.

Every effort should be made on the part of defensive players to prevent the attack from receiving the ball within 15 ft. of the basket. In order to accomplish this task it seems helpful to think of the correct defensive position in terms of the opponent's position in relation to the ball. It is necessary to differentiate the defensive responsibilities when a player is guarding an opponent who is one or two passes away from the player with the ball. No player is ever more than two passes away from the ball if the ball is passed to the pivot player. The position of defensive players opposing wings and guards will be discussed in the following section. Positioning for guarding a post player will be discussed later in the chapter.

One Pass Away from the Player with the Ball

An attack player is "one pass away" when she is near the player with the ball and is a logical receiver of the next pass. The ball need not be relayed to her by another attack player. When defending against a player who is one pass away, the defender's position depends upon whether she is defending against a guard, wing, or pivot player. Her positioning and tactics can also be determined by which player has the ball at that particular instant.

Defense Against the Offside Guard Who Is One Pass Away

When the other guard has the ball (in a double guard front), the defender drops back to a position slightly ball side of a line between her opponent and the basket, where she can see both her opponent and the ball. From this position she can defend against a cut by her opponent following a pass to the other guard. Anticipating and preventing the guard cut is one of her major responsibilities. From this position she can also prevent a pass into a high post, thus limiting the extent to which the opponents can use the scissor maneuvers. She also is in position to help if the ball handler drives down the lane. Her job is to help and recover to defend against her own opponent. She must also anticipate lateral moves by the two guards and be prepared to reduce their effectiveness.

If the defensive team is pressing, the defensive player does not drop back as far and plays a step closer to the ball handler. In this way she can more effectively harass her opponent by closing the direct passing lane and forcing (to a greater degree) her opponent to maneuver to become free for a pass. Nevertheless, she still is responsible for helping on a drive down the middle.

If the wing has the ball, the defensive player drops back, opens her stance, and has three responsibilities:

1. She protects against the wing passing the ball into the medium or high post and assists her teammate if the wing drives toward the lane.
2. She anticipates any two-player maneuvers by her opponent and the wing with the ball and attempts to beat her opponent in her desired cut.
3. If the guard moves away from the wing with the ball, the defensive player adjusts her position as necessary so that she can continue to see the ball and her opponent. The further away the guard moves from the ball, the further the defensive player positions herself from her opponent, and the more weak side help she can give.

If the post player has the ball in a high or medium post position, the defensive player drops back and attempts to harass the pivot player to limit her maneuverability. She must continue to face her own opponent but reaches backward toward the pivot player to limit movement in her direction. At the same time she must anticipate a scissor maneuver by her own opponent as soon as the pivot player receives the ball, and she must know the type of team defense to use against this tactic. She must be ready to return quickly toward her opponent if the ball is passed to her. She must also be alert for any cut that her opponent may make.

Defense Against a Wing Who Is One Pass Away

When the point or near side guard has the ball, the defensive player positions herself so that her rear foot splits the stance of the wing and her forward foot is in front of the wing's front foot. The arm nearer the ball extends forward with the hand and forearm rotated to face the ball. If the right foot is forward, the right arm is also forward (Fig. 2.5).

This position takes away the passing lane to the wing and forces her to go backdoor or to maneuver in some fashion to become free. It may force the wing to go wider to receive a pass; thus causing her to be beyond her shooting range.

Overplaying the wing to this extent does make

Fig. 2.5 *Playing the Passing Lane. Dark 6 keeps her body and arm in the passing lane as the offensive player tries to get free for a pass (a–d).*

Fig. 2.6 *Defense Against a Backdoor Cut. The defender is denying the ball (a–c). As the wing cuts backdoor, the defender opens to the ball (d) and continues to overplay her (e).*

the defender susceptible to a backdoor cut, but she knows there is weak side help if she needs it. As the wing attempts to become free, the defender should allow her to take her first step toward the goal without reacting. As the second step is taken, the defender must immediately pivot on her rear foot opening to the ball and slide to the lane in this open position. She must then pivot on her rear foot again and return to the closed position to cover her opponent as she cuts across the lane. Contact with the opponent must be maintained during the cut; otherwise, she may be free for a lob pass when there is no weak side help. If the ball remains on the opposite side of the court, the defender does not follow her opponent out of the lane since she now becomes the weak side help (Fig. 2.6).

The coach must establish definite rules of how wide (close to the sideline) and how high (above the free throw lane extended) the overplay position will be maintained. Usually the overplay position is used when the wing is below the free throw line extended and within ten to twelve feet (laterally) of the free throw lane. If the wing goes beyond this area, the coach may wish to direct defensive players to sag until the wing moves into shooting range.

If the post player has the ball in the low or medium post position, the defensive player must drop off her opponent to help her teammate defend against pivot maneuvers. The defensive player must be alert for a scissor maneuver or any other type of cut by her opponent when the pivot has the ball. She also must be ready to return quickly to her opponent if the ball is passed to her.

Defense Against a Corner Player Who Is One Pass Away

When the wing has the ball, the corner defender overplays her opponent in the same manner as the wing defender overplayed her opponent when a guard or point player had the ball. She must disallow the penetrating pass to the corner. If team tactics dictate considerable pressure to be exerted against a low post, the corner defender sags off her opponent to front the low post. If this is the case she must quickly return to her own opponent when she receives a pass.

If the low post gets the ball, the corner defender sags off her opponent to help against the post. She must be alert for a scissor maneuver and also a cut by her opponent. If the post passes the ball out to the corner, the defender must return quickly before the shot can be attempted.

Drills for Defense Against a Player Who Is One Pass Away from the Ball

Players should practice their positioning and moves in the position(s) where they are most likely to be playing. Therefore, the drills are established by position.

Point Player or Guards

1. Groups of four — two guards and their opponents or a point and wing and their opponents. The ball is passed from guard to guard slowly so that the defender can move to the correct position and corrections made if necessary. The speed of the passes is increased to gamelike conditions and corrections continue. Alternate on offense and defense.

2. Same as drill 1 above except the ball handler attempts to drive the middle and the sagging defender helps and then recovers to her own opponent. Repeat with the other defender performing the help and recover action.

3. Same as drill 1 only substitute a point and a wing or one guard of a two-guard front and a wing.

4. Same as drill 2 above with a point and wing and their opponents.

Wings

1. Individually practice the forward and backward movement necessary in the overplay position. Practice on both sides of the court.

2. Pairs — the offensive player works on fakes and cuts to the basket followed by a cut to the wing position. The defender retains proper overplay position. Alternate positions. Change sides of the court.

3. Pairs — the offensive player executes backdoor cuts and the defender uses the opening and closing actions necessary. Add another player who passes to the wing when she is open. Then allow the players to go one on one if the wing receives the ball. Alternate positions and sides of the court.

4. Groups of three — the wing, her defender, and a post. The ball is passed into the post and the wing defender sags off and returns to her own player when she receives a pass. Exchange positions and sides of the court.

Corners

1. Individually practice the forward and backward movements necessary in the overplay position. Practice on both sides of the court.

2. Groups of three — wing, corner player, and the corner player's defender. The corner player practices fakes and moves to the basket as well as the backdoor cut while the defender maintains good position. Exchange positions and sides of the court.

3. Groups of three — corner player, her defender, and a low post. As the ball is passed into the post the defender sags to help and returns to her own player when she receives a pass. Exchange positions and sides of the court.

Two Passes Away from the Player with the Ball

There are only a few occasions when a defensive player is guarding an opponent who is two passes away from the ball. This situation occurs most often when the ball is on the far side of the court; it may also occur when the ball is at the point or in the corner when the opposing team plays with a point, wing, and corner player. Regardless, the only way the defender's opponent can receive a pass is by means of a relay pass from another teammate or a high lob pass. Basically, when a defensive player is guarding an opponent two passes away, the defensive player's primary task is to help out on team defense. She drops off her opponent further than usual so that she can help double-team an opponent or guard a player who has evaded her opponent. Obviously, she must be aware of the ball's movement and of her opponent so that she may return to a better defensive posture as the ball moves to a position only one pass away from her opponent.

Defense Against an Offside Guard Who Is Two Passes Away

Either a corner player or a low or medium post on the far side of the court has the ball. When this occurs, the defensive player drops back into the free throw area and opens her stance toward the ball. She is in a position to observe her opponent and the movement of the ball. She must beat the opponent on any cut toward the ball and, from her position in the free throw area, tries to intercept or deflect passes into this area.

Defense Against A Wing or Corner Who Is Two Passes Away

This situation occurs when any player on the far side of the court has the ball. When this occurs, the defender drops off her opponent so that both feet are in the lane, and she is ready to assist any teammate if necessary.

When the ball is above the free throw line, the weakside defensive player has both feet in the lane on her side of the basket. When the ball is dribbled or passed to an area between the baseline and the free throw line extended, the weakside defensive player moves to a position ball side of the basket in the lane and on a line between the ball and the basket.

The weakside defensive player is alert for reverse cuts by the far side guard or wing who does not have the ball and lob passes into the post player when she is being fronted. If she anticipates and moves into position, she may force a charging foul by an unalert opponent. She will also help to stop any opponent who is driving in the lane. The weakside defensive player must also be alert for a pass to her own opponent. If this occurs, she must return quickly to her opponent; but her approach must be made with her weight balanced so that the opponent cannot fake a shot and drive for an easy layup.

The defensive player must also be particularly alert for a weakside cut made by her opponent through the lane. The attack player may be cutting through the lane to move to the ball side; she may return to the offside and replace herself; or she may be a flash post. When the opponent cuts, the de-

---

Drills for Defense Against a Player Who Is Two Passes Away from the Ball

1. Groups of five — two guards and their opponents, and one wing or corner player without an opponent. The guard on the same side of the court as the wing starts with the ball. The guard may pass either to the other guard or to the wing, with the defensive players moving accordingly. At first the three offensive players should remain stationary while the defender two passes away from the ball becomes accustomed to her move as the ball is passed to the wing. Later, the guard two passes away should attempt to cut through the lane toward the ball for a pass while the defensive player tries to check the path of her opponent. After repeating the drill a few times, move the wing (corner) to the other side of the court so that the other defensive player is able to adjust her position when the ball is two passes away from her opponent.

2. Same as drill 1 above, only replace the wing without an opponent with a low or medium pivot.

3. Same as drill 1, only the guard on the weakside does not have an opponent, and a defensive player guards the wing. Now the emphasis is on the position of the defender guarding the wing.

4. Same as drill 1, only substitute two wings (corners) and a pivot player with one of the wings without an opponent. Emphasis is on the position of the defender against the other wing. The wing without an opponent should occasionally try a cross-court pass to her other wing and a pass into the pivot who relays it to the wing being guarded. Emphasis is on the defender preventing the desired cut by the wing. Later, the post player moves into a low or medium position on the weak side and the defender tries to prevent the wing from cutting over the post for a pass from the wing on the other side.

5. Same as drill 4, but substitute a point, wing, and corner player, leaving one offensive player free.

6. Same as drill 5, but allow the corner to drive and practice help and recover techniques for the point defender.

7. Five defensive and five offensive players. Any attack player may start with the ball and the teacher/coach calls out when a pass may be made. Emphasis is on the defensive position of the player(s) who is (are) two passes away from the ball.

8. Groups of three — one wing with the ball, and offside wing (corner), and her defender. Practice flash pivot moves and defense against them.

fender must front her when she is within ten feet of the basket. This means that she must anticipate her cut, beat her to the cutting lane she desires, and remain in front of her as she goes across the lane (Fig. 2.4). This places her in position to discourage a pass and forces the opponent to take an alternate route. If the attack player receives a pass in this area, she is likely to score regardless of the efforts of the defensive player. If the wing continues to cut up toward the free throw line rather than going behind the defender, the defensive player overplays her. Once the wing posts up, she is played like any other post player. Beyond the 10-ft. range, the defender should overplay her opponent in the same manner. The defensive player's teammates must warn her of a potential double screen that her opponent may use. She must also be alert for a cut around a low or medium post when the ball is on the weak side.

GUARDING A PLAYER WITH THE BALL

Each player should recognize that her opponent has three alternatives when she has the ball: she may dribble, pass, or shoot. It is each defensive player's responsibility to analyze the strengths and weaknesses of her opponent in relation to these possibilities. She should learn very quickly if her opponent is a good ball handler and can maintain poise under pressure. She should learn in what direction her opponent prefers to dribble and whether she can dribble equally well with both hands. She

should learn the type of shot that her opponent prefers and from what location on the court her shots are usually attempted. She should learn how well she shoots off a drive to each side. The defensive player must ascertain whether the player cuts after she passes or whether she tends to remain stationary or replace herself. The defensive player must also determine whether her opponent is a play maker. If so, she will need help from her defensive teammates in preventing her opponent from getting the ball. They should attempt to block the passing lanes to the play maker as much as possible. Whenever the play maker gets the ball her opponent should exert extreme pressure against her so that she will have difficulty in giving an accurate pass.

When an offensive player receives the ball it is because the defender was unable to maintain the overplaying position or she was sagging to help a teammate. If she was overplaying and forced her opponent wide to receive the pass, the defender must quickly move to prevent the baseline drive (Fig. 2.7). If she was sagging, she must hustle out to her opponent and land in a jump stop which takes away the baseline drive (Fig. 2.8). If the defender stops directly in front of the opponent, the offensive player can drive in either direction; this is not desirable. As she lands, the defender must have her weight low and balanced to defend against the drive.

The defense player takes her stance so that she forces her opponent toward the middle of the court. (If the reader prefers to force the opposition

a   b

Fig. 2.7 *Defender Obtaining Good Position Against a Ball Handler. The defensive player denies the wing the ball and forces her beyond the free-throw line for a pass (a). As the wing receives the ball, the defensive player takes away the baseline drive (b). (Note how the wing has squared to the basket as she received the pass.)*

toward the sideline, the following descriptions for overplaying should be reversed so that the defender is inside her opponent.) Overplaying a ball handler is accomplished by playing half a player to the outside of her opponent. This means that the defensive player is slightly outside of her opponent and closer to the sideline instead of being directly in line between the opponent and the basket. The defensive player should have her inside foot approximately in the middle of the opponent's stance and her outside foot outside of her opponent's outside foot (Fig. 2.9). If it is found that the opponent prefers to cut toward the sideline or to drive toward the sideline, it may be more desirable for the defensive player to play a full position outside of her opponent. This means that her inside foot is opposite her opponent's outside foot (Fig. 2.10). This technique of overplaying the offensive player dictates the manner in which the offense must be developed. It forces the opposing players to pass toward the center of the court and also to drive in that direction.

The overplaying position described in the above paragraph is a basic one. It is one that should be

Fig. 2.8 *Defender Going to the Corner. The weakside defensive player has sagged into the lane (a). The ball is passed around the periphery as the defender moves toward her opponent (b) and approaches on the baseline side (c); good defensive position is gained as the corner player prepares to make a move (d).*

Fig. 2.9 *Overplaying Half a Player. The ball handler prefers to drive to her right. The defender takes her stance half a player in that direction—i.e., her right foot is midway between her opponent's feet, and her left foot is to the left of her opponent's feet.*

Fig. 2.10 *Overplaying a Full Player. The defender places her right foot opposite the right foot of her opponent and her left foot outside either of her opponent's feet to encourage the dribbler to drive toward the sideline or her nonpreferred direction.*

Fig. 2.11 *Poor Defensive Position. The defender has her weight forward as she reaches for the ball, which makes her susceptible to a fake and drive.*

used under most circumstances. For reasons of team defense it may not be used by all players at all times. If a team wishes to trap the offensive players at the sideline, they would overplay to the inside. When a defender is guarding a weak shooter, she may drop her to close passing lanes to other more dangerous players. A team may believe that it must close off the passing lane to a pivot player, in which case the defender guarding the player with the ball may take exception to the outside overplaying position. All of these decisions are matters of team defense, however, and will be discussed more fully in another chapter.

From her basic defensive stance the defender keeps her eyes focused on her opponent's hips. She makes upward jabbing motions at the ball to disconcert her opponent. In so doing, though, she must not overcommit herself and allow her weight to move onto the balls of her feet (Fig. 2.11). As she makes the jabbing motions, her weight must remain back so that she can retreat quickly. At no time in her effort to contact the ball should she move so that she is no longer between her opponent and the basket (Fig. 2.12). This is often done by beginners and permits the ball handler to pivot and drive for the basket. Emphasis must also be placed on the proper weight distribution described previously. Beginners often let their weight advance to their

a b c

Fig. 2.12 *Poor Defensive Action. The defender is in a good position (a). The ball handler pivots away from the basket, and the defender moves with her in an attempt to tie the ball (b). The defender places herself in an extremely poor position, as dark No. 3 can continue pivoting toward the lane and be free for a drive or shot (c).*

forward foot, and this is exactly what a ball handler hopes for. A simple fake and she is able to leave the defender behind. By keeping weight back, knees flexed, and hips low the defender can prevent this action by the ball handler. The defensive player must also be aware of the possible fakes that an opponent might use. She should not be deceived by the jab, crossover, or rocker steps, and must not become susceptible to head fakes. Keeping her eyes on the hips of her opponent helps her distinguish between a ruse or an intended move by the opponent.

The position of the defensive player and the constant upward jabbing motion at the ball should cause the opponent some concern. The defender wants to harass her to such a degree that it is diffi-

---

Drills for Defending Against a Pass and Cut

1. Two attack players — guard (point) and wing, point and post, or wing (or corner) and post — and one defensive player guarding the ball handler. The defender harasses her opponent, trying to make it difficult to pass accurately, and immediately slides back to prevent the pass and cut. Emphasis is placed on the quick movement backward. Alternate positions.

2. Two attack players opposed by two defensive players in any of the positions described in drill 1. This drill is identical to drill 1, except that the pass and cut is attempted by the attack players. Following the pass to her teammate, the player immediately cuts for the basket to receive a return pass. Emphasis is on the defensive player retreating as soon as her opponent makes the initial pass and preventing or intercepting the return pass to her.

a   b

c   d   e

Fig. 2.13 *Defensive Footwork. On a pass-and-cut tactic by the ball handler, the defender has successfully beaten her opponent to the ball.*

cult for her to make an accurate pass. Once the offensive player releases the pass, the defensive player must quickly move several steps backward and in the direction toward the ball (Fig. 2.13). This will place the defender in a good position to guard against the pass and cut play. If the offensive player makes no effort to cut toward the basket, then the defensive player can be ready to assist her teammates if necessary.

Opponent Shoots

There are several circumstances for which a defender must attempt to harass a shooter. Each will be discussed in turn.

When the offensive player has completed her dribble, the defensive player must "belly up" to her immediately. As the term implies, the defender steps close to her opponent so that the two players are "belly to belly." At the same time the defender raises her arms directly overhead to discourage a shot. With the defender in this position the offensive player is unable to get the ball into shooting position (Fig. 2.14). In order to use this technique successfully, the defender must step in before the offensive player can raise the ball for the shot.

Once the attack player has raised the ball, the defender must jump to block the shot only after her opponent has jumped or released the ball. Every defensive player must practice time and again in

a

b

c

d

Fig. 2.14 *Belly Up After a Dribble. The ball handler has completed her dribble and the defender "bellies up" (a and b). The pass is successful and the defender maintains a denying position (c and d).*

Fig. 2.15 *Blocking a Shot. The defensive player has "bellied up" to the shooter with arms straight overhead. No downward movement is made.*

one-on-one situations so that she gains experience and does not fall victim to a fake shot. No defensive player should ever jump into the air until the ball is on its way toward the goal. When the jump is made, it should be vertical with the arms overhead. The hand does not move downward to try to block the shot; rather, the ball is allowed to advance toward the hand to be blocked. To be successful, the defender must be close to the shooter so that the ball does not have time to rise above the defender's arm on its flight toward the goal (Fig. 2.15). This action will save many fouls.

If the defensive player is in poor position to the side of the shooter, she can attempt to harass the shooter with an upward motion made with her right hand. This causes the defender to turn partially in the air and will place her in position to rebound. Few blocked shots will occur when the defender must resort to this technique, but some pressure

can be exerted against the shooter and the defender will not foul as a result (Fig. 2.16).

Occasions do arise when an offensive player is free to take a shot. About the only thing a defender can then do is to run hard to the shooting side of the player and jump as high as possible. The defender's momentum will carry her beyond the player, avoiding a foul, but also taking her beyond a position to block out or to rebound. The movement of the defender may have a psychological effect on the shooter and at least cause her to hurry her shot (Fig. 2.17).

Another situation that may arise occurs when the defender tries to draw a charging foul as a player drives toward the basket. As the defender sees the opponent driving free, she must establish her position and be stationary when the contact occurs. Her base should be wide to provide balance and her arms should be extended overhead (Fig. 2.18).

Fig. 2.16 *Attempt to Block a Shot. The defender is evaded (a–c). She tries to block the right-hand shot with her right hand (d and e). This causes her to turn slightly to avoid a foul and places her in position to rebound.*

a

b

c   d

Fig. 2.17 *Defender Attempting to Block a Corner Shot. The defender is sagging off her opponent or playing the deep defender in a one-three-one-zone (a). As the ball is passed to the corner, the defender realizes she will be late and moves toward the shooting side of the opponent (b); attempts to block the shot (c), and avoids fouling (d).*

a

b

c

Fig. 2.18 *Taking a Charging Foul. The ball handler has evaded her defensive player (a) and drives toward the basket. The weakside corner player has moved into the lane (b) and takes the charge (c). The ballside defender against the wing moves down to cover the free corner player.*

DEFENSE AGAINST THE DRIBBLER

Defending against a dribbler might have been included under the discussion of defense against a player with the ball, but it is considered of such importance that it is discussed separately. Every player on the court must be able to stop the advance of a dribbler. When an offensive player can constantly drive against her opponent, the defense is placed in an untenable position. It means that there can be no effective harassment of the player prior to a pass or shot, and it places extreme pressure on the other defenders to assist in the defense against the dribbler. It means that the defense is porous and susceptible to many varied attacks. Because of this,

players must be determined in their efforts to halt the dribbler and practice religiously until they acquire the skill to do so.

Body Position Against a Dribbler

Of greatest importance is that the defender is low. Her arms should be out to the side so that she does not reach for the ball or place a hand on the dribbler's back and commit a foul as a result. Only when the ball is truly exposed for a steal should the defender attempt it with the near hand.

Her weight must be evenly balanced and her feet must be moving constantly so that she can change direction with the dribbler. Psychologically she must think in terms of beating the dribbler wherever she goes. This can be accomplished by keeping the defender's nose over the shoulder of the dribbler's hand. To do this the defender must take a quick exaggerated stride on each change of direction and continue to slide her feet as fast as the dribbler progresses forward. She must not allow her opponent to beat her at the sideline or at the baseline. As the dribbler approaches either of these two boundary lines, the defender beats her by putting her foot on the line and forcing the dribbler inside.

On a change of direction toward the defensive player's forward foot, the defender should use a drop step to regain proper defensive position. This is done by pivoting on the rear foot and dropping the front foot back to the rear and sliding. This move must be made quickly and with the exaggerated step so that the dribbler does not gain an advantage (Fig. 2.19).

If an opponent is considerably faster, the defensive player may have to play her slightly loose. This means that the defense is weakened to that extent, but it is better to keep the dribbler under control in this fashion than permitting her to constantly evade a slower defensive player.

Against a spin dribble, in which the ball is well protected, the defender should drop back a step at the onset of the spin. This action does not allow the dribbler to pin her opponent behind her as she completes the spin. The drop step allows the defender to maintain good position.

It is difficult to keep an exceptional dribbler checked all of the time. If a dribbler starts to gain an advantage on the defender, it may be necessary for

the defensive player to run a few steps to regain her defensive position and then continue with the sliding technique to keep the dribbler under control (Fig. 2.20). A defensive player should call for help when she loses her opponent. When a teammate "stops the ball" the defender who sought help hurries to guard her teammate's opponent. The defense against a dribbler becoming free due to a screen will be discussed in another chapter.

Teammates must warn a player who is defending against a dribbler of the development of screens. Some ball handlers are particularly adept at driving their opponent into a lateral or rear screen set some distance from the ball handler. In order to cope with this situation the defender must have verbal help to learn where the screens have been set. It is also important for the defender to know in which direction her opponent prefers to drive. Most often players prefer to dribble to their right because they tend to be better dribblers with the right hand. This conjecture cannot be taken for granted until the action of the dribbler bears it out. Defenders should also know that most players shoot right-handed and are freest when moving to the right. When driving to the right with a half-step advantage the shooter's right hand is free for an attempted shot. When driving to the left with a half-step advantage and shooting with the right hand, the shooter actually brings the ball back in range for the defender to block. For this reason defenders should be prepared to defend against the move by the opponent to her right to a greater extent than one to the opponent's left.

The defensive player should also know the favorite spots from which the dribbler likes to shoot.

a

b

Fig. 2.19 *Defense Against a Dribbler. The dribbler moves to her right (a), and the defender "beats" her by taking a large step; arms are to the side (b).*

Fig. 2.20 *Defender Regaining Position Against a Dribbler. The defender reaches for the ball (a), and the dribbler does a crossover dribble (b) to elude the defender. The defender runs to regain position (c), prepares to regain a sliding position (d), and re-establishes position against the dribbler (e).*

a

b

c

Fig. 2.21 *Flicking the Ball Against a Dribbler. The ball handler starts a spin dribble (a); the defensive player is unable to move her feet to recover position and reaches behind the dribbler (b) to flick the ball toward a teammate (c).*

She can expect the dribbler to use a variety of fakes or screens — to free herself so that she can dribble to or receive a pass in those positions. If the defender recognizes those favorite spots, she is less susceptible to fakes away from them and can better cope with the offensive players' ruses. She also may guard the dribbler differently if these spots are known. For example, if the dribbler likes to shoot from the top of the circle and starts to dribble toward the sideline to her left, the defensive player

may overplay her toward the center so that she is unable to change direction and drive to that spot. The defender has violated one of the previously stated principles by undertaking this overplay position toward the inside. In this case, however, such action has merit.

When guarding a dribbler, the defensive player must be alert for the opponent to come to a quick stop and execute a jump shot. For this reason, it is important for the defensive player to know the positions on the court where the offensive player is likely to attempt her shots. When the dribbler picks up the ball (catches it), the defender should belly up immediately to prevent the opponent from raising the ball to shooting position and to exert pressure on the ball.

As an element of surprise, when an opponent does not protect the ball when using a spin dribble, the defender may take a step forward (away from the basket) and reach carefully behind the back of the dribbler to bat the ball toward a teammate (Fig. 2.21). A dribbler who does not protect the ball when

Drills for Guarding the Dribbler

1. Pairs. One dribbler and an opposing defensive player. The dribbler starts at one end of the court and dribbles toward the opposite basket. She is required to stay within half of the court divided lengthwise. If the offensive player evades the defensive player, she should stop her dribble, permit the defensive player an opportunity to regain good defensive position, and then recommence her dribble. When the players reach the other end of the court they exchange responsibilities.

2. Same as drill 1 above, except the offensive player continues to drive toward the basket for a layup if she evades her opponent. The defensive player runs to catch up and slides as good defensive position is attained.

3. Pairs. A dribbler is opposed by a defensive player who must keep her hands on her waist or hips. The dribbler starts at one end of the court and uses a change of pace and change of direction as she proceeds down the court. The purpose of this excellent drill is to teach defensive players the need for retaining good body position in relation to the dribbler. It is easy to spot those defensive players who rely on an extension of their arms to keep a dribbler from penetrating.

4. A dribbler and an opponent in either corner position. The dribbler attempts to drive the baseline. By proper footwork and positioning, the defensive player prevents that baseline drive and forces the opponent in toward the lane. Players should alternate positions.

5. A dribbler and opponent anywhere on the court. The dribbler is instructed to change direction several times and to suddenly pick up the ball. The purpose of this drill is to force the defensive player to make several directional changes and to move in quickly toward the dribbler once she picks up the ball. Change positions.

6. Groups of three — two attack players and one defensive player guarding the dribbler. The dribbler is instructed to make several directional changes, pick up the ball, pass to her teammate, and cut for the basket. The defensive player maintains good body position as she dribbles; moves in close to her when she picks up the ball; and, following the pass, immediately retreats several steps to prevent the give and go. Exchange positions.

7. One column on the baseline at opposite corners of the court. First player in each group is the dribbler; second player is the defender. Emphasize as many directional changes as possible. If the defender is beaten, she must sprint and assume good defensive position again. Exchange responsibilities. Shoot a jump shot at one end of the court and layup at the other. Move columns from the right to the left side of the court.

8. Same as drill 7 but defense waits for her opponent at the center line. She must start moving her feet as the opponent approaches.

9. One on one; the defender is not permitted to use her hands. When the dribbler picks up the ball, the defender bellies up and blocks out on the shot. Exchange positions.

a   b

c   d

Fig. 2.22 *Stealing a Dribble. A defender approaches from the rear and to the side of the dribbler (a and b). She reaches forward with her inside hand (c) to bat the ball to a teammate and stops quickly to reverse direction (d).*

advancing downcourt may be surprised by a defender approaching from the rear who bats the ball to another defensive player (Fig. 2.22).

Guarding a Single Player on the Fast Break

It is essential that a defender get back when an opponent steals the ball. The player closest to the center line must retreat to the foul line. It is important that the defender races to that point and not attempt to guard the dribbler until she nears the lane. She wants to prevent a layup and she should not

chance getting beaten some distance from the basket. Once back the defender overplays the dribbler toward the middle and attempts to force her toward the sideline so that her route to the basket is lengthened. By keeping her hands active the defender may be successful in causing the dribbler to pick up the ball and shoot beyond the layup range or to wait for a trailer.

GUARDING THE POST PLAYER

Guarding an active post player who maneuvers well and who has a variety of shots is a difficult assignment. The most important task for the defender is to prevent the pivot player from receiving a pass. Since she operates primarily within 15 ft. of the basket, she is in an excellent scoring position should she get the ball. Nevertheless, it is extremely difficult to maintain a good defensive position against a post player who keeps moving.

Defense Against a Player in a High Post Position

An offensive player is in the high post position whenever she is 15 ft. or more from the basket. She stands with her back to the basket just beyond the free throw line or its extension. She may also move laterally or forward (away from the basket) to set a screen. Regardless of her exact position, she is considered to be in a high post position whenever she is beyond the free throw line. The ball is usually passed in to a high pivot by a guard, point, or wing.

The defensive player guarding a high post takes her stance on the ball side of the post player. One foot is in front of the post player's foot and the other foot is to the rear of the pivot player. The arm on the ball side is extended in front of the pivot player, and the other arm is to the rear of the pivot. By keeping an arm in front of the pivot, the defender can discourage passes to her or force them to the weak side of the pivot (Fig. 2.23). If a guard passes to the other guard the defensive player slides behind the post player and returns to the same relative defensive position on the other side. On initiating the slide across, the first step is always taken with the rear foot.

When a player is in a high post position she is generally used to feed cutters and is often outside her normal shooting range. Therefore, when the high post player receives the ball the defensive player can safely move 1 or 2 ft. behind her. The high post player is permitted to shoot from that position and is encouraged to do so if she lacks success. Of course, if successful on a number of shots the defensive player will be forced to contest each shot. However, if unsuccessful in her shooting attempts, the defender can drop off and assist her teammates as cutters scissor off her.

If a player in a high post position moves away from the free throw line either laterally or forward, she is generally moving in this direction to set a rear screen for a teammate. When this occurs the player guarding the post must warn a teammate of a possible screen and be ready to help and recover or switch. If the pivot player is forced to cut toward the

outer edge of the restraining circle to receive a pass, the defender has accomplished her purpose extremely well.

Defense Against a Player in the Medium Pivot Position

The medium post area is between 9 and 15 ft. from the basket. This area includes the area from the third lane space mark out to the free throw line and includes the portion of the restraining circle contained within the lane area. Because the medium post player is in an excellent position to shoot and pass off, it is extremely important that the defensive player prevent her from receiving the ball. Other defensive players must help to close the passing lanes into the medium pivot. The ball may be passed to a medium pivot by a wing, guard, or corner player.

The defender must play on the ball side one-half player to the side of the post player. This means that her feet straddle either the rear foot (the one closer to the basket) or the forward foot of the pivot, depending upon the position of the ball. The defender has her front arm extended in front of the post player to deter any passes to her. The other arm is behind her (Fig. 2.24). She is effective in preventing a direct pass into the pivot from this position. This position, however, makes her vulnerable to a lob pass and she must have confidence that there is weak side help.

If the ball is passed around the perimeter to the other side of the court, the defensive player must go behind (basket side of) the pivot before she regains her correct defensive position. If she goes in front of the pivot she is too susceptible to the lob pass. And, this is difficult to defend against from the middle of the lane.

If the medium post gets the ball despite the efforts of the defender, the defender should move a step behind her and try to force her toward the sideline. By overplaying her, she tries to prevent her from moving into the lane area where the shooting percentage is much higher. This is particularly true when the pivot is to her left of the basket. When she is to her right of the basket and prefers to move to her right, the defender may overplay her toward the baseline and allow her to move toward the lane, which should be more effective defensively.

The defensive player should be aware of any shooting limitations of the pivot. She should know the range from which she can shoot; and, when she is beyond that, the defender should allow her to shoot freely and protect against the post passing off to cutters. She can be extremely effective in this capacity.

a   b   c

d   e   f   g

Fig. 2.23 *Guarding a High Post. Light 6 retains good position against a stationary post as the ball is passed from one side to another (a–c). Light 6 maintains good position against a high post cutting across the free throw line as the ball is passed around the top of the key (d–g).*

a   b   c

d   e   f   g

Fig. 2.24 *Guarding a Medium Post. Light 6 overplays the post (a and b), realizes she cannot intercept the pass, and begins to move behind the post (c and d) and obtains good position against a ball handler (e). When a post is on the off side and cuts to the ball, the defender must overplay her (f and g).*

Defense Against a Player in the Low Post Position

The low post area is within 9 ft. of the basket. Generally a player is in this position to maneuver for good shots. She is rarely used as a passer to cutters because the passing lanes usually are closed due to the relatively close position to the basket. In this position the ball is passed in to the pivot from a corner, and when the pivot is unable to shoot she usually returns the ball to a corner player or wing.

Because any shooting done from this area generally results in a score, the defensive player must prevent her opponent from receiving a pass. This means that the defender plays either in front of her opponent or three-quarters. If a defender chooses to play in front of her opponent, she may either face the ball or her opponent. By facing the ball she is better able to see the total play and to assist in blocking shots near the basket. She cannot be as aware of her opponent, however. She can keep her opponent under control by facing her, but will be of little help to team defense. If her teammates can rebound well and it is important to prevent the low post from receiving a pass, this defensive posture may be advisable. Most often though, the defender plays her opponent three-quarters. The defensive

player's rear foot is opposite the rear foot of the pivot and her other foot is comfortably advanced. Her arms are extended in the usual manner (Fig. 2.25).

When the opponents cannot pass the ball to the pivot from one side, they often pass it around the perimeter to the wing on the other side and try to make the entry from there. When the ball is reversed to the other side, the defender must move in front of the pivot player rather than behind her. Lob passes are not as dangerous when the player is in this position because of the player's proximity to the basket. As the pivot player maneuvers to the opposite side of the free throw lane, the defending player steps in front of her by taking the first step with the rear foot. She slides across the free throw lane and then resumes her three-quarter defensive position by stepping back with the opposite foot. In the process of moving across the lane the defensive player must not permit the pivot to receive a pass. The defender must stay ball side (in front) of her opponent as she moves across the lane. Once the low post player gets the ball she should be forced toward her weakest shooting side. Generally when the pivot is to her right of the basket, the defender should force her back toward the middle by overplaying her toward the baseline. When the pivot is to the left of the basket, the defender usually

a   b   c

Fig. 2.25 *Guarding a Low Post. With the ball at the wing position, the defender denies the ball to the post (a); as the ball is passed to the post, the defender steps around the post (b) and deflects the ball to a teammate (c).*

should overplay her toward the middle and force her toward the baseline. If the pivot player's actions do not substantiate this action by the defense, the defender should adjust her position to become more effective.

Other Thoughts About Post Defense

Against a pivot player in any position the defender guards her with one arm extended in front of her. The purpose of this posture is to discourage a pass to the pivot. The pass must be toward the weak side and extremely accurate in order to be successful. This often causes the pivot player to fake and/or cut to another position so that she might be free before the defender can resume this position. This constant pressure becomes frustrating to a pivot who has difficulty getting free.

One of the real advantages of this posture is that it forces the pivot to readjust her position frequently. If she is not trained to accomplish this, she may be rendered ineffective for the game. Of course, the defender cannot hold the pivot in any way as she attempts to maneuver. The defender must lower her arm but try to interject her body in the path her opponent wishes to take. Employing this action causes the post to recut and maneuver to become free. This tends to affect the timing of offensive team play, which, of course, is favorable for the defense.

Whenever the ball is on the weak side, the defender should anticipate a cut by the pivot player to receive a pass. The defender should ascertain where the cutting lane exists and beat her opponent to the position where she would like to receive

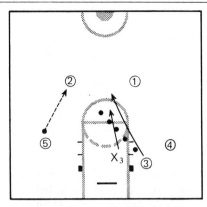

Fig. 2.26 *Defense Against a Pivot to Force Her Wide of Her Desired Cut. The dotted line shows the cut desired by 3. By floating away from 3, player X_3 can beat her on her cut and force her path to be altered.*

the pass. A pivot should never be allowed to cut where she would like. The defender must contest the cut legally and be one step ahead of the pivot. By floating away from her opponent when the ball is on the weak side, she is able to gain this desirable position (Fig. 2.26). It is imperative that the pivot be unable to receive a pass in the lane. Her favorable position almost assures her of scoring.

The defender against the pivot should never leave her opponent to help a teammate unless an opponent is going in for an uncontested shot. In this case she may attempt to harass the opponent or block the shot, but a weak side defender must block out the pivot player.

Drills for Guarding the Post Player

1. Two guards and one pivot player in a high post position, each with a defender opposing her. The two guards pass the ball back and forth to one another and attempt to get the ball to the post player. The defender against the post player changes her position as the ball is passed from one guard to another and tries to prevent the ball from being passed to the post player. If the post player receives the pass, the defender moves back a step and allows the post to take a shot from that position. If the pivot player decides not to shoot but to drive, the defensive player guards her and tries to force her away from her most successful shooting spots. After the shot is taken, the defensive player blocks her opponent out. The two guards are not permitted to cut toward the basket at this stage. The purpose of this drill is to assist the post player's opponent in regaining proper defensive position as the ball is passed from one guard to the other.

2. Same as drill 1, but substitute a point and two wings for the two guards.

3. Five offensive players and five defensive players. No cutting is permitted by the offensive players. Their purpose is to pass the ball around the perimeter in an attempt to find an opening to get the ball to the post player. The post player starts in a high post position and may move to any position she desires in order to receive a pass. The defensive player must play her accordingly.

4. Five offensive players against one defensive player guarding the post player. The post player plays only in a medium post position and maneuvers from one side of the lane to the other in order to receive a pass. The purpose of this drill is to assist the defensive player in moving from playing the post player half a player on the left side of the court to playing half a player on the right side of the court. Emphasis must be placed on the defensive player moving behind the post player when she moves across the lane and regaining proper positioning as rapidly as possible. She also must understand that while she is maneuvering behind the post player under normal conditions she will have defensive help from her teammates so that it is not as easy to get a pass to the post player as it appears in this particular drill.

5. Five offensive players and their opponents with the pivot player in the low post position. The offensive players pass the ball around the perimeter in an attempt to get the ball into the post by means of a pass from one of the forwards. The post player maneuvers from one side of the key to the other but tries to stay in a low post position. The defensive player moves in front of the pivot in this instance so that she is between the ball and her opponent to prevent a pass from reaching the pivot while she is in the lane. The defensive player constantly tries to front the pivot whenever she is in a low post position. If the post player gets the ball, the defender tries to force her in the appropriate direction.

6. A wing player with the ball and a low post and her defender on the offside. The post cuts to the ball and the defender legally obstructs the path she wishes to take and regains good defensive position as she posts up.

DEFENSIVE REBOUNDING

Individual defensive players must learn the value of good defensive rebounding. Defensive players will often concentrate and work extremely hard to prevent their opponent from receiving a pass or prevent her from taking a high percentage shot. Frequently, however, as soon as a shot is attempted, they relax slightly, permitting the offensive players to maneuver for the rebound. This can be extremely disheartening for a defense that has caused the opponents to work for 20–25 seconds and forced an outside shot, only to find they score a rather easy layup following the rebound.

Blocking Out

It has been said many times and by many people that many games are won or lost "on the boards." Although this statement applies to both offensive and defensive rebounding, the implication for su-

perior defensive rebounding is clear. Regardless of the type of defense being played, the defensive players are closer to the basket than their opponents (except a defender against a low or medium pivot) and, therefore, are in a better position to secure the rebound. Whenever a shot is attempted, they must continue to exert pressure so that their opponent cannot move in toward the basket to obtain the rebound. This pressure is established by moving into the path of the opponent, thus preventing her from gaining that advantage. The concentration and effort that rebounding demands can be developed if players acquire the attitude that the opponents should never get a second shot. They will not always succeed, but if *every* defensive player concentrates on blocking out her opponent on *every* attempted shot, there will be few easy offensive tip-ins or rebounds. There is a high correlation between the emphasis placed on rebounding and the percentage of rebounds a team recovers.

When playing man-to-man defense, rebounding

assignments are relatively easy to establish. Each player is responsible for keeping her opponent away from the backboard. This can be accomplished if each defensive player always keeps her eye on the ball. By doing this she can see each time a shot is taken and can turn immediately so that one shoulder is perpendicular to her opponent. From this position she can see in what direction her opponent starts to cut toward the basket. As the offensive player makes her move, the defensive player pivots directly into her path so that the defensive player is facing the basket with her opponent behind her. The defensive player pivots on one foot, swings her other leg across in front of the opponent's path, and assumes a wide stance to cause the opponent to move in a wide arc around her (Fig. 2.27). As the offensive player maneuvers toward the goal, the defender uses sliding steps to retain her favorable position. Once this position is attained the assigned defensive players move toward the basket for the rebound. Some teams assign only three players to obtain the rebound while other teams use four. Regardless of the number who advance toward the basket, the passing lanes should be open so that a pass can be made successfully toward the sideline once the rebound is gained.

Each time a player blocks out an opponent who makes no effort to rebound, she remains in her position perpendicular to her opponent no longer than two seconds. She can estimate that time by counting one thousand and one, one thousand and two, and then pivot to face the basket so that her attention is focused on the ball as it hits the backboard or rim. If she delays longer, she will not be in position to rebound, and a smart offensive player who observes a defender's tardy pivot will continue to maneuver on subsequent shots so that the defensive player does not pivot in time to be of assistance in rebound responsibilities. The two-second period is an arbitrary one that is usually used on long shots for the time it takes the ball in flight to reach the goal. On shorter range shots the time should be reduced to one second more or less. As players gain experience in playing, they will acquire the timing necessary to be in proper position.

Specific Rebounding Responsibilities

Guards or Point

A team that can rely on its front line players to secure the rebound should not require either of its guards or point to rebound. Their responsibility is

a   b   c

Fig. 2.27 *Blocking Out. The player shoots (a), dark 6 pivots against her opponent (b), and blocks her out (c).*

to cut to receive the outlet pass and try to start a fast break attack. If a team does not possess strong rebounders, one of the guards may be assigned to cover the area near the free throw line. The offensive team usually keeps one of their guards back for defensive measures in case the ball is lost, so that one defensive guard generally does not move for a rebound. A point player never rebounds unless her opponent takes her to the boards.

Once the ball is shot the guards block out their opponent, look to retrieve a loose ball or rebound, and start a fast break. If the ball is rebounded by any of their teammates, the appropriate guard cuts to the sideline for the outlet pass. Once the ball is shot a point player will block out her opponent and then cut for the outlet pass.

When one of the offensive guards shoots, she generally rebounds so that her opponent must use correct blocking out techniques. The other offensive guard will remain back and her opponent pivots after two seconds and is prepared to cover a wide rebound or move for the outlet pass.

Wings and Corner Players

Wings and corner players usually have rebound responsibilities, and their opponents must block them out on every shot. If a defensive player's opponent shoots, or if any other offensive player one pass away shoots, the defensive player is close to her opponent and can follow the techniques described to block her out. If the defensive player is weak side she will have sagged off her opponent. Therefore, she takes a step or two toward her opponent so that she meets her sooner than if she waited for her opponent to move toward the basket. As she approaches her opponent, she pivots in to her path and retains her favorable position as she moves toward the basket.

Post(s)

The opposing post player always rebounds so that her opponent must block her out on every shot. Basically, her opponent is never more than one pass away from the ball; therefore, the defensive player has little opportunity to sag off her opponent. Therefore, she utilizes the same technique described previously to block out her opponent. This task is easiest when the opposing pivot is playing in the high post position. Here the defensive player is behind her or closer to the basket and in a good position to block out properly. As the offensive post moves down to the middle or low post position, the defender's problems are increased. By playing one-

half, three-quarters, or a full player in front of the offensive pivot in these positions the defender no longer is closer to the basket than her opponent and the offensive player has a clear advantage in rebounding.

When the post player is in a medium pivot position and a shot is taken on the far side (side away from the pivot), the post defender should be between her opponent and the ball and able to obtain good rebounding position. When the medium pivot player shoots or the shot comes from the near side the defender will be half a step in front of her. She must obtain good rebounding position as best she can. She pivots on her rear foot, swings her other foot across to form a wide stride, and tries to keep her opponent behind her.

When the offensive pivot player is in the low post position, she is always in better rebounding position than her opponent regardless of who shoots since her opponent plays her three-quarters to a full player in front. This means that when a shot is taken, the defender must attempt to neutralize the effectiveness of her opponent's rebounding efforts. At the same time the offensive pivot player is in position to block out the defensive player's moves. Nevertheless, the defender must pivot, preferably toward the middle, attempt to position herself beside her opponent, and put one foot in front of her so that she can gain the rebound. If this cannot be accomplished, she must maneuver to find an opening. If the offensive post successfully blocks out the defender, a weak side player must block out the post and the defensive post will hustle to block out her teammate's opponent.

Obtaining the Rebound

Although it is not always possible, ideally, a defensive player should be moving forward at the time she goes up for the rebound. This means that as she moves toward the backboard for the rebound she should slow down or stop about 7 ft. from the basket if she has arrived before the ball will descend. She takes a firm side stride position with her knees and hips flexed, arms raised, and elbows at shoulder height. From this position she can jump forward for the rebound. This action prevents a taller opponent from reaching over her head to obtain the rebound or tie it up. She must not allow the offensive player to push her under the basket where the ball will rebound over her head. As the defensive player jumps forward with her arms stretched high and forward, her legs also reach forward so that her body is in more or less a V position with the but-

a b c d

Fig. 2.28 *Rebound and Outlet. The defender goes up for the rebound (a), pivots in the air and looks for a free teammate (b and c), and passes (d). During game play, the ball is rebounded by dark 42 and she turns toward the corner. Note how all defensive players have good block-out position (e). The outlet pass is made, and all players have begun the transition. Light 30 has remained to try to delay the outlet (f).*

e

f

tocks forming the point of the V. In this position the ball can be grasped firmly and the rebounder may turn on her descent to make a quick outlet pass toward the sideline before she returns to the floor. Obviously, she must have good body control in order to make the turn in the air and she must be certain that the passing lane is open before passing to a teammate. This type of outlet pass following the rebound is of great value for any team that likes to use a fast break (Fig. 2.28).

There are those who declare the rebounding area as "war on the boards." Thus, it is essential that a rebounder gain firm control of the ball. Grasping the ball should be done with both hands simultaneously. It is not as spectacular as the one hand grab and slap into the other hand, but it does provide better protection of the ball. If a rebounder cannot control the ball herself, she should tip the ball to a teammate. Rebounding is a game of inches!

Once the rebounder has gained control she must pass the ball while in midair only if the passing lane is open. Lacking this, she should return to the floor and pass to a free teammate in an open passing lane. If this remains blocked the rebounder should quickly dribble the ball out of the lane while looking for a free teammate. A pass should be made as soon as possible.

When the area near the rebounder is congested she should pull the ball in to her abdomen, flex her elbows outward and flex at the waist to protect the ball. If necessary she may pivot away from the greatest opposition. Once the area has cleared the rebounder may either dribble or pass to a free teammate.

Drills for Defensive Rebounding

1. Each player does a series of ten short jumps followed by ten high jumps. Repeat this process for a designated number of times or until a predetermined time has elapsed. The purpose of this drill is to develop both leg strength and the explosive power necessary for rebounding.

2. The sargent jump and reach test or other similar test can be used to measure a player's jumping ability or to record progress.

3. Columns of four or five players. The first player in each column has a ball. That player tosses the ball against the backboard and each player in turn moves forward, jumps, tips the ball against the backboard, and tries to keep the ball in play. Continue until the ball can no longer be controlled; restart the drill.

4. A player with the ball near the backboard tosses the ball and, by constantly tapping the ball against the backboard, keeps it in play as long as possible. Allow players to rest while others attempt the same drill. To increase the difficulty of the drill once players acquire success, the player should attempt to tap the ball from the right side of the basket to the left side and continue to alternate sides as long as possible.

5. Two wings and a pivot player and their opponents. The teacher/coach has the ball. A shot is attempted whereupon the defensive players pivot slightly so that one shoulder is perpendicular to the opponent. They eye their opponent for a split second and then pivot in the direction of their opponent's cut for the rebound. As a defensive player gets the rebound, she should return to the floor with her elbows extended outward.

6. Two wings, a pivot player, and their opponents. One of the attack players has the ball and is permitted to shoot. The defensive players immediately block out and move for the rebound.

7. Columns of four to five players standing 8–12 ft. from the basket and behind lines placed on the floor 4–5 ft. in front of the basket on each side of the basket. In turn players run forward to the line, jump for the rebound, and attempt to gain the V position. Later a ball is tossed toward the backboard so that the player may time her jump with the descent of the basketball.

8. One wing or pivot player and her opponent. The attack player tries to maneuver one on one and follow her shot for the rebound. The defensive player blocks her out; after gaining possession of the rebound, she pivots away from the offensive player who attempts to guard her.

9. Two attack players and two defensive players playing two on two. Any time the offensive players attempt a shot, the defensive players block out and move into position for the rebound. Later, add another attack and defensive player.

10. Two defensive players, preferably one wing or a pivot player, stationed 5–6 ft. from the basket. A guard or point is stationed near one of the sidelines. A third player or manager tosses the ball against the backboard while the pivot player (wing) moves in for the rebound. The rebounder attempts to acquire a secure grasp on the ball, turns in the air, and passes to the outlet near the sideline. During the early learning stages of this drill, the shooter must insure that the ball rebounds on the same side of the basket as the outlet is located so that poor passing techniques (passing the ball across the basket) are not developed or encouraged.

11. Same as drill 10 above, except the point starts out in front of the keyhole prior to the time the shot is taken. As it becomes apparent that the pivot player is going to gain possession of the rebound, the guard cuts to the sideline to receive the outlet pass. Later, if desirable, another guard or wing is added so that she can cut toward the middle of the court to receive the second pass for the start of a fast break.

12. Same as drill 11 above, only add opponents against players involved. Following the shot, defensive players must block out prior to their assigned moves.

13. Five attack players and five defensive players. The offensive players run a designated set of offensive plays or maneuvers and attempt shots whenever the opportunity arises. Emphasis is placed on the defensive players blocking out, rebounding properly, and making a quick outlet pass.

2

Two-, Three-, and Four-Player Tactics

3

Pass and Cut

There are several tactics that an offensive player can use in combination with one or more teammates that may prove successful against varying types of defenses. The maneuvers that will be described are basic to all offensive tactics. Some are more useful against man-to-man defense whereas others are equally effective against both man-to-man and zone defenses. The pass and cut, screens, and running screens are effective against both types of defenses; scissoring and screens encouraging a switch of defensive player assignments are effective only against man-to-man defenses.

PASS AND CUT

Once beginners learn to cut they are then ready to execute the most elementary of all offensive plays — the pass and cut maneuver (often called the give and go) in which a player passes to a teammate and then cuts for the basket. It is a play in which the original passer reacquires the ball in a position closer to the basket, either to shoot immediately or to drive closer to the goal. Either the front or reverse cutting techniques may be used, depending upon the position of the defensive players. The back door cut is open against a defender who turns her head in the direction of the pass. The offensive player simply cuts hard for the basket as soon as she sees the defender's head turn. This move can also be executed by an attack player who runs directly at her opponent, and does a reverse pivot to place the defender behind her.

This play is executed most often with the guard starting the play by passing to a wing. If the defense guards this maneuver well, the cutter must continue her cut to a position near the end line and then clear the area. In so doing she may clear to the opposite side of the court or stay on the same side of the court and set a running screen for the player with the ball (Fig. 3.1). It may also be successful when executed by the two guards if the pivot player has cleared the lane. A wing passing to a corner player is another option used commonly against both man-to-man and zone defenses.

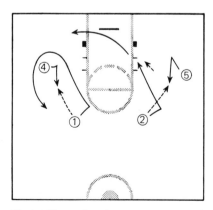

Fig. 3.1 *Players 2 and 5 execute a pass and cut play. If 5 cannot pass in to 2, 2 may clear to the opposite side; player 1 started a pass and cut with 4 but was not free, so she set a running screen for 4 and then buttonhooked and replaced herself.*

123

a

b

c

Fig. 3.2 *Defense Against a Pass and Cut. A point player passes to a wing and the defensive player moves toward the ball (a); she stays between her opponent and the ball (b); forces her to go backdoor and continues to deny her the ball (c).*

Defense Against the Pass and Cut

As soon as an attack player passes the ball, the defender must take a step back and a step toward the ball to disallow the offensive player from cutting in front of her. Successful completion of a pass and cut play must be eliminated.

The footwork is simple. As the pass is made the defender slides diagonally backward toward the ball one to two steps. As the cutter moves toward the ball, the defender continues to slide and beats the offensive player. When the offensive player cuts to the basket, the defender pivots on her rear foot and overplays the cutter through the lane (Fig. 3.2). If the opponent goes out of the lane on the weak side, the defender stays in the lane to provide weak

side help. If the cutter replaces herself, the defender follows principles based on an opponent one pass away from the ball.

BLAST

The blast is a variation of the pass and cut in which a pass is made and another player makes a basket cut. This tactic is particularly effective when the ball is passed to the post. It is also extremely effective when a team normally screens away from the ball and the defense is lulled into this maneuver. At an appropriate time a player cuts to the basket and leaves her defender behind.

The weak side guard can effectively cut to the

basket when the ball is passed in to a high post. With the post in the low or medium position, a wing or corner can effectively blast, particularly when their opponent is helping with a troublesome post player.

Defense Against the Blast

Since the blast is generally attempted when a defender has sagged off her opponent, it is important that defenders always are able to see both the ball and their opponent. Although defenders have help-

ing responsibilities, their primary responsibility is to stay with their own opponent. Therefore, as soon as an opponent starts to cut, the defender must move close to the cutter and overplay her. Giving her too much space keeps the passing lane open.

This is another situation in which a cutter should not be free. The defender should always be closer to the ball than her opponent and should be able to regain good defensive position to prevent the blast from being successful. Only when a team wants a particular player to shoot should the play be allowed.

4

Screening

Screening is the premier means for freeing a player against a man-to-man defense. The purpose of screening is threefold:

1. To provide a teammate with the ball the opportunity to shoot or drive for goal
2. to free a teammate without the ball for a pass
3. to go behind a teammate to receive a hand-off with the option of shooting or driving for goal

Some teams use screening tactics against teams that switch defensive assignments to cause a mismatch in size of opponents. Unless the height differential is significant, height mismatches produce only negligible gains by the offensive team. Perhaps more important is a speed differential that can be exploited. If a quick guard or point screens a slower opponent, a significant advantage may be realized when the opponents switch.

There are three ways of setting a screen. The player sets the screen:

1. to either side of her teammate's opponent (lateral screen, Fig. 4.1)
2. closer to the basket than her teammate's opponent (outside or rear screen, Fig. 4.2)
3. between her teammate and her teammate's opponent (inside or back screen, Fig. 4.3)

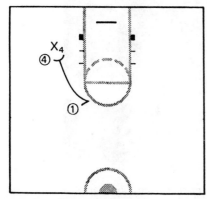

Fig. 4.1 *Player 1 sets a lateral screen for player 4.*

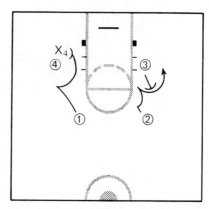

Fig. 4.2 *Player 1 sets an outside screen for player 4. Player 3 moves up to set a rear screen for player 2.*

127

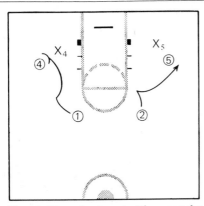

Fig. 4.3 *Player 1 sets an inside screen for player 4, and player 2 cuts behind player 5 to effect an inside screen variation. Player 5 actually provides the screen for 2.*

SETTING THE SCREEN

The position of the teammate's opponent is the deciding factor in determining where the screen is set. When an opponent is guarding loosely or sagging, the inside screen is generally used. When guarded closely, players generally use the outside, rear, or lateral screens. The reason for this will be shown in the description of each screen.

The player may set the desired screen in either of two ways. She may cut over to set the screen on the defensive player or she may dribble into position for the screen. Both techniques may be employed to set either a moving or stationary screen although the dribbling technique usually involves a moving screen. Screen plays may involve two, three, or four players. Beginners should learn how to screen first with two players; once the moves and timing are acquired, three-player screens may be attempted, followed by four-player screens —commonly called double screens.

Certain techniques apply to setting a screen. The screen must be set so that a defensive player will have difficulty getting around the screen. Too often beginning players set the screen on their own player or on "air." If the defensive player is not positioned where the screener thinks she should be, the screener must go find the defender and set the screen on her.

The screen must be set at an appropriate angle. The angle is determined by which of the screens is being used and the path that the offensive player wishes to follow. This factor will be discussed in greater detail under each type of screen.

Position of the Screener

The screener must have good body position so that if the defensive player makes contact she doesn't lose her balance. Her stance must be wide to give her a wider base of support and to cause the defender to go further to get around her. The screener's knees should be flexed to provide better bal-

Fig. 4.4 *Position for a Lateral Screen. The stance is taken so that the opponent's near foot is midway between the screener's feet. The arms are folded and in contact with the chest. A wide stance is taken, and knees are flexed to provide balance.*

ance. If the screen is set facing the defender, the screener should cross her arms in front of her body with each hand in contact with the opposite shoulder and the elbows in contact with the abdomen (Fig. 4.4). This method provides protection for the screener.

A screen may be set either facing the defender or with the screener's back to the defensive player. If set with the back to the defender, the screener is in position simply to cut to an advantageous position following the use of the screen (Fig. 4.5). The drawback of setting a screen in this manner is that the screener may have to look over her shoulder to follow the action of the player using the screen if the player cuts away from the screen. Also, good balance is more difficult to maintain when contact

is made from the rear rather than from in front. If the screen is set facing the defender, the screener may simply cut to an advantageous position while looking over her shoulder for a pass after the screen has been used or she may roll by pivoting on the foot closer to the basket.

One of the errors made by the screener is cutting (or rolling) in the same area as the player for whom the screen was set. If the player using the screen goes low off the screen, the screener should go high; if the player using the screen goes high, the screener should go low.

Whenever a screen is set, the player for whom the screen is set is responsible for using it. When the screen is set on the ball, the player must cut off the screen to relieve congestion in the area and to

Fig. 4.5 *Lateral Screen Set with Back to the Defensive Player. A weakside player prepares to set a screen on the ball (a). The ball handler sets up her opponent (b); the screen is set (c); and the screener cuts for a pass as the defensive players switch opponents (d).*

relieve defensive pressure on the ball. To use any screen effectively the player must fake, cut, or maneuver in such a way that she takes her opponent into the screen. Frequently, good screens are set but the offensive player does not force her opponent into the screen.

Screens may be set on or off the ball. A screen set on the ball involves only two players. A screen off the ball involves either three players or four players for a double screen.

LATERAL OR SIDE SCREENS

A lateral screen (often called a pick) is executed either for a player with the ball to drive or shoot, or away from the ball to free a player to receive a pass. The lateral screen is effective when the defensive player is guarding closely.

Setting the Pick on the Ball and Subsequent Movement

When screening on the ball, the player sets her body perpendicular to her opponent and as close as possible while avoiding a foul. She approaches the defender so that as she plants her feet the defender's feet will bisect her stance (Fig. 4.6).

After setting the screen, the player holds it until her teammate starts her drive. She then moves to an open area on the court, going high if her teammate

a

b

c

Fig. 4.6 *Lateral Screen. Dark 21 passes to her teammate (a); moves to set a screen for her (b), pivots on her back foot (c), and rolls for a pass (d). The screen is made off the ball as dark 6 passes to dark 5 (e), sets a screen low (f), pivots, (g), rolls for a pass (h), and is free for a shot (i).*

d

e

f

g

h

i

Fig. 4.6 *(continued)*

goes low and going low if her teammate goes high so that congestion does not occur and a passing lane is open.

Rolling

If the screen is set with the left foot closer to the basket than the right foot, the screener moves her left foot slightly to the left to assure that the defender being screened is forced to remain behind the screener. After taking the slight move to her left, she pivots on her left foot and cuts for the basket with her right foot. If the screen is set on the other side of the court when the player has her right foot closer to the basket, the screener moves her right

foot slightly to her right, pivots on her right foot, and starts for the basket with her left foot. If the defensive player is close to the defender it is not necessary for the screener to move her rear foot slightly to the side to keep the opponent behind her (Fig. 4.6).

Cutting

Rather than rolling, the screener may simply cut to the basket by pushing hard off the high foot, pivoting on the foot closer to the basket, taking the first step with the high foot, and extending the arm on the same side (Fig. 4.7).

The player with the ball generally cuts toward the

a

b

c

d

Fig. 4.7 *Lateral Screen and Cut. Light 32 moves over to set a screen on the ball (a and b); as 32's defender edges to help against the screen, light 32 cuts for the basket (c), receives a pass, and has an easy shot (d).*

side of the screen, thus forcing her opponent into the screen. The screener is free on her roll or cut if the defenders switch opponents. The player for whom the screen was set is free if the defenders stay with their own opponent.

If a defensive player anticipates a screen and moves toward the screening side before the screen is set, the player with the ball should cut away from the screen and should be free on her drive toward the basket (Fig 4.8).

For a lateral screen to be successful it is important that the player for whom the screen is set looks away from the site of the forthcoming screen and fakes in another direction. For example, if the screen is coming from the player's left, she can look toward the basket or to her right, fake to her right, and then cut left around the screen. Otherwise the defender is alerted for the screen and can take measures to reduce its effectiveness.

It is the responsibility of the player for whom the screen is set to avoid causing a foul. She must wait for the screener to come to a stationary position before the cut or drive is made. If she starts her cut or drive around the screen too soon, her teammate is likely to be called for blocking if contact results between her and an opponent.

There are a number of possibilities for using lateral screens. They may be used by a guard setting the screen for another guard, a guard screening for a forward, a pivot player screening for a forward, or

a b

c d

Fig. 4.8 *Lateral Screen. Dark No. 2 passes to her teammate and moves to set a screen (a and b). Light No. 1 anticipates the screen and moves toward the direction of the anticipated drive (c). Dark No. 1 drives away from the screen (d) and is free for the layup before the defense can recover (e–g).*

e f g

Fig. 4.8 *(continued)*

a b

c d e

Fig. 4.9 *Lateral Screen Away from the Ball. The wing is being overplayed (a); a teammate moves over to set a screen on the low side (b and c); the wing runs her opponent into the screen (d); and is free for a pass (e). The defensive player against the wing is sagging (f). The wing takes her opponent lower (g) and cuts back to use the screen (h and i). The wing moves around the screen as the other defender helps temporarily (j and k). The wing is free for the shot (l and m).*

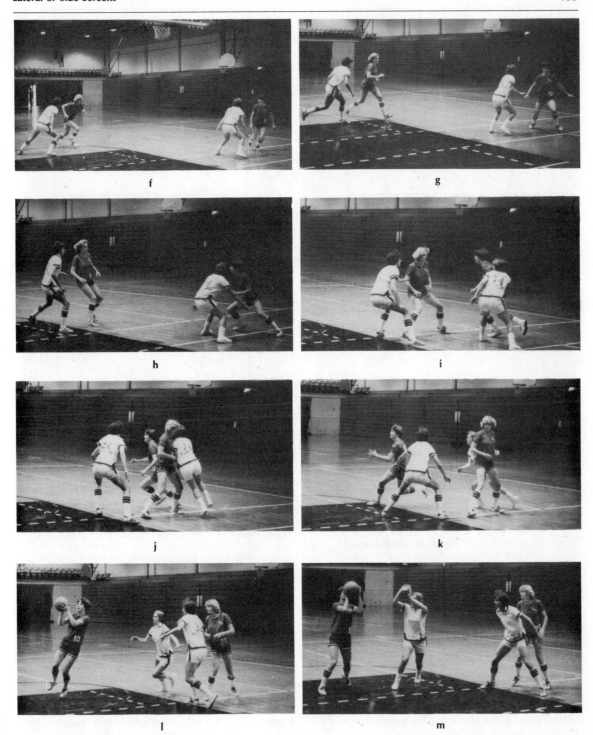

f

g

h

i

j

k

l

m

Fig. 4.9 *(continued)*

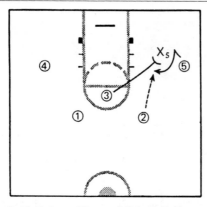

Fig. 4.10 *Lateral Screen Off the Ball. Player 3 sets a screen for 5. 5 fakes away from the screen and cuts back for a pass from 2. If 5 is not free, 2 can pass to 3 on her subsequent move.*

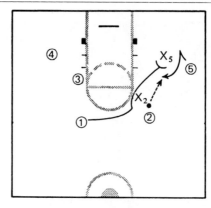

Fig. 4.11 *Lateral Screen Off the Ball. Player 1 cuts behind X₂ and continues to set a screen for 5. Player 5 fakes and cuts around the screen for a pass from 2. Player 2 also has the option of passing to 1 on her subsequent move.*

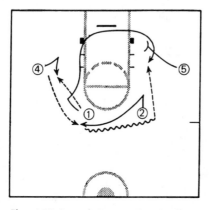

Fig. 4.12 *Lateral Screen Set in Open Space. Player 1 passes to 4 and cuts for the basket. Player 2 fills the space, and 4 passes back to 2. 5 moves toward the lane and sets a diagonal screen for 1 to cut around. 2 dribbles to her right and passes to 1 or 5 on her subsequent move.*

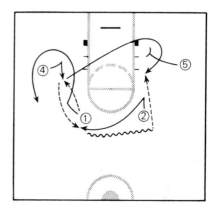

Fig. 4.13 *Variation of Fig. 4.12. Player 1 passes to 4 and cuts for the goal. When 1 does not get a return pass, she buttonhooks back as 4 passes to 2. Player 2 dribbles to her right and passes to 4 as she cuts around 5's screen, or she may pass to 5 if she is free on her subsequent move.*

a wing screening for a corner player. Use of the lateral screen is made to a lesser extent by a wing screening for a guard or a pivot screening for a guard. In both of these instances, the rear screen is more effective. A lateral screen is an effective means for freeing a corner player who is close to the baseline. Because of her inability to cut toward the endline side, when she is in this position the only effective screen is the lateral screen.

Setting the Pick Off the Ball

When screening off the ball, the player sets her body perpendicular to the path that the defender would follow to stay with her opponent (Fig. 4.9). Examples of lateral screens off the ball are shown in Figures 4.10 to 4.13. Following the screen, the screener may roll or cut to a new position.

DEFENSE AGAINST SCREENS

The means of coping with the offensive action is dependent upon the type of screen that is set, and is partially dependent upon the site of the screen. Basically, there are four ways of defending against screens. The defender being screened may

1. move over the top of the screen (stay between her opponent and the screener)
2. slide through (go between the screener and the screener's opponent)
3. slide behind the screen (go behind the screener and the screener's opponent)
4. switch (exchange opponents)

Going over the top must be used when an opponent is in shooting range. Sliding through and sliding behind the screen are not effective when the opponent is in scoring range. When the opponent is beyond shooting range, the defender can slide through and move up on her. Switching is less effective than going over the top.

A screening situation may arise any time a player dribbles or cuts toward a teammate. When this occurs the defensive players must anticipate a screen whether or not it actually develops.

When an offensive player sets a screen, her opponent is responsible for warning her teammate of the impending screen. She calls out "Screen" or "Pick." Her teammate will know from which side the screen will be set depending on the direction from which her voice comes. Some teams prefer to call "Screen left" or "Screen right" to designate the direction from which the screen is coming. Regardless of the technique used, the defensive player guarding the screener is responsible for informing her teammate of the potential screen so that she may take measures to avoid or at least minimize the screen's effectiveness.

Defense Against a Side or Lateral Screen (Pick) on the Ball

The greatest pressure can be exerted against the side screen when the defensive player goes over the top of the screen. This means that she must go between her opponent and the screener. By doing this, she forces the offensive player to protect the ball to a greater degree and may cause her opponent to move slightly wider of the screen. If the offensive player has a good outside shot, this method of dealing with the screen may be necessary. On the other hand, if the offensive player is much quicker than the defensive player or the defense is slow to

react to the screen, this method may be treacherous. The offensive player may gain a half-step advantage due to the screen and may be beyond the defensive player before she can maneuver into good defensive position.

Over the Top

This may be facilitated by any one of several practices. First, the defensive player to be screened may take a step back from her opponent as she hears her teammate call "Screen." She takes a step forward toward her opponent just before the screen is set. A lateral screen is most effective when the defensive player is guarding her opponent tightly; it is much less effective when the defensive player is guarding loosely, because there is space into which the defensive player can move. By taking the backward step the defensive player places herself in a looser defensive position and, therefore, can more easily go over the top of the screen. By delaying her move over the top until just before the screen is set, she can force the screener to continue in her same predetermined path; thus, the screen will be set behind the movement of the defensive player (Fig. 4.14). If the screener changes her path at this stage, she probably will be called for blocking because the defensive player has already started to move in a new direction.

The defensive player guarding the player to be screened may also move up close to her opponent as a means of coping with the lateral screen. If this technique is used, the defender must have help from her teammate who jumps in front of the offensive player freed by the screen for an instant to delay her progress and then quickly returns to guarding her own player. This action provides the defender who is screened with time to go over the top of the screen to stay with her own opponent. This tactic is commonly called "help and recover." It is necessary against teams that screen extensively (Fig. 4.15). Much practice must be devoted to this method, for the timing of the moves is critical.

Another method that aids the defensive player in going over the top is by her moving one-half or whole player to the ball side of her opponent. This action forces the screen to be set further from the player for whom it is intended, and forces the offensive player to take more steps before she is around the screen. This provides the defensive player additional time to move over the top to stay with her opponent. This position by the defensive player makes her vulnerable to a cut or drive away from the screen, so she must anticipate this action by her opponent.

a

b

c

d

Fig. 4.14 *Going Over the Top. Dark No. 5 moves to set a lateral screen (a and b). Light No. 3 anticipates it, moves closer to her opponent (c), and is in good defensive position against her opponent (d).*

To help her get over the screen, the defender straightens, takes short quick steps and uses her arms to help her get around the screener. She must trail the ball handler slightly, particularly if she has help from a teammate. Otherwise, the ball handler will cut back, reversing her direction and she will be free for a drive toward goal.

Behind the Screen

A weaker means of dealing with the side screen occurs when the screened defensive player goes behind the screen. This movement permits the offensive player to take an outside open shot. If she is inaccurate from this range, however, nothing is lost. This method may be desirable when the defensive player is much slower than her opponent.

In order to defend effectively in this manner, the defensive player to be screened must move one-half to a whole player to the ball side of her opponent before the screen is set. She also opens toward the direction from which the screen is coming so that she can move more quickly behind the screen (Fig. 4.16). By moving toward the screener she forces the offensive player for whom the screen is set to take additional steps before she can utilize the screen. Once again this maneuver allows the defensive player time to recover good defensive position, but she must be alert for a cut away from the screen. To counteract this defensive move, the ball handler

Fig. 4.15 *Going Over the Top. Light No. 5 is guarding dark No. 3 (a). Light No. 3 takes a step out in front of the ball handler to force her to go wide around the screen (b and c). This enables light No. 5 to go over the top (d and e) and regain good position (f). In (d–f), note that light No. 3 has moved quickly to front her opponent, although she should be closer to her opponent in (e and f).*

a

b

c

d

e

Fig. 4.16 *Going Behind the Screen. Defender No. 5 has moved half a player toward the direction from which the screen is coming (a and b). As her opponent drives toward the screen, light No. 3 takes a step back which allows light No. 5 to slide through (c and d), and regain position (e). Dark No. 3 failed to read the defense. She should have noticed the defender going behind in (c) and (d) and taken her shot at the top of the circle. In (e) she is dribbling directly toward her opponent.*

should shoot while the defender is behind her teammate. It is from this position that she is free.

An occasion may arise in which the defender's teammate does not provide sufficient space for her to slide through. In this case she must fight around both the screener and her teammate. She can do this most easily by utilizing a reverse pivot to get behind both players and hustle to regain defensive position. Obviously, this is a very weak defensive posture which allows the opponent to shoot free on the outside.

The technique of overplaying (moving one-half or a full player) toward the side of the screen is useful when backcourt players are setting screens for each other. It is less useful and probably undesirable when a backcourt or pivot player sets a screen for a forward in the corner. Since the screen generally comes from the middle area, it leaves the baseline open for the forward to drive away from the screen. Most coaches prefer that the offense be stopped at the baseline and therefore would not encourage or permit their players to utilize this practice in this situation.

Defense Against a Ball Handler Who Dribbles to Set a Side Screen

The same defensive tactics are used when a ball handler drives toward a teammate's defender and sets a side screen as she hands off. One defender must help and recover while the other fights over the screen if her opponent is in scoring range or slides through if she is not. The defenders must not make their moves until they see the ball handed off. If they move too soon, the dribbler will not hand off and will continue to drive free.

Defense Against a Side Screen Away from the Ball

At no time should a player who is two passes away from the ball be screened. A successful screen against her indicates that she has a poor defensive position (Fig. 4.17). A defensive player who is two passes away from the ball should sag or float away from her opponent and open slightly toward the ball (Fig. 4.18). In this position, the defensive player can see any potential screener approaching and should be able to avoid the screen by sliding through. It is unnecessary to go over the top on a screen off the ball.

All players should be alert for this tactic because it is frequently used whenever a team operates with a double post as high post screens for low, or less

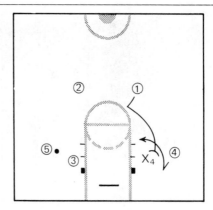

Fig. 4.17 *Poor Defensive Position by Player X_4, Who Is Guarding 4, a Player Two Passes Away from the Ball. Her poor positioning allows player 1 to set a lateral screen to free player 4. This should never occur under these circumstances.*

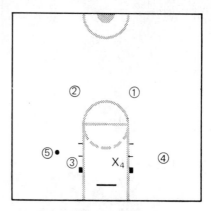

Fig. 4.18 *Proper Positioning by Player X_4. Her opponent 4 is two passes away from the ball, so X_4 has floated toward the ball. If player 1 attempts to screen X_4, it will be ineffective, as X_4 has plenty of space to avoid the screen or may slide through if the screen is set.*

often low screening for high. It is also the premise that for the passing game all screens are off the ball. Wings screen for a corner, point for a wing and posts for anyone.

Switching

A switching defense is another means of counteracting a screen's effectiveness. Switching simply implies that the two defensive players exchange op-

a   b

c   d

e   f

Fig. 4.19 *Switching. Dark No. 3 is guarded by light No. 3 (a and b). Dark No. 5 sets a screen on light No. 3 (c). Light No. 5 switches to guard dark No. 3 (c and d). Light No. 3 moves quickly to front her new opponent, dark No. 5 (e), and makes the interception (f). Jump Switch (g–l). Light No. 5 sets a lateral screen for No. 3 (g and h). Dark No. 5 jumps out to switch opponents and stop the drive (i and j). Dark No. 3 moves to get ball side of her new opponent, light No. 5 (k and l).*

g

h

i

j

k

l

Fig. 4.19 *(continued)*

ponents following a screen on the ball. This technique should be used rarely and then only when absolutely necessary. In other words, it should not be used as the fundamental method for dealing with the screen. It is never used when the screen is off the ball. It may be necessary when the defensive player being screened has not adequately avoided the screen.

It should be apparent that a defensive switch between two guards may not be as dangerous as a switch between a guard and a wing. In the latter instance, one defensive player is often left guarding a player much taller than she. If an opposing team knows that a team normally switches on screen maneuvers, they will plan to utilize guard-to-wing screens to effect this height advantage.

Generally, it is the responsibility of the defensive player guarding the screener to call for the switch. However, some coaches believe that either player should be given that privilege. In any case, the teammate must react to the switch once it is called, and carry out her new responsibility regard-

less of whether she thought the switch was necessary. There is no time to question the decision. Once the switch is called, the defensive player guarding the screener must move close to the screener so that the other offensive player cannot drive between her and the screener. From this point she must maintain good defensive position against her new opponent. The defensive player being screened must move quickly to the rear of the screener immediately after the switch is called so that she will be able to defend against the subsequent roll. At the same time she must also be ready to guard her former opponent if she decides to drive away from the screen (toward the opposite side). As the screener moves to a free area, the defender must work to get in front of her and prevent a bounce pass to her. Her teammate must prevent the lob pass. She does this by raising her arms high in the air as soon as the dribbler catches the ball (Fig. 4.19). The two defensive players involved may obtain additional help from a weak side defender when the switch is necessary.

Drills for a Lateral or Side Screen

The technique for executing and counteracting this type of screen should be clearly presented to the students on a blackboard or magnetic board, in a "live" demonstration, or a combination of these means. Only one method should be introduced and then practiced. Other methods may be presented and practiced later. The following drills provide a progression that is adaptable for any of the methods described.

1. A point guard and a wing and their opponents. One guard passes to her teammate and walks over to set a screen. The defender moves over the top of the screen as the dribbler moves slowly. The screener rolls toward the basket and her opponent stays ball side of her. Repeat to the other direction. Substitute using two guards or a wing and a corner player.

2. Repeat drill 1 above, but permit the players to move at normal speed.

3. Repeat drill 2 above, but the dribbler moves away from the screen.

4. Repeat drill 2 above, but allow the dribbler to move in either direction.

5. One offensive guard and one offensive forward and their opponents. Repeat drills 1 and 2 above.

6. Repeat these drills, utilizing the sliding through technique of combatting the screen. Adjust the spacing on the floor so the ball handler will be out of scoring range. Later, move players within shooting range so offensive players learn to read the defense and react properly to it.

7. Repeat these drills with a ball handler dribbling to set a screen.

8. Repeat the drills on a screen away from the ball.

9. A point guard, two wings and their opponents. Offensive players execute a weave on the outside and the defensive players switch opponents.

Jump Switch

A jump switch may be used in defense of a lateral or inside screen executed by two guards. Because the jump switch involves an exchange of opponents, it is not often used when other players are involved in a screen maneuver. The jump switch is used when a teammate is guarding her opponent closely. As the screen is set, the defender guarding the screener jumps forward and places herself in the path of the ball handler for whom the screen was set. This action should stop the forward drive of the ball handler and, as she picks up the ball, her new opponent raises her arms to prevent the overhead pass. Meanwhile the other defender quickly gets ball side of her new opponent (the screener) and anticipates a bounce pass to her (Fig. 4.19 g–l).

A more daring jump switch involves double-teaming an opponent. The purpose of the two-player jump switch is to force the ball handler to stop her drive and make it difficult for her to make a subsequent pass. Because of the dangers involved, this tactic is rarely used throughout an entire contest. It is generally designed for use during specific times — at the beginning of a period, after a time out, or at some other predetermined time. It can be extremely effective with the element of surprise.

The jump switch is started in much the same manner as the one previously described, with the exception that the defensive player guarding the screener may start her move an instant sooner. She forces the driver to stop her dribble and catch the ball as she jumps into the path of the driver. As this occurs the driver's own opponent has time to approach from the other side, and the two defensive players form a V and pressure the ball handler. The timing of the formation of the wedge is critical! While in this position the two defensive players make no attempt to tap the ball out of the player's hands. They keep their arms moving and high so that the ball handler's vision is obstructed. This, of course, delays her pass and gives the defensive players' teammates time to cover the free player close to the ball. These players must be alert for a bounce pass because the players forming the wedge should prevent the overhead pass. With anticipation and good timing, a defensive player may be able to intercept a pass. Because of the dangers involved, this maneuver should be used sparingly and then only when teammates have acquired excellent timing. It is used most often by guards to trap at the sideline, or by a guard and wing to trap at the wing or corner position, or by a wing and corner player to trap in the corner.

OUTSIDE SCREENS

The outside screen is set basket side of a teammate's opponent and is used when the defensive player is guarding a teammate closely. It may be used in preference to a lateral screen since the outside screen is more easily disguised and the opponent is not as aware that a screen has been set. The outside screen may be executed either moving or standing still, and may be initiated by a player dribbling or cutting into position for the screen.

Setting the Outside Screen

When setting an outside screen, the screener must be certain that she is on a direct line between the player screened and the path that her teammate would like to take. That path may be toward the basket, to the high post area, or any other place, depending upon the location of the ball. It is important that the screener take her stance at the proper angle. (Note the angle of the screen in Figures 4.20 to 4.22.) When possible, she should face the basket. The screen is extremely effective either when set for a player with the ball or when set for a player away from the ball who may then cut off the screen for a pass. The screen can be used effectively by any two or three players on the court. When set for a ball handler, the screen must be set 15 ft. from the baseline so that the ball handler has the option of going in either direction. For this reason it should never be set for a corner player with the ball. However, if a three-player outside screen is set, it may be set anywhere on the floor, including the corner.

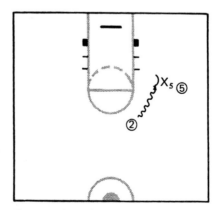

Fig. 4.20 *Outside Screen. Player 2 dribbles and sets the screen for 5, who fakes in either direction to receive a hand off.*

When using the screen it is necessary to fake or cut a few steps beyond the screen and then cut back in order to force the opponent into the screen. The player for whom the screen is set must always cut off the screen and continue away from it. This relieves congestion in the area and enables the screener to step in front of the closer opponent and roll or cut to a free area.

One guard may dribble over behind her teammate's opponent and stop to set a stationary screen at that point. The screened player then utilizes fakes to force her opponent into the screen and cuts in the opposite direction to receive a hand-off from the ball handler (Fig. 4.20).

The same options are available when the ball is passed from a guard to a wing as shown in Fig. 4.21.

a

b

c

d

e

Fig. 4.21 *Outside Screen. Light No. 5 passes to her teammate (a) and moves over to set a screen behind dark No. 4. No. 3 fakes and drives, causing dark No. 4 to move into the screen while her teammate fakes (b and c). No. 3 drives, forcing her opponent into the screen (d) and is free for the layup (e). As No. 3 drives low, No. 5 should cut high to open a passing lane.*

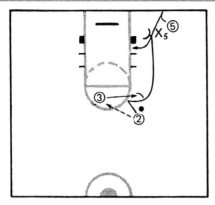

Fig. 4.22 *Three-Player Outside Screen. Player 2 passes to 3 and cuts down to screen for 5. Player 5 fakes and cuts around the screen forcing X₅ into it.*

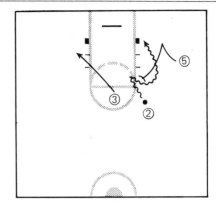

Fig. 4.23 *Rear Screen. Player 3 cuts to the weak side. Player 5 cuts to set a rear screen for player 2, who dribbles her opponent into it and drives around the screen for a shot.*

A three-player screen may be set by a guard who passes to a post and cuts down to set a screen for a corner player. The corner player maneuvers her opponent into the screen, cuts around it, and receives a pass from the post player (Fig. 4.22). This tactic is also effective for an out-of-bounds play.

Rear Screen

The principles and options for the rear screen are the same as those described for the outside screen, except the rear screen is always set at a distance from the player with the ball, or at a distance from the player for whom the screen is intended. It is most commonly set by a corner player or a post player who is closer to the basket than the player for whom the screen is set. The rear screen can be a highly effective tool when set for a player who works one on one effectively. A rear screen is always set in a stationary manner in an uncongested area on the court. Again the angle at which the screen is set is vital.

Possible Uses

A guard has possession of the ball and a player cuts out from her corner position to an uncongested area 15–18 ft. from the basket, generally at an extension of the free throw line. She sets her screen and the guard dribbles her opponent into the screen thus allowing the guard to continue her drive around the screen for an attempted shot (Fig. 4.23). If the defensive players switch, the screener steps in front of her new opponent, cuts for the basket,

and should receive a pass. The pivot player clears to the other side.

A variation of this play is executed when the corner player cuts up toward the guard and the guard passes to her. The ball handler immediately pivots to face the basket and the guard maneuvers her opponent into the screen and cuts in the opposite direction around the player for a hand-off. If the defenders switch assignments, the corner player is free to shoot a jump shot or drive for the basket.

Pivot for Guard

Similarly, the post player may cut diagonally up toward the guard or laterally to an extension of the free throw line to set the rear screen. The near side forward clears to the far side of the court (Fig. 4.24).

A three-player screen may be set as a post player sets a rear screen at the extension of the free throw line. A guard passes the ball to a wing and cuts off the screen for a return pass. The pivot player then cuts for a free area. A pass is made to whichever player is freer (Fig. 4.25).

Defense Against an Outside or Rear Screen

The defense against both of these screens is identical. The defender being screened must go over the top of the screen since the screen is usually set within shooting range.

The screener's opponent must alert her team-

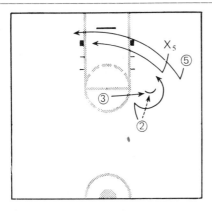

Fig. 4.24 *Player 3 cuts to set a rear screen for player 2. 5 clears to the opposite side. 2 passes to 3, who pivots to face the basket. 2 forces her opponent into the screen and receives a hand-off from 3.*

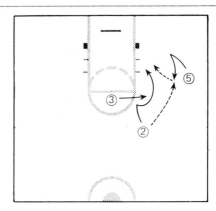

Fig. 4.26 *Three-Player Rear Screen. Player 3 cuts to set a rear screen. Player 5 does not clear, and 2 passes to her. 2 cuts off the screen to receive a pass from 5. If 2 is not free, 5 can pass to 3 as she cuts to a free area.*

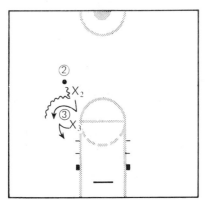

Fig. 4.25 *Defense Against a Rear Screen. Player 2 dribbles toward the inside of 3, but X_2 prevents her drive in that direction. As 2 drives to her right, X_3 hedges to the outside to force 2 to go wider. This allows X_2 time to move over the top of the screen and regain good defensive positioning. X_3 recovers to her own player immediately.*

mate of the impending screen, and she must also help her teammate after the screen is set. As the offensive player uses the screen, her defensive player must stay between her and the screener; she must go over the top. The screener's defender steps out to help her teammate by forcing the opponent to go wider and then recovers on her own opponent as her teammate regains good defensive position (Fig. 4.26).

INSIDE SCREENS

An inside screen is executed by a player moving between a teammate and her opponent who is guarding loosely, and is most commonly used by two guards or by a guard and a wing. The

---

Drills for an Outside or Rear Screen

Each of the possible screens should be practiced. Offensively, emphasis is placed on setting the screen at the proper angle, proper use of the screen, i.e., running the opponent into the screen, reading the defensive reactions, and the screener moving high if her teammate goes low and moving low if her teammate goes high. Defensively, emphasis should be placed on the defender going over the top, the screener's defender helping and recovering, and constant defensive pressure being maintained.

1. Four players — one guard or point player and wing and their opponents. The guard or point player dribbles over and sets an outside screen for the wing. Alternate players and exchange sides of the court.

2. Same as drill 1, but the point guard passes the ball to the wing.

3. Four players — a high post and a point guard and their opponents. The point guard passes to the post at the extension of the free throw line and cuts off her. Alternate sides of the court.

4. Six players — one guard, post, and wing and their opponents. The guard passes to the post and sets a screen for the wing. Exchange sides of the court.

5. Six players — point guard, wing, and post and their opponents. The point passes to the wing as the post sets a rear screen. The point player cuts off the screen and receives a pass from the wing.

screen may be established by a player cutting between her teammate and her opponent and stopping to form a stationary screen, or the screen may be set as a player cuts between a teammate and her opponent or dribbles between the two players, thus forming a moving screen. In all cases the screener should face the basket.

Stationary Inside Screen

If the inside screen is set by a player who passes to a teammate and cuts in front of her and stops, the player with the ball has several options. If she is within her shooting range, she may shoot from behind the screen. If either defensive player moves around the screen to place more pressure on her, she can drive in the opposite direction. If neither defensive player moves in to defend, she may drive in either direction.

It is easily understandable that the alternative chosen by the player with the ball depends upon the defensive moves of the opponents. This is also true of the subsequent action of the screener. If either defensive player moves to guard the player with the ball, the screener blocks out the other defender so that she (the screener) should be free for an ensuing pass. Having set the screen while facing the basket, the screener will have both defenders in front of her and probably side by side. If the defender on her right moves in to guard the player with the ball, the screener quickly steps forward with her left foot to place the defender on her left behind her. She is then free for a quick pass. If the defender on the screener's left moves in to guard the player with the ball, the screener then steps forward with her right foot to block out the defender on her right. The blocking out and move toward the

basket is started as soon as the switch in defensive assignments is made, and the pass to the cutting player must be made immediately (Fig. 4.27). A bounce pass is usually most effective. If the pass is delayed the defensive team has time to reposition and possibly intercept the pass.

Moving Inside Screen

The moving screen is more commonly seen in double guard maneuvers. The guard with the ball dribbles between a teammate and her opponent (or cuts between them). The teammate then cuts in the direction from which the dribbler came, receives a hand-off, and drives for the basket. Her own opponent should be at a defensive disadvantage or, if the opponents switch, her teammate should have a half-step advantage on her new opponent (Fig. 4.28). (Note: The two defensive players came shoulder to shoulder before the switch was started.) If the defensive players had anticipated the screen and if the dribbler's opponent had started her switch too soon, this would have permitted the dribbler to cut between the two guards after her hand-off, thus affecting an outside screen and enabling her to be free for a subsequent pass (Fig. 4.29).

Three-Player Inside Screen

This play may be executed by a post, guard, and wing. As the pivot player receives the pass the guard cuts down and sets the inside screen for the wing. The same options are available for the wing and the pivot player looks for either the wing or the guard — whichever player appears to be more

a

b

c

d

e

Fig. 4.27 *Inside Screen. Dark No. 5 moves over to set a screen against defender No. 3 who is guarding loosely (a and b). As No. 3 moves toward the ball handler, No. 4 drives in the opposite direction (c). No. 5 (dark uniform) has pivoted on her left foot to block out her opponent (d). The pass is made for the layup (e).*

a   b

c   d

Fig. 4.28 *Inside Screen. Dark No. 5 has dribbled over and handed the ball to No. 4 (a). As both defenders are concerned with the drive (b), No. 4 passes (c), to her free teammate (d).*

a

b

c

d

e

f

Fig. 4.29 *Inside Screen. Dark No. 5 dribbles toward her teammate (a and b). She has handed the ball to No. 4 and sees that the two defenders have not moved shoulder to shoulder (c). No. 5 cuts between the defenders (d), receives the pass (e), and shoots (f).*

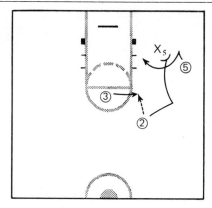

Fig. 4.30 *Three-Player Inside Screen. Player 2 passes to 3 and cuts down to set an inside screen for 5. Player 3 passes to either 5 on her cut or to 2 on her roll.*

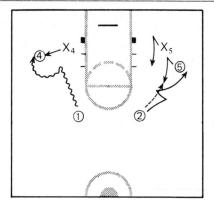

Fig. 4.31 *Player 1 dribbles toward 4 to set an inside screen, but X_4 moves to guard closely so 1 dribbles behind 4 to effect a variation of an inside screen. Player 2 passes to 5 and tries to set an inside screen but goes behind 5 as X_5 moves in to guard closely. Players 2 and 5 demonstrate a similar variation of an inside screen.*

free. The pivot player should be particularly aware of any mismatches in defensive assignments that may develop (Fig. 4.30).

Inside Screen Variations

Variations of an inside screen occur when a player cuts behind a teammate in possession of the ball, or when a player with the ball dribbles behind a teammate (Fig. 4.31). In both cases the options are the same as those that occurred with the inside screen.

DEFENSE AGAINST AN INSIDE SCREEN

To defend against an inside screen in which a player moves between a teammate and her opponent, the defense has two choices:

1. they may permit the long shot and protect against the drive and screener's move
2. they can prevent the long shot and recover against the screener's move

If the defense selects the former method, they must know that the player, who is freed by the screen, does not have an accurate outside shot or that she is beyond her normal shooting range. As the offensive player moves to set the inside screen, the two defensive players move shoulder to shoulder to prevent a cut between them. Once they attain this position they remain there and encourage the player with the ball to take the long shot. If the of-

fensive player chooses not to do so and starts to drive, her own opponent must quickly maneuver to guard her. There is no problem if she cuts away from the direction from which the screen was set. If she moves toward the direction from which the screen was set, her teammate must drop back a step to allow her to slide through between her teammate and the screener. The other defensive player moves quickly to get ball side of the screener (her own opponent). For these situations, neither defensive player should have difficulty in regaining good defensive position.

If the player for whom the screen is set is a good outside shooter, the problem for the defense is magnified. As the screen is set the two defenders once again must come shoulder to shoulder to prevent the cut between them. Then, one of the defenders must move to guard the outside shooter. If the game plan calls for forcing the attack toward the middle, the outside defender (the one closer to the side line) makes the first move. As this is done, the offensive player with the ball will probably commence her drive in the opposite direction — i.e., toward the middle. The defensive player must hustle to attain a good defensive position but needs help at this stage to delay the drive of the player with the ball. The defender's teammate helps by jumping forward, causing the dribbler to slow her progress and make a wider turn than she desires. This provides the dribbler's opponent with the time neces-

a

b

c

d

e

f

Fig. 4.32 *Inside Screen. Light No. 5 moves to set an inside screen (a and b). Dark No. 5 steps forward to cause light No. 3 to make a wider arc on her drive as No. 3 moves around the screen (c and d). Dark No. 3 regains position as her teammate returns to her own opponent (e and f).*

Fig. 4.33 *Inside Screen. Light No. 5 dribbles, hands off, and sets an inside screen for No. 3 (a–c). Dark No. 3 starts to move around the screen (d). Dark No. 5 moves to stop the drive of No. 3, as dark No. 3 moves to get ball side of her opponent (e–f).*

sary to regain good defensive positioning. Following the jump forward, the other defensive player quickly retreats and stays ball side of the screener (Fig. 4.32).

There is an alternate method of defending against this situation. The procedure is identical to that already described — up to the point where one guard moves forward to prevent the long shot and her teammate jumps forward to delay the offensive player's drive for the basket. At this stage the defender who jumps forward continues to defend against the dribbler while the other player quickly adjusts her position to get ball side of the screener. This method may or may not result in a switch of defensive assignments, depending upon which de-

fensive player initially confronts the player with the ball. If it is team practice to force the opponents toward the inside, a switch in assignments will occur with use of this practice.

If a screener dribbles over to set an inside screen and hands off to a teammate behind her, the defense usually switches to counteract this action (Fig. 4.33).

Defense Against the Inside Screen Variation

The basic defense against the inside screen is known as "slide through."

The defensive player guarding the player with

a

b

c

d

Fig. 4.34 *Inside Screen Variation. Light No. 5 passes to her teammate and starts behind her (a). As her intention becomes clear, dark No. 3 takes a step back (b) to allow her teammate to slide through as the ball is handed to light No. 5 (c). Dark No. 5 has regained defensive position (d).*

the ball takes a step back toward the basket to allow her teammate to slide through between her and the player with the ball. As the defensive player slides through, she keeps her hands active to discourage the ball handler from shooting. As she slides through she must be alert to a change of direction by her opponent and a cut back toward the side from which she started. This action is not usually taken by the offense; but, if the defensive player predetermines where she will move on a specific play, she leaves herself open to the directional change. When the player completes her slide through, both defensive players return to their normal defensive positions (Fig. 4.34).

Drills for an Inside Screen

1. Two offensive guards (or one wing and one guard) and their opponents, both of whom are guarding loosely. Neither offensive player has a good outside shot, so the defense allows the long shot. One player dribbles over between her teammate and her opponent and hands off to her teammate. Emphasis should be placed on the defender guarding the dribbler to move shoulder to shoulder with her teammate. From this position they allow the long shot. Repeat in the other direction.

2. Same as drill 1 above, but the offensive player recognizes that she has not been successful in shooting from that distance and is instructed to move away from the side from which the screen was set. Emphasis is on her defender moving with her (which should not be difficult) and on her teammate obtaining a position between the screener and the ball.

3. Same as drill 1 above, but the offensive player with the ball moves toward the direction from which the screen was set. Emphasis is placed on the player guarding the screener retreating one step so that her teammate may regain defensive position more quickly. The defender against the screening player must then maintain a fronting position on her opponent.

4. Two offensive guards and their opponents, both defending loosely. The two attack players are known as good outside shooters; the defenders, therefore, must utilize a different method of defense. The team has decided to force the dribbler toward the middle, so the outside defender moves to guard the player with the ball. Emphasis is on the timing of the moves of the defenders — the move forward by the outside defender, the jump forward by the other defender, and her quick return to her own opponent while her teammate gains good defensive position. Repeat to the other side.

5. Same as drill 4 above, but the inside defender moves forward to guard the player with the ball and the outside defender jumps forward to delay her. Repeat to the other side.

6. Same as drill 4 or 5 above (stipulate which one), but allow the dribbler to maneuver if she can and reverse direction on her dribble. Repeat on the other side.

7. Two offensive guards (or one wing and one guard) and their opponents, both defending loosely. This drill is the same as drill 4 above, but the defender who jumps forward to delay the dribbler stays with her while her teammate must front the other attack player. Emphasis is on the timing involved. Repeat on the other side. Repeat also with the other defender jumping forward.

8. Two offensive guards (or one wing and one guard) and their opponents, both defending loosely. Allow the player with the ball to dribble in any direction and reverse direction if possible. The defender in the better defensive position guards her while the other defender obtains a fronting position on the screener. Repeat on the other side.

9. Two offensive guards (or one wing and one guard) and their opponents. One guard passes to her teammate and cuts behind her for a hand-off. The screener's defender moves one step back to permit her teammate to slide through. Emphasis should be on the timing of the defender's backward and return step so that she does not leave her opponent with the ball unguarded either before or after her teammate has moved through. Repeat in the other direction.

10. Same as drill 9 above, but permit the player who receives the hand-off to reverse direction so that the defender must adjust.

11. Same as drill 9 above, but let the player receiving the hand-off move in any direction she wishes.

12. Same as drill 9 above, but the player who receives the initial pass fakes the hand-off and retains possession and attempts a shot if she is free or dribbles in any direction.

DOUBLE SCREENS

A double screen always requires four players and because of the number of players involved, the timing of this screen is more difficult than any of the others. Two players are always used to form the screen as a third player cuts behind the screen to receive a pass from the fourth player. Basically, the purpose of the double screen is to permit a player to be relatively free for an immediate shot. If this does not materialize, the player can drive beyond the screen for a short jump shot or continue to drive for the basket. If the defensive players switch, then the appropriate screener should move to receive a pass.

Double screens are usually formed when a guard has possession of the ball and a post and wing or post and guard set the screen. Following the double screen, players must hasten to regain court balance in case the ball is intercepted or the opponents recover a rebound.

Because of the nature of double screens, they are used less often than other screens. Their use is limited in terms of frequency and position on the court where they can be set. The double screen is always set along one of the lane lines or at the free throw line.

One example of a double screen utilizes a post player moving to a low post position and a wing on that side cutting to the lane line beside the post for the double screen. The strong side guard or a point guard has the ball and the wing on the weak side cuts through the key and behind the double screen to receive the pass. She either shoots from behind the screen or drives around it (Fig. 4.35).

Another double screen is possible when the

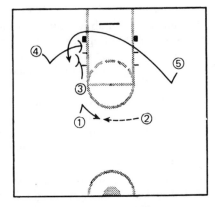

Fig. 4.35 *Double Screen Along the Lane. As player 2 passes to 1, 3 and 4 both cut to set the double screen. 5 cuts around the double screen. Player 1 passes to 5 or to 3 or 4, depending upon the action of the defense.*

guard on the strong side passes to the weak side guard and immediately cuts along the key beside the pivot in the low or medium post position. The strong side forward then cuts around the screen to receive a pass from the guard.

A third example of a double screen occurs when a wing has the ball. A guard and post form a double screen at the free throw line and the weak side wing cuts up and around the double screen for a pass (Fig. 4.36). The same situation can develop with the pivot and wing forming the screen at the free throw line and the weak side guard cuts around it for the pass.

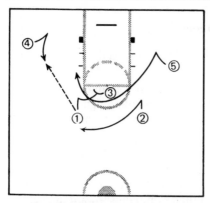

Fig. 4.36 *Double Screen at the Free Throw Line. Player 1 passes to 4 and screens beside 3. Player 5 cuts around the screen for a pass from 4.*

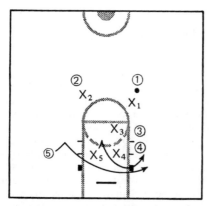

Fig. 4.37 *Defense Against a Double Screen, Along the Lane. As the double screen is set, X_3 and X_4 warn their teammates. Player X_4 hedges to force 5 to go wide of the screen. Player X_5 has floated, anticipates 5's cut, and forces her wide around the screen. This allows X_5 space to go over the top of the screen.*

Defense Against Double Screens

Double screens can be extremely troublesome to the defense, particularly the double screen set along the lane line.

The defensive players guarding the screeners must alert their teammates as the double screen is set. The defender guarding the screener closer to the basket may also hedge slightly toward the base-

line to force the cutter to go wide around the screen. The defensive player guarding the ball handler helps by pressuring her opponent to delay the pass to the wing cutting behind the screen so that the wing's opponent has time to cut around the screen and prevent an open shot. The defensive player guarding the weak side wing should sag off her opponent when the ball is passed to the strong side. She can anticipate the direction of the wing's cut and beat her to the double screen (Fig. 4.37). By combining this action with the help of her teammates, she may be able to force her opponent to cut to the inside of the screen where she is more easily defended.

When the double screen is set at the free throw line, the defensive players guarding the screeners must alert their teammates to the offensive maneuver and also drop back a step from their opponents and slide toward the ball side. This generally congests the area so that the ball handler cannot pass to the cutter (Fig. 4.38).

Progression for Learning Screening Tactics

The success of any of the screen plays is entirely dependent upon the timing of the cuts, the proper stance for the screen itself, the correct use of the screen, and the ability to read the reaction of the defense. This means that considerable practice time must be devoted to the two- and three-player screens by the players involved so that they may develop the game sense necessary for proficient execution. While two guards or a guard and wing are

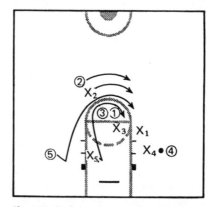

Fig. 4.38 *Defense Against a Double Screen at the Free Throw Line. The defenders guarding the screeners drop off their opponents toward the ball side to congest the passing lane.*

Drills for Double Screens

The defense against the two types of double screens should be practiced on each side of the court.

1. Players necessary for a double screen along the lane line and their opponents. Emphasis should be placed on the defender against the ball handler guarding tight and the defender guarding the player to receive the pass anticipating the screen and beating her opponent to it.

2. Same as drill 1 above, but the defender should allow the wing to go behind the screen and maneuver to defend against her.

3. Players necessary for a double screen at the free throw line and their opponents. Emphasis is placed on the screener's defenders sagging off their opponents toward the ball to cover the passing lane to the cutter moving around the screen. Practice on both sides.

4. Same as drill 3 above, but permit the ball handler to pass to either screener if the defender's action leaves them free. Emphasize a quick return to guarding their own opponent.

practicing various screens, the post and one forward may also work on their screen moves. At another time a guard and wing on each side of the court can work on their moves while the post player may be working on her individual moves at another basket.

At the initial stage of learning, the position of defensive players in relation to ball handlers must be stipulated so that the two offensive players may practice a designated screen. For example, if two players are preparing to practice an inside screen, the defensive player must be instructed to sag so that there is space in which the inside screen may be set. Later the defenders should be instructed to press or play closely so that the offense may use a lateral, outside, or inside screen variation as instructed.

Initially, the defensive player should be instructed to play strict man-to-man with help and recover tactics so that the offense can learn how to react to this situation. Later, the defense should be instructed to switch each time the screen is practiced so that the offensive players can practice the roll (or cut) and subsequent pass. Somewhat later the defensive players can be encouraged to use their own discretion and play either strict man-to-man or switching defense so that the offensive players learn to recognize which tactic is being

used and learn to combat it.

After the offensive players have gained some wisdom and skill in the use of these screens, the defensive players can be encouraged to attempt to counteract the desired screen that the offense wishes to employ. For example, if a defensive player is sagging and can see that an inside screen is desired by the offensive players, she can move up to a position closer to the offensive player so that the offense must then set a different type of screen in order to be effective. In this particular situation as the defensive player moves close to the offensive player, the screener can then change from an inside screen to an inside screen variation, a lateral screen, or an outside screen.

There is no question that considerable time must be devoted to two- and three-player maneuvers in practice sessions. Offensive players must be able to react to whatever defensive tactics are employed and be able to change their tactics to counteract those of the defense. Understanding and acquisition of these skills takes time and considerable team work among the players involved. All of these screens are the heart of offensive patterns that may be selected for team use. They must be learned and practiced to the extent that players can react instantly to any defensive tactic employed by the opponents in a game situation.

5

Scissoring or Double Cut Off the Post

Scissoring is a maneuver involving the post player and two other players who cross and cut on either side of the pivot. The purpose is to free one of the cutters for a pass or an attempted shot for the basket. The players involved with the post may be two guards, a point guard and a wing, or a wing and corner player.

SCISSOR AT THE HIGH POST POSITION

With the post playing at the free throw line the double cut is made with two guards. If the post plays at the free throw line extended at the side of the lane, the double cut is made by a guard and a wing.

The play is initiated by one of the players who passes the ball into the pivot who has moved to the high post position with her back to the basket. The player who passes in to the post *always* makes the first cut. She fakes down her side of the court and then cuts around and as close as possible to the post player. The other player delays her cut momentarily and then fakes down her side of the court and cuts "off the back" (very close behind) of the first cutter to the other side of the pivot. The pivot player may pass to either player, whichever one appears to be more free. Generally, the second cutter will be the freer player since her opponent should be forced into the screen provided by the first cutter (Fig.

5.1). It is important that the cutters move as close as possible to the pivot player so that their opponents cannot maneuver between them and the pivot player. (Beginners tend to cut in a wide arc and this must be corrected immediately.)

Variations

Whenever the scissor maneuver is executed, the offensive players should be aware of how the defense attempts to defeat the effectiveness of the scissor play. Defensive players often try tactics to prevent the success of the scissor maneuver. In one such tactic the pivot player's opponent anticipates the pass to the second cutter and moves slightly in that direction to help. Since the pivot player has her back to the basket, she must use her peripheral vision to observe the defensive position of her opponent. As she sees her move to help, the pivot player should fake a hand-off to the second cutter and then pivot and take a jump shot immediately; or, if the lane is open she should drive for a layup or a short jump shot (Fig. 5.2).

Occasionally, the defense tries to counteract the scissor play with the cutter's defenders dropping back in front of the pivot so that they may switch opponents when the opponents cross. If this occurs, the first cutter makes her normal cut and the second cutter starts her usual cut; instead of continuing around the pivot player, however, she reverses

161

Fig. 5.1 *Scissor Play: No Defensive Help. The wing receives a pass (a). The post maneuvers for a pass as the point player cuts away from the ball (b). As dark 20 cuts around the post, her opponent maintains good defensive position (c); dark 20 screens the point's defender (d), allowing the post to pass to the point for an easy layup (e).*

a

b

c

d

e

Fig. 5.2 *Scissor Play: Post Helps but Does Not Recover. The post receives a pass (a) the point and wing cut (b); dark 20 screens the point's defender (c); the post player's defender helps with the free cutter and the post drives (d); for an easy layup (e).*

a · b · c

d · e

Fig. 5.3 *Scissor with the Defenders Dropping Back to Switch Opponents. The ball is passed to the pivot (a). Both guards move back in front of the pivot in position to switch opponents as they cross (b). The ball cannot be handed to the first cutter (c). The second cutter observes the defensive plan and changes direction (d). She cuts in the same direction as the first cutter (e) and receives the hand-off (f). She drives and is free to shoot as dark No. 2 screens out her new opponent (g–i).*

f

g

h

i

Fig. 5.3 *(continued)*

her cut and cuts down the same side of the post as the first player. The pivot player hands off to the second cutter who should be free for a jump shot or a drive for a layup (Fig. 5.3).

If the defense fears the effectiveness of the scissor play, one defender may drop back to help protect against the ball being passed into the pivot. This means that the player without the ball is left open. As the ball is passed to the pivot, the non-ball handler may quickly blast (cut down her side of the court in executing a backdoor play). In this instance, she does not time her cut after the passer starts, but moves immediately as the pass goes successfully to the pivot. The pivot player passes quickly to her for the layup or short jump shot (Fig. 5.4). In order for this play to be effective, a corner

player must clear that side of the court or her opponent will sag and be in a position to prevent the layup or at least reduce its effectiveness.

The other way in which the defense attempts to counteract the scissor is by sending the second cutter's opponent behind the post player so that she is not screened by the move of the first cutter. By moving behind the pivot, she is in position to recover good defensive position as the second cutter moves past the pivot. When the first cutter observes this action she should stop behind the pivot player to form a double screen. The second cutter delays her cut and stops behind the double screen to receive a hand-off. She then may execute a set shot or utilize any of the other options that are useful from a double screen position (Fig. 5.5).

Fig. 5.4 *Scissor with the Weak Side Defender Helping on the Post. The ball is passed to the pivot even though defensive guard (light No. 1) has retreated to hinder this move (a). Dark No. 1 observes the position of her opponent and cuts directly for the basket (blasts) (b). The pivot passes to No. 1, who is free to shoot (c–e). Notice that the player who passed to the pivot altered her usual move and cut down the other side of pivot.*

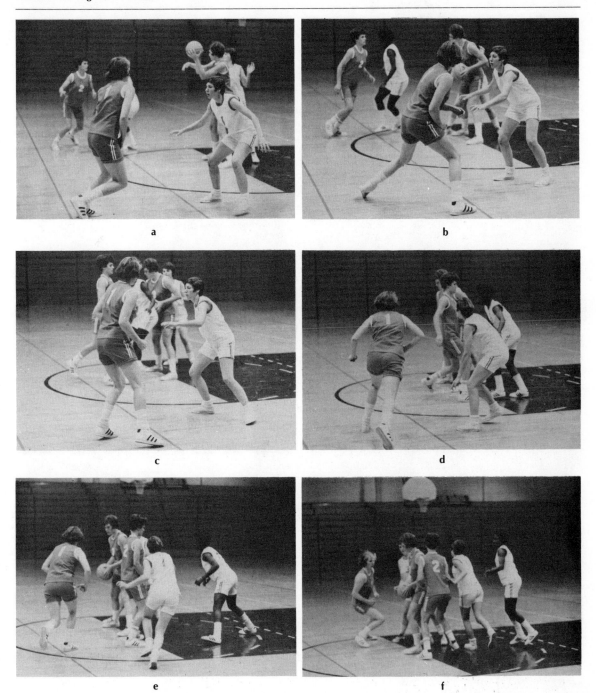

a

b

c

d

e

f

Fig. 5.5 *Scissor with the Defender Going Behind. The ball is passed to the pivot and the cutters start their usual moves (a–d). Light No. 1 cuts behind the pivot to meet her opponent on the other side (e). Dark No. 1 observes this action and changes direction (f). Dark No. 2 moves to set a double screen with the pivot (g and h). No. 1 is free for a shot (i and j).*

g   h

i   j

Fig. 5.5 *(continued)*

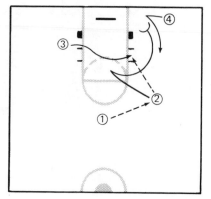

Fig. 5.6 *Scissor Off a Medium Post. As 1 passes to 2, 3 cuts, 2 passes to 3, cuts around her, and sets a pick on 4's defender. Player (4) is free for a pass or hand–off from 3.*

Scissor at the Medium Post Position

The same scissor maneuver and all of its variations may be used by a pivot player and a wing and corner player. Usually the ball starts with the wing who passes to the pivot in a medium post position along the lane line. Again, the pivot player receives the pass with her back to the basket. Following the pass in, the wing fakes a cut inside and cuts around the post to the outside. The corner player delays the baseline cut and then cuts around the post. She should be free as the first cutter picks off her opponent (Fig. 5.6). Defensive players can use any of the options previously described to counteract those moves.

DEFENSE AGAINST SCISSOR MANEUVERS

Scissor maneuvers, if allowed to materialize, can be exceedingly dangerous. They provide opportunities for driving layups and short jump shots for both the cutters as well as the pivot player. Whenever the ball is passed into a high or medium post, strong side defenders should be alert for the double cut maneuver and all of its variations. The post player's defender is responsible for warning her teammates whenever a double cut starts.

Defense Against the Scissors Off a High Post

The best defense against this maneuver is to prevent the pivot player from receiving the ball. Certain precautions may be necessary against a team that uses the double cut effectively. First of all, the player defending against the high pivot plays in her normal defensive position, on the ball side with her arm extended to discourage a pass into the pivot. The defender against the ball handler plays half a player toward the inside and has her inside arm extended to discourage a pass into the pivot. The defender against the other player sags off her player and opens toward the middle and the pivot player. She has her outside arm reaching toward her opponent and her inside arm toward the pivot player (Fig. 5.7). Hopefully, the defensive position of these three players will discourage a pass to the pivot and force a pass elsewhere. If, however, the ball handler chooses to pass to a guard, the defenders must reverse their positions. The danger period occurs while the pivot player's defender moves behind her opponent to the other side. The defender (opposing the ball handler) must quickly open and retreat toward the pivot player to partially close the passing lane during this process.

If, despite the efforts of these defensive players, the ball is successfully passed into the pivot, the de-

Fig. 5.7 *Defensive Help Against the High Post. When the wing has the ball, the point defender sags off her opponent to help prevent the pass in to the post.*

a

b

c

d

e

Fig. 5.8 *Scissor Play with the Defensive Post Player Helping and Recovering. The scissor develops (a–c); the defensive post moves to help against dark 21 (d) so that dark 21's opponent can regain defensive position (e).*

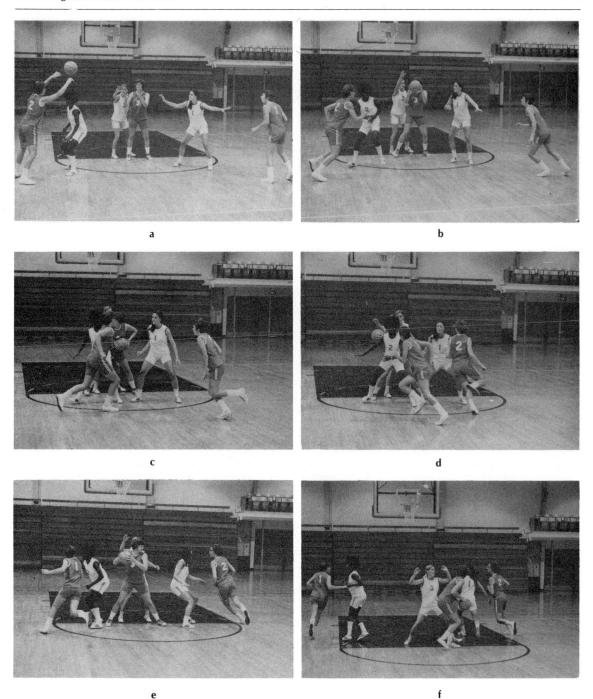

a

b

c

d

e

f

Fig. 5.9 *Defense Against a Scissor with the Defenders Dropping Back. The ball is passed to the pivot (a). Both defensive players slide back one full step in front of the post (b and c). As the offensve players cross (d), the defenders switch opponents and maintain the inside position (e and f).*

fender against the pivot must quickly move one step back from her opponent in line with her and the basket. She must immediately call out a warning to her teammates if the opponents start to cut. The two defenders opposing the cutters must retain their position half a player toward the inside of their opponent in an attempt to discourage them from crossing. If the offensive players are able to cross, the defensive player guarding the player who passed the ball to the pivot should have no difficulty maintaining defensive position, as she is easily able to go over the top of the screener (the pivot player). The problem for the other defensive player is con-

siderably greater. If the scissor maneuver is well timed, she will be cut off from her opponent by the action of her teammate's opponent. Nevertheless she must go over the top of the screen while forcing her opponent as high above the screen as possible. The player guarding the post player helps to force the second cutter wider of the screen, thus allowing the cutter's opponent to slide closer to the screen and regain good positioning more quickly (Fig. 5.8).

An alternate method of dealing with the double cut is for both defenders to drop back a full step in front of the pivot player with the ball. With upward jabbing motions at the ball, they attempt to force

---

Drills for a Scissor (Double Cut) Maneuver

1. Two offensive guards (or guard and wing) and a pivot player in the high post and their opponents. The offensive players pass the ball back and forth between them, making no effort to get the ball in to the post. Emphasis is on the movement of the post's defender as she moves from side to side, and on the defender who sags toward the pivot to close the passing lane.

2. Same as drill 1 above, but the offensive players pass in to the pivot whenever the opportunity arises. Emphasis is the same as previously described and on the pivot defender taking one step back as soon as her opponent gets the ball.

3. Same as drill 2 above, with the attack players executing the double cut. Emphasis is on the pivot player helping toward the side of the second cutter and both defenders going over the top of the screen. Offensively, emphasis is on the fakes, timing of the cuts, and cuts close to the post player.

4. Same as drill 3 above, but the cutter's defensive players step back in front of the post after she receives the pass. The attack players are instructed to cross. Emphasis is placed on forcing the cutters wide and not permitting them to cut between the defenders and the pivot.

5. Same as drill 4 above, but instruct the cutters to cut to the same side (the side of the first cutter) and let the defenders adjust to this action. Emphasis is placed on reading the defensive tactic and the defender's ability to anticipate the cut to the same side and adjust quickly.

6. Same as drill 4 above, but instruct the cutters to cross or cut to the same side at their discretion.

7. One wing, corner player, and pivot player in the medium post and their opponents. The wing and corner player pass back and forth, making no attempt to pass in to the pivot. Emphasis is on the position of the post's defender and the wing's defender during the exchange of passes. The pivot defender moves behind her opponent each time to get one-half player on the ball side of her. The guard's defender drops back to help prevent a pass in to the pivot from the corner. The corner players's opponent does not do this, as the ball is returned to the wing.

8. Proceed as in drills 2 through 7 above to gain confidence in dealing with the tactics between these three players.

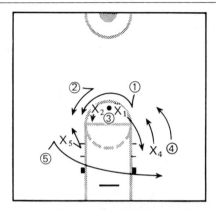

Fig. 5.10 *Defense Against a Scissor When Both Players Cut to the Same Side. Player 1 passes to 3. When 2 sees that both defenders drop back in front of 3 she fakes her normal cut but cuts to the same side as 1. Meanwhile, 5 clears the area but X_5 does not follow and remains in position to guard 2. At the same time, X_1 drops back to defend against 5.*

the post to pass immediately. If this is not successful and the offensive players start their double cut around the post, the defensive players switch opponents as they cross. By being a full step in front of the pivot, their defensive position forces the offensive players to make a wide cut around the post. This position also allows the two defenders to stay

between the ball and their opponent (Fig. 5.9). However, if both defenders drop back in front of the pivot, both cutters may choose to go to the same side of the post. Therefore, defensive players who choose this alternate method of defense against the double cut must be aware of this offensive option so that they can move to regain defensive position against this maneuver. When the defensive players are playing in this fashion, the defender against the weak side corner player should be cautious of clearing the area. From her position, she can assist her teammates if both players cut to the same side (Fig. 5.10). If she clears the area, the second cutter should be relatively free.

If the offense can shoot from the 18-ft. range, the defense should not slide behind the post. On the other hand, if the team cannot handle the double cut in any other manner, it is preferable to allow the outside shot instead of a short one.

When the double cut in the high post area emanates from a wing pass to the post, the defense has to be most concerned about the guard involved as she most likely will be the second cutter.

Defense Against the Scissors Off a Medium Post

The double cut off the medium post is played in the same fashion as the maneuver off the high post. The player to be most concerned about is the corner player who usually is the second cutter.

3

Team Offense and Defense

6

Fast Break

The purpose of the fast break is to provide the attack with a player advantage. It usually results in a two-on-one or three-on-two situation. The fast break is the quickest means of advancing the ball downcourt and may be started any time the defense acquires the ball in its backcourt. This may occur following a steal, rebound, violation, missed free throw, or any type of score. It must be started quickly so that the defense can be outnumbered.

This style of play produces many advantages. First, and quite obviously, it produces many scoring opportunities. Many easy layups should result with the opponents at a player disadvantage. If a team uses the fast break extensively, it forces the opponents to begin thinking about defense before they lose possession of the ball. Often after they shoot they begin to fall back to prevent the fast break and fail to rebound properly. Although this may limit the number of fast break opportunities it affords, it almost assures the fast breaking team of acquiring a large number of rebounds thus keeping the opponents' offensive rebounds at a minimum. Because the fast break is a running style of play, it forces the opponents to play at a fast tempo and they may become fatigued in the later stages of the game and commit an unusual number of ball handling errors. The fast break also allows scoring to be distributed among a number of players, and those who are not high scorers enjoy this. It also allows players to free lance and to use their own initiative — particularly the middle player. She is the ball handler and can help distribute the scoring by various means.

The fast break can be used as the primary style of offense. In other words whenever a team obtains the ball, they think *fast break* and try to initiate it. Only when it is halted does the team consider a controlled style of play. Other teams use the fast break only when a specific situation arises in which they can easily gain the player advantage.

The fast break does have some disadvantages. Players must be in excellent physical condition in order to use this style of play as the primary offense. If not, they will begin to commit ball handling errors and traveling violations, thereby negating the advantages that it may produce. The fast break is also frustrating to teach and learn during the beginning stages because players commit so many ball handling errors. They run at full speed, and the timing of passes and judgment of speed is far more difficult than under normal conditions. Players and the teacher/coach must be patient until the skills are developed for using the fast break effectively.

The fast break requires only one good ball handler. A team with two or more good ball handlers is particularly capable of using this style of play. The opposing team knows that the best way to prevent a fast break is to stop it before it gets started, so they will take some means to accomplish this. if a team has more than one player who can assume the responsibility of the middle player, they are less likely to stop the break by tightly defending one player.

This is an excellent offense to use when a team has small, quick players and must face much taller opponents. They are able to play them on a more equal basis by racing down the court for uncontested layups.

DEVELOPMENT

There are five important aspects to the success of a fast break: rebound, outlet, middle player, trailer, and safety. Assuming a team has two ball handlers who can play the middle position, the team can utilize the following procedure. As one player gets a rebound, another player cuts into a free space and calls "outlet." At the same time, a ball handler is cutting to the middle and calling "middle." After the ball is passed to the outlet player and middle player, the outlet player cuts down one sideline as a wing player, and another player fills the other wing. Whichever player can move to the second wing position the fastest should race to that position. The next player who can make the transition from defense to offense follows the group of three down the court and calls "trailer" as she approaches the top of the circle. She should be ready for a pass and a short jump shot. The safety player follows the other players downcourt. She is usually the rebounder although if she is quick it is conceivable she could become a wing or the trailer. For the fast break to be successful these positions must be filled.

The most important factor for the success of the fast break is to start it quickly. If the play starts from an out-of-bounds situation, the ball must be inbounded immediately. The player closest to the ball catches the ball as it passes through the net and passes it in as rapidly as possible. If the fast break starts from a rebound, as is the case most of the time, the rebounder looks long and gives a lob pass which will bounce up in the hands of the receiver. (A baseball pass should not be given as it will rebound over the endline.) If no one is free downcourt, the outlet pass is made quickly. When the rebounder secures the ball she wishes to pass immediately toward the nearer sideline. (She rarely passes down the middle because of the imminent danger in this direction.) The rebounder may be able to turn and pass while she is still in the air, although this practice is not recommended for anyone except the highly skilled (Fig. 6.1). In order to pass quickly (even after she has returned to the floor) the rebounder must be assured that a player will be cutting to the sideline and in position to receive the outlet pass. In order to accomplish this purpose the fast breaking team must assign someone to be in that position. Two players are generally

Fig. 6.1 *Rebounding to Start a Fast Break. The player has gained good rebound positioning (a). She rebounds, turns in the air, and makes the outlet pass to a cutting teammate before landing from her jump (b).*

a

b

designated to receive the outlet passes. This may be accomplished in two ways: either player may be assigned to be in a certain spot or each player is assigned a designated side of the court. Depending upon the system selected, the rebounder either passes to a spot and to the player who is there or looks down one side of the court for a specific player. In either case, the outlet player must free herself because the defenders will attempt to prevent this initial pass. Either system may be used, or they may be used interchangeably.

When a team is using a zone defense it is usually easy for the top players to get into position quickly for the outlet pass. When playing man-to-man, opponents may cut under the basket which takes the usual outlet receivers out of position. In this case any player who has replaced the defender in an outside position cuts for the outlet pass if the other guard is not in position to do so. If the rebounder is closely guarded she may have to dribble toward the sideline before she can pass. She must hurry however, because any delay reduces the success of the fast break.

Once the rebound is secured and the outlet pass is made, players endeavor to fill the three lanes as fast as possible. A ball handler moves to the middle position while the outlet player fills one wing position and the closest player fills the other wing so that three players move down the court in line with one another. The ball should be passed or dribbled into the middle position as quickly as possible. The next player follows the front line downcourt by about 10 ft. She is the trailer to whom the middle player may pass if the opponents succeed in getting back three players. The fifth player, usually the rebounder (or in-bounder), follows the others downcourt in a safety position in case the ball is intercepted and the opponents start a fast break. Fig. 6.2 shows the relative positions of the fast breaking team as the top of the circle is approached.

There are several points of view on which player should be in the middle position. Some believe that the best ball handler should always move into the center position. If another player receives the outlet pass, the best ball handler cuts to the middle to receive the subsequent pass. However, if the ball is rebounded on her side of the court the best ball handler must break to the sideline for the outlet pass. She then would dribble the ball into the middle position and continue downcourt. This method allows a team to always have the same player in the middle so that she can gain experience in analyzing the defense and deceiving them. Others prefer to allow any good ball handler to act as the middle player.

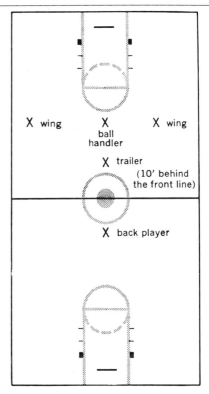

Fig. 6.2 *Position of Players as They Approach the Top of the Circle on a Fast Break.*

The desirability of utilizing one method in preference to another is a philosophical decision that must be made by the teacher/coach. If a team possesses one outstanding ball handler, it may be desirable to have her in the middle all of the time. If it is difficult to determine who is the better ball handler, then a team might choose to use anyone, depending upon the situation at the time.

During a fast break it is important that the ball be dribbled down the middle of the court. If the ball is advanced by one of the wings near the sideline, the opponents find it easier to defend since a pass can be made in one direction only; if the ball is brought down the middle, the pass can be made to either side — which complicates the task for the defense. There are some coaches who advocate passing while the ball is advanced. This action seems somewhat questionable since players are moving at top speed and the more players handling the ball, the greater chance there is for a ball handling error.

Fig. 6.3 shows the movement of players as they

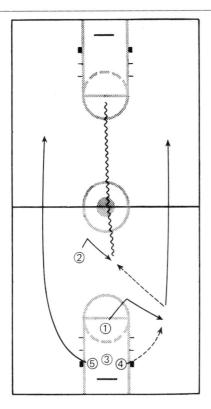

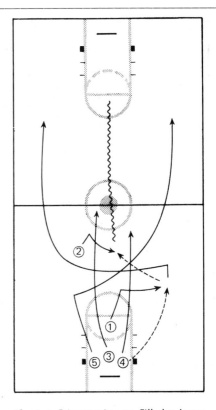

Fig. 6.3 *Filling the Lanes on the Fast Break. Player 1 cuts for the outlet pass and passes to 2 as she cuts to the middle. Player 5 hurries downcourt to fill the third lane. Player 3 becomes the trailer as rebounder 4 becomes the back player.*

Fig. 6.4 *Crisscrossing to Fill the Lanes. Player 4 rebounds and passes to 1 who cuts for the outlet pass. 1 passes to 2 and 1 crosses to the left side of the court. Player 5 starts up the left side and then crosses to the right. Players 3 and 4 follow in the usual manner.*

start downcourt to fill the closest lanes that allows the players to fill the lanes in the quickest way possible. Another method used is that of crisscrossing the wings as shown in Fig. 6.4. This method takes slightly longer than the other and forces the players to run further but may be used for variety.

As the middle player approaches the top of the circle, both wings should be even or slightly ahead of her. One defensive player will generally step out at this point to stop the advance of the ball. As this occurs, the ball handler should pass to either wing. She first must read the defense to ascertain whether the defender moving toward her actually commits herself. If so, one of her wings will be free if there is only one additional defender back (Fig. 6.5). The ball handler must read the action of the back defender before committing herself to pass to either wing. If the back defender anticipates to which wing

the ball will be passed and moves in her direction, the ball handler must pass to the other wing.

After the pass is made, the middle player moves to the edge of the free throw lane on the side to which she passed the ball. She is available for a return pass if the wing is unable to shoot. It is the middle player who is most likely to be free as the defender generally attempts to prevent the opposite wing from receiving a subsequent pass. If more than two passes are required before someone is free to shoot, the fast break probably has not materialized effectively.

The middle player must alter her actions so that the defense cannot anticipate accurately what the offense intends to do. Too often the ball is passed to the right. The middle player must distribute passes to both sides. The ball can be passed off the

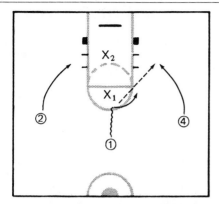

Fig. 6.5 *Fast Break — Three-on-Two. As 1 approaches the top of the circle, X_1 moves to defend against her. Directly from her dribble, 1 passes (with her right hand) to 4 for the layup. Had she passed to 5, the pass would have been made with her left hand. After her pass, 1 stops at the side of the free throw line.*

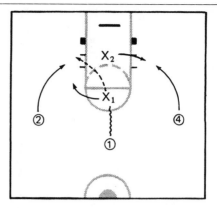

Fig. 6.6 *Fast Break — Three-on-Two. Player 1 stops and fakes a pass to 4 which draws X_2 toward 4. Player 1 passes to 2 for the shot.*

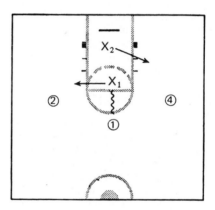

Fig. 6.7 *Fast Break, Three-on-Two. Player 1 stops at the free throw line and fakes a pass to 4, which draws X_2 toward 4. X_1 anticipates a pass to 2 and floats toward her. Witnessing the action of the defenders, player 1 shoots a jump shot.*

dribble with the right hand to the right side and the left hand to the left side if the defender commits herself early. Otherwise, the ball can be caught and a bounce pass given to the free wing.

There are other options that the offense should become familiar with. If the defender who moves out to guard the middle player is slow, the middle player may fake and drive around her for the layup. If the second defender interferes with her drive, the middle player passes off to either wing for the layup. The middle player may also stop at the free throw line and fake to one wing to determine what the defense will do. If one opponent moves to guard her and the other one edges toward one of the wing players, a bounce pass to the opposite wing should be successful (Fig. 6.6). If the front defender sags after the dribbler catches the ball to prevent a pass to a wing, the dribbler should shoot a jump shot from the free throw line (Fig. 6.7).

Should the front defender move out to defend against the dribbler before she reaches the top of the circle, the ball handler should pass immediately to one of the wings who should pass without hesitation to the other wing for the shot. This wing will be free because the front defender has too great a distance to recover to prevent the wing to wing pass. If the offense has been delayed slightly in advancing the ball downcourt, there may be three defenders ready to combat the fast break. This should not deter the offense. The trailer is approaching and should be calling "trailer right" or "trailer left"

whichever the case may be. The ball handler simply delays passing until the trailer moves to a position near the lane and slightly ahead of the ball handler. The pass is given to the trailer for a short jump shot (Fig. 6.8).

A team that is fast breaking must learn to recognize when they no longer have a fast break situation. As soon as the defense has more players downcourt than does the offense, the fast break has not developed and the middle player should stop the fast break by dribbling to any free space. She

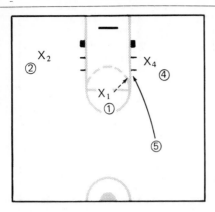

Fig. 6.8 *Fast Break. Three defenders are back. Player 1 waits for the trailer and passes to 5 for the jump shot.*

waits for the rest of her teammates to move downcourt and sets up the offense.

A three-on-two situation may develop near the division line in which one of the opponents attempts to delay the middle player. This leaves the defense extremely vulnerable, but a team may attempt this tactic against an inexperienced fast breaking team. The offense should take immediate advantage of the opponents' vulnerable position. The middle player should pass to one of her wings without delay so that they may proceed downcourt in a two-on-one situation. The two players should remain well spread, and the ball handler should drive for a layup. If she draws the lone defender she should pass to her teammate for the layup. The middle player may follow downcourt in a trailer position but should remain well to the rear of her teammates so that her opponent cannot guard her and one of her teammates.

THE SHOT

In a three-on-two or four-on-three situation, the offensive team should score on a short jump shot. Although a layup may result against poor defense, the offense should not force the ball in close for the layup. The 10–15 ft. jump shot is usually open.

Need for a Rebounder

Any team that has great success with a fast break must have an outstanding rebounder. As has been stated previously the most important element for

the development of a fast break is the quick outlet pass. For utmost speed in starting the fast break a pass receiver must be in position for the outlet pass as the rebounder catches the ball. This means that she cannot wait to see if her team obtains the rebound. She must cut considerably before that. In order to do this a team must have a player on whom they can rely to obtain almost every rebound, or they must be willing to gamble. If either of these conditions exist, the outlet receivers generally block out their opponent only for an instant and then cut for the pass. If a team does not have an exceptional rebounder or is not willing to take many chances on rebounds, the outlet receivers should continue to block out and delay their cut until they see that a teammate has acquired the rebound.

With an outstanding rebounder it may be possible for a player to release downcourt on occasion following a shot. She does not block out her opponent at all and cuts downcourt as soon as a shot is taken. She may be open for a long pass and an easy layup. The long pass is extremely difficult for most players with small hands to throw with accuracy, and teachers may wish to prohibit its use; but there is no need to do this if a player has success with it. Another problem with the long pass is that a player telegraphs her intention as she draws her arm back for the overhand throw. She must be free so that an opponent cannot approach from behind and tap the ball from her hand or block the pass.

THE SIDELINE BREAK

Some coaches prefer to run the break down one side of the court rather than taking the ball to the middle. There are also occasions when it is impossible to get the ball to the middle because of the recovery pattern of the defenders. In this case the outlet may be made as usual. The middle player acknowledges that she is covered and continues to the sideline to receive a pass near the center line. She can dribble the ball to the corner and pass to a free player as she reaches scoring range.

It is also possible to release one of the outside players and send her downcourt to the corner. The closest player cuts for the outlet and another player cuts to the sideline to receive the ball at the center line. The ball is passed to the corner. Players move downcourt to fill the areas in the low post, weak side rebound, edge of the free throw line and point position (Fig. 6.9).

The sideline break forces the pass in only one

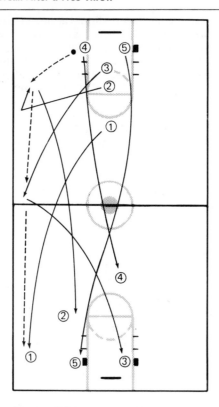

Fig. 6.9 *Sideline Fast Break. Player 4 re-bounds and passes to 2, who passes to 3 and on to 1. Players fill the key positions as shown.*

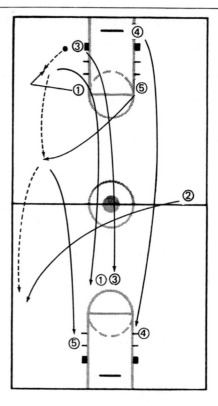

Fig. 6.10 *Fast Break from a Missed Free Throw. Player 3 rebounds and passes to 1 at the sideline. Player 5 cuts for a subsequent pass. 5 passes to 2 and players fill the lanes.*

direction but it does present a different look to the defense which is used to the break approaching from the point position. Often the defense allows the ball handler to drive in from the side or over, commits itself toward the dribbler, and allows the weak side wing to cut into the lane. Adoption of this break may give a team its primary break pattern or a variation when the middle break is not open.

FAST BREAK AFTER A FREE THROW

Teams may try to break after each free throw attempt. If the free throw is successful, the break may be started and executed in the same fashion as when a field goal is scored. If the free throw is missed, the fast break may be initiated as shown in Fig. 6.10. Variations may be created to best utilize the talents of the players.

Other Fast Break Situations

Fast break opportunities will arise from steals, which result in fewer players involved in the fast break. If a player steals a pass at the top of the circle or near the free throw area, she should dribble downcourt as rapidly as possible and maintain her speed as she goes up for the layup. A teammate should race downcourt to try to move legally into the path of the defender who is trying to catch the dribbler. This places the offensive team in position for the rebound should the layup be missed.

In a one-on-one situation the dribbler should zig-zag as she moves downcourt to cause the defender to lose good position. If this proves to be the case, the dribbler should have an easy layup. Meanwhile her teammates should be hustling downcourt. If the dribbler's opponent maintains good defensive position, she should hand the ball off to a trailing teammate for the layup.

When a two-on-one situation arises, the players should pass the ball back and forth while progressing downcourt. At the same time they must read the position of the lone opponent. (Should a team not have players who handle the ball well, the better ball handler should dribble the ball downcourt. Since the ball remains in the possession of one player the defense has an easier time adjusting as the top of the circle is reached by the offensive play-

ers.) The attacking players should approach the top of the circle about 15 ft. apart. This forces the defender to commit herself to one or the other player. The attack should always get a layup in this instance. If the defensive player sags off the ball handler, the dribbler continues for the layup. Should the defensive player ever be even with the dribbler, the ball handler has beaten her and should continue for the layup. Once the defender moves to stop the ball, the dribbler should pass off to her teammate for the layup.

Drills for Fast Break

All drills should be practiced to the left and right sides.

1. Columns of four players 6 ft. in front of each basket, with another player tossing the ball against the backboard. The first person in each column moves forward observing correct rebounding technique and jumps for the rebound, lands on the floor, and immediately pivots toward the near sideline ready to pass. She should pivot toward the corner of the court and away from the middle or the under-basket area. She gives the ball back to the tosser, who repeats the drill with each succeeding player. As experienced players rebound, they can pivot in the air and land facing the near sideline.

2. Same as drill 1 above, but another player is positioned about 6 ft. in from the sideline and about 20 ft. from the basket. The same drill is repeated, but the rebounder passes to the outlet receiver.

3. Same as drill 2 above, but an opponent stands behind the rebounder and tries to harass the outlet pass. The rebounder may have to take a bounce in order to make an accurate pass.

4. One offensive player; three defenders, including a player loosely guarding the shooter. The offensive player shoots; her opponent blocks out, obtains the rebound, pivots, and passes to her teammate who has cut to the near sideline. The other player cuts to the middle and toward the division line for the subsequent pass.

5. Same as drill 4 above, but add another rebounder. The player who does not rebound and the player receiving the outlet pass must move into the wing positions as the middle player dribbles downcourt to the free throw line. Emphasis should be placed on the timing of the cuts and the quick start to move up on a line with the middle player as fast as possible.

6. Ball handlers dribble down the center of the court to the free throw area and stop; fake a pass to the right and left and go up with a jump shot.

7. Partners; one player dribbles downcourt with her teammate in the wing position. At the free throw line the wing cuts in, receives a pass and takes a jump shot (Fig. 6.11).

8. Group of three doing a figure 8 full court. No more than five passes may be made and a layup completes the break. Players return downcourt continuing with the figure 8 and layup.

9. Groups of three; three players on the court facing the basket. The middle player tosses the ball against the backboard, rebounds it, and passes to the player calling "outlet"

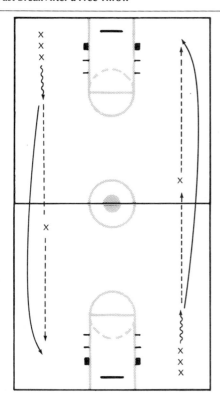

Fig. 6.11 *Player Dribbles, Passes to a Teammate Who Returns the Pass. The receiver must shoot from wherever she receives the pass without a dribble. Alternate sides of the court.*

(on the rebounder's side of the court). The third player cuts to the center while calling "middle." The outlet fills the wing position on her side of the court and the rebounder fills the other wing position. The middle player dribbles to the free throw area and gives a bounce pass to one of the wings for a jump shot. Repeat coming back.

10. Same as drill 9 above, but place one defensive player at the free throw line to challenge the dribbler as she approaches.

11. Same as drill 9, with two defensive players in a front and back position at the defensive end. The middle player reads the defense and uses a variety of methods to obtain the shot such as
    a. pass to the wing on her left
    b. pass to the wing on her right
    c. against a slow front player, change the pace of the dribble and drive by her
    d. stop at the free throw line
        1) pass to a wing if the front player moves to guard the middle player
        2) shoot if the front player sags to prevent a pass to a wing
    For all of these drills involving defensive players, the instructor should inform the defenders of the actions they should follow. At first they should be instructed to stay in the middle of the lane with the front player guarding the dribbler. Later the back player can be instructed to edge toward one wing or the other to see if the middle player can recognize the opening to the other side. The front player may also be instructed to sag

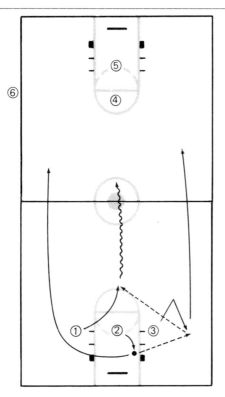

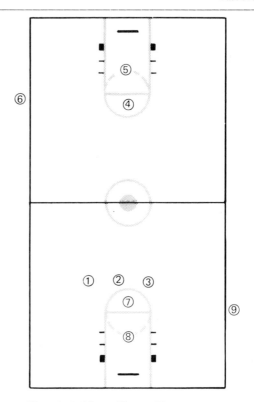

Fig. 6.12 *Six Player Fast Break. Players 1, 2, and 3 execute the fast break against 4 and 5. When the defense acquires the ball, they go down court two-on-one against 6; players 4, 5, and 6 return against 1 and 2. Continue.*

Fig. 6.13 *Nine Player Three-on-two. Players 1, 2, and 3 execute a fast break against 4 and 5; 4, 5, and 6 break against 7 and 8; 7, 8, and 9 break against 1 and 2. Continue.*

as the dribbler approaches. Finally the defenders can move as they wish. In this way the middle player can recognize where the opening exists under a designated condition. Later when the defenders move as they wish she must make the correct deccision to any number of variables.

12. Three defenders at the defensive end playing man-to-man. Three attack players start at the division line with a trailer 10 ft. behind. The middle player dribbles down the court flanked by the wings and followed by the trailer who indicates "trailer right" or "trailer left." The middle player times her pass to the trailer as she moves beyond the free throw line.

13. Two offensive players against one defensive player. One of the attack players has the ball at the division line and dribbles downcourt using proper techniques for scoring.

14. Five players in their backcourt in normal positions on defense. Another player tosses the ball against the backboard and the players react immediately for the start of the fast break. Emphasis should be on the wings hustling to position, the trailer about 10 ft. behind and the rebounder about 15 ft. behind the trailer.

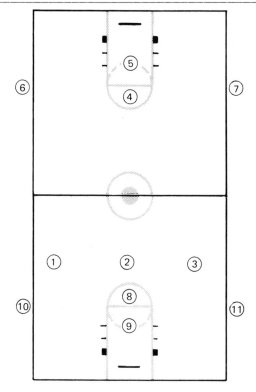

Fig. 6.14 *Eleven Player Fast Break (Three-on-Two). Players 1, 2, and 3 move down court against 4 and 5. Whoever gets the rebound goes down court with 6 and 7 against 8 and 9. The rebounder at this end goes down court with 10 and 11. Continue.*

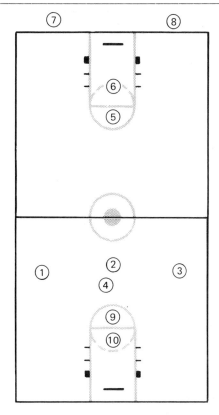

Fig. 6.15 *Four-on-Two. Players 1, 2, 3, and 4 go down court against 5 and 6. When either defender gets the rebound both go down court with 7 and 8 against 9 and 10. Players call "outlet," "middle," and "trailer." The group of four alternates playing defense and going out of bounds. Continue.*

15. Two teams at one end of the court. A player on the attacking team shoots and the opposing team immediately starts to fast break. The team that attempted the shot delays for a count of two and tries to recover. Again, emphasis is on the positioning of the attacking team.

16. Three-on-Two; Two-on-One. Proceed as above in the three-on-two drill. When either of the two defenders intercepts or gets a rebound (or after a field goal), she moves downcourt against the point player who becomes a defender. The next group of three moves out to start the drill again.

17. Six player drill as shown in Fig. 6.12.

18. Nine player drill as shown in Fig. 6.13.

19. Eleven player drill as shown in Fig. 6.14.

20. A four-on-two drill as shown in Fig. 6.15.

DEFENSE AGAINST A FAST BREAK

Once a fast break has developed, the defense against it is most difficult. The defense must have a little bit of luck to be successful! The best way to defend against a fast break is to prevent it from starting! One of the requirements for this is the maintenance of defensive balance while a team is on offense. On any offensive play two players must remain near the top of the circle in case ball possession is lost. If a fast break is started the defenders have at least two players to force an outside shot rather than a lone defender.

It may be possible for a team to make certain adjustments on offense when it has to contend with a good fast breaking opponent. There are several steps that may be taken to cause certain key players on the opposing team to be out of position to start the fast break. A team may play its pivot in a high post position to lure the opposing player away from the backboard and out of good rebounding position, thus reducing the opportunity for that team to start a fast break. This tactic may prove successful if a team has forwards who are equal or better rebounders than the opponents. If this tactic also pulls its best rebounder away from the basket, thus reducing its own rebounding strength, it may not be worthwhile. A team may also try to maneuver the opposing ball handlers into the corners so that they are not in a favorable position to receive an outlet pass to start a fast break when their team rebounds. This tactic may be effective against a man-to-man defense; against a zone, of course, players are not that maneuverable.

Utilizing methods such as those described may limit the number of fast breaks the opponents start, but it may also reduce the effectiveness of the offense of the team employing them. Such maneuvering may necessitate special offensive plays, the timing of which may not be fully developed. It may also maneuver some of the better offensive players out of position and psychologically affect their offensive contributions. Many teams find that the values accrued from these measures do not outweigh the problems created in structuring a different offense.

The tactics used most often against the fast break include four measures.
1. The team rebounds strongly. If unable to obtain the rebound, a player or players guard the rebounder aggressively. They overplay her passing arm with arms extended overhead and try to stall the rebounder from making her outlet pass.
2. The first player retreats down the middle of the court and attempts to stop the progress of

the ball. Other players retreating try to force the dribbler to move laterally or pick up her dribble.
3. The defenders guard the receivers for the outlet pass. Very soon after a game begins, it should be evident which players are the usual recipients of the outlet pass. Whenever the ball is lost, players are then assigned to guard them closely following a rebound, thus slowing the start of the fast break. They may also attempt to draw a charge if the outlet (or middle player) invariably pivots and puts the ball to the floor.
4. Another method of dealing with the outlet receivers may be used. It should be obvious where the opponents generally receive the outlet pass, and players may then be designated to move in to the intercepting angles.

By a combination of the first and second and either the third or fourth measures, the fast break effort should be delayed long enough so that other defenders have ample time to recover downcourt.

Should a team make a mental or physical error resulting in a fast break by the opponents, the defense will be subjected to a situation where the offense has more players than the defense. This is likely to occur sometime during the course of a game. It may happen when the opponents intercept a pass or when a player falls mentally asleep and fails to maintain defensive balance. From an offensive point of view, a team should score whenever it has a one- or two-player advantage. It is the objective of the defending team to delay the offensive players and force as many passes as possible before a shot is attempted. The more passes made by the offense, the more time the other defenders have to recover. At the same time, the defense is also trying to force the outside shot and prevent the layup.

There are many situations that may arise — one-on-none, two-on-one, three-on-one, three-on-two, four-on-two, four-on-three, and five-on-four. Some of these occur rather infrequently; therefore, attention will be given only to those that are most likely to occur.

One-on-None

This situation may occur when a player taps the ball away from an opponent or intercepts a pass and makes a clear breakaway downcourt. The defensive player nearest the action must retreat as fast as possible and attempt to disconcert the shooter. Once the shot is taken, the defensive player should attain rebounding position so that the ball does not rebound over her head. In beginning play the shooter and defensive player are often running at such speed that neither can stop after the shot and both continue to run out of bounds. This means that another offensive player hustling downcourt may obtain the rebound and score an easy layup. This should never be permitted. The defensive player must slow her forward speed so that she is positioned for the rebound.

Two-on-One

When this happens the lone defensive player must run backward as rapidly as possible to the top of the free throw circle. She should not attempt to harass the dribbler while she maneuvers at midcourt. This can be extremely dangerous for obvious reasons. If the two offensive players are passing, the defender may anticipate and intercept a pass but she must be 100 percent sure of stealing the ball. The defender meets the dribbler at the top of the circle and retreats with her. She may make feinting motions at the ball, but her weight always remains to the rear. She does not commit herself to either player and stays at least 6 ft. from the dribbler until she is within that distance of the basket. By sagging off the dribbler and opening toward the cutter with one arm pointing in her direction she can deter a pass to her. As the cutter is the more dangerous player since she is closer to the basket, the defender wants to cut off the passing lane to her. The defender tries to force the dribbler into catching the ball. If successful, she quickly retreats toward the cutter to encourage an outside shot by the dribbler. As she retreats, she stays in the lane and waits for the cutter to come toward her. Moving out of the lane opens a passing lane closer to the basket. Basically the defender is trying to delay the offense by using feinting techniques and cause the offense to make an extra pass. If the defensive player succeeds in preventing a layup shot, she has demonstrated excellent defense regardless of whether a long shot is successful. Once the ball is shot, the defender blocks out the nonshooter.

Three-on-Two

There are two ways of combating a three-on-two advantage. One method calls for an up-and-back system while the other places players parallel. The former method is the one generally preferred. When a three-on-two break occurs, the two defensive players must hurry back to the free throw line. One player stops inside the top of the circle while the other one moves back in the lane about 8 ft. in front of the basket. It is the front defender's task (at the top of the circle) to stop the dribbler by the time she

reaches the free throw line and cause her to pass. The more passes that the defenders can force, the more time their teammates have to recover. Usually the offensive advantage is lost after the second pass.

The back player is responsible for guarding whichever player the dribbler passes to. She must not commit herself too soon but wait until she actually sees the ball released so that she is not susceptible to a fake and pass in the opposite direction. As soon as the dribbler passes, the front player retreats down the middle of the lane about 8 ft. in front of the basket to protect the passing lane to the offensive player cutting toward the basket on the other side. This player is now responsible for guarding whichever player is the receiver of the next pass. These two defenders continue to exchange positions until additional help arrives (Fig. 6.16). The next defender back should hasten down the middle of the court to the free throw area.

The parallel system of defense may be used against a poor fast break team or when a poor ball handler is in the middle position on offense. The two defenders position themselves at the corners of the free throw line and open toward the cutter on their side, but keep their eyes on the player with the ball. They must prevent the dribbler from driving between them. The defender on the ball side of the dribbler makes feinting motions to cause the dribbler to pass. As the pass is made, the defender closer to the receiver prevents the easy layup while the other defender drops back in the lane to cut off the passing lane to the cutter on her side. If the ball is passed back to the former dribbler at the free throw line, the defender who dropped back goes out to guard the dribbler unless a teammate has recovered in time.

Three-on-One

When a situation like this occurs, the lone defender is really at the mercy of the opponents. She must run back to the defensive lane and force the ball handler to make a pass from the free throw line. The offense should score on a layup but the defender may cause a bad pass and she should hold her position and try to draw a charge after the middle player passes.

Four-on-Three

Zone principles must be applied in this situation also. A triangle zone is established by the defense, with the front player one step beyond the free throw line and the other two players 8 ft. in front of

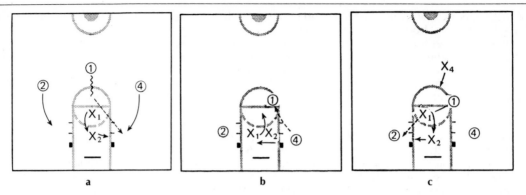

a   b   c

Fig. 6.16 *Defense Against a Fast Break. As player 1 passes to 4, X_2 moves over to defend against 4. Player X_1 drops back to cover the passing lane to 2 (a). Player 4 is unable to shoot and passes back to 1. Player X_1 must move out to guard her as X_2 moves back into the middle of the lane so that she can guard whoever receives the next pass (b). As player 1 passes to 2, 2 moves to the edge of the lane to guard her as X_1 drops back again. After this number of passes, another defender should be retreating. In this instance, X_4 is moving to cover a return pass to 1 (c).*

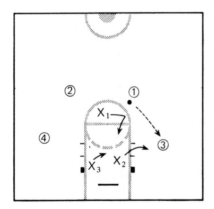

Fig. 6.17 *Defense in Four-on-Three Situation When Opponents Use a Two-Two Alignment. Player X_1 must guard either player 1 or 2 if she has the ball. If 1 passes to 3, X_1 drops back as X_2 guards 3. Player X_3 moves into the lane and covers the passing lane to 4 or 2 if either cuts into the lane.*

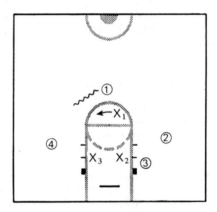

Fig. 6.18 *Defense in a Four-on-Three Situation When the Opponents Are in a One-Two-One Alignment. Player X_1 overplays to force 1 to dribble toward the weak side. After 1 passes, the responsibilities of the defensive players are the same as previously described.*

the basket and at the edge of the lane on their side. While the three defenders counteract the moves of the first three attack players the defense must be alert for the trailer. They must help and recover until they get further defensive help. If the opponents move downcourt in a two-two alignment (Fig. 6.17) the front player must chase between the two out-

side players. If they use a one-two-one, the front defender tries to force the dribbler toward the weak side — the side with fewer offensive players (Fig. 6.18). All defenders open toward the ball and try to prevent a pass in to a cutter moving across the lane. The defenders must protect against the high percentage shots and allow the long shot.

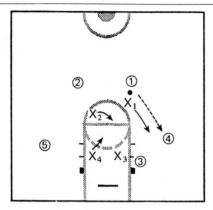

Fig. 6.19 *Defense in a Box Zone in a Five-on-Four Situation with the Offense in a Two-Three Alignment. If player 1 passes to 4, the defenders reposition themselves as shown. Players X_2 cuts off the passing lane to 1 or 2 on a cut through the lane. Player X_4 cuts off the lane to 5.*

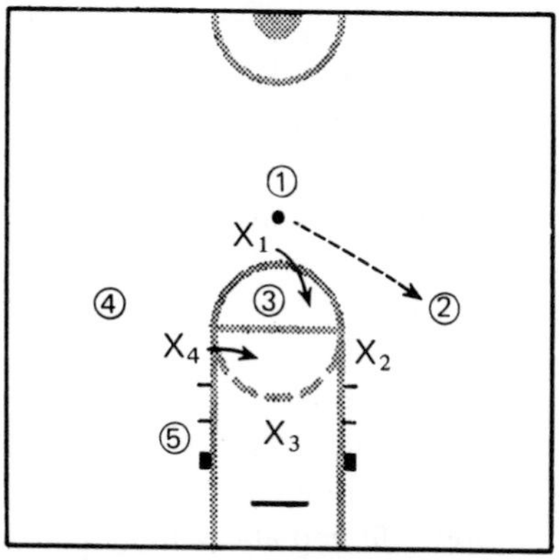

Fig. 6.20 *Defense in a Diamond Zone in a Five-on-Four Situation with the Offense in a One-Three-One Alignment. If player 1 passes to 2, X_2 moves to guard her; X_1 drops back and X_4 floats over. Emphasis is on delaying a shot until the fifth defender recovers.*

Five-on-Four

A box zone may be used when defenders are confronted with this situation and when the opponents are in a two-three alignment (Fig. 6.19). The two outside defenders start one step in front of the free throw line on their side while the back players are 6 ft. in front of the basket at the edge of the lane on their side. Again they try to encourage as many passes as possible and prevent the easy shot. If the opponents are in a one-three-one or one-four alignment, the diamond zone may be a better posture from which to start (Fig. 6.20). The zones are similar after the initial pass.

Drills for Defending Against an Offensive Advantage

1. Groups of three — two attack players and one defensive player. A defensive player starts running backward from the center circle toward the top of her defensive circle. The two attack players pass and dribble downcourt, attempting to score. The defender uses correct techniques to prevent the layup and force the outside shot. Rotate.

2. Groups of five — three attack players and two defensive players. The two defensive players start at the defensive end in their up-and-back (or parallel) position. The three attack players start at the top of the free throw circle at the other end and bring the ball downcourt with the middle player in possession by the time they reach the offensive circle. The defensive players use correct techniques to cause as many passes as possible.

3. Same as drill 2 above, but the defensive players start at the division line and must hurry back to get in proper position to defend against the approaching attack players.

4. Same as drill 3 above, but add another defensive player starting at the free throw line behind the attack players. She is in pursuit and races down the middle of the court to recover at the defensive free throw line. Later, at a sideline or in a corner, start this defensive player from other positions behind the attack players.

5. Groups of seven — four offensive players against three defensive players at one end of the court. The three defensive players use a triangle zone and try to force the outside shot and as many passes as possible before a shot is attempted.

6. Same as drill 5 above, but add another defensive player starting 6 ft. in front of the basket at the other end. She races downcourt and tries to assist her teammates before a shot is taken.

7. Two teams without a defensive pivot — nine players, all at one end of the court. The defense forms a box zone and tries to force as many passes as possible before a shot is taken. Later, replace a forward with the pivot who has been out of action.

8. Same as drill 7 above, but start the defensive pivot 6 ft. in front of the basket at the opposite end and see if she can recover before a shot is attempted.

9. Three columns of players at one endline and three defensive players on the court at the free throw line. A manager passes the ball to the first player in one of the columns. She and the first player in the other two columns fast break down the court. Two of the defensive players talk as they retreat to gain good defensive position. The third defensive player must touch the endline and retreat the full length of the court to help her teammates on defense.

7

Basic Offensive and Defensive Principles

BASIC OFFENSIVE PRINCIPLES

When building any type of offense the teacher/ coach must consider her players' abilities and potential development. The devised offense may be either simple or complicated. It may range from the use of give-and-go tactics only to a pattern offense that utilizes cuts of all kinds and various screening maneuvers. Regardless of the offense selected there are certain aspects that should be emphasized and basic principles that are applicable to any offensive system.

Ball Handling

1. Ball possession must be considered extremely important. A team cannot score unless it has possession of the ball, and opponents cannot score when they do not have the ball. The importance of gaining the ball and keeping it once it is gained until a score is made must be impressed continually upon the players. They must recognize the importance of good ball handling skills and how poor ball handling jeopardizes the entire offensive structure of the team.
2. All passes must be accurate and crisp. Lob passes should be made with caution, as they allow the defense time to realign and lead to interceptions. Short passes tend to be more accurate than long ones. Passes should be made to where a player is moving, not where

the passer wishes she were. A pass interception, a pass that goes out of bounds, or a pass that is fumbled by the receiver is almost always the fault of the passer rather than the receiver.
3. Pass receivers must move to meet the ball. A pass should rarely be made to a player who is standing still. If the defense is passive (sagging or playing loosely), cutting to meet the ball may not be as necessary; but, offensive players should not be deceived by the defender's apparent position. It may only be a ruse so that an interception may be attempted. When the defense is playing aggressively, offensive players must cut to meet a pass and the pass should be made toward the "off" shoulder (shoulder away from the opponent).
4. Pass receivers should be facing the basket when they receive a pass (with the exeception of the pivot player). Receiving a pass with her back to the basket is a great weakness of many beginning players — particularly wings and corners. This action limits offensive play considerably. The player with the ball is unable to see any teammate cutting free for the basket and she is not in a position to shoot. This means that the defensive players have an opportunity to regain a good defensive position while the ball handler contemplates her next move. When the defense is sagging a player should have no difficulty in receiving a pass while facing the basket. The cut to meet the ball should be made on a diagonal so that as

193

a   b

Fig. 7.1 *Receiving a Pass. The player receives a pass (a). She pivots immediately to face the basket (b).*

the player stops she can be facing the basket. The same action should be followed by a player who is closely guarded. She must cut on a diagonal to receive a pass which should be aimed at her "off" shoulder. The foot position on her stop should allow her to face the basket as she receives the pass. If not, she should land facing the passer so that a short pivot permits her to face the basket (Fig. 7.1). If a potential receiver sees that her defender is pressing often, she should cut backdoor. Do not continue to fight pressure.

5. Players should dribble the ball only for a specific purpose. It may be to advance the ball downcourt; to balance the court or reset offensive positions; to gain a better passing angle; to drive for the basket; and to force a defensive player to commit herself. An "alive" player (one who has not dribbled) is more dangerous than one who has already dribbled and caught the ball. A reception of a pass followed by an immediate bounce is a sign of an ineffective player and this habit must be corrected quickly. A player should not stop dribbling until she is ready to pass or shoot. This keeps her alive and discourages double-teaming efforts by the opponents. When

challenged by a defensive player, beginning players often stop dribbling, whereupon one or more defensive players guard her closely, frequently causing a violation or a bad pass. Players must acquire an early understanding of the values and disadvantages of the dribble, including when and how to use it effectively.

Positioning and Cutting

1. Whatever offensive system is utilized, it must contain both ball and player movement. An offense where players basically stay in the same position is far easier to defend than one in which the defense must be aware of the changing position of players and ball. This is true for both an offense against a man-to-man and zone defense. Players must pass and cut to force the defense to readjust constantly. They must keep the defense busy physically and mentally.

2. At the start of any offensive thrust players should remain apart 15 ft. or more. They must make every effort to discourage double-teaming tactics and to keep the defense spread so

that one defender cannot guard two offensive players. Beginning players tend to edge toward the ball and/or the lane, thus bringing the defensive players in tighter and closing the passing lanes. Following cuts or screens, players should realign so that the 15 ft. spaces can be retained.

3. Cuts on offense must be well timed. This is one of the most difficult aspects for players to learn. This is also what makes teaching offense more difficult than teaching defense. How often one sees two or three beginning players cutting for a pass and all arriving in the same spot at practically the same time! This must be avoided! One player may cut to a space and when she clears it another player may cut through the space — but not both at the same time! As one player leaves a spot, another player may fill it.

4. Players should understand and be able to move quickly into their offensive alignment as the defensive alignment is determined. Players must then know the responsibilities of their position. Either a pattern should be devised or certain rules must be applied to a free lance or motion offense. In any attack system the movements of the individual players are devised so that players remain spread. This prevents crowding in a particular location, opens cutting lanes, and helps players to acquire the timing for an offensive thrust.

5. Under most circumstances a player cutting for the ball should receive a pass from a player whom she is facing. This is the easiest way for a receiver to catch a pass and it is also the easiest way for a player to give an accurate pass. This means that generally when a pivot cuts to the high post position she should receive a pass from a player in the guard position. As a guard cuts for the basket she should receive a pass from a player in the corner, wing, or low or medium pivot position. As a player in the corner position makes a cut through the lane under the basket or makes a cut up and through the lower half of the restraining circle, she should receive a pass from a player in the opposite corner or in the low or medium post position on the side toward which she is cutting. Although passing in this manner is desirable and most maneuvers should be designed with this principle in mind, it is not always possible or desirable to follow. For example, use of a roll following a screen on the ball, scissor maneuvers, and reverse cuts all necessitate a pass being received as a player is cutting away from the ball. This type of pass is most difficult to give accurately and should be used only when necessary.

6. The ball should be passed back out when continued penetration is not feasible. Ideally, the attack wishes to pass the ball toward the basket until a score can result. This may not always be possible. A defense may adjust to the ball and player movement so well that continued advancement of the ball toward the basket would result in a charging foul or pass interception. In this case the ball should be passed back, forcing the defense to realign and making it possible to start an offensive thrust again. The action may be started again on the same side, or the ball may be reversed from the strong side around the perimeter to penetrate from the weak side.

7. Players should clear the area when a player is driving. Teammates should cut away from the dribbler to draw their opponent with them and prevent the defense from collapsing around the dribbler. This is particularly important against a zone defense. If a player can penetrate the perimeter of the zone, she will draw another defender; this will allow a teammate to cut into a seam of the zone to receive a pass. The cut must be made so that the same defender cannot guard both players. Against a man-to-man defense it is possible to free one player to operate one-on-one if the ball is passed to the weak side, providing the other player clears the area (Fig. 7.2).

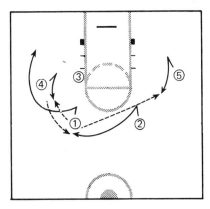

Fig. 7.2 *Pass to the Weak Side to Allow a Forward to Work One-on-One. Player 1 passes to 4 and cuts to the corner. 4 passes back to 2, who passes to 5. Player 5 can work one-on-one against her opponent.*

Shooting

1. A team must have players who can shoot accurately from the inside and outside. Long shots do not produce a high scoring percentage, and a team that must rely on these for

scoring will not win many games the ability of the Asiatics notwithstanding. Likewise the team that can shoot only from within 10–15 ft. of the basket will have difficulty in scoring, as the defense will collapse to this area and permit and encourage longer shots.

2. Whenever a tall player shoots, she should use her height to advantage and execute overhead layups, jump shots, and set shots. When a short player moves through the lane she probably will have the greatest success by faking an overhead layup and using an underhand shot or by stopping short of the layup and taking a jump shot 8–10 ft. in front of the basket.

3. Although a team may possess good outside shooters, it should continually attempt to free players within the 10-ft. range. Shots taken from this area will produce a high percentage for success. If shots cannot be attained from this area, the next highest percentage area falls between 10 and 15 ft. The least desirable shooting distance would be from 15–21 ft. Few shots should be taken from beyond this area (Fig. 7.3).

4. Patience must be the byword of an attacking team. They must not hurry their scoring thrust but cut and pass to obtain the high percentage shot. Offensive maneuvers must be designed with this in mind and will provide many opportunities for players to be free within a short distance of the basket.

5. The offense should be devised to give every player an opportunity for scoring. This helps team morale. A team that has only two or

three good shooters must provide those players with most of the scoring opportunities, however. A team should not reduce its scoring effectiveness to satisfy the desires of inaccurate shooters.

6. Players should not shoot if another player is free and in a better position to do so. Unselfishness is a characteristic that players must be taught if they do not already possess it. A player who is free under the basket is more likely to score than another player 10 ft. from the basket.

7. Whenever a shot is attempted, four conditions must be met:
   a. the shooter must be in a better position than any other player to shoot
   b. she must not be hurried or off-balance as she attempts her shot
   c. she must be within her shooting range
   d. rebounders must be in position unless the shooter is attempting a layup or a shot within 5 ft. of the basket

A team usually has worked hard to obtain the ball and to get it in position for a shot. It is senseless to take a shot that has little possibility of scoring, and it is even more questionable to take it without rebounders in position.

8. Unless directed otherwise, any player who shoots should follow her shot for the rebound. She is in the best position to know where the ball is likely to rebound if it is unsuccessful. Other players should be assigned rebounding responsibilities. In reality it makes little difference whether the first or fourth attempt at a field goal in the same possession is successful.

General

1. Field goal shooting percentage and number of points scored per possession are vital statistics in determining offensive capability. Teams that rank high in these areas possess good discipline and shot selection. They also play good defense that causes turnovers and enables layups to be scored.

2. Screens should be considered a vital part of any offensive system. Contrary to the beliefs of some coaches, screens are effective against both man-to-man and a zone defense. Many zone offenses utilize running screens to free players effectively. Against a zone, screens are also set at a spot to prevent a zone defender from moving to her new position as the ball changes position. The value of screens against a man-to-man defense is unchallenged. Their use should be perfected to garner advantages against both types of defense. To make the screen effective, a player must fake away from the screen prior to using

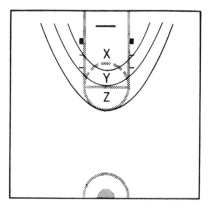

Fig. 7.3 *Shooting Distances. Area X contains the area within 10 ft. of the basket. Most shots should be taken from within this area. Area Y includes the area between 10 and 15 ft. of the basket. Area Z includes the area 15–21 ft. from the basket. Few shots should be attempted from beyond this area.*

it and must not alert an opponent that a screen is being set.

3. Maneuvers that are designed to use a screen and roll should be started approximately 15 ft. from the basket. If started closer than this, there is not sufficient space for the screener to roll toward the basket and receive a pass. The area within 8–10 ft. of the basket is generally congested.

4. Any designed offense should exploit the strengths of the offensive players. Maneuvers should be designed to free the best shooters. Advantage should be taken of good ball handlers, and an effort should be made to hide weak ball handlers and shooters. These players should deploy their defenders by fakes and cuts to keep their opponents occupied. The best rebounders should be placed in a position favorable for this task. All players understand the role they play in the offensive system. Rather than scorers or rebounders, some players will be effective as ball handlers and passers. Every player should recognize how she can contribute to the team effort. Team understanding and respect should evolve.

5. An offense should not only exploit the strengths of its own players but also the weaknesses of the opponents. If the opposing team has one or more weak defensive players the scoring thrusts should be made in their direction. Soon better skilled teammates will try to help them, thus weakening their own defensive responsibility. If the opponents are slower, the ball should be advanced quickly downcourt. Players can use various cuts to get

free and drives to gain a step advantage. If the opponents lack height or jumping ability, taller players may be assigned those positions that bring them close to the basket, and passes should be directed to them.

6. A team must provide defensive protection while it is on offense. There must be at least one or two players 20–25 ft. from the basket at all times. As a guard cuts toward the basket, she is replaced by another player and that player is replaced by another. Fig. 7.4 shows how this may be done during a simple, common maneuver. It is evident from this diagram that this deployment does not involve the same players at all times, although the guards are likely to be in this position more often than the others. Essentially, the purpose of this tactic is twofold:

   a. it provides the offense with a trailer who can receive a pass when forward penetration with the ball is not feasible
   b. it serves as a safety valve in case the ball is intercepted. All offensive maneuvers must use this very important principle.

7. Above all, players must understand the importance of team cooperation and recognize the contribution that each player makes in the total offensive effort.

OTHER CONSIDERATIONS

Getting the Ball from the Backcourt to the Frontcourt

A team may acquire the ball in its defensive end by intercepting it, obtaining a rebound, or by getting the ball out of bounds following a violation or score. There are two ways to advance the ball — either by means of a fast break or a controlled style of play. If the team uses a fast break, the passes are made quickly to gain a player advantage. On an out-of-bounds play a forward (or pivot) puts the ball in play, as she is the closest player to the endline. The ball is in-bounded as rapidly as possible so that the fast break can be initiated.

If a team chooses to use a controlled type of offense, the ball is given to the best ball handler while the rest of the players move to the frontcourt and get into position. The player with the ball dribbles into the frontcourt and sets up the attack. If the ball is put in play from out-of-bounds the best passer is given this assignment. The ball is in-bounded to a ball handler while other players move to the frontcourt.

Following a score, the team putting the ball in play from out-of-bounds may need more help if the opponents press them. In this case the forwards

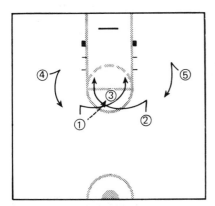

Fig. 7.4 *Players Filling the Spaces to Retain Defensive Balance. On a scissor maneuver by the guards, the two forwards clear the area and come back to provide defensive balance. Fig. 7.2 shows player 2 providing balance.*

may remain in the backcourt to assist in beating the press. The post moves to the frontcourt as usual. The manner in which a team beats a press is discussed in Chapter 10.

The 30-Second Clock

The 30-second clock is used in college and international play. Since it has not been adopted for high school play, coaches of those teams need not be concerned with its effect on play.

The purpose of the clock is to force the ball to exchange hands reasonably often and, as a result, to prevent any type of stall offense to develop for more than 30 seconds. Although the purpose of the clock is to speed up play, there are few occasions when a team is unable to establish its offense in the manner in which it would like and obtain a high percentage shot. Thirty seconds is a long time, when one considers that it takes only 4 or 5 seconds (or less) to advance the ball into the frontcourt when a team is not pressed.

Coaches should impress upon their players that there is no need to hurry an attack and that they should be patient in maneuvering for an open shot. Although a pressing defense may delay the crossing into the frontcourt, there still should be ample time to develop the offense in the usual manner. Many teams have been clocked on the time it takes them to obtain a shot, and most are amazed with the alacrity with which they shoot. It is not unusual for a team to shoot within 15 seconds of the time they obtain the ball. If for some reason a team is slow in obtaining a good shot, it is wise for substitutes or a manager to inform the players when there are only 10 seconds left, if the 30-second clock is not visible to the players. Counting down the last 10 seconds is also helpful.

Determining the Type of Defense Being Used

On each offensive possession the attack should determine specifically what type of defense is being played against them — man-to-man, switching man-to-man, the type of zone, or a combination defense. Each is attacked somewhat differently. If a defensive player follows each cutter, the opponents are using some type of man-to-man defense. If they do not follow each player they are either playing a zone or a combination defense. The nature of either of these must be determined.

As a team moves into its offensive end, it should try to determine the defense being played. It should

then run its offense against that type of defense to verify its judgment. If the defense changes into a different system, the offense must be changed.

There are other times when the defense may change alignment, but the start of each period is a logical one and the attack should be prepared to identify it immediately. Following a time out or other suspension of play are other times when the attack must be particularly alert for a change. Of course, some teams can make the transition from one defense to another without benefit of a time out. Any time an attack player observes a different alignment she should notify her teammates if the coach has not already done so.

Use of Signals

The practice of using signals of some description to designate a particular offense or defense is familiar to all. Signals may be verbal or visual. Names of schools, colors, animals, athletes, and numbers are common verbal signals. The main criticism against the verbal signal is that it may not be heard above the crowd noise. The visual signal is preferred. One finger, two fingers, a closed fist, or other hand signal may be used to designate the tactic.

BUILDING AN OFFENSE

Innumerable offenses have been constructed over the years. Many used today are variations of those designed some years ago. The basic question the coach must resolve is whether to employ a pattern offense or a free lance system with rules, such as the motion offense. Once this question is answered, the coach can design an offense that will be best suited for the team's personnel. In general, the free lance style may take longer to teach because players have more freedom of movement. The value of devising a pattern lies in the continuity of motion of the players as one move leads into the next. Players know their exact responsibilities on every maneuver and recognize that if a scoring opportunity does not develop on one move it will on another. The continuity offense has an inherent disadvantage in that the opponents can identify the basic pattern and structure their defense to limit its effectiveness. However, if the attack utilizes options from the continuity and executes properly, defensive modifications to overcome the pattern should be nullified.

In the construction of any offense, certain principles should be followed:

1. There should always be defensive balance. This may necessitate a forward moving back to the top of the circle on a cutting maneuver by a guard.
2. A scoring thrust should be made on the initial maneuver, i.e., there should be immediate player movement to free a player for a shot after two or three passes.
3. Opportunities should be provided for both long and short shots. The best shooters on the team should be freed for these scoring attempts.
4. Player movements should include diagonal and vertical cuts and should take advantage of the individual assets of various players. Ball movement should include the potential for passing into the lane area and reverse movement.
5. Rebounding strength should be provided at all times. Care must be exercised to assure that all of the best rebounders are not pulled away from the basket at the same time.

Teaching an Offense

The instructor/coach should be thoroughly familiar with all movements as a pattern is presented and should be particularly aware of the desirable timing of the sequential moves. The coach should be able to visualize the pattern in operation from both the right and left sides, although all patterns are devised to circulate predominantly in one direction to take advantage of player strengths.

It is desirable to circulate diagrams of the movements to the players so that they can follow them while the teacher describes them either on the blackboard or with an overhead projector. Each diagram should contain only one or two movements by each player so that the student can easily follow the drawing. Subsequent action can be included in other diagrams, and players can take the diagrams home for additional study.

Once the pattern has been reviewed orally and diagrammatically, players should be placed on the court in their proper positions and allowed to walk through the movements. This should be followed by running through the pattern, with careful attention given to the timing of the moves both toward and away from the ball. Defensive players should be added and instructed to be passive and not interfere either with ball or player movement. They maintain proper position but do not play at all aggressively. At this time particular emphasis should be placed on the players' sequential movements. The pattern should be broken down into its parts whenever

necessary to obtain the desirable moves and timing by the players involved. As soon as parts have been learned the whole pattern should be reviewed once again. Defensive players can then be instructed to defend in their usual manner.

It is important that attack players be successful with the pattern as they are learning it. They must develop confidence in its ability to penetrate the defense and see evidence that many natural scoring opportunities can arise through its normal movement. By instructing the defense to remain stationary or passive, the attack can gain confidence in its use. Following this initial learning period, the attack must work the pattern against a more normal defense so that they can adjust to whatever defensive feints or moves they may encounter during a game situation.

When the teacher is satisfied that the players have acquired the desirable level of competency with the pattern, options should be learned. The same progression the players experienced while learning the pattern itself should be used while learning the various options. After a period of time, a different style of defense should be employed to provide the players with an opportunity to gain poise in coping with it.

Although far more experience can be gained in learning the pattern by playing five-on-five, it is important during the learning stages that the players play full court also so that they must advance the ball downcourt and set up the offense. The instructor may initially suggest that the ball be advanced to the frontcourt in a controlled manner so that each time ball possession is gained, the pattern or one of its options may be worked. Later, the team may fast break whenever the opportunity arises and slow down to the pattern offense when the fast break does not materialize.

BASIC DEFENSIVE PRINCIPLES

Team defense requires the active participation of all five players. This is unlike the offense, which utilizes only two- or three-player involvement at any one time (in most instances). On defense, however, a team is considerably weakened when one or more players is out of position or has a mental lapse. Each player must react to every movement of the ball and her opponent (or the opponent in her zone). The defense is weakened any time a player fails to fulfill her responsibility in this respect.

A team must cultivate pride in its defensive ability. Teammates must recognize and accept their defensive strengths and weaknesses and should be ready to assist those players whose skills are inferior. They must also be ready to help a teammate who has a particularly difficult defensive assignment.

Players must strive to develop the tenacity and aggressiveness that distinguish a truly great defensive player from any other. When playing a man-to-man defense, players must not be permitted to develop the attitude that they are only responsible for "following" a player or guarding her when she has the ball. Often it is more important what a player does when her opponent does not have the ball! When playing a zone defense, players should not move merely from one position to another, but "attack" each position and any player who enters her zone. "Attack" means that no defensive player should let the offense run their patterns as they wish. The defense must anticipate where they would like to cut to receive a pass and beat them there. They must learn to disrupt the general offense of their opponents!

Defensive players must recognize that causing opponents to commit violations is the easiest way of gaining possession of the ball. Once they develop this concept they will have advanced in their defensive thinking. The next step is to acquire the readiness and anticipation to prevent their opponent or any opponent in their zone from receiving a pass. The cultivation of this concept leads to interceptions and forcing turnovers. As these attitudes are developed along with the necessary skills involved, a team will be on its way toward improving its overall defense.

In competitive play, one type of defense is no longer adequate to confound the offense of the opponents. A highly skilled team should be able to utilize two or three different types of defenses in any one game with equal ability. They should be proficient at some type of man-to-man defense, one or more zones, and a pressure defense. Development of skill in a variety of defenses takes considerable practice time; unless this is available, a team probably would perform better by using only one or two defenses well.

The author is a firm believer in the necessity of developing sound individual defensive skills and therefore is a proponent of starting with a man-to-man defense. Beginners must learn the fundamental concepts of this defense before they can successfully use a zone defense or any of the pressure defenses, for in any zone defense a player with the ball must be guarded with man-to-man principles. Once these concepts are acquired they can be incorporated into other types of defenses.

Identification of important principles follows:

1. A team must prevent or, once started, hinder fast break opportunities and any other offensive advantage. To prevent these from occurring, mental errors must be eliminated on offense. These occur in any of three ways.

   a. Defensive balance must be maintained, i.e., on every offensive thrust, two players should be deployed in the area near the top of the circle to prevent a fast break by the opponents if they should intercept a pass or obtain a rebound.

   b. Players must exercise good judgment in recognizing when a player is free or, more important, when a player is *not* free to receive a pass. Interceptions lead to many instances where the opponents gain an offensive advantage.

   c. When a team loses possession of the ball they must retreat rapidly to a position 6–8 ft. in front of the basket and look for any free opponent (Figs. 7.5 and 7.6). If there

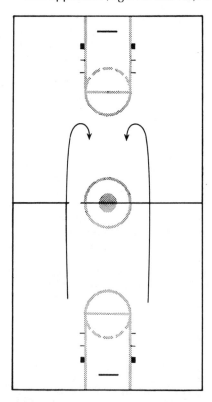

Fig. 7.5 *Poor Defensive Retreat by First Players Back on Defense. Players retreat only to the top of the circle to meet their opponents.*

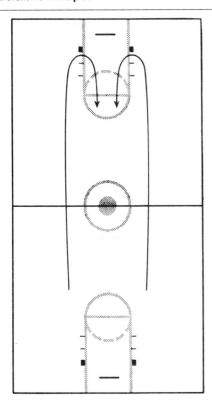

Fig. 7.6 *Good Defensive Retreat by First Two Players Back on Defense. Players recover downcourt to point within 6 ft. of the basket and then move out to their defensive positions. This technique precludes a long pass downcourt to a free player for a layup.*

is one, a defender moves to guard her while calling to her teammate the number of her own opponent, so that she may guard her. If the team is playing a zone defense the player may return to her own position once the position near the basket is filled. Free and uncovered opponents cannot be permitted to penetrate the area near the basket while a slower defender recovers downcourt.

d. The team retreating on defense must "stop the ball." Stopping the ball implies slowing the forward progress of the ball so that all of the defensive players have time to gain good defensive position. If the offensive player is dribbling, her opponent must delay her as much as possible; she cannot allow the dribbler to beat her. If the ball handler's opponent is unable to guard her for any reason, some other defensive player must delay the dribbler's forward progress, if only temporarily. She does this by taking one or two steps with the dribbler and then leaves the ball handler to retreat and guard her own opponent or take her position in the zone. This slight delay should allow her teammate to recover against the dribbler.

2. A team must force the opponents to alter their desired offensive maneuvers. They can cut off their normal passing lanes, double-team a high scorer or playmaker, float to the middle to eliminate cuts or drives through the middle of the lane, force the opponents to speed up their play by pressing them if they prefer to use a deliberate passing attack, or slow them down by cutting off the passing lanes if they prefer a fast break style offense. A team should analyze the opponents' strengths and take measures to minimize their effectiveness. It should also analyze their weaknesses and take measures to exploit them.

3. A team must prevent the cheap baskets that result from a fast break, tip-in, rebound, lob pass to a post, drive into the lane, or free throw follow-up.

4. A team must also prevent easy baskets taken within 12–15 ft. of the basket. Every possible measure should be taken to prevent a player from dribbling into this area or from receiving a pass within this area. The team should attempt to close the passing lanes into a player in this area and also to force the opponent in that area to alter the path of her cut away from her desired direction. If the offense gets the ball in this area, the defense should sag to force the ball out, tie it up or cause a 3-second violation. The defense does not want to be penetrated in this area. A team that permits a number of shots from this range will not win many contests.

5. A team must force the opponents to shoot long shots. By congesting the lane area and by contesting shots within 15–18 ft. of the basket, the opponents should be forced to shoot from a distance greater than this. Unless they prove successful in shooting beyond 21 ft., encourage them to shoot from that distance by not moving beyond that distance to guard them. Tactics must be changed if one or more players scores consistently from this distance.

6. A team must rebound well. The defensive aim should be to allow no more than one shot any time the opponents are on offense. A team must block out well and move to the areas where the ball rebounds. They must not allow themselves to get caught too far under the basket, and they must make pro-

visions for blocking out the offensive pivot player who shoots from a low or medium post position.

7. A team must learn good defensive techniques so that they will commit few fouls. Defensive fouls are generally caused by poor position, laziness, or poor position by a "helper." A team that commits fewer fouls than the opponents will force the opponents to make more field goals in order to win.

8. A team that plays good defense can control the tempo of the game. It seldom allows an easy basket and keeps fast breaks at a minimum. By placing pressure on the ball handler and playing "hard nosed" defense, a team can limit the number of shots the opposing team takes, which will in effect decrease the number of points they score.

9. A team on defense *must* talk. There must be communication between players so that players know when: a pick might be set; a cutter cuts across the lane; a shot has been taken; an opponent is free; when to help; and when to help and recover.

10. By using multiple defenses a team may place the opposing team at a disadvantage, if only temporarily. The time it takes the opponents to adjust cannot be used for effective scoring thrusts. If it takes the opponents several possessions to adjust, the defense gains an edge psychologically and scorewise.

TEAM REBOUNDING

For most players the blocking out process is not a natural one and must be cultivated by extensive practice. The procedure and drills for becoming proficient in this vital technique are discussed in Chapter 2 if the reader needs review. Unless a team develops proper blocking out techniques it can never become a good rebounding team.

Generally a team assigns three players as their primary rebounders, while a fourth player moves near the free throw line to recover any shot that rebounds hard off the backboard or rim. The fifth player moves to her assigned position outside of the lane, or cuts to receive an outlet pass. Some teams rely wholly on three rebounders; this is desirable if a team has strong rebounders, for it allows the outlet pass to be made further downcourt. Generally, the two forwards and pivot player are given the primary responsibility for rebounding; but there may be occasions when a guard has cut through the lane and is in better position to rebound than a forward.

Most authorities agree that when playing man-to-man defense all players should block out their opponent immediately after a shot is taken. There are two theories on the tactics that follow, however. One suggests that defenders should block out their opponents, keep them blocked out in that position until the ball rebounds, and then move to obtain the ball. The other proposes that the opponents should be blocked out momentarily and that the rebounders should then move toward the ball. This latter technique is easier since body contact need not be maintained as long. However, it does allow both defensive and offensive players to move closer to the basket sooner and, as a result, may limit the passing lanes once the ball is secured. It is better to maintain contact with the offensive player as far away from the basket as possible and then go for the rebound. This prevents the offensive players from pushing the defenders under the basket and maintains open passing lanes when the ball is rebounded. As soon as a rebounder obtains the ball, she should pass it quickly toward the near side line.

Defensive players must be aware of free opponents in the scoring area and be ready to block them out on any shooting attempts. Players must be ready to cross-block under these circumstances.

Because a player is not responsible specifically for any one opponent, zone defense screening responsibilities are more difficult. As a matter of fact, the offense has a better chance of obtaining a rebound against a zone defense than it does against a man-to-man defense. Because defenders are not responsible specifically for any one opponent, it is more difficult to keep the offensive players away from the logical rebounding areas. This is one of the disadvantages of a zone defense, but if player personnel qualifications make the zone defense desirable, this aspect must be overlooked in determining the type of defense to be played overall.

A team using a zone defense may establish its rebounding responsibilities in either of two ways.

1. It may assign its best rebounders to specific positions in a triangle in front of the basket. A fourth player may also be assigned to a position near the free throw line. Those who believe this tactic is effective maintain the philosophy that if the rebounders position themselves in these vital positions the ball must rebound to one of them.

2. A team may block out the nearest opponent before moving into rebound position. If a zone is overloaded, it may not be possible to block out all players. Nevertheless, blocking out some may be better than none!

This second method is better, since it momentarily stalls the forward movement of the attack players and keeps them behind the defenders as they move toward the backboard. It may also prevent complacency from developing and the resulting poor positioning of the defenders.

Regardless of the technique used to block out, rebounders should react immediately. They should operate under the philosophy that no shot will be successful and obtain proper position against an opponent rapidly.

8

Man-to-Man Defense and Offense

A man-to-man defense is considered the fundamental defense upon which others can be developed. It places the responsibility for an opponent on each player and tends to develop a greater pride in individual defensive ability. It also uncovers those players who have defensive deficiencies.

ADVANTAGES OF MAN-TO-MAN DEFENSE

1. It permits players to be matched with regard to several factors — height, speed, quickness, jumping and rebounding ability, and defensive skill against a drive.
2. It fixes responsibility and encourages a player to improve her defensive fundamentals.
3. It places more pressure on all players continually.
4. It is effective against a stall and is absolutely imperative when a team is behind in score in the last few minutes of a game.
5. It has many variations for which the transition can be made easily.
6. Zone principles may be applied by sagging and floating.

DISADVANTAGES OF MAN-TO-MAN DEFENSE

1. It takes time to become proficient in the individual skills and basic principles.

2. It is susceptible to screens and double cuts.
3. Players tend to commit more fouls than when playing a zone defense.
4. More players generally are forced to move greater distances and expend more energy than when playing a zone defense.

BASIC PRINCIPLES FOR MAN-TO-MAN DEFENSE

1. A player is responsible for her opponent first and the ball second.
2. A player is always in a triangle formed by the ball, her opponent, and the basket. Her exact position in this triangle varies according to where her opponent is in relation to the ball and basket. The further her opponent is from the ball, the further she is from her opponent, for she must be able to see the ball and her opponent at all times without turning her head.
3. Basic principles previously discussed in Chapters 2 to 5 apply. These chapters deal with guarding a ball handler, guarding a player who is one or two passes away from the ball, defense against screens, scissors, or pass and cut tactics.
4. A player should quickly analyze the strengths and weaknesses of her opponent and that of the entire offensive team. If her opponent is weak she may concentrate on helping teammates or in double-teaming.
5. Players utilize sagging and floating principles

Fig. 8.1 *Sagging of the Defense. The far side defenders sag from their opponents.*

when their opponents are two passes away or when they are beyond scoring range.

a. Sagging occurs when a player moves away from her opponent toward the basket (Fig. 8.1). Guards use this technique more than other players in order to keep their opponent and ball in sight.

b. Floating takes place when a player moves laterally across the court toward the basket. It is used extensively by all weak side players so that they are in a "helping" position (Fig. 8.2). The tactic also places the defensive player in good position to front her opponent on a cut across the lane toward the ball.

c. Use of both of these principles allows the defense to congest the area within 15 ft. of the basket, thus preventing the high percentage shots and cutting down the lane. It permits one or more defensive players to concentrate on interceptions. It is extremely effective against a team that uses a cutting offense or has an effective driver. It uses some zone principles while employing pressure man-to-man tactics near the ball.

6. All players must understand and perfect the techniques involved with screens and double cuts. The method of dealing with these two tactics was discussed in Chapters 3 and 4.

7. Players may influence the direction of the ball. They can influence the offense to pass the ball in a certain direction by overplaying in a designated manner. This may be done for several reasons. Other defensive players may be alert for interceptions. It may also be desirable to direct the ball away from a high scorer, toward a poor ball handler, toward a particular side of the court, away from a weaker defensive player, toward a side line, toward the middle, or away from the baseline.

8. Players may also influence the direction of the dribbler by overplaying her (Fig. 8.3). This may be desirable because she does not dribble well with one hand or for any of the reasons stated above.

9. Whether a team is going to force the opponents toward the middle where there is help or toward the sideline where there are fewer passing lanes must be determined. Regardless of which philosophy is adopted, the defense can never give up the baseline.

10. A decision must also be made on the distance from the lane that the strong side forward will be overplayed. A distance should be designated so that players have an understanding of their responsibilities in this respect. The distance may be altered against a particularly dangerous opponent.

11. The degree to which the post player is fronted must be determined. In the high post position one foot of the defender should be behind the opponent so that the team is not vulnerable to the lob pass down the lane. In the medium post and low post positions, the defense must decide whether to play behind the post and allow the defender against the wing or corner player to sag and front the post; or whether the post defender will front her opponent and receive weak side help if the ball is lobbed. Allowing the post defender to play behind her opponent places her in good blocking out and rebounding position. However, against a team that has strong outside shooting, it may not be desirable to have the defender against the wing or corner player sag off her player. If the post player is primarily a rebounder and not a shooter, it would be wise for the post defender to play behind her to keep her off the boards. This would also allow the wing and corner defenders to put more pressure on their opponents. Against a team that shoots well from the outside and has a high scoring post, it is wise to keep pressure on the outside players, which forces the post to front her opponent and demands weak side help. When a player is in good weak side help position she can move to draw a charge on the lob pass. When the weak side defender's opponent is in the corner it is also difficult for the opponents to pass to her; as a result, the defense is not really hurt by this positioning. When there is weak side help against the post and a shot is taken, the weak side guard must block out the weak side forward. The offensive team can counteract this tactic by bringing the corner player high and forcing the weak side help away from the basket.

12. When the post receives the ball in the medium or low position, a defender against a wing or corner player must understand her responsibilities. She must know whether she is to play tight or play the passing lane against her opponent, or whether she should sag in and help against the post. Tactics in relation to the defender's position may be altered dependent upon the strengths of the post and the wing and corner players. Against a high scoring post, it may be desirable for the wing to sag and help against the medium post. If the post is low and a good

Fig. 8.2 *Weakside Help. Defensive players are overplaying any opponent one pass from the ball handler. The weak side corner defender has sagged into the lane.*

scorer, either the wing or corner defender (or both) may sag to help. A team may choose to sag the corner defender only, forcing a pass to the corner where the possibility of a trap results. If the corner player is a greater scoring threat than the wing, and the trap is not successful, it would be wiser to have the defender against the wing sag to help on the post.

13. When the corner has the ball and the post is low, the wing defender must be familiar with the game plan. She must know whether she is to sag off her opponent to help against a drive by the corner player or whether she is to overplay her opponent who is one pass away from the ball. Again this decision is based on the abilities of the opponents. If the corner player rarely drives or is not a good ball handler, the wing defender may continue to put pressure on her opponent, thereby encouraging the drive by the corner opponent. If the corner player is a danger to drive or if the wing is to put pressure on the post when she receives the ball, the wing defender must sag off her opponent and allow the pass back to her.

14. A similar decision must be made by the weak

a

b

c

Fig. 8.3 *Overplaying the Dribbler. The defensive player against the ball handler has been instructed to overplay light 21 to the right (a); as the dribbler is cut off (b), she dribbles to her left and is prevented from going back to her right (c).*

side guard when the opponents play with a double guard front. When the strong side guard has the ball, the weak side guard normally sags off her player to help against a drive down the lane or help on a pass into a high post. Defensing in this manner utilizes the principle that penetrating passes or moves should be prevented while passes away from the basket are allowed. On the other hand if a defensive team wishes to exert pressure on the guards at all times, the defensive players will not sag to help. Instead they will overplay their opponent, denying the ball at all times. In order to use this tactic, the defensive players against the guards must be skilled against a drive and be able to contain their opponent.

15. When a wing has the ball, the strong side guard must understand whether she sags to help against a drive or a pass to a high post or whether she continues to overplay her opponent who is one pass away from the ball. Basic philosophy calls for her to sag, but if her opponent is exceedingly dangerous, tactics may call for her to deny her the ball at all times.

16. On a screen away from the ball, the defender guarding the player who is screening must take a step and a half and deny the passing lane to the player for whom the screen was set. She then recovers on her own opponent and denies the pass to her (Fig. 8.4).

17. Defensive players must be prepared to help

Fig. 8.4 Denying the Pass. Player 32 passes (a) and moves away from the ball to screen as her teammate sets up her opponent (b); the screen is set (c), and 32's opponent denies the pass temporarily over the screen while allowing her teammate time to regain defensive position (d and e).

a

b

c

d

Fig. 8.5 *Weak Side Help. Players one pass away from the ball are in good defensive position (a). The ball handler eludes her defense player and the weak side corner player helps against the drive (b). Meanwhile, the weak side guard moves back to cover the free corner player (b and c), intercepts the ball (d), and the transition to the other end is made quickly.*

and recover on their own player whenever an opponent dribbles behind another offensive player or when an opponent does a reverse dribble. Basically defenders must be ready to help on any drive by an offensive player.

18. When the opposing team utilizes a weave offense, the defenders must know whether to stay with their own player or whether to switch automatically. Often coaches choose to have players switch opponents automatically if the weave is horizontal but not switch when the weave is vertical. This means that guards will switch with guards but will not switch onto a forward. This principle is utilized so that a height disparity does not

occur. If there is little difference in the height of all players, there is reason for all players to switch automatically.

19. When a corner or wing player has the ball and drives toward the goal, weak side forward help may be necessary. As help is given, the weak side guard must slide down the lane to prevent a pass to the "free" forward (Fig. 8.5).

NORMAL MAN-TO-MAN DEFENSE

Under normal circumstances defenders contest the passing lane to their opponent on any penetrating

Drills for Man-to-Man Defense

Players should review the techniques and drills found in Chapters 2 to 5. There is no need to repeat those drills here. Normal man-to-man alignment should be learned before any of the other man-to-man styles. The tight style should be attempted only when players are highly competent in man-to-man techniques.

1. Four offensive players and their opponents; no pivot player on her opponent. The four offensive players can take their position on the court with any one having the ball. On signal from the instructor, they pass the ball around the periphery. No offensive player may cut, and the ball may not be passed until the signal is given. By using this method each player's move can be observed and corrections made. Attention is focused on the defender guarding the ball handler, the contesting position of players near the ball, and the position of the weak side players.

2. One pivot player and either a guard or wing and their opponents. This drill can be done simultaneously with drill 1 if two separate areas are available. The wing or guard attempts to pass to the pivot while the defenders try to prevent it. This should be practiced at the high post between the pivot and guard, and at the high and medium post with the pivot working with a wing.

3. Five offensive players and their opponents. The drill is the same as drill 1, with the addition of the pivot player who has freedom of movement.

4. Same as drill 3, but allow the offense to pass at their own discretion.

5. Same as drill 3, but allow all players to maneuver as they wish. At first the instructor may wish to limit the types of screens that can be set and gradually add all of them.

6. Two teams on the court, with offensive players attempting double cuts whenever possible. Emphasis is placed on the correct action of the defenders directly involved and the sagging and floating of teammates to help.

7. Two teams — the offensive guard with the ball at the top of the circle and one step inside (closer to the basket than) her opponent. She tries to drive down the lane for a layup. Defensive players sag and float to prevent this action. Practice from both sides.

8. Same as drill 7, but a wing has the ball and is one step inside her defender. Later, place a player in the corner position and repeat the drill.

9. Two teams with the offense trying to get a lob pass into the medium pivot. Emphasis is on the floating of the weak side forward to guard the pivot as she receives the pass, (or cause a charge), and on the sagging of the weak side defending guard to cover the passing lane to the forward.

10. Six players — corner, wing, and post and their defenders. The ball is passed to the post and the wing and corner players react according to team strategy. The ball is returned to the original ball handler and defenders adjust their positions accordingly. Later, allow the three offensive players to pass the ball more quickly among themselves with the defenders reacting properly. Still later, let the three players maneuver on one-fourth of the court so that the defenders must react under more gamelike conditions.

11. Same as drill 10, but utilize four offensive and four defensive players, none of whom are in the post position. Use two guards and two wings or one point guard, two wings, and a corner player.

pass when their opponent is one pass away from the ball. This means that a wing would contest a pass when the ball is at the guard position; the corner would contest when the ball is at the wing position. The post player contests any pass since she is always one pass away from the ball.

Against a player who would receive a nonpenetrating pass, defenders generally sag to help against a drive or a pass into the lane. When the wing has the ball, the near side guard sags into the high post area; when the corner or post has the ball, the wing sags toward the lane to be in a helping position.

When a player is two passes away from the ball, her defender floats or sags into the lane to a helping position. There she is in position to help against a lob pass or to block her opponent cutting through the lane toward the ball.

Once a ball handler picks up her dribble, the defender should play her tight to place as much pressure as possible on her and possibly cause a ball handling error; but the defender *must not* foul.

TIGHT OR PRESSING MAN-TO-MAN DEFENSE

This style of defense places considerable pressure on the ball handler and those offensive players only one pass away from the ball. The defender guarding the ball handler plays tight on her even before she has dribbled. Since all other defenders near the ball are also playing tight against their opponents, there is no close help if the ball handler eludes the defender.

The team has the option of playing all players tight or having those defenders guarding players two passes away from the ball to float or sag into the lane to help. The latter tactic seems more advisable. At least some help is available on a drive, backdoor cut, or lob pass. Because of the pressure it exerts against the offense, it is a particularly good style of play to use against a poor ball handling team. Players may lose their composure and commit ball handling errors.

The pressure defense may also be used when a team must gain possession of the ball when it is behind in score. It also is useful to influence the ball to be passed in a predetermined direction. By playing tight against the better players and loose against the less skillful players, the defenders may influence the ball toward the poorer players.

MAN-TO-MAN OFFENSE

Against a man-to-man defense, teams rely on cutting maneuvers, screens of various kinds, and scissor maneuvers to free a player for a high percentage shot. Whenever a man-to-man defense is encountered, a team should quickly analyze whether the opponents play tight or loose, whether they sag and/or float, under what conditions (if any) they switch, which players possess defensive weaknesses, and which defenders are the primary rebounders. Whatever defensive weaknesses are discovered should be exploited.

Basic Principles to Follow Against a Man-to-Man Defense

1. The basic technique to free a player is by means of a screen. The type or types of screens selected depend upon the offensive system devised, but any or all of them are effective against this type of defense. As the reader knows, the screen may be set toward or away from the ball, and the screen need not be set necessarily where a defender is positioned. A player should roll after she sets a screen on the ball. One of the offensive players involved in the screen should be free if the timing of the moves and cuts is perfected.

2. Lateral or rear screens may be set anywhere on the court for a teammate to use. If a player has a favorite place on the court from which to shoot, a teammate may set a screen at that site to free the player for a shot from that position. A screen of this nature may also be set to allow a cutter to cut off it or to allow a dribbler to drive around the screen. The purpose of both tactics is to free the attack player momentarily from her defender.

3. Prior to using a screen the player for whom the screen is set must always fake in the opposite direction. She is responsible for making use of the screen. She must run her opponent into it. This tactic is necessary if the screen is to be effective.

4. The player being guarded by the weakest defensive opponent should be encouraged and given opportunities to work one-on-one against her. This is done by clearing one side of the court to provide the offensive player with space in which to maneuver against her opponent.

5. If the defenders use sagging and floating techniques, the offensive players being guarded by this method should maneuver to become free. By cutting away from the ball, they force their opponent to move away from the ball also, thus making their sagging and floating techniques less effective. Teammates can also set screens away from the ball to allow the offensive players being guarded in this manner to use them to free themselves for a pass.

6. There are two effective ways of dealing with a team that uses pressing measures in the frontcourt. A team may use lateral screens near the ball or rear or lateral screens away from the ball to free the offensive players. When guarding closely, defenders are less able to avoid lateral screens. The attack players should also be skilled in backdoor maneuvers and use them effectively. A few successful layups scored by this means tend to make the defense a little more "honest" (guard more loosely). Players must learn not to fight the pressure, but to go backdoor or screen for a teammate.

7. If the defense overplays against lateral screens on the ball to make the screen less effective, the attack should cut away from the screen on numerous occasions. This move also tends to force the defense to guard in a more normal manner.

8. The offense should maneuver to acquire a disparity in heights and/or abilities against a team that utilizes a switching man-to-man defense. The offense should use numerous guard-forward, guard-pivot, and pivot-forward screens. This action should produce a height advantage for one of the attack players, and this tactic should be exploited.

9. The offensive team should employ lob passes over the defender's head against a team that fronts the pivot player in the medium or high pivot position. Whenever the weak side forward views the pivot being played in this manner, she should cut toward the strong side so that her opponent cannot float and intercept the pass to the pivot or be in a position to challenge the pivot once she receives the pass.

10. Once a player receives the ball, she must square up to the hoop. This position makes her potentially more dangerous and also allows her to pass in a number of directions. The player is far less likely to have a pass intercepted when she assumes this stance. Once square, she wants to look for her shot, a drive or to pass; and after looking to pass, she must also reconsider her other options because a defender may have opened the possibility of a shot or drive by moving to cut off a passing lane. This ability to read a change in a defender's position is a sign of an experienced player.

11. A player with the ball must fake adequately before passing. All fakes should be made with wrist action so that the ball may be released quickly. The ball must remain in the center of the body, either at chest level or overhead, so that the ball may be released quickly in any direction.

12. Offensive balance must be maintained so that players are in position to rebound and to hustle back on defense should the ball be intercepted. When running a motion offense, particular attention must be given to this aspect. When using a pattern, players tend to retain better balance because the pattern is devised with this principle in mind.

OFFENSIVE ALIGNMENTS

When playing a motion or pattern style of play it is possible to establish the offense with different alignments. The selected alignment is based on player personnel and their attributes. For example, a team with a tall, rather immobile player should choose an alignment that would permit her to maneuver under the basket. A team without tall players would benefit from playing from a posture other than a pivot.

The alignments are named by designating the number of players furthest from the basket (closer to the division line) first followed by those closer to the basket. For example, a three-two alignment would have three players on the outside and two players closer to the basket.

One-Three-One

The alignment shown in Fig. 8.6 offers good possibilities for a double post to work in tandem (one high and the other low). An offense can be designed in which the pivots interchange; or, if one pivot is less agile, she may remain primarily in the low post while the other is assigned the high or medium post position. This is a good formation for a team with three small players and two tall players. The best

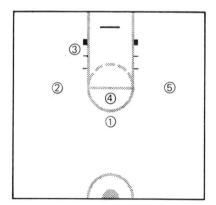

Fig. 8.6 *One-Three-One Offensive Alignment.*

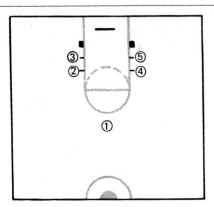

Fig. 8.7 *One-Four Offensive Alignment (Stack).*

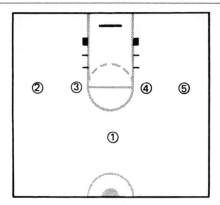

Fig. 8.9 *One-Four Offensive Alignment (Free Throw Line).*

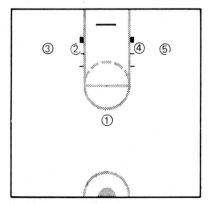

Fig. 8.8 *One-Four Offensive Alignment (Baseline).*

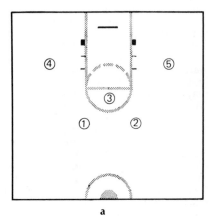

a

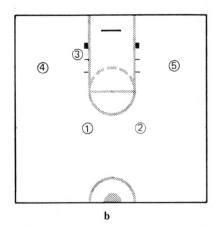

b

Fig. 8.10 *Two-Three Offensive Alignment. Possible placement of players: 3 is in the high post position (a); 3 is in the low post position (b).*

ball handler of the three small players should be in the middle with the other two at the wing positions.

One-Four

This configuration popularized by Cousy is also called the stack offense. It is an excellent formation for a team with one good ball handler and four tall players. The position of the players is shown in Fig. 8.7. Rarely seen is the baseline one-four alignment shown in Fig. 8.8. The free throw one-four alignment shown in Fig. 8.9 is seen more often.

Two-Three

This formation utilizes two players on the outside with three close to the basket and generally involves

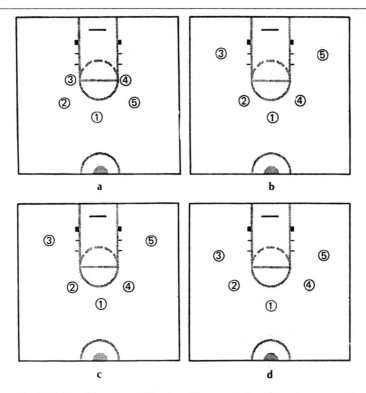

Fig. 8.11 *One-Two-Two Offensive Alignment. Possible placement of players: 3 and 4 are playing a double pivot in parallel positions (a). All align without a pivot player to allow drives and cuts through the lane and to permit a flash pivot (any player moving into pivot position) (b–d). Players 3 and 5 may interchange positions as the ball is reversed.*

a post player at the high, medium, or low post position. This alignment provides good rebound strength and is effective for a team with two short players and three good rebounders. Fig. 8.10 shows possible placement of players for this formation.

One-Two-Two

This alignment provides numerous possibilities for player positioning. It can be initiated from a double post (Fig. 8.11a). It may also be initiated without post players and all players on the outside (Fig. 8.11b and c). Another alternative is to utilize a corner player. The post and corner player may interchange positions when the ball is reversed or the corner player may move from one corner to the other if the post player does not have the attributes to go to the corner (Fig. 8.11d). A team with three small players and two tall players may choose an alignment utilizing the double post. A team with all short players may

select any of the formations where all the players are on the perimeter. A team with a good corner shooter should take advantage of her assets.

Four-One

Fig. 8.12 shows the basic formation. This alignment is often used against a zone defense because it involves overload principles. It is not used as often against man-to-man defense although the Drake Shuffle is an outgrowth of this alignment.

SELECTING AN ALIGNMENT

Before choosing an offensive alignment from which to start, a coach must carefully evaluate the team's personnel. Ball handling ability, including both passing and dribbling ability, shooting, and rebounding strengths must be carefully assessed.

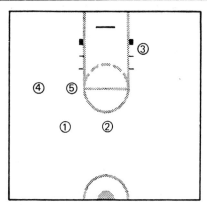

Fig. 8.12 *Four-One Alignment (Overload).*

Once this is done the coach should have sufficient data on each player to develop an offense that is suitable and effective for the team members. It is extremely important that an offense is developed for the personnel rather than trying to mold personnel into a particular offense. This is particularly true at the high school level where coaches must utilize the players available. It is somewhat different at the college level where coaches can recruit the types of players who will fit into the offense that the coach prefers.

If the analysis of personnel suggests that the tall players are better than the small players, the coach should consider a double post or triple post offense. If only one tall player is available, it should be obvious that a single post offense must be introduced. When a team has no inside strength, it may choose a spread offense without a post player. When three small, quick players are highly skilled, a coach may choose to go with a three-guard offense.

Once the abilities of players and the team as a whole are assessed the coach needs to consider which of the offensive alignments will best suit the team's efforts. If the team plans to operate with a single post, a two-three or a one-three-one with a corner player are the most useful alignments. The four-one alignment is also a possibility.

To utilize a double post, the one-three-one, and one-four are the most commonly used alignments. The stack is also a possibility, but often the stack rotates into a one-four or one-three-one alignment after the first pass. To run a triple post offense the stack concept with modifications is generally used. If a spread offense is desirable, a one-two-two alignment may be used to force the opponents away

from the basket and nullify some of their strength (although it might also cause the opposition to play zone).

The coach must recognize that in order to use a point offense (one-four, one-three-one or one-two-two), the team must have an exceptionally good ball handler. Otherwise the defensive team will place a great deal of pressure on the ball handler, which should lead to a number of turnovers. When a point player makes a bad pass, it usually results in an easy layup for the opponents. Lacking a good ball handler, a team should use a double guard front.

When a double or triple post offense is chosen, there is less opportunity for drives by outside players because the lane is more clogged. A corner offense provides the opponents with opportunities to trap in the corner, particularly if the corner player is short. The corner player also is placed at a disadvantage for rebounding.

After carefully weighing all of the factors involved, the coach must then proceed to developing an offense.

DEVELOPING AN OFFENSE

Undoubtedly one of the most important decisions a coach must make is the style of offense that the team will run. Perfecting an offense takes considerable effort because of the timing involved in both player movement and ball movement. It is difficult to change offenses midseason, although if an offense is producing little in the way of desirable results, it may be better to attempt a different offense. Some teams with veteran and highly skilled players may run two or three offenses. All teams do not have the talent to attempt this. It is far better to execute one offense well than several offenses in a mediocre manner. A coach must also remember that the opposing team may know the offense as well as the team running it, but proper execution will still beat the defense. Execution is the key!

When selecting an offense the coach may choose one that is very simple with only two or three basic moves. This choice might be wise with inexperienced players and only one or two talented individuals. A more complex offense would be selected for more gifted players. Again it should be emphasized that the offense must be suitable for the players involved. The coach may find an offense in a textbook that meets the needs of team personnel or the coach may decide to develop an offense. More coaches should use their own creativity and use the principles of cutting, screening, and scissoring found in Chapters 2, 4, and 5 to develop an offense based on the talents of team personnel. Certain cuts and screens can be incorporated into the offense which will maximize the talents of the players.

SET PLAYS VERSUS CONTINUITY OFFENSE

In general, offenses are no longer established with a series of set plays, which are totally unrelated to each other. There are times when set plays are utilized, particularly when maneuvering for the last shot to tie a game or go ahead; to exploit a poor defensive player or one in foul trouble; or after a time-out. However, these instances fall into the category of special situations and do not occur continually throughout a contest.

Most offenses devised today have some degree of continuity. A basic pattern is run and players move from one position to another in a predetermined fashion. Certain options are developed so that advantage may be taken of the way in which the opposition tries to defend the maneuvers. By running a continuity offense, the players can keep the court balanced for rebounding and defensive purposes. Player movement is constant, and players know where to go and what to do on each pass.

The motion offense, which is popular today, is not really a continuity offense but does utilize certain principles so that court balance can be maintained.

PROVEN OFFENSES

There follows a series of suggested offenses that have been proven over the years. Space does not permit the inclusion of all of the popular offenses, although an attempt will be made to discuss at least one offense using the most popular alignments.

DOUBLE POST OFFENSE

This type of offense is excellent for use with two tall players who can maneuver and shoot within the lane area and three other players who are mobile and able to interchange positions. The post players may play in a tandem position (one high and one low), in a double high post, or double low post position. Which position is selected for the post players depends on their abilities. If they are both agile, a double high post or tandem position can be used. If neither is agile, a double low post should be used.

Use of the double pivot offense places much stress on the defense because two players are always close to a high percentage shooting area. This tends to make the opponents sag and float and to provide opportunities for medium range shots for the other three attack players. It is also a good posture from which to operate when the opponents are playing a zone defense.

ONE-FOUR OFFENSE

Options are determined by what the point player does. If a pass is made to the post, one option is initiated. If the point dribbles toward a wing, another option is started. If the point passes to a wing, two other options are possible. Therefore, all players' moves are determined by the first pass by the point. The offense is as successful as the point player in exploiting defensive weaknesses and the ability of the two post players to work together. This is a complex offense with many options all of which retain a double post alignment with both posts high or a high-low alignment.

Certain rules are followed:

1. After passing the ball, move to a new position.
2. After receiving a pass, work with the player who passed to you.
3. The wing must clear every time the point dribbles toward her (unless she calls "back").
4. The onside post player must screen for any player who dribbles near her and then the post must roll.
5. Players 1, 2 and 3 interchange positions.
6. Rebounding assignments:
   a. No. 1 always moves to the free throw line.
   b. Nos. 4 and 5 always go to the side position; if one shoots, she goes to the front position.
   c. Nos. 2 and 3:
      1) the onside wing goes to the front rebound position unless a post shoots, in which case, she goes to a side position.
      2) the weak side wing goes back to the deep position.

Several options may be developed, only a few of which are shown:

Fig. 8.13a–d shows the options for the Post Series.

Fig. 8.14 shows the options for the Drive Series. Fig. 8.14a–d shows options when the point drives with the aid of a screen, and the defenders switch opponents. Fig. 8.14e–g shows options when the defenders do *not* switch opponents.

Figure 8.15 shows the Go Behind Series. Fig. 8.15a shows the options the wing has. Fig. 8.15b and

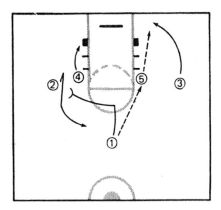

Fig. 8.13a *Post Series. Player 1 tries to hit either post; 3 cuts backdoor and receives the pass. If X_4 takes her, 3 passes to 4.*

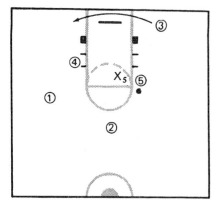

Fig. 8.13b *Player 5 has the option of going one-on-one. She looks to see where X_5 is playing and executes a power move to the hoop (to the right if X_5 is positioned as shown). If 5 cannot pass to 3 or make a power move, she turns to face the basket and goes one-on-one after 3 clears.*

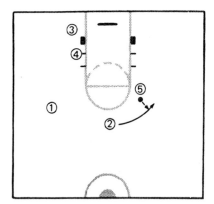

Fig. 8.13c *If 5 cannot go one-on-one, 2 continues back of 5 for a jump shot or drive.*

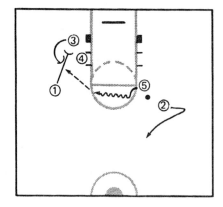

Fig. 8.13d *If the pass to 2 is not open, 5 dribbles along the free throw line and passes to 3 who comes off 1's screen. If nothing materializes, 1 can clear and 3 dribbles back to the wing and players are positioned for another effort.*

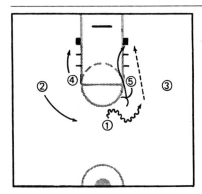 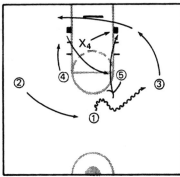 

Fig. 8.14a Drive Series. When the point cannot get the ball into the post, 1 continues to dribble and one of the posts screens for her which keys the series. If X_1 anticipates the screen, 1 must go left. Player 5 rolls close to the lane line and 1 must get the ball to 5 if X_1 and X_5 switch.

Fig. 8.14b If X_1 and X_5 switch, 5 must work to get free. Player 3 clears. If X_4 helps on 5, 4 cuts to high post for the pass.

Fig. 8.14c If X_3 does not clear, 1 goes to weak side by dribbling and passing to 3.

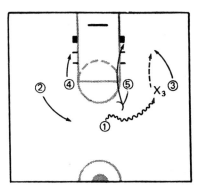 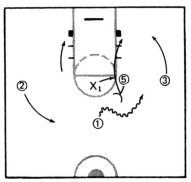 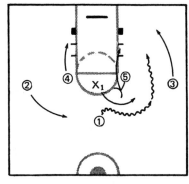

Fig. 8.14d If X_3 stops 1, 3 goes backdoor.

Fig. 8.14e If X_1 goes behind the screen, 1 shoots a jump shot behind the screen.

Fig. 8.14f If X_1 goes over the top of the screen, 1 drives. Player 5 stays high.

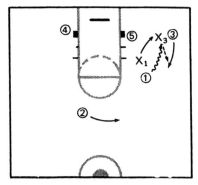

Fig. 8.14g If 1 is unable to pass to 3 or 5, 1 drives at X_3 and hands off to 3 who shoots, passes to 5 or out to 2. If 2 cannot shoot, continue the dribble interchange with 1 until an opening occurs.

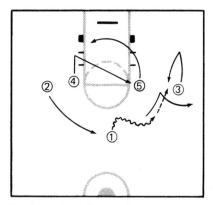

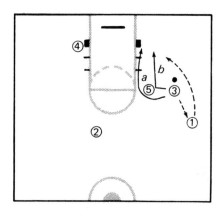

Fig. 8.15a *Go Behind Series. This series is useful when the post's defender switches on screens with the wing but not with the point. Player 1 cuts inside of 3 and calls "back" and moves behind 3. Player 3 has the option to drive baseline or drive off the post; pass to the post and go behind; pass to the post and screen for her or cut to the basket; or pass back to 1.*

Fig. 8.15b *Player 3 takes path a on cut to basket. If X_3 sags off to help on post, 3 cuts at X_3, reverses and takes path b. If 3 has a height advantage, she works to get free in the low post area; otherwise, she clears.*

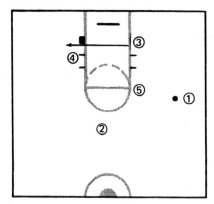

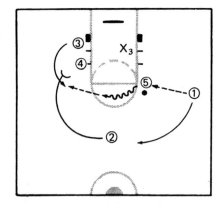

Fig. 8.15c *Player 1 now has the same options as 3 had in 8.15a.*

Fig. 8.15d *If the ball is passed in to 5, 1 can cut behind 5, screen for 5 or cut to the basket; but if X_3 does not clear, 5 enters into the weak side series.*

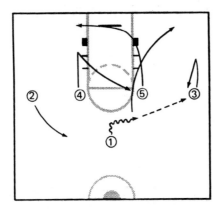

Fig. 8.16a *Corner Series. On pass to wing, 1 calls "corner" and cuts.*

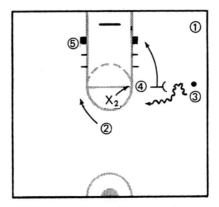

Fig. 8.16b *Player 4 screens and 3 shoots behind it or drives to hoop if there is no switch and X_2 does not sag. If X_4 switches, 3 passes to 4; or if X_2 sags, 3 passes to 2. If the pass goes to 2, 2 drives and 5 screens and rolls.*

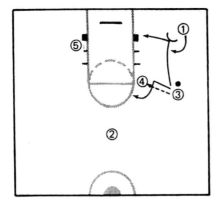

Fig. 8.16c *Player 3 may pass to 4 and go behind or 3 may screen for 1 and roll.*

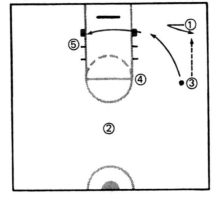

Fig. 8.16d *Player 3 can pass to 1 and clear. Player 1 can pass to 3 if free. If not, 4 screens and rolls for 1.*

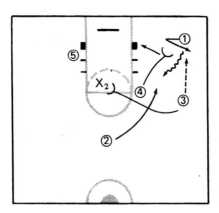

Fig. 8.16e *Player 3 can pass to the corner and screen opposite when X_2 sags. Player 4 screens for 1 and rolls as 3 screens for 2.*

c shows the options if the ball is passed back to player 1 and 8.15d shows the options when the ball is passed into the post.

Fig. 8.16 shows the Corner Series. Fig. 8.16a–e shows the options available to the wing.

ONE-FOUR OFFENSE FROM A STACK

This offense has been run by Notre Dame; its virtue is its simplicity. It is played with a double post with both post players high or one high and the other low. Basically there are two options. When the ball is passed in to the post from the point player, a scissor maneuver is initiated (Fig. 8.17a–c). When the ball is passed to a wing, the point shuffles off the post and posts low. If the wing passes to the post, the wing screens low (Fig. 8.18a–b). Weak side moves are shown in Fig. 8.18c–f. Whenever one post has the ball, the other post and weak side wing execute one of the possible options for freeing a player on the weak side. The strong side wing and point player may also utilize weak side options to free each other.

Fig. 8.17 shows the Notre Dame offense. Fig. 8.17a shows the starting alignment (which may also flex into a one-three-one formation).

Fig. 8.17b and c shows the moves when the point passes in to the post.

Fig. 8.18 a and b shows the options of the strong side players when the ball is passed to the wing who passes it to the post.

Fig. 8.18d–f shows the weak side options.

ONE-THREE-ONE

A double post in this alignment is very common. It provides opportunities for both posts to play high and low and opens numerous scoring opportunities. If one post player is a better passer, an attempt should be made to run the offense to her side so that she can operate from the high post position. The offense does demand the interchange of the high and low post positions. It provides opportunities for a strong wing player to go one-on-one in each of the options.

Fig. 8.19 shows the basic starting position.

Fig. 8.20 shows the Corner Series. Fig. 8.20a and b shows a pass to the high post and the options off it; Fig. 8.20c–e shows the options when the ball is passed to the corner; and Fig. 8.20f and g show the options when the ball is reversed.

Fig. 8.21 shows the Guard Behind Series. Fig. 8.21a–c shows the options when the defense switches; Fig. 8.21d and e shows a screen for the high post; and Fig. 8.21f and g shows the use of a high post screen.

Fig. 8.22 shows the Screen Away Series. Fig. 8.22a–c shows the options if the defenders do *not* switch. Fig. 8.22d–f shows the options if the defenders switch.

SINGLE PIVOT OFFENSE

A team that chooses to use a single post offense has one player who operates at an optimum level within 15 ft. of the basket. She generally is not sufficiently

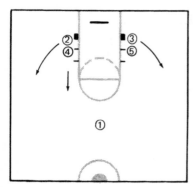

Fig. 8.17a *One-four offense started from a stack with 2 and 3 cutting to the wing position.*

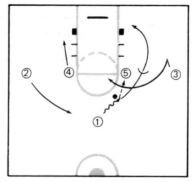

Fig. 8.17b *Player 1 passes to 5, and a scissor action (split the post) is started. Player 1 screens for 3 and continues to basket. Player 3 cuts off the screen and around 5.*

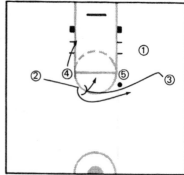

Fig. 8.17c *If neither player is open, 3 screens for 2 and rolls as 4 cuts.*

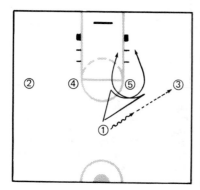

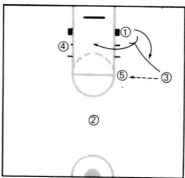

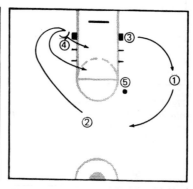

Fig. 8.18a *Player 1 passes to a wing and shuffle cuts off the post. Player 1 reads how X_1 is playing and cuts to the other side of 5. Player 3 passes to 1. If X_5 helps against 1, 3 passes to 5 for a shot. If 5 is overplayed, 5 exchanges with 4.*

Fig. 8.18b *When 3 passes to 5, 3 screens for 1 and rolls; screener will often be free. With any weak side move (shown in c–f) 5 has two players moving high and two players cutting into the lane. The timing of the cuts is crucial.*

Fig. 8.18c *If 1 or 3 is not free, 5 looks to the weak side. Player 4 screens and rolls and 2 cuts.*

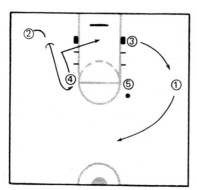

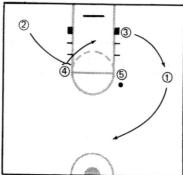

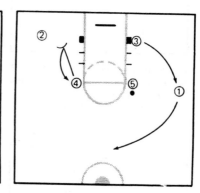

Fig. 8.18d *Player 4 holds high; 2 sets a screen; and 4 cuts off it for a different weak side move.*

Fig. 8.18e *Player 2 fakes a rear screen and cuts for a weakside move.*

Fig. 8.18f *Player 4 fakes a screen for 2 and cuts back for the pass.*

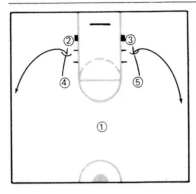  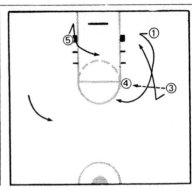

Fig. 8.19 *One-Three-One with a Double Post. Players 4 and 5 downscreen to free the wings. The ball side post cuts high.*

Fig. 8.20a *Corner Series. Player 1 passes to 3 and cuts to the corner. Player 5 screens for 4 who cuts high.*

Fig. 8.20b *Player 3 passes to 4 who may shoot or pass to 3 or 1 on the splitting move or to 5. If nothing materializes, 1 continues to the point position, 3 goes out to the wing, and the original alignment is restored.*

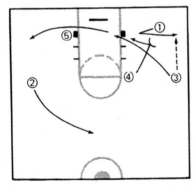 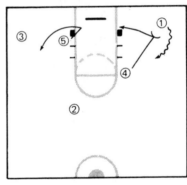 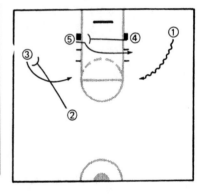

Fig. 8.20c *If 3 cannot pass to 4, 3 passes to 1 in the corner and cuts for the basket. If 3 is not open, 4 screens the corner and rolls to the hoop.*

Fig. 8.20d *Player 1 drives over the screen. If a shot is not open, 1 continues to dribble.*

Fig. 8.20e *As 1 comes off the screen, 2 screens down for 3 who cuts for a jump shot at the foul line. At the same time 4 continues her roll and screens for 5. Player 1 can pass to 5 or 3.*

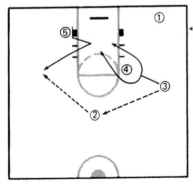

Fig. 8.20f *If 3 cannot pass to 4 or to 1, 3 passes to 2 who looks for 5 either cutting out or going backdoor. Player 5 looks for 3.*

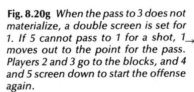

Fig. 8.20g *When the pass to 3 does not materialize, a double screen is set for 1. If 5 cannot pass to 1 for a shot, 1 moves out to the point for the pass. Players 2 and 3 go to the blocks, and 4 and 5 screen down to start the offense again.*

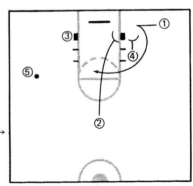

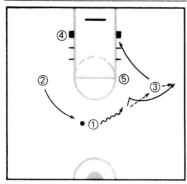 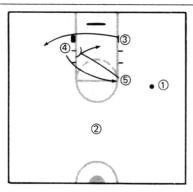 

Fig. 8.21a *Guard Behind Series. Player 1 passes to 3, goes behind and receives a pass from 3. If the defense switches players, 3 cuts to the basket for a return pass.*

Fig. 8.21b *If 1 cannot pass to 3, 5 downscreens for 4 and 5 rolls if the defense switches.*

Fig. 8.21c *If neither 4 or 5 is open, 4 continues and screens for 1 and rolls to the basket.*

 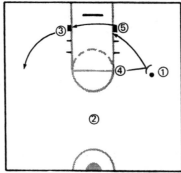 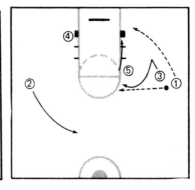

Fig. 8.21d *If the defense does not switch, 3 screens along the lane for 5. If 5 is not open, 3 continues and screens for 4.*

Fig. 8.21e *If 4 is not open, she continues and screens for 1. Player 5 clears so 4 can roll.*

Fig. 8.21f *Another route which 3 can take is to cut over the top of 5 for a jump shot if X_3 sags or to cut baseline if X_3 plays tight. Player 5 may be open if the defense helps.*

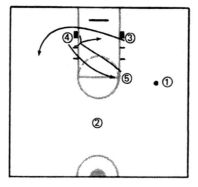

Fig. 8.21g *If 3 or 5 are not open, 5 downscreens and the same options open as before. Throughout this series, 1 may need to dribble to prevent a violation and to keep her defender occupied.*

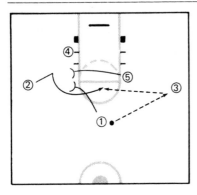
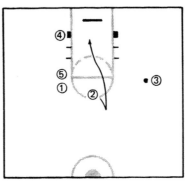
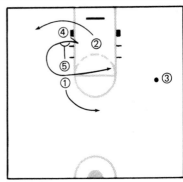

Fig. 8.22a *Screen Away Series. Player 1 passes and screens for 2. Player 5 also moves to screen.*

Fig. 8.22b *If 2 is being overplayed, she takes X_2 higher and cuts backdoor.*

Fig. 8.22c *If 2 is not open, 5 down-screens for a pass to 4.*

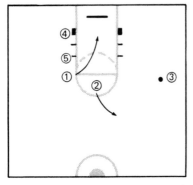
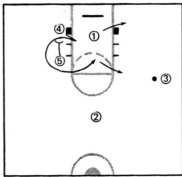
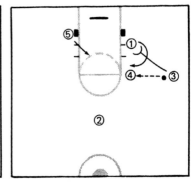

Fig. 8.22d *If the defenders switch on the double screen, 1 rolls. If X_4 helps against 1, 1 should pass to 4.*

Fig. 8.22e *If 1 is not open, 5 screens down for 4. If 4 is not open, 4 stays in the high post for a pass.*

Fig. 8.22f *Player 3 passes to 4 and 3 screens for 1. 4 passes to 1 or to 3 who posts up or to 5 cutting into the lane. Player 1 fills the wing spot, and 3 fills the opposite wing.*

mobile to maneuver as effectively outside of the lane area. She is often the tallest player or the best shooter on the team in this area. She should be the strongest rebounder on the team because, by virtue of her position in relation to the basket, she is in the best position to rebound and is involved in rebounding on every play.

When she plays in a high post position her main function is to feed cutters as they cut off her or as they utilize a screen from another player to free themselves for a pass. When playing in the medium post position, the pivot is in an excellent position to shoot or to pass to cutters. When cutting across the lane in this position she must have the ability to fake and front her opponent so that she is free in this high percentage shooting range. When in the low

post area she must maneuver constantly to get free to receive a pass. She is too close to the basket in this position to allow players to cut off her. When she gets the ball she must shoot or pass back out if she is double-teamed and unable to obtain a good shot.

Regardless of the position she is playing she must use various tactics to free herself from her opponent. The pivot is always guarded closely unless her opponent has been forced into a screen. This means that she must acquire a number of different moves to get free and be able to move or drive either to her left or right. She must be able to protect the ball well in this congested area. She must rarely take more than one bounce on any offensive move.

A team must work to pass the ball in to the pivot player. Because of her position in relation to the basket, she is always within a good shooting distance. In addition to the scoring possibilities this presents, it also forces the defense to make some adjustments. When a pivot player is successful in shooting, defensive players guarding other opponents sag or float away from their opponent to assist their teammate in limiting the effectiveness of the post player. When this happens, other offensive players are freed by the very action of the defensive players. If a pivot receives the ball and defenders sag on her, she should immediately pass the ball to one of her free teammates. The faster the post is able to find a free teammate, the greater exploitation can be made of the defender's action. As the opponents learn that their sagging tactics permit outside shots, they should begin to delay their moves against the pivot; this in turn should open the passing or cutting lanes to the pivot once more. Providing a team has accurate outside shooting and an effective pivot player, extensive pressure is placed on the defensive team to limit the scoring of their opponents. Because of the effectiveness of this style of offense, it is one of the most widely used today.

SINGLE POST FROM A ONE-THREE-ONE ALIGNMENT

This offense utilizes a post player who starts high and slides around the lane to the ball, a point player who always remains in that position, a corner player who moves to the ball side, and two wing players who exchange sides of the court.

The offense is designed to take advantage of a strong wing player and a good shooting corner player. The play should be directed toward the strong side at the outset. It allows the strong side wing to shoot on the outside and to receive the ball on a cutting maneuver. The defense has difficulty in counteracting both effectively. The accurate shooting corner player entices the defense to play tight instead of sagging against the cutter. The point player is utilized primarily as a passer but should be able to shoot from the top of the key if the defense sags off of her.

The pattern is basically very simple and easy to learn. Fig. 8.23a shows the basic starting alignment. Fig. 8.23b shows the options when the ball is passed to the corner. Fig. 8.23c–e shows the continuity when the ball is reversed. Fig. 8.23f shows the realignment of players when the ball is reversed

again. The pattern demands patience in waiting for a good shot and requires the reading of the defense for effective execution.

SINGLE POST FROM A TWO-THREE ALIGNMENT

Although the two-three alignment is not retained throughout the offensive thrust, it does provide some flexibility in allowing initial penetration from either side of the court rather than from the point position. Two ball handlers are used and they may play either at the point or on the wing. Two forwards play at either wing position and on occasion at the high and low post. Opportunities are provided for the wing to go one-on-one.

The offensive moves eliminate some weak side help. It therefore is effective against a team that is not particularly strong on straight man-to-man coverage. As is the case with most offenses, it is designed to exploit a particular defensive weakness. Scoring thrusts in the lane are designed for each position.

Fig. 8.24a–c shows the options to free a wing. Fig. 8.24d–f shows the options for a guard and Fig. 8.24g–i shows the options for freeing the post player.

TWO-THREE CORNER OFFENSE

This offense utilizes two ball handlers, either one of whom goes to the corner. If a team has a short player and wants to use the basic principles of this offense, the short player should be designated as the point player and the other guard should go to the corner on the strong side. This strategy would eliminate encouraging a trap against a short player in the corner.

Basically there are three options run from this formation and opportunities should occur for all players to obtain good shots in the lane. The offense is primarily geared toward screens away from the ball, although the pinch post series is also used on the reverse option. The position of the players should provide good offensive rebounding.

Should the defense deny certain passes, an entry for an option may be precluded; therefore, it is possible that wings and guards may interchange positions. It may be undesirable to have a wing at the point position (depending upon her ball handling abilities). If this is the case, an adjustment can be made. It is quite conceivable, however, that the wing may end up in the corner. Strong shooting and

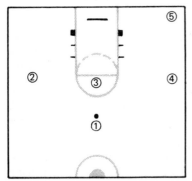

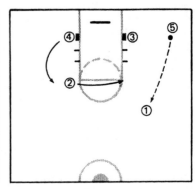

Fig. 8.23a *One-Three-One Offense with Single Post. Whenever possible the ball is passed to the strong side. This eliminates the need for 5 to cut to the other side.*

Fig. 8.23b *Player 1 passes to 4, and 3 cuts to the edge of the lane. Player 4 passes to 3 if she is free. If not, 4 passes to 5 and cuts. Player 3 slides down the lane. Player 5 looks to either 4 or 3.*

Fig. 8.23c *Player 5 passes to 1. Player 2 cuts to fill the high post, and 4 fills the wing.*

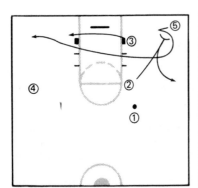

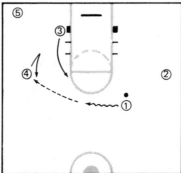

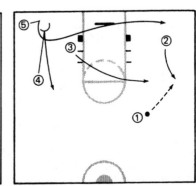

Fig. 8.23d *Player 2 continues and downscreens for 5, who cuts to the opposite corner. Player 2 fills the wing.*

Fig. 8.23e *If Player 1 reverses the ball, 3 cuts up and the offense can be run to the other side with 4 again in the strong side wing position.*

Fig. 8.23f *If 4 is being overplayed, 1 passes to 2 as she pops out. Player 4 downscreens for 5 who cuts to the corner, and 4 fills the wing. Player 3 cuts to the high post, and the offense can be started again.*

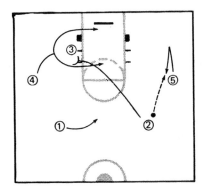 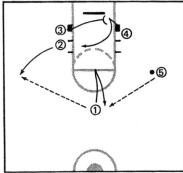 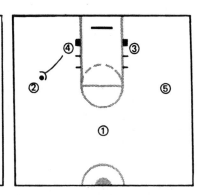

Fig. 8.24a *Single Post from a Two-Three Alignment. Wing cut. Player 2 passes to 5 and sets a double screen with 3; 4 cuts off the screen. If X_3 helps, 5 should lob to 3.*

Fig. 8.24b *If 4 is not free, the ball is reversed through 1 to 2. Player 3 screens for 4.*

Fig. 8.24c *The ball may be reversed or 2 and 4 can work two player moves.*

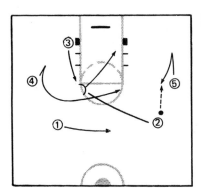 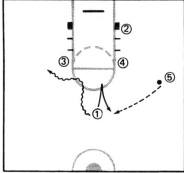 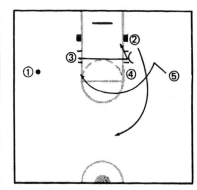

Fig. 8.24d *Guard Cut. Player 2 passes to 5 and sets a double screen with 3. Player 4 cuts over the screen, and immediately 2 cuts down the lane. If 2 is not free, 5 and 4 can utilize two player moves and 2 clears to the corner.*

Fig. 8.24e *Player 5 passes to 1 who works the pinch post or other two player moves with 3.*

Fig. 8.24f *If nothing materializes, 3 sets a double screen for 5 to cut over, and 3 cuts to the basket. Player 2 moves to the point and the pattern continues.*

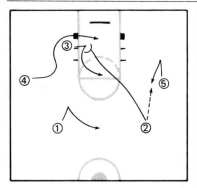 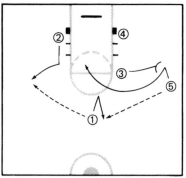 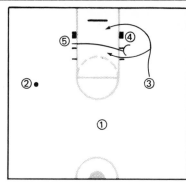

Fig. 8.24g *Center Cut. Player 2 passes to 5 and screens for 3; 4 cuts off 3, and 3 cuts over the top of 2.*

Fig. 8.24h *If nothing opens, the ball is reversed. Player 3 screens for 5 who cuts while looking for a pass from 2.*

Fig. 8.24i *Player 5 cuts over to set a double screen for 3.*

driving from the corner are essential to make this offense effective.

Fig. 8.25a shows the initial thrust. The guard who passes the ball to the wing always cuts to the corner. Fig. 8.25b–d shows the post option. Every effort should be made to pass the ball in to the post as often as possible. If the wing cannot pass in to the post, she reverses the ball as shown in Fig. 25e–g. The third option is the pass to the corner as shown in Fig. 8.25h–k.

TRIPLE POST OFFENSE

The value of a triple post offense lies in its rebounding potential and the pressure it places on the opposing defense. This type of offense is usually selected when a team has three tall players who are reasonably agile. A triple post offense requires one of the post players to play at the wing or corner position, depending upon the choice of the coach. Added pressure is placed on the defense when all of the posts can interchange positions. This means that defensive players must be equally adept at playing in the post and outside. Not all players have this capability! The disadvantage of this type of offense is that a team may sacrifice speed and quickness for height.

Two examples of a triple post offense are shown. In one offense a post goes to the wing and in the second offense a post goes to the corner. In either offense all three posts may be in the position outside the lane or the offense can be adjusted so that only one player moves to the wing or corner position. The first offense has a simple design while the second offense has more options.

TRIPLE POST WITH A POST TO THE WING

Fig. 8.26a–e shows the basic continuity of the offense. An attempt should be made to enter the ball on the side with the single post. She should be the best wing player of the three. The ball should not be forced to that side however, as one of the posts on the stack side can cut out to the wing.

Options may be developed from this alignment. For example, in Fig. 8.26c the low post can cut high to alleviate pressure if the ball cannot be entered in that position. In Fig. 8.26d the ball handler can dribble to the corner and allow the other two posts to screen for each other in the low post area. During any of the manuevers, the ball should be passed inside whenever possible.

TRIPLE POST WITH A POST TO THE CORNER

The strongest corner player is always positioned in the low post on the stack side. The wing player always goes to the same side as the single post. To vary the side to which the ball is entered, the single post must exchange sides of the lane with the stacked posts. It is the single post who dictates the side to which the ball in run.

The basic offense is run from the corner option shown in Fig. 8.27a–c. The offense can be adjusted if all posts cannot play equally well in the corner. One post can move from side to side. Options are designed to counteract pressure placed on the point player as shown in Fig. 8.27d–f. The wing

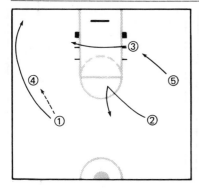

Fig. 8.25a *Two-Three Corner Offense. The guard who passes to the wing goes to the corner. If 2 passed to 5, 2 would go to the corner. On the pass, 3 cuts ball side, 5 goes to the low post, and 2 takes X_2 down and comes back.*

Fig. 8.25b *Post Option. Player 4 passes to 3 and screens for 1. Player 1 cuts for a jump shot and if the defense switches, 4 rolls. Player 5 clears.*

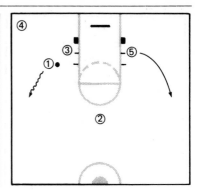

Fig. 8.25c *If nothing develops, 1 dribbles out and a new thrust is started.*

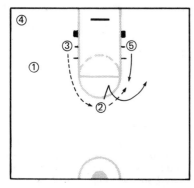

Fig. 8.25d *If 3 cannot pass to 1, she passes out to 2; 5 cuts to the high post. Player 2 can either pass to 5 and cut off her or dribble around her. Player 2 can go one-on-one if there is no switch or pass to 5 on the roll if the defense switches.*

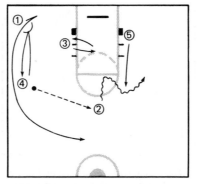

Fig. 8.25e *Reverse Option. Player 3 is not free so 4 reverses to 2; 2 passes to 3 who cuts half-way across the lane and clears to the same side. If 3 is not free, 2 uses 5 as a pinch post as described in Fig. 8.25d. As 2 uses the post, 4 downscreens and replaces herself as 1 goes to the point.*

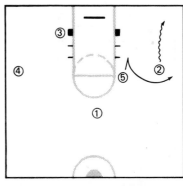

Fig. 8.25f *If nothing materializes, 2 dribbles to the corner; 5 goes to the wing, and the offense can be restarted.*

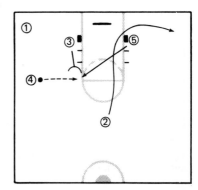

Fig. 8.25g *When 4 cannot get the ball to 3 or 2 because they are overplayed, 5 cuts to the high post. Player 2 cuts back door for a pass, and 3 screens for 5.*

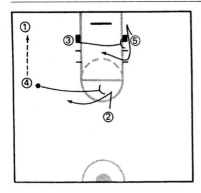

Fig. 8.25h *Corner Option. Player 4 passes to 1 and screens away for 2; simultaneously 3 screens for 5.*

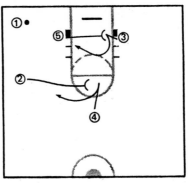

Fig. 8.25i *If nothing materializes, repeat.*

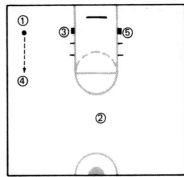

Fig. 8.25j *If the pass is made to the wing, any of the three options may be reinitiated.*

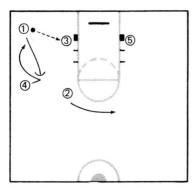

Fig. 8.25k *When 1 passes to 3, 1 screens for 4. Player 3 should be free as she comes off consecutive picks by 2 and 1.*

Fig. 8.26a *Triple Post. Player 1 passes to 3; 4 cuts across lane; and 5 cuts high.*

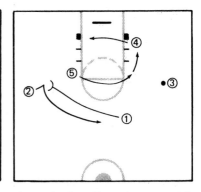

Fig. 8.26b *If 4 is fronted, 3 gives a lob pass. If nothing materializes, 4 clears and 5 makes her cut. When 1 is pressured, she exchanges with 2.*

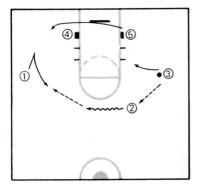

Fig. 8.26c *The ball may be reversed and passed to 5 for a short jump shot.*

Fig. 8.26d *Player 5 looks weak side for 3 as 4 clears. If 3 is not free, she cuts ball side.*

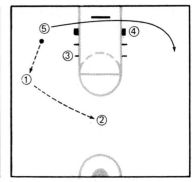

Fig. 8.26e *The ball is reversed and the options continue. If only 3 can play effectively on the wing, 5 stays in the low post and 3 can cut off 4 for the reversal action.*

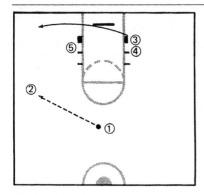

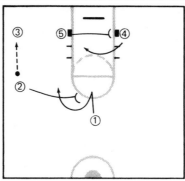

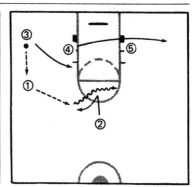

Fig. 8.27a *Triple Post. As 1 passes to 2, 3 cuts to the corner. Player 2 can pass to 3 or 5.*

Fig. 8.27b *Corner Option. If 2 passes to 3 and 5 is not free, she screens for 4. When the defense plays tight, 2 and 1 exchange positions.*

Fig. 8.27c *If a post is not free, the ball may be reversed. Player 4 cuts to the corner and 3 goes in to the post. If all post players cannot play in the corner, 3 can cut to the opposite corner.*

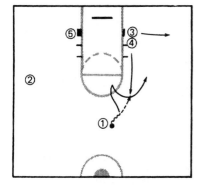

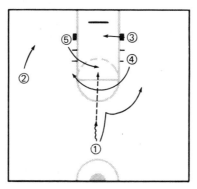

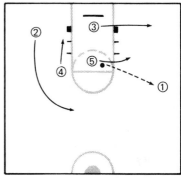

Fig. 8.27d *Guard Drive. When 1 is pressured, 4 cuts up for pinch post moves (1 either driving or passing to 4 and cutting off of 4). Player 3 cuts to the corner, and 1 and 4 have two player options. If the ball is passed to 3, the options shown in (b) and (c) are used.*

Fig. 8.27e *Post Option. When pressure is exerted early against 1, 5 cuts high, 2 goes back door, 4 and 3 cut.*

Fig. 8.27f *If none of these players is open, the ball is passed out to 1 and the continuity is restarted. Player 1 may also use 5 for pinch post moves or other two player options.*

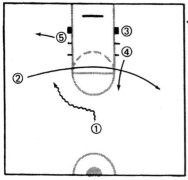

Fig. 8.27g *Wing Clear. This series is keyed by 2 clearing. This allows 1 to work one-on-one or use two player options with 5.*

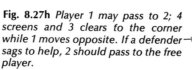

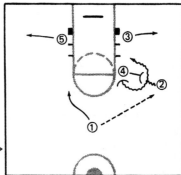

Fig. 8.27h *Player 1 may pass to 2; 4 screens and 3 clears to the corner while 1 moves opposite. If a defender sags to help, 2 should pass to the free player.*

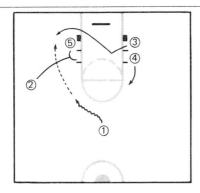

Figure 8.27i *Double Screen. Player 2 screens along the lane; 3 cuts behind the double screen for the pass. If nothing materializes, 1 can reverse the ball to 4 and use the options discussed in 8.27d.*

player keys the one-on-one option by the point player shown in Fig. 8.27g and h, and a double screen as shown in Fig. 8.27i.

MOTION OFFENSE

The motion offense is listed separately only because it can be used with a single or double post; or it can be played without a post or with a triple post. Players on the periphery can move into the lane and post up at any time which is the reason for the leniency in number of post players. Basically most motion offenses are run with a double post although one of the posts may be a peripheral player who posts up.

The offense does have certain advantages. It is a free lance offense employing certain rules. It has no set pattern, no predetermined series of moves and therefore is not easily scouted. Since there is constant movement of players, all players have scoring opportunities. It may be possible for the defense to contain a great scoring threat but other players should be free for short range shots. Since it is not a continuity offense, it is difficult for the defense to close off a pass to a particular position. The offense is designed to react to the position of the defensive players on the court.

Disadvantages of the offense include the difficulty in maintaining court balance. Particularly with inexperienced players, eight or ten players may be very close to the ball. Because of the manner in which the passing game develops, there may be times when key players are out of position to recover downcourt when the ball is intercepted or rebounded. It is also true that rebounders are not always in the best position to attack the boards.

Rules for the Motion Offense

1. General
   a. Move every time a pass is made.
   b. Screen away from the ball — never on the ball.
   c. Complete at least four passes before attempting a shot, unless a layup is open.
   d. Pass to the post one in every four passes.
   e. Play the post when it is vacant.
   f. Do not fight pressure if overplayed; cut backdoor or screen for teammate.
   g. Use the dribble *only* in the following situations:
      1) Against full court pressure.
      2) Drive to the basket.
      3) Improve passing lanes.
2. Perimeter Players
   a. Maintain 15 ft. spacing.
   b. Hold the ball for a count of two to allow teammates to use screens; if a player is open sooner, pass to her.
   c. Screen away from the ball:
      1) Set the screen low when the defense is overplaying.
      2) Set the screen high when the defense is sagging.
   d. Make a cut when not screening:
      1) Cut to the baseline so you can come off a screen.
      2) Cut for the basket.
      3) Cut for the basket using the high post to vertical rub.
      4) Replace yourself when nothing else is available.
      5) Do not make a cut in the same direction as a teammate.
   e. Set opponent up when a screen is set for you; V cut and run your defender into the screen.
   f. Cut to the high post when it is vacant.
   g. Screen for the nearest teammate or cut to an open area in the perimeter when the ball is passed in to a post.
3. Post Players
   a. High Post:
      1) Go to the ball side; if you receive the ball, look low.
      2) Slide low on the ball side.
      3) Screen away for the low post and stay in the low post.
      4) Screen for a player on the perimeter.

5) Relieve pressure by stepping out of the high post to receive the ball; face the basket and look low.
6) Serve as a relay passer to the weak side.
7) Cut to the basket when the ball is passed low.

b. Low Post:
1) Start on the side opposite the ball.
2) Cut to the high post when it becomes vacant.
3) Cut to the high post when screened by the high post.
4) Screen for a perimeter player.
5) Post up when the ball is at the high post or wing; screen away if you do not receive the ball within a count of three.

6) Try for a three-point play when you get the ball.

As is true of any offense, it takes time to develop positioning, timing of moves, and particularly reading the defense and reacting accordingly. When choosing this offense, the coach must use discipline to see that something more than "street ball" is played. Most coaches generally find that a team has greater success with the offense in the second year of its use. One of the values of the offense is that players tend to revert to its principles when they are engaged in a "pickup" game during the off season.

9

Zone Defenses and Offenses

ZONE DEFENSE

In a zone defense, players play the ball instead of a specified opponent. Everyone faces the ball and moves in relation to its position on an assigned area of the court. The purpose of a zone defense is to defend from the basket area outward, with emphasis on preventing short shots and permitting long ones, if necessary. A zone defense should be learned only after players acquire skill in individual defensive techniques.

Advantages of a Zone Defense

1. Players can be assigned to a position on the court to utilize their strengths.
2. It is an effective defense to use against a team that dribbles, cuts through the lane, and relies on high percentage shots.
3. Weaker defensive players can be "hidden" to a greater extent than in a man-to-man defense.
4. It reduces the number of fouls called and protects those in foul trouble.
5. Many zones afford opportunities for a fast break since players are assigned definite positions at the top of the circle.
6. It is easy to make the transition from offense to defense, since players run back to an assigned position on the court rather than look for a particular opponent when they reach the defensive end.

7. In a zone, players in certain positions are required to cover little space and therefore find it less tiring than man-to-man defense.
8. It may provide a psychological barrier to the opposing team.
9. It may help a team secure more interceptions.

Disadvantages of a Zone Defense

1. All zones are vulnerable at certain positions; they tend to be weak against long shots at the top of the circle, shots from the corners, or both.
2. A zone is weak against a fast breaking team because it does not have time to set up.
3. A zone does not place pressure on players outside the perimeter and allows them to pass with little interference.
4. A zone may not encourage players to improve their own defensive skills.
5. A zone may permit players to become complacent as they move from one assigned position to another. Players may lose their aggressiveness.
6. A zone may overcommit itself by being drawn out too far or by sagging too far.

Basic Principles for a Zone Defense

1. Players are responsible for guarding the ball first and an opponent second. They always face the ball and are responsible for covering

237

the passing lanes and intercepting the ball if it is passed within the perimeter of the zone.

2. The zone's configuration should be maintained with the correct spatial relationship. The zone should not be overextended beyond the 21 ft. area. Shots should be permitted from beyond that distance.
3. The stance assumed by players is higher than for man-to-man defense, and the arms are spread in a legal manner to give an impenetrable appearance to the zone.
4. Players should quickly retreat to the defensive end when they lose possession of the ball to establish their defensive position.
5. Defenders guarding a player with the ball move their arms in windmill fashion, trying to deflect the ball or force a high pass.
6. Players moving in a zone must be aware of the position of attack players in their zone. They play an attack player who is one pass away one-half step ball side, and try for an interception if possible, knowing that there is another defender behind.
7. Players should not permit an attack player to receive the ball in the free throw lane. If she does, all players sag and float toward the ball.

SPECIFIC ZONE DEFENSES

Zone defenses are named according to the configuration of the zone starting with players closest to the center line. For example, in a three-two zone, three players form the front line near the free throw line and two players are closer to the basket. Zone defenses are characterized by having an odd front line or an even one. Examples of zones having an odd front line include the three-two, one-two-two, and one-three-one zones. Even front lines include the two-one-two, two-three, and two-two-one zones. Choice of the zone depends on the individual abilities of the defensive players, considering both their physical and mental attributes. It also depends on the capability of the opponents.

Each zone has certain strengths and weaknesses depending upon the deployment of the players. A zone is strong where it has the greatest concentration of players and weak where fewer players are positioned. The strengths and weaknesses of the popular zones will be discussed with diagrams presented to show the movement of the players in relation to the ball. The positions for each player shown on the diagrams are basic and should be adjusted slightly depending upon the position of an opponent within that area. Numbers 1 and 2 represent guards, 4 and 5 represent forwards, and 3 is the post.

The position of players in each zone can be adjusted to provide more pressure against certain offensive positions. For example, all of the zones can be started higher to force the opponents out of position. The zones can be "pinched," brought in tighter against inside scorers or they can be spread against outside shooters and nondriving teams. When utilizing a two-three zone, the top two players can pinch a point player and try to cause a turnover. A perceptive coach may make other adjustments, depending upon the strengths of the opponent.

Two-One-Two Zone

This zone is one of the most popular in use today. It combines some of the advantages of the three-two and two-three zone. It is strong near the basket and in the lane, and therefore is useful against a pivot offense. It also provides good rebounding strength and opportunities for a fast break to develop as either player 1 or 2 is in position to start downcourt following a shot. It is weak from the point position and in the corners. Fig. 9.1a–i shows the movements of players and Fig. 9.2a–e diagrams the position of players as the ball moves around the perimeter of the zone.

Two-Three Zone

In many respects, the two-three zone is similar to the two-one-two zone. The primary difference between the two zones is that player X_3 plays closer to the basket in the two-three zone and therefore it is stronger against low or medium pivot moves and weaker at the free throw line. Because player X_3 is deeper in this zone, X_4 and X_5 need not cover as much area. This makes the zone somewhat stronger in the corners than the two-one-two. When the ball is at the wing, one of the top players must front a high post at the edge of the free throw line. When the ball is in the corner, the back middle player must front a low post.

The two-three zone has good fast break potential. It is weak to the side of the lane in the medium post area. It has good potential for double-teaming in the corners.

Fig. 9.3a–e shows the position of the players as the ball moves around the perimeter of the zone. Fig. 9.3f–g shows the coordination between the back and front line players when the ball is reversed while the attack is in a one-three-one alignment. Fig. 9.4 shows a double-team tactic in the left corner.

Fig. 9.1 *Two-One-Two Zone. Players 1 and 2 are the front line, 3 is in the middle line, and 4 and 5 are the back line.*

f

g

h

i

Fig. 9.1 *(continued)*

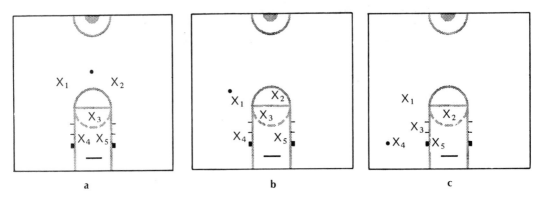

a

b

c

Fig. 9.2 *Two-One-Two Zone.*

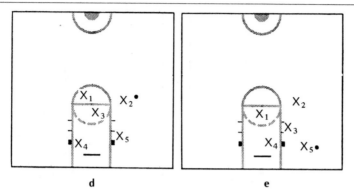

Fig. 9.2 *(continued)*

Fig. 9.3 *Two-Three Zone.*

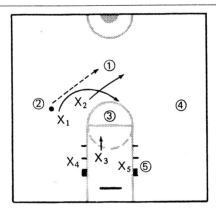

Fig. 9.3f *Player 2 has the ball with X_1 pressuring her and contesting the high post. 2 passes to 1 and X_2 moves out on her while X_1 moves back on 3.*

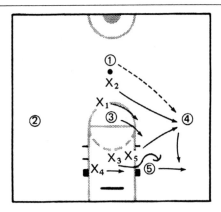

Fig. 9.3g *When 1 passes to 4, X_5 moves out until X_2 recovers on 4. X_5 slides down. X_1 has moved to front the high post; X_3 moves to front a low post. If the ball is lobbed into 3 as she moves into the low post, X_4 tries to draw a charge, and X_1 is responsible for blocking out 2 if she rebounds.*

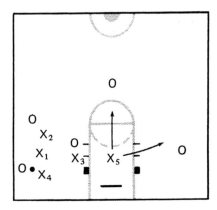

Fig. 9.4 *Two-Three Zone with a Double-Team in the Left Corner. Player X_1 slides down to help X_4 double-team; X_2 slides over to play an opponent in that area aggressively; X_3 fronts the post; X_5 zones against the two players furthest from the ball.*

Two-Two-One Zone

This zone resembles the two-three, although it is stronger in the medium pivot area and weaker under the basket. It is a good zone to use when a team has one player whose greatest asset is her rebounding ability. It may also be used by a team that has one tall player and four short, quick ones. It provides opportunities for double-teaming and fast breaking. It is weak beyond 18 ft.

Fig. 9.5 shows the players' positions as the ball moves around the perimeter of the zone.

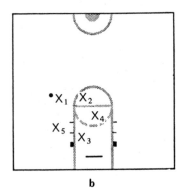

a

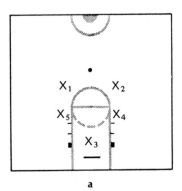

b

Fig. 9.5 *Two-Two-One Zone.*

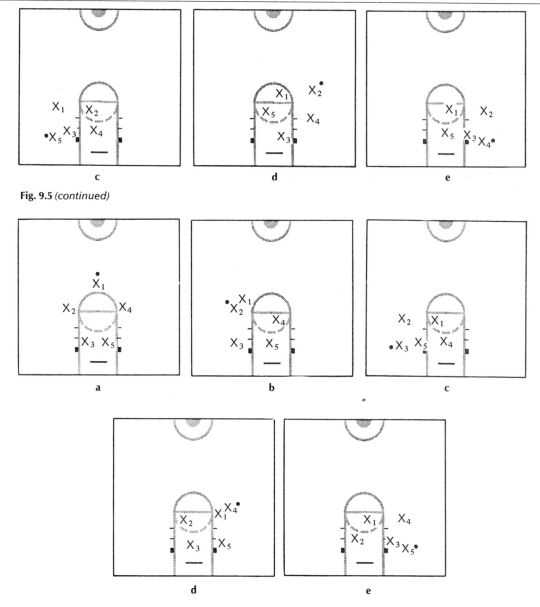

Fig. 9.5 *(continued)*

Fig. 9.6 *Three-Two Zone.*

Three-Two Zone

This zone is extremely strong at the free throw line and is excellent to use against a high post player. The three quickest players are assigned to the front line positions; the rebounders are in the back line. If the rebounders are strong, this zone is an excel-

lent one for fast breaking. It is strong against outside shooters from the top of the circle and the free throw line extended. It is weaker once the front line has been penetrated, and is not a particularly strong rebounding defense.

Fig. 9.6 shows the positions of the players as the ball moves around the perimeter of the zone.

One-Two-Two Zone

This zone is similar to the three-two zone, but is stronger in the medium post area outside the lane and is weaker beyond the free throw line. It is good against a medium or low pivot. It provides better rebound positioning than the three-two zone and is stronger in the corners. It is weak against outside shooters at the top of the circle, as they move away from the point position.

Fig. 9.7 shows the positions of the players as the ball moves around the perimeter of the zone.

One-Three-One Zone

This zone is effective against a high scoring pivot player. It is strong at the free throw line and at the wing positions, but is weak in the corners and at the top of the circle. It is not a strong rebounding or fast breaking alignment.

Fig. 9.8 shows the positions of the players as the ball moves around the perimeter of the zone.

Drills for Any Zone Defense

Prior to presenting a zone defense to a group, the teacher should prepare a mimeographed (or dittoed) diagram of the zone for every student. If this is too costly, each team of five players should have a copy and additional copies might be placed around the gymnasium for easy reference. A series of diagrams show the position of the defensive team in a zone when the ball is in the corners, wings, or at the point position. It should also include diagrams showing the positions of the individual players when the ball moves to each of these positions. The teacher may add other pertinent information.

Before introducing a specific zone, general principles related to all zone defenses should be discussed. Then a specified zone may be introduced to a class. Its advantages, disadvantages, and reasons for selection should be presented. Diagrams for the zone should be distributed to students at this time if not done previously.

Players should then be permitted to get into groups of five, if they have not already done this. The ability necessary for each position should be discussed, and the students should decide on which player should play each position. Time should then be provided for each student to mentally gain a picture of her moves when the ball changes position.

Each team should be assigned to a free throw lane area for practice. If there are not a sufficient number of these, additional ones may be taped on

the floor in extra space. If this does not provide enough areas, teams will have to rotate. Once the teams reach their assigned area, all players sit down under the basket behind the endline, with the exception of the player in the No. 1 position. She takes her starting position on the court and the teacher verifies that all players be ready with "arms out." Slowly, and in turn, the teacher calls out "Right wing," "Right corner," "Right wing," "Point," "Left wing," "Left corner," etc. As all X_1's move to a new position, time is taken to verify that they have moved to the correct position. This is continued until they have moved to each position twice (or more). The signal to move to a new position may be speeded up if they seem ready. Again the calls should be made in order around the perimeter. This process is repeated for No. X_2's, X_3's, X_4's, and X_5's.

This technique is repeated, starting with the X_1's once more. At first the signal should be to move to the adjacent position in one direction only. After the students have acquired some confidence, however, the teacher may alternate direction — for example, she may call left wing, point, and left wing again. At this time, she should only signal for a move to a position "one pass away."

It is now time for all five players to assume their starting position and, on signal, move to a new position. All players' arms should be outstretched in a legal manner to give the appearance of impenetrability and unity. As players gain confidence, the teacher can change direction frequently and increase the tempo of the signals.

Now half the teams are asked to put on pinnies and move to an adjacent court to be attack players against the zone defense. One player for each attack team gets a ball and the attack players take their places on the court in their usual positions. The attack players are informed that they may not dribble or cut. They must be stationary and pass to an adjacent player only when a signal is given.

When all teams are ready to start the teacher may call, "Pass"; the defense reacts to the ball's new position. A signal is given again, and this process is continued. Following each pass, the teacher checks the positioning of as many groups as possible. The tempo of the signals is increased. The teams alternate and the same process is repeated.

Next in the progression is the permission for the attack players to cut as they please. Again, they may only pass on signal. With these directions the process is repeated for both teams. Following this drill, players should be ready to practice on their own with five-on-five, and the teacher moves from group to group to correct positioning when necessary.

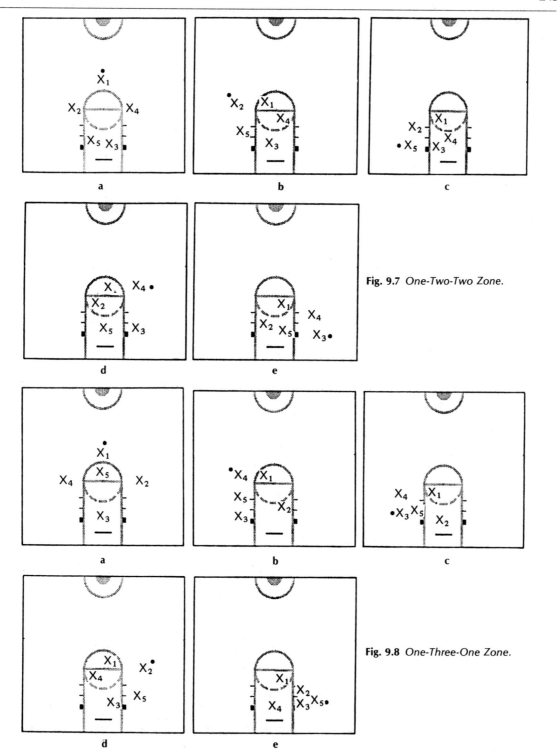

Fig. 9.7 *One-Two-Two Zone.*

Fig. 9.8 *One-Three-One Zone.*

MATCHUP DEFENSES

A matchup defense implies that the defensive players position themselves in a zone defense that is similar to the alignment of the offensive team. Thus, if the offense comes down and sets up in a one-two-two position, the defense moves into a one-two-two zone. When the offense comes down into a one-three-one alignment, the defense counteracts

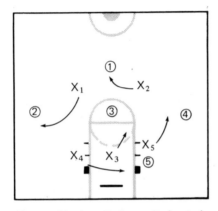

Fig. 9.9 *Matchup Defense. Defensively the team is playing a two-three zone. As the offense aligns into a one-three-one formation, the defense flexes into a one-three-one zone. Defensive players move in a counterclockwise fashion to their new positions.*

with a one-three-one zone. Matching the offensive alignment disallows the offense from filling the gaps in the zone unless they realign into another offensive formation. However, as they do realign, a good defensive team will flex into the new offensive alignment to continue to matchup. This positioning provides the defense also with an appearance of man-to-man. Nevertheless, the offense should identify a zone when the same defensive player does not follow a cutter through the lane.

Fig. 9.9 and Fig. 9.10 show examples of matching up.

COMBINATION DEFENSES

This type of defense combines man-to-man and zone principles. Normally, it is not appropriate for teaching in physical education classes but may prove valuable in competitive play. A teacher with imagination can devise a number of combinations that should prove effective against a particular offense. An example of a combination defense is four defenders playing a box or diamond zone and the fifth defender playing man-to-man against a high scorer or outside shooter.

Advantages of Combination Defenses

1. The advantages of principles for both man-to-man defense and zone defense are realized.
2. A defense can be devised to reduce the effec-

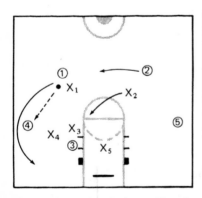

Fig. 9.10a Matchup Defense. The offense aligns into a 2–3 formation, and the zone matches with a two-three zone. After 1 passes to 4, she cuts to the corner and 2 moves to a point position.

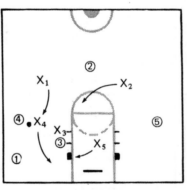

Fig. 9.10b *As player 1 cuts to the corner, X_1 slides down, tells X_4 she has 4, and X_4 slides back into position for a one-three-one zone with the ball at the wing. X_2 slides over while X_3 and X_5 reposition slightly.*

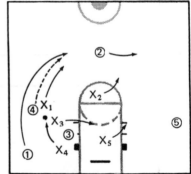

Fig. 9.10c *Should the offense realign into a 2–3 formation, the defense players simply move clockwise to match up.*

tiveness of one or more particular players.
3. It provides opportunities for double-teaming.
4. It is a special defense for which the opponents may not be prepared; thus, it may take them time to solve it.

Disadvantages of Combination Defenses

1. It takes special preparation and time to learn.
2. If the opponents can counteract the defensive deployment, an easy basket usually results.
3. If the defense misjudges the potential of each opponent and utilizes an inappropriate defense, an easy basket will result.
4. Disadvantages of man-to-man defenses are apparent for those players utilizing man-to-man tactics.
5. Disadvantages of zone defenses are apparent for those employing zone tactics.

SPECIFIC COMBINATION DEFENSES

Some of the more popular combination defenses are described briefly. For clarification purposes the defenses are named by identifying the zone first followed by the man-to-man coverage.

One and Four

The defensive player assigned to guard the poorest shooter becomes a "rover" and, in a sense, a zone player. She gives the outward appearance of guarding her assigned player when the opponents are setting up on offense. When they start their offensive thrust she sags off her opponent and is free to move wherever she can assist other defenders. Among other things she can help double-team an effective scorer or pivot player, cover the passing lane into the play-maker, or cover a favorite shooting position of one of the opponents. She is given unlimited freedom in her movements; for this reason, the player assigned to this position is usually quick, agile, and has the ability to be in the "right place at the right time."

Two and Three

In this defense three players play man-to-man while two back players play in an up-and-back position in the lane play zone. This can be effective against a team that has two players with weak shooting and ball handling techniques. The players using zone principles stay in the lane ready to assist on cuts or drives through the lane. Both players start in the middle of the lane — the front player 12 ft. from the basket (3 ft. behind the free throw line) and the back player 6 ft. in front of the basket. The front player must be agile and the back player should be a strong rebounder (Fig. 9.11). If one of the opposing strong players is a pivot, this defense permits double-teaming her, regardless of her position in the lane.

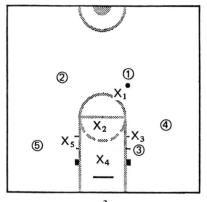
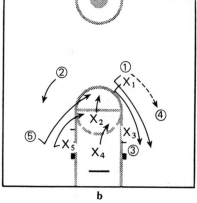

a   b

Fig. 9.11 Two-and Three-Combination Defense. Players 2 and 4 are considered weak ball handlers or poor shooters as they allow X_2 and X_4 to zone in the lane (a). Player 1 passes to 4, who remains unguarded unless she dribbles in to the lane. X_1 and X_5 continue to guard their opponents closely. Note that X_2 helps X_5 cut off the passing lane to 5 (b).

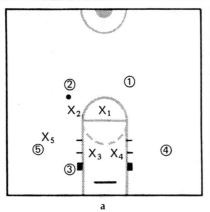 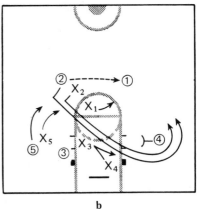

a   b

Fig. 9.12 *Triangle and Two — Combination Defense. Players 2 and 5 are considered to be the only dangerous offensive players. They are guarded man-to-man while the others play a triangle one-two zone (a). Player 2 passes to 1 and cuts diagonally through the lane. X_2 fronts her as X_4 moves up and follows 2's cut through the lane to discourage a lob pass. Player X_1 moves up to prevent 1 from dribbling into the lane. Meanwhile X_5 continues to play 5 man-to-man (b).*

Triangle and Two

In the triangle zone one player takes her position at the free throw line, and the other two players are 6 ft. in front of the basket; each stands astride the free throw lane on her side. The front player must be quick and possess good game sense. The back players should be the best rebounders. The remaining two defenders play man-to-man against the most dangerous opponents. It is common to chase two guards or one guard and one forward although chasing a post in this alignment is not recommended. From this posture the defense can dictate which opponents shoot (Fig. 9.12).

If the opponents utilize a one-three-one offensive alignment, the triangle should be inverted with two players at the free throw line and one player deep, as shown in Fig. 9.13.

The triangle and two can also be used as a trapping style of defense. The two players who can trap the best are given that assignment while another player who has the ability to anticipate and intercept is placed at the top of the triangle with the best rebounders in the back of the triangle. The back player who is more mobile should play on the side the offense generally attacks. One of the trapping players on occasion falls back into the zone while the top player of the zone becomes a trapper. Therefore, all three players need to become adept at trapping techniques and the principles of the zone.

Examples of defensive positioning are shown in Fig. 9.14.

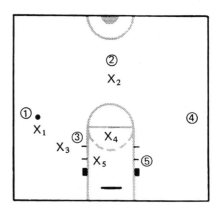

Fig. 9.13 *Triangle (2–1) and Two Combination Defense. Players 1 and 2 are guarded man for man while X_3 and X_4 play the front of the zone and X_5 plays the back.*

Box (or Diamond) and One

The box or diamond zones should be familiar to most readers. In a box zone the front players start a step in front of the free throw line with the inside foot on the lane line on their side. The back players are 6 ft. in front of the basket and have their outside foot on the lane line on their side. The two front players should be quick and aggressive while the two back players should be the best rebounders. The other defender may either be assigned to guard

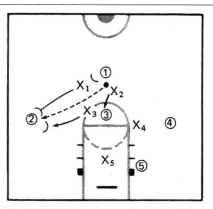

Fig. 9.14a *Triangle and Two Trapping Defense. Against a two-one-two offensive alignment, X_1 and X_2 trap. X_3 and X_4 overplay on the ball side. As the ball is passed to 2, X_2 and X_3 trap; X_5 moves out on 5; X_4 moves up to cover 3 until X_1 gets back; whereupon X_4 retreats to the middle of the lane.*

Fig. 9.14b *Against a one-three-one alignment, the triangle is inverted with X_3 and X_4 playing at the top and X_5 underneath. As the ball is passed from 1 to 2, X_1 and X_3 move to trap and X_2 falls back into the zone.*

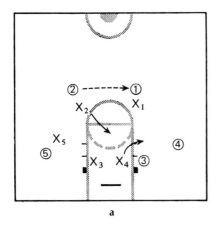

a

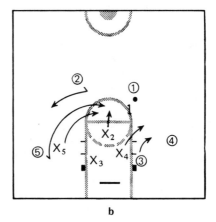

b

Fig. 9.15 *Box and One — Combination Defense. Player 5 is the best shooter and is played man-to-man by X_5. Note that X_4 has modified her starting position slightly because of the position of 3. After 2 passes to 1, X_2 retreats (a). As the ball is passed to 1, 5 cuts up, guarded by X_5, who is assisted by X_2. Since no player is in the corner, X_4 can afford to place pressure on 3 as she makes a cut (b).*

a high scorer and place extra pressure on her or may be free to rove anywhere (Fig. 9.15). If the choice is the latter, the player should be the quickest one on the team with good anticipatory characteristics. When the opponents shoot, she may have the opportunity to cut downcourt for a lead pass and an easy layup.

If a team prefers the diamond posture to the box, the front player takes her position halfway between the free throw line and outer circle. The back

player is in the center of the lane 6 ft. in front of the basket, and the two middle players are just inside the free throw lane with their outside foot on the lane line on their side (Fig. 9.16).

The diamond zone is strong against shots from the side, but has some weakness in the medium and low post area. It is often used against a three-two offensive alignment. The box is strong under the basket but is weak in the 18 ft. range to the side of the free throw line.

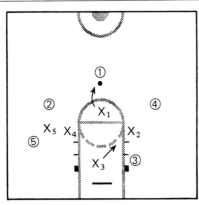

Fig. 9.16 *Diamond and One—Combination Defense. Player 5 is guarded closely by X_5. X_3 has adjusted her position slightly due to the position of 3.*

Drills for Combination Defenses

Because these defenses are extraordinary, sufficient time must be spent in practice so that the players have complete confidence in their ability to apply the principles involved correctly while under stress. As explained previously, in learning any zone it is possible to have the players move individually through their pattern — particularly, with the three- and four-player zones. Then, all zone players should practice moving as a unit before the man-to-man players are added. This should be done next, with attention being given to the defensive positioning of all players as an opponent guarded man-to-man cuts through the lane. Time should be devoted to this phase as well as to any other potential double-teaming opportunities.

The two-player zone can be introduced in the same manner but is somewhat more dependent upon the position of the opponents since two players are covering a larger zone and must position themselves within an area occupied by an opponent. During the early stages, strong emphasis should be placed on the principle that neither player in the zone leaves the lane area regardless of where the other opponents are. If attention is given to the two players involved with the zone alone, soon their actions should be integrated with the other defenders. This is probably the best way to practice the one-and-four combination defense also.

ZONE OFFENSE

A team on offense must determine why the opponents have chosen to play a zone defense. The primary reason for its selection is that the offensive team does not have an accurate outside shooter. Other reasons include a player in foul trouble, one or more players with individual defensive weaknesses, or a desire simply to protect a lead or to disrupt the offensive style of attack. If possible, once the reason for the zone's use is identified, the offensive team should exploit the opponent's vulnerable positions.

Basic Principles to Follow Against a Zone Defense

1. The easiest way to defeat the effectiveness of the zone is to beat it downcourt. As soon as possession of the ball is obtained either from an interception or an out-of-bounds play, the ball should be advanced as rapidly as possible downcourt, and a scoring thrust must be attempted before the zone can be established. A long pass to a player in the corner is effective if the defenders are not alert as they recover downcourt.

2. The offensive team must be able to penetrate the zone. This can be accomplished by means of passing to a player in the zone or by having a player dribble into the zone. Once the zone is penetrated, other defensive players are drawn toward the ball. This opens a passing lane toward the new perimeter of the zone which allows players on the perimeter of the zone to shoot with less pressure and generally from a shorter distance.

3. A team must possess at least one player who can successfully shoot from the 21 ft. range. By demonstrating an ability to score from this range the defense is forced to spread their zone to a greater degree which, in turn, opens the zone for greater penetration.

4. Because the defense is basically playing the ball, the zone can be penetrated from the weak side and with cuts from behind the zone (from the baseline). This type of cut can be particularly effective.

5. It is extremely important that all players, with the exception of a pivot player, face the basket when they receive a pass. This allows them to spot a free teammate quickly and pass to her before the zone has time to readjust their positions.

6. It must be remembered that a zone moves primarily with ball movement. Therefore, if the offense can move the ball quickly, the

defense should be slightly behind the position of the ball since they cannot slide as fast as the ball can be passed. This advantage is lost any time a player holds the ball, fumbles a pass, or dribbles without penetrating the zone because the defense has adequate time to reposition. This means that players must pass quickly after receiving the ball, but their passes cannot be stereotyped. A player may have a preconceived idea as to where she would like to pass, but the pass cannot be made automatically until it is determined that the passing lane to that position is open. It also means that all passes must be accurate so that the ball is not fumbled; and, it means that dribbling would be eliminated except to drive toward the goal or to move the ball away from excessive defensive pressure.

7. The offense should be patient in maneuvering for a good scoring opportunity and not shoot hurriedly unless in college play the 30-second clock is due to sound. The offense should make every effort to enter the zone for a high percentage shot and shoot long shots only when absolutely necessary or in a desire to demonstrate effectiveness from this range in an attempt to spread the defense to a greater extent.

8. Definite rebounding assignments should be made on each scoring thrust. The defensive players are frequently drawn away from desirable rebounding positions, and the offense should take advantage of this. Furthermore, the defense is often not in a position to block out the opponents even temporarily so that the offensive player often is able to move into rebound position uncontained by the opposition.

9. Any offense against a zone must utilize cuts. Maneuvers that utilize diagonal cuts through the lane should be developed, as well as the following: parallel cuts to the ball, vertical cuts toward the basket outside the lane, vertical cuts away from the basket through or along the lane, and lateral cuts across the lane (often behind the defenders).

10. Screens should be employed against a zone defense. These may include running screens, particularly outside screens and also screens set at a seam in a zone so that a defender is temporarily delayed in moving to her new position as the ball is passed. This is an excellent technique, and greater use should be made of it.

11. The overload principle may be applied to attacking a zone. One area is flooded with more offensive players than defensive players assigned to that part of the zone. The temporary advantage in numbers (for the zone will react to the overload) may free a player for a shot, or one of these players may screen a defensive player to allow a pass, cut, or drive. Quick reversals of the ball will often leave a weak side player free for a shot.

12. There must be both ball movement and player movement against any type of zone defense. A zone attack that involves ball movement only is an easy one against which to defend.

Selecting an Offensive Alignment to Attack a Zone

The reader knows that every zone has one or more weakness. Because it depends upon the manner in which each is played, one can only generalize about the weaknesses in each type of zone. The most vulnerable areas in most zones are either from the corners or in the area at the top or to the side of the circle. Some zones also have weaknesses in the medium pivot range. The offensive team must recognize where these areas are and take measures to exploit them. In order to do this the teacher/coach must devise scoring thrusts at the places where the zone is most vulnerable, or devise scoring efforts at defenders who are in foul difficulty or who have particularly weak individual defensive skills. To gain the greatest advantage against a specific zone alignment, some coaches select an offensive formation with an odd front line if the opponents are using an even front line or a formation with an even front line if the defense has an odd front line. Table 9.1 shows possible offensive alignments against various zones and the general weaknesses of each zone and, therefore, where they should be attacked if the individuals in the zone have no identifiable weaknesses.

As stated previously the one-four stack alignment may be used to defeat almost any of the zones.

Another factor that should be considered in the decision for choice of an offensive alignment against a zone is the alignment used for the primary offense. The closer the zone offensive alignment comes to the one generally used, the easier it is for the players to learn. It should also be understood that an offensive alignment will not in itself defeat a zone. Player movement must be designed to take advantage of the original positions in the formation to exploit the weaknesses of the defensive movements. Formations other than the ones suggested above may provide equally good results against any zone if appropriate player movement is devised.

One other factor should be considered. Few

Table 9.1 *Zone Alignments, Their Weaknesses and Suggested Alignments for Attacking the Zones*

Zone Alignment	Area of Weakness	Offensive Alignment to Attack the Zone
2–1–2	at the top of the circle; in the corners	1–3–1; 2–3
2–3	at the free throw line; medium pivot position outside the lane	1–3–1; 3–2; 2–3
3–2	medium pivot outside of lane; after front line is penetrated	2–3
2–2–1	top of the circle; in the corners	1–3–1; 3–2
1–2–2	top of the circle as a player moves away from the point position	2–3
1–3–1	top of the circle; in the corners	1–3–1; 2–3

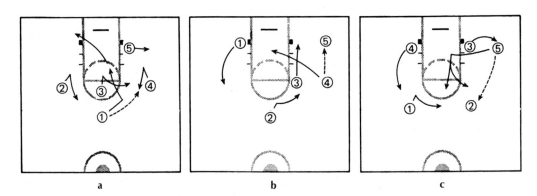

a   b   c

Fig. 9.17 *One-Three-One Continuity Zone Offense. As 1 passes to 4, 3 fakes and cuts to the edge of the free throw line; 1 fakes and cuts through the lane as 2 replaces her and 5 cuts toward the corner (a). 4 passes to 5 in the corner and cuts down, posts up temporarily, and clears the lane; 1 clears the lane and returns to a wing position as 2 slides over; 3 cuts down the side of the lane (b). 5 passes back to 2 and 4 clears to a wing position and 1 moves to the top of the circle. After passing, 5 cuts to a high post position off 3 and then 3 replaces 5 in the corner (c). This offense can be used when 3 and 5 can both play effectively from the corner. The offense utilizes vertical cuts through the lane, vertical cuts on the side of the lane and diagonal cuts.*

teams are able to perfect offensive tactics from a number of alignments, and few teams can perfect a different offense to cope with every zone defense. Therefore, it may be wise for a team to develop one zone offense that can exploit the weaknesses of several different zones. Devising a series of options is one way to accomplish this purpose. A continuity offense with options is another. If the latter technique is selected, the player movement should exploit the weaknesses in any zone.

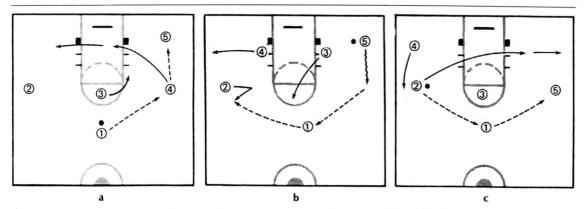

Fig. 9.18 Continuity Offense from a One-Three-One Alignment. The fundamentals of this offense are used in many variations. Basically the two wings and corner player interchange positions. The point and post remain in their own position, 1 passes to 4 who passes to 5, 5 looks for 4 in the low post, followed by 3 (a). If neither is free, 5 dribbles to the wing position and reverses to 1. If 2 is not free on her move toward the free throw line, she cuts out to receive the pass from 1. 4 cuts to the corner (b). 2 reverses to 1, who passes to 5. 2 cuts out to the corner as 4 replaces 2 at the wing (c).

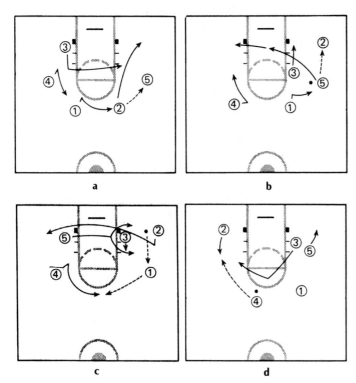

Fig. 9.19 Two-Three Continuity Zone Offenses. Player 2 passes to 5 and cuts for the corner. 1 replaces 2; 4 replaces 1 and 3 fakes and cuts across the lane (a). 5 passes to 2 in the corner and 5 cuts through the lane; 1 replaces 5 as 4 cuts in the opposite direction, 3 slides down the lane (b). 2 passes back to 1 as 5 makes a return cut across the key using 3 as a screen; 1 passes to 4 and 2 cuts across the lane (c). 4 passes to 2 as 5 moves toward the baseline, and 3 fakes to the free throw line and then cuts to the edge of the lane (d). 3 slides down the lane and then clears to the opposite side as 5 cuts off her; 2 returns a pass to 4 (e). 4 passes back to 1 as 2 cuts around 3; if nothing has materialized during this sequence, 1 may dribble the ball while all players return to their starting positions (f).

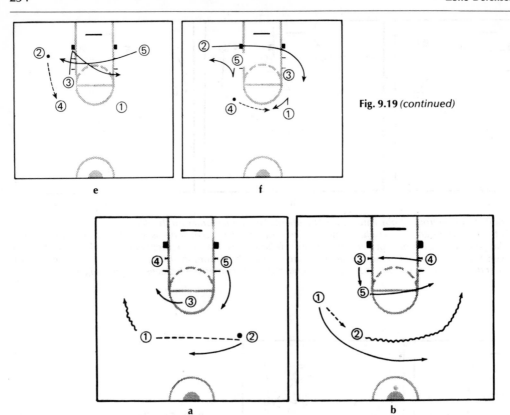

Fig. 9.19 (continued)

e   f

a   b

Fig. 9.20 Overload Offense with a Triple Post. The post players continually rotate to the ball while filling the high and low post on ball side. Player 2 passes to 1 who dribbles down to the wing position and 2 slides over. The posts continue to rotate as 1 and 2 pass (a). If the entry cannot be made from that side, the top players take the ball to the other side and attempt it from there as the post players reverse their direction (b).

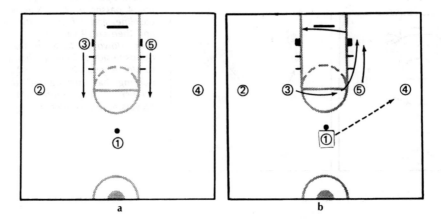

a   b

Fig. 9.21

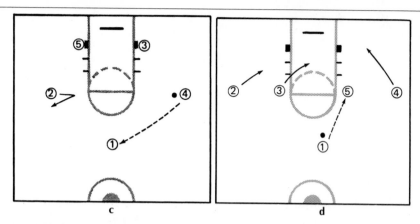

Fig. 9.21 *Continuity Offense from a One-Four Alignment. This offense retains the basic posture of a point and two wing players with a double post rotating to the ball (a). Player 1 passes to 4. 5 slides down and 3 cuts to fill the high post. 5 slides across the lane as 3 slides down (b). As 4 reverses the ball, 2 may be free at the free throw line. If not, 2 cuts out for the pass and the continuity is continued (c). If the ball is passed in to a post, the other post cuts low, and the wings move into gaps in the zone (d).*

One-Three-One Zone Offense

This alignment is one of the most popular in use today. Player 1 should be the best ball handler on the team, while players 2 and 4 should be good cutters and good shooters. Players 3 and 5 are the tallest players and remain close to the lane most of the time. In many cases players 3 and 5 interchange positions, as do players 1, 2, and 4. Fig. 9.17 shows a basic continuity offense.

Two-Three Zone Offense

This alignment is also popular, using a single pivot player who maneuvers from the low post to high post position. The guard and wing positions are somewhat interchangeable, but the forwards return to the corner and wing positions as soon as possible. Player 1 should be the best ball handler and player 2 is generally the other guard. Players 4 and 5 are the forwards while player 3 is the post player. A continuity offense is shown from this posture in Fig. 9.19. Fig. 9.20 shows a two-guard front with a triple post.

One-Four Zone Offense

This alignment of players retains two posts inside who rotate to high and low post. The point player must be a good ball handler. The wings should be good outside shooters. Fig. 9.21 shows a basic pattern.

10

Pressure Defense and Offense

PRESSURE DEFENSES

Although there may not be a need to teach a pressure defense in physical education classes, almost all highly competitive teams utilize some type of pressure defense in every game. Some teams use it throughout an entire game while others use it as a surprise measure at different times during a contest. There are two basic types of pressure defenses — man-to-man and zone. Each may be employed full court, three-quarter-court, or half-court. A full court press is started at the endline in a team's own frontcourt; a three-quarter press is started at the top of the circle in a team's own frontcourt; and a half-court press is initiated at the division line or one step into a team's own frontcourt.

The type of pressure defense employed by a team depends upon the qualifications of the players. Players must possess better individual defensive abilities if they choose a man-to-man press. It is easier to "hide" a weak defensive player in a zone press defense.

Regardless of the type of pressure defense a team chooses to play, the further downcourt it can initiate the press successfully (full court rather than half-court), the more effective it is in accomplishing its purpose. It also follows that in order to use a full court press a team must possess better defensive personnel than if they are using a half-court press. Because any pressure defense takes time to set up, it is used only after a successful field goal or free throw, a time out, or any other situation causing a temporary suspension of play.

The purpose of any pressure defense is to cause the opponents to use more energy — both physical and mental — before gaining position to shoot. In so doing the defense hopes to cause them to make tactical errors and turn the ball over to them. The pressure to get the ball over the division line has considerable significance at the high school level because of the 10-second rule. Although that rule does not apply at the college level, the college team has the pressure of shooting within 30 seconds. Thus, at either level, a pressure defense may cause the opponents to consume more time in advancing the ball into their frontcourt.

A team that selects to play a zone press has several alignments from which it may operate. The most popular ones are the two-two-one and the three-one-one, (one-two-one-one), which may be used from the full, three-quarter, or half-court posture. Other possibilities for a half-court press include a two-three and a one-one-three. Therefore a team may choose to use a zone press with an odd or even front line. The choice may be made on the basis of team personnel, the strengths or weaknesses of the zones in question, or the offensive alignment of the opponents. If an opposing team relies on one player to receive the in-bounds pass, the defensive team may attack it with an equal number of front line defenders. Hence their choice would be an even front line. If the offensive team sends two

257

players to help the in-bound passer, the defense might counteract with a three-one-one alignment.

While utilizing a pressure defense, the coach must analyze its usefulness in terms of the effect it has on the composure of the opponents as well as the number of points the team utilizing the pressure is gaining from the press as compared with the points scored by the opponents. The press should be continued only if the balance of judgement favors the pressing team. To help in making an objective evaluation statistics can be kept on points scored by both teams while the press is used.

As has been the case throughout the text, in all diagrams that follow, players who normally play in the guard position are X_1 and X_2, forwards are X_4 and X_5, and the post is X_3. Their placement in a zone press depends upon their inherent qualifications.

Advantages of Pressure Defenses

1. It is offensive in nature; it is fast, exciting, and provides continuous action over the entire court (or most of it).
2. It is a highly effective defense to use against a weak ball handling team or an inexperienced team. It causes them to commit ball handling errors that lead to easy scoring opportunities for the team using the pressure defense.
3. It is effective against a team that has a height advantage or against a slower team.
4. The team that uses the pressure defense tends to control the tempo of the game.
5. It is a defense that causes the opponents to become both physically and mentally fatigued. They are given no time to rest, relax, or think; this pressure often leads to the demise of all but the most poised teams.
6. The defense often causes the opponents to call a time out to solve the defense. This means that they have one less time out later in the game.
7. It is the most effective defense to use in the last few minutes of a game when a team is behind.
8. It is effective against a college level team that uses a controlled style offense because it helps to consume part of the 30 seconds.
9. It may also be used as an antidote to a team's own lethargic play.

Disadvantages of Pressure Defenses

1. The defense takes time to set up, so it cannot always be used when a team is forced to go on defense.
2. It requires a great deal of endurance and may be inappropriate for a team that has little practice time.

3. When the opponents solve the defense, they may create many offensive advantage situations — four-on-three, three-on-two, etc.
4. When any member of the defensive team makes a mental or physical error or fails to hustle, an easy scoring opportunity for the opponents results.

MAN-TO-MAN PRESSURE DEFENSE

In order to use this defense effectively, all players must be well skilled in fundamental defensive techniques. They must be quick and aggressive and possess good body control. Players must be exceptional to play a man-to-man press full court. It is difficult to control from this posture, and players need extraordinary stamina. A team also must have a number of substitutes who can press well so that the starters may be given short, periodic rests if necessary.

In whatever posture (full, three-quarter, or half-court) a team establishes its press, defenders must be able to stop a dribbler. If any player is unable to contain her opponent, the man-to-man pressure defense is useless. If a dribbler should evade her opponent, the defender must retreat quickly and force her opponent toward a side line, which helps curtail the dribbler's forward progress. The defender must then regain good defensive positioning.

An opponent who has not as yet dribbled must be approached cautiously. Once the player starts to dribble, the defender attempts to influence her in a predetermined direction. With a man-to-man press most teams choose to direct the ball toward the middle rather than the side line. However, a team may choose to force a particular opponent to dribble with her weak hand; regardless of the direction, this influences her. As the dribbler is forced to catch the ball, other defenders overplay their opponents at an intercepting angle to force them to make a reverse cut requiring a lob pass from the ball handler. After the dribbler passes off, her opponent must drop back immediately so that she does not succumb to a give-and-go pattern.

When using the man-to-man defense full court it is extremely vital that the guards are quick, agile, and can stop a dribbler. The forwards must also be quick, but height to match their opponents is not as vital. Due to the press their opponent is forced out further from the basket where the value of their height advantage is reduced. The center should be a good rebounder and possess good reflexes and powers of anticipation, for most likely she will be confronted with several two-on-one situations.

As the opponents put the ball in play, a team using a full court press may choose to guard the passer and make it difficult for her to in-bound the ball and possibly commit a 5-second violation; or, the team may choose not to guard the in-bound passer but to double-team the receiver and cause a 5-second violation or errant pass.

The half-court man-to-man pressure defense is not as strong against a taller team because it does not often draw the offensive players out far enough from the basket to reduce the effectiveness presented by their height advantage.

Trapping from a Man-to-Man Pressure Defense

When utilizing man-to-man pressure a team may choose to increase the pressure by trapping at designated places on the court. It may trap when the ball goes to the sideline, at the wing or corner position in its own backcourt. These are the most common locations to set a trap although some teams may trap in the point position. Other teams may trap in the low post area or may trap a high scorer whenever she gets the ball regardless of her location on the court.

Trapping techniques involve a second player close to the player with the ball who moves over to help double-team the ball handler. Together the defenders stop the dribble and belly up to the ball

handler with their arms extended high overhead to encourage the lob or bounce pass or to cause a held ball. Meanwhile the other defenders rotate to the ball and overplay offensive players near the ball handler and anticipate an interception. One defender is left to zone against the two offensive players farthest from the ball. An example is shown in Fig. 10.1. A team that does not have a very mobile post player might choose not to trap under these circumstances. Rather, they might limit their trapping to the corner (Fig. 10.2).

Trapping is effective against a team that has not practiced against pressure defenses. It is also effective against a poor ball handling team. Used sparingly against better ball handling teams, it may be effective once or twice and could result in two to four points, which might be the difference in the game's final score. It is only useful, however, when the other three defensive players are alert to the situation and move to cover the passing lanes to the opponents closest to the ball handler. If the passing lanes are not cut off, the obvious danger exists for a four-on-three offensive situation to arise.

Run and Jump

A modification of a man-to-man pressure defense is known as the run and jump defense. The name may be a misnomer since a player does not literally jump at an opponent, but that was the name popularized with this type of defense. It is a rotation style of de-

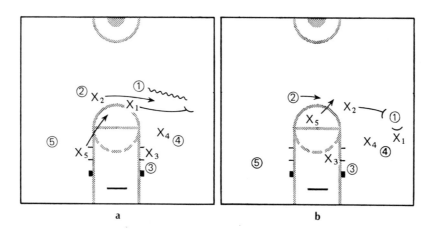

Fig. 10.1 *Trapping Man-to-Man Defense. Player X₁ overplays 1, forcing her toward the side line. While this is occurring, X₂ drifts away from 2 to help double-team 1 at the side line. At the same time, X₅ moves up toward 2 to guard her (a). As 1 pivots, X₂ meets her to complete the trap. X₅ anticipates a pass to 2. X₄ contests a pass to 4. X₃ is responsible for zoning against both 3 and 5. She is more concerned with 3 because she is closer to the ball and the basket (b).*

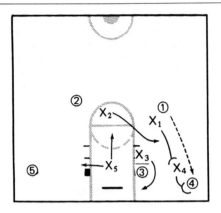

Fig. 10.2 As 1 passes the ball to the corner, X_1 slides down to trap with X_4; X_2 hurries to cut off the passing lane to 1; X_3 contests against 3; X_5 zones against 2 and 5; and X_5 is ready to intercept a lob pass to either.

fense when a jump is initiated. The run and jump technique is used only when the ball is dribbled by an opponent. It may be used full court, three-quarter court, half-court or only at special predetermined times. It is a gambling style defense used as a surprise tactic to force turnovers. When employed in the backcourt, defensive errors occur more often, but a team is not often hurt by these errors since there is time to recover.

The run and jump is effective against a dribbler who reverses. It also is effective against a team that screens on the ball. The pick never gets set because of the jump and rotation by the defense to a new player. It is a defense that must be used to surprise the opponents and cannot be used as the primary defense.

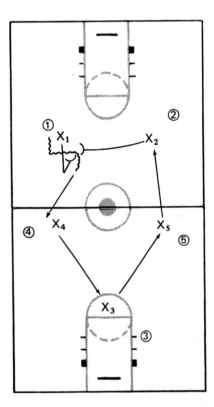

Fig. 10.3 Run and Jump. X_2 runs at 1. All players rotate to a new opponent counterclockwise.

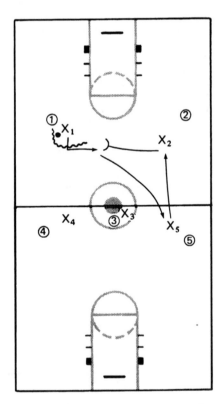

Fig. 10.4 If an opponent moves into the middle, her defender does not rotate. Only three defenders are involved in this rotation. X_2 must temporarily cut off the passing lane to 5 while X_1 has time to recover deep enough in the passing lane.

Basically when a dribbler is moving slowly, the jump is made by a defender when she is approximately 5 ft. from the dribbler. When the dribbler is moving more quickly, the jump is made when the dribbler is approximately 10 ft. away. Basically the defense wishes to keep the ball out of the middle.

Fig. 10.3, Fig. 10.4, and Fig. 10.5 illustrate the use of the run and jump. Note that the entire defense must be set in order to initiate the run and jump. The defender must allow the dribbler a few steps and then she must run fast toward her and land in good defensive position. As soon as the remaining defenders see a teammate run toward the dribbler, they rotate. The only time an offensive player is open is at the instant of the double-team to cause the dribbler to pick up the ball and then only the player opposite the ball is free.

Fig. 10.6 and Fig. 10.7 demonstrate two- and three-player run and jump tactics in the backcourt.

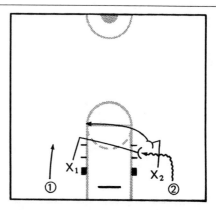

Fig. 10.6 *Two-Player Run and Jump in the Backcourt. X_2 must force 2 toward the middle. X_1 runs directly at 2. X_1 and X_2 double until 2 picks up the ball whereupon X_2 moves to cover 1. If 1 and 2 cross, X_1 and X_2 switch opponents.*

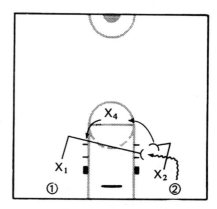

Fig. 10.7 *Three-Player Run and Jump in the Backcourt Against Two Opponents. As X_2 forces 2 toward the middle, X_1 jumps and X_4 moves to intercept a pass to 1. X_2 replaces X_4 and X_1 stays with 2.*

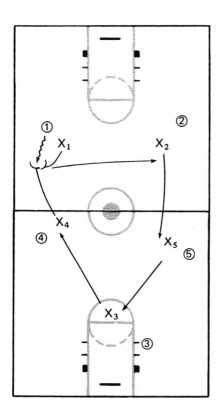

Fig. 10.5 *X_4 runs directly at 1. In this case, the rotation is in a clockwise direction.*

Other Man-to-Man Stunts

The term "stunt" is commonly used to identify an unorthodox tactic used to surprise the opponents. As the definition implies, stunts are utilized in specific situations and cannot be used continually.

Forcing a wing backdoor cut is shown in Fig. 10.8 and Fig. 10.9.

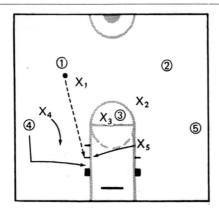

Fig. 10.8 X_4 overplays 4 to force a back-door cut. X_5 moves over to intercept the pass. Defenders recover into a zone as shown in Fig. 10.9.

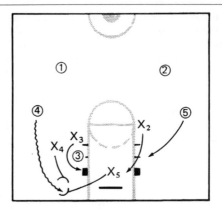

Fig. 10.10 X_4 allows 4 to drive. X_4 and X_5 trap at the baseline. X_3 overplays 3 and X_2 moves to intercept the pass to 5.

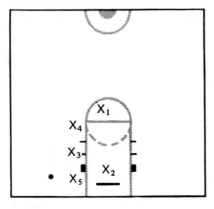

Fig. 10.9 Position of defensive players as they rotate into a one-three-one zone following the backdoor stunt.

Allowing a wing to drive the baseline is shown in Fig. 10.10.

Another stunt that can be used against a pattern team is to double-team the recipient of the first pass with the remaining defenders overplaying the passing lanes. The defender can return to man-to-man coverage or fall back into a zone.

ZONE PRESSURE DEFENSE

This type of pressure defense may be played by a team that has one weak defensive player who is placed in the zone where she can do the least amount of damage. This placement depends upon which of the zone defenses is used. With more than one weak player it is doubtful that a successful zone press can be maintained.

The purpose of a zone press is to have two defenders double-team the ball handler and zone the rest of the opponents, i.e., to play the intercepting angles to them. Two defenders cover the passing lanes to the two opponents closest to the ball handler. The remaining defender must cover the passing lanes to two opponents, must play closer to the player nearer the ball, but must be ready to retreat to the player closer to the basket. By double-teaming the ball handler and closing the passing lanes, the defense tries to force the opponents to use lob or bounce passes that are more easily intercepted.

The method used for double-teaming a player depends upon whether the ball handler has dribbled. If an opponent receives a pass and has not dribbled, two defenders approach cautiously and form a wedge in front of her with their inside feet touching and the inside hand low so that the opponent cannot dribble between them. The other arm is held high. If an opponent has dribbled and a defender forces her to catch the ball, a teammate approaches from the blind side. If the ball handler pivots, the approaching defender should try to tap the ball or tie it up. If this is not successful, the two players form a wedge in front of the ball handler, but their inside feet need not be touching (since the ball handler has already completed her dribble). Both players hold their arms high to force a high pass. Because of the double-teaming tactics the zone press uses, it is considered a better pressure defense to use than a man-to-man against a good dribbling team.

Full Court Pressure Zone Defenses

The in-bounds passer is not generally harassed for any of the zone pressure defenses. The defenders drop back to their starting position and allow the initial pass inbounds and then move to trap the pass receiver. If a player dribbles, the defenders influence her in a predetermined direction and try to stop the dribble as quickly as possible. The remaining defenders play in front of the opponents in their zone and try to intercept the pass. After the ball has cleared one line of the zone, those players retreat quickly in a straight line back toward the basket. At no time should the defense allow the opponents to pass over a zone. In Fig. 10.11 it should be relatively

easy for player 1 to pass over the heads of the front line and/or the second line of defenders. With the offensive players in these positions, the defenders should adjust their position as shown in Fig. 10.12. The back player in any of the alignments must protect the goal and prevent any full court passes. She must be particularly skillful in playing a two-on-one situation, for she will be confronted with it when the defense breaks down.

In any zone press, it should be recognized that considerably more energy is expended on the part of all players than in a normal zone defense. Players must have considerable endurance and often must sprint to their new position. Sliding techniques usually employed on defense are too slow. Once an attacking team has penetrated to the top of its offen-

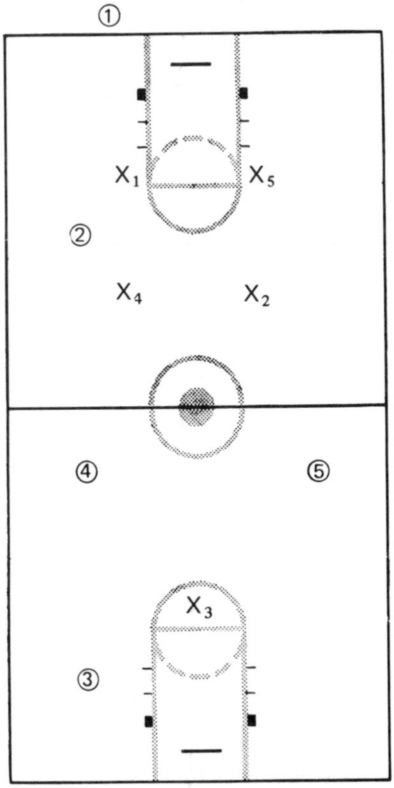

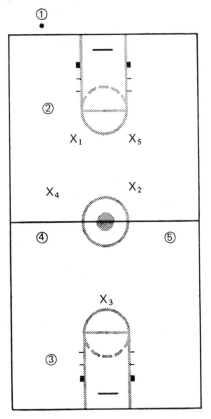

Fig. 10.12 *Modified Positioning of a Zone Pressure Defense So That the Opponents Cannot Pass Over a Line. X_4 and X_2 are in position to intercept a lob pass over their heads to 4 or 5. The starting position for any zone press must be modified to prevent the ball from going over a line.*

Fig. 10.11 *Poor Positioning by Zone Pressure Defensive Players. Player 1 can pass the ball over the first line of the press to 2 or over the second line to 4 or 5.*

sive circle area, the defenders may continue the press or revert to a normal zone defense.

A team must also understand that permitting the ball to be in-bounded to the defender's right weakens the defensive posture considerably because of the qualifications of players in those positions. If the inbound player starts to the defender's right of the basket, the defensive wing players (and the front line in the two-two-one) can reverse positions to counteract this move.

The two full court zone presses utilized most frequently are the two-two-one and the three-one-one. Each will be discussed separately.

The Two-Two-One Zone Press

The two-two-one zone press contains three "lines" of defenders who take their starting positions as shown in Fig. 10.13. X_1 and X_5 compose the front line, X_2 and X_4 the wing line (or wings), and X_3 is called the back player. The peculiar numbering system occurs because the numbers represent the usual playing position for each player. As the reader recalls, X_1 and X_2 are guards, X_3 is the center, and X_4 and X_5 are forwards.

*Qualifications for and
Responsibilities of Each Position in
the Zone Press*

Player X_1

1. She should be the quickest guard.
2. It is her responsibility to direct play up her side of the court. She forces a pass to be received in front and to her left.
3. With the help of X_5 she does not allow a pass to go between them.
4. She permits the receiver to dribble beyond the free throw line and then moves quickly to help X_4 with the trap.
5. If the ball goes downcourt she retreats quickly to the medium post position on the ball side.

Player X_5

1. She is the taller of the two forwards.
2. With X_1's assistance she prevents a pass from going between them.
3. She prevents a pass to the in-bounder.
4. She protects the middle while X_1 double-teams.
5. If the ball is passed in on her side, she double-teams with X_2 as X_1 covers the middle area.
6. If the ball is advanced downcourt she retreats quickly straight downcourt to a position about 6 ft. in front of the basket.

Player X_4

1. She is the quicker and more agile of the two forwards.
2. She prevents a pass from going between them with X_2's help.
3. She allows the ball to be in-bounded in front of her; if no opponent is in front of her, she drifts back so that the ball cannot be passed over her head.
4. She prevents the receiver from dribbling downcourt between her and the sideline. She helps double-team with X_1.
5. If the subsequent pass is on her side of the court, she double-teams with X_2.

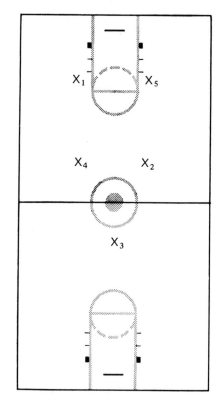

Fig. 10.13 *Basic Positions of Players for a Two-Two-One Zone Press. These positions may be altered, depending upon the positions of the opponents. X_1 and X_5 represent the front line, X_4 and X_2 the wings, and X_3 the back player. X_1 and X_5 take their position astride the lane line; X_4 and X_2 are directly behind X_1 and X_5, approximately midway between the top of the circle and the division line; X_3 is in the back court half of the center circle.*

6. If the ball is advanced downcourt she retreats quickly in a straight line and is prepared to double-team in the corner on her side; if the ball is on the far side, she retreats to the top of the circle and moves down the lane to about 6 ft. in front of the basket.
7. If the ball is in-bounded on the other side of the court, her duties become the same as those of X_2.

Player X_2

1. She is the second guard.
2. With the help of X_4, she prevents a pass from going between them.
3. She moves up near the division line on the ball side to zone any opponent in that area.

4. If no opponent is in her area she adjusts her position to cover any free opponent so that the ball cannot be passed over her head.
5. If an opponent receives a pass in her area, she prevents her from dribbling downcourt between her and the sideline. She double-teams with X_4.
6. If the ball advances downcourt, she retreats to front any player in the medium post position on the ball side.
7. If the ball is in-bounded on her side of the court she assumes the responsibilities of X_4.

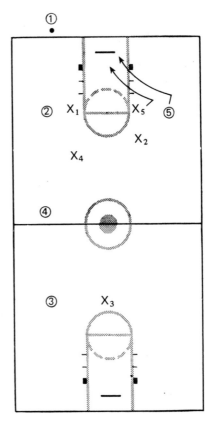

Fig. 10.15 *If the attack is having a difficult time advancing the ball downcourt, they may send 5 back to receive the in-bound pass. In this case, X_5 anticipates 5's cut into the lane and beats her there, forcing the pass to go to 2. Time is an asset to X_5 since 1 has only 5 sec. to in-bound the ball. While X_5 covers 5's cut, X_2 edges over to help X_5, since no one is in her zone. Her responsibility is to prevent a lob pass over X_5 to 5 if she cuts back toward the division line.*

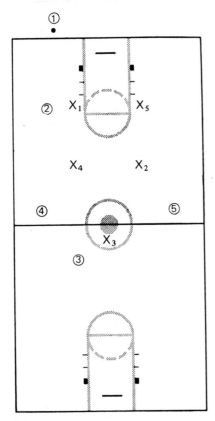

Fig. 10.14 *The defensive team wants the ball to be in-bounded to their left. Therefore, X_1 allows 1 to pass to 2. X_2 and X_5 prevent 5 from cutting in to the middle; X_5 also covers the passing lane to 5 if she cuts down her side of the court toward the end line. X_4 prevents the pass to 4. X_3 can prevent the full court pass to 3.*

Player X_3

1. She is both center and safety valve and must protect against any easy field goals. She must be skilled in playing two-on-one.
2. She must prevent any full court passes. If she cannot intercept them she must at least deflect them away from an opponent.
3. When playing in front of her opponent she must not allow a pass to go over her head; if she does, it is almost a sure two points.
4. As the ball crosses the division line she should

anticipate a pass into the corner and try to intercept it. Her timing on the interception must be perfect, or the opponents should score easily.
5. She must be a good rebounder.

In Figs. 10.14 to 10.23, the attack players are also included so that the reader can better visualize the relative positions of a defender to an opponent. In this zone the defenders do not allow the ball to be advanced down the middle of the court, and direct all ball movement toward the sideline.

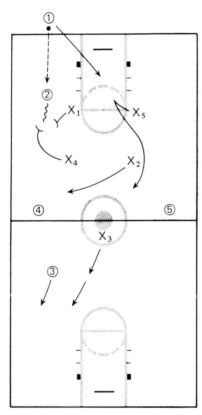

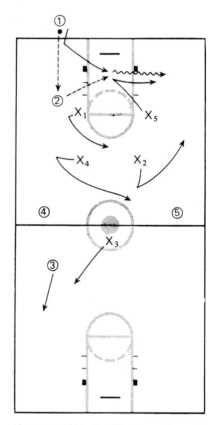

Fig. 10.16 X_1 allows 2 to receive the pass and dribble beyond the free throw line. X_1 delays her move toward 2 to discourage a return pass to 1. X_5 moves toward 1 for the same purpose. As 2 dribbles, X_4 moves over to prevent her from driving by; X_1 moves over to double-team. At the same time X_2 moves over to prevent the pass to 4 and X_5 moves to the intercepting angle so that 5 is not free; X_1 and X_4 have arms high trying to force a lob pass.

Fig. 10.17 If 2 in Fig. 10.16 cannot pass to 4, she may return a quick pass to 1. X_5 must not permit her to drive down the middle. She must overplay her and force her to the defensive right side. There the trap and other coverage can be re-established; X_2 reverses her direction to assist X_5 with the trap; X_4 reverses her direction to cover the passing lane to 5; X_1 recovers down the middle.

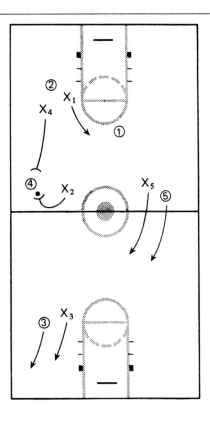

Fig. 10.18 *If 2 succeeds in passing to 4, X_2 approaches cautiously so that she is not subject to a fake and drive by 4. At the same time X_4 moves up from behind. If 4 pivots, X_4 attempts to tie up the ball. If not, both players raise their arms high and try to force a lob pass. X_2 and X_4 must not let 4 dribble between them. At the same time, X_1 cuts down the center of the court, filling in where needed. X_5 and X_3 cover the passing lanes to the opponent in their zone.*

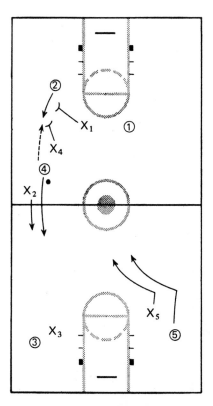

Fig. 10.19 *4 is unable to pass to 3 or 5 and is forced to pass backward. X_1 has zoned well against 1, so 4 returns a pass to 2. (When 4 has the ball in this position, X_1 tries to zone against both 2 and 1, but must be more concerned with 1 because the defense does not want the ball to be passed in to the middle.) Once 4 passes to 2, X_1 and X_4 double-team 2 while X_2 zones 4. X_3 cuts oi the passing angle to 3 and X_5 cuts off the angle to 5. If 4 succeeds in passing to 1, X_1 forces her toward the defensive right sideline; X_2 moves over to help X_1 while X_4 plays zone between 2 and 4.*

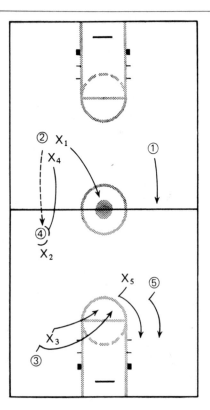

Fig. 10.20 *2 returns the pass to 4 and players resume their same relative position as described in Fig. 10.18. X_1 must be ready for a pass back to either 2 or 1.*

Fig. 10.21 *4 succeeds in passing to 3. X_3 and X_2 trap 3 while X_4 cuts ball side of 4. X_5 moves over near the free throw line covering the passing lane to 5 and is ready to help if 3 eludes the trap. X_1 breaks down the middle to help where necessary.*

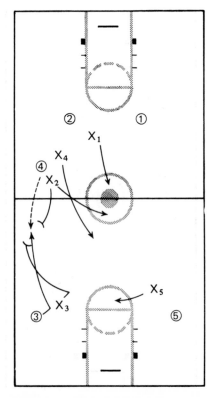

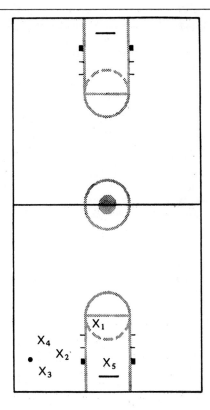

Fig. 10.22 *Position of the Players If the Ball Moves to the Defensive Left Corner. X_2 fronts any player in the medium post position. X_1 adjusts her position according to the position of the opponents.*

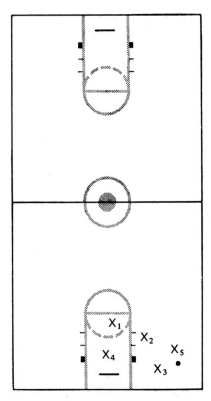

Fig. 10.23 *Position of the Players If the Ball Is in the Defensive Right Corner. When the ball is successfully advanced downcourt, the defense has the option of continuing with the press or reverting to a normal zone defense.*

The One-Two-One-One Zone Press

This press also has three lines of defense, as shown in Fig. 10.24. The player in X_1 position will be referred to as the top player, X_4 and X_5 are the wings, X_2 is the middle player, and X_3 is the back player. Although the one-two-one-one alignment differs from the two-two-one, basically the same zones on the court are covered with this zone as the one previously described. Placement of personnel may make one of the zone presses more desirable and effective than the other. This zone permits the initial trap to be made sooner than does the two-two-one. The two zones resemble each other after the in-bounds pass is made.

Qualifications for and
Responsibilities of Each Position in
the Press

Player X_1

1. She should be the quickest guard; she may be a tall, agile forward or post.
2. It is her responsibility to direct play to her left, and she forces the in-bound pass to that direction.
3. She prevents an immediate return pass to the inbounder.
4. She allows the receiver to obtain the pass and double-teams with X_4.
5. If the ball is returned to the in-bound passer, she forces her to the defender's right and traps with X_5. It takes time to set the trap, so the players involved should not be too hasty in their moves or the dribbler will escape the trap.
6. She protects the middle area whenever she is not involved in a trap.
7. When the ball is advanced downcourt she retreats quickly to the medium post position on the ball side.

Player X_4

1. She is the quicker and more agile of the two forwards; she must be skilled in one-on-one defensive techniques.
2. She allows the ball to be in-bounded in front of her; if no opponent is in front of her, she drifts back so that the ball cannot be passed over her head.
3. Once the ball has been in-bounded in front of her she sets a trap with the help of X_1. She must be certain that the dribbler does not

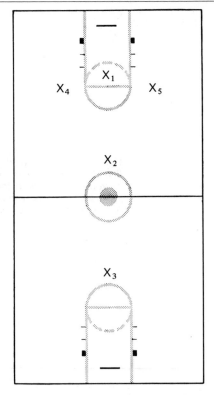

Fig. 10.24 *Basic Positions for a One-Two-One-One Zone Press. X_4 is the better defensive forward as the defense tries to force the ball to their left.*

evade the trap by dribbling between her and the sideline.

4. If the subsequent pass is on her side, she double-teams with the help of X_2.
5. If the ball is advanced downcourt on her side, she retreats quickly to help X_3 trap in the corner. If the ball is on the far side of the court she retreats to the top of the circle and moves down the lane to about 6 ft. in front of the basket when the ball is in the far corner.
6. If the ball is in-bounded on the other side of the court, her duties become the same as X_5.

Player X_5

1. She is the second forward; it is helpful if she is tall.
2. She prevents a pass from being in-bounded on her side.
3. While X_1 and X_4 are double-teaming, she protects the area at the top of the circle.

4. If the ball is returned to her side of the court through a pass to the in-bounder, she prevents the ball handler from dribbling between her and the sideline. With the help of X_1 they trap the ball handler.
5. When the ball is advanced downcourt on the other side, she retreats quickly to the top of the circle and moves down the key to about 6 ft. in front of the basket as the ball is passed to the far corner. When the ball is on her side, she helps double-team any player who has the ball.
6. If the ball is in-bounded on her side of the court, her duties become the same as X_4.

Player X_2

1. She is the quicker of the two guards and should have outstanding anticipation; she has a large area to cover.
2. When the ball is in-bounded to her left, she prevents a subsequent pass up that side of the court. She overplays any opponent in that area.
3. If the opponent receives the ball she prevents her from dribbling downcourt between her and the side line. She helps trap with X_4's assistance.
4. If the ball is passed back to the in-bounder and is dribbled up the far side of the court, she crosses to the other side at midcourt to overplay a logical receiver in the area.
5. When the ball is advanced downcourt, she retreats quickly to the ball side and moves down outside of the lane as the ball moves into the corner.

Player X_3

1. She is the pivot player and the best rebounder.
2. She must protect against any long downcourt pass, but her timing for an interception must be exceptional so that an easy layup does not result.
3. She must anticipate and fake well in a two-on-one situation.
4. She must anticipate a pass into the corner and contain the ball handler until she has help in a double-team effort.
5. She must not let a pass go over her head while she is overplaying a potential receiver.

In Figs. 10.25 to 10.34, the defenders' positions are shown as the ball is passed downcourt.

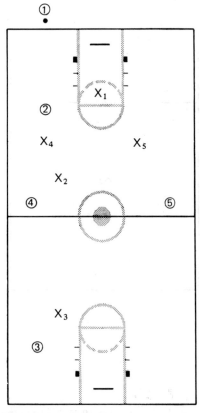

Fig. 10.25 *Modified Starting Position When the Offensive Players Start Behind the Free Throw Line. The defense must not allow a pass to go over a zone, so they drift back to force the pass to be made in front of them. X_5 prevents a pass to 5, and X_4 forces the in-bounds pass to go to 2.*

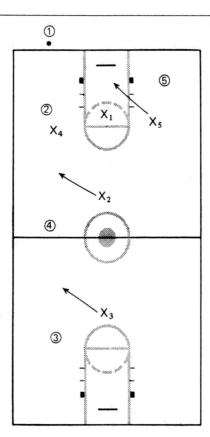

Fig. 10.26 *If the attack is having difficulty advancing the ball downcourt, they may send another player to receive the in-bound pass. The defenders want the ball in-bounded and brought down the court to their left, so X_5 cuts off the passing lane to 5.*

Fig. 10.27 *X_1 allows the ball to be passed in to 2 and cuts down the lane to prevent a return pass to 1 and then helps X_4 double-team 2. As the ball is in-bounded to X_2's left, she moves over to cover the passing lane to 4. X_5 edges back to cover the passing lane to 5. X_3 moves over to prevent a pass to 3.*

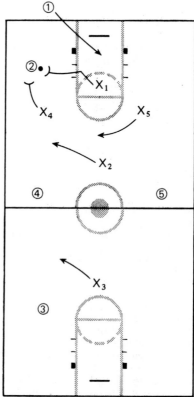

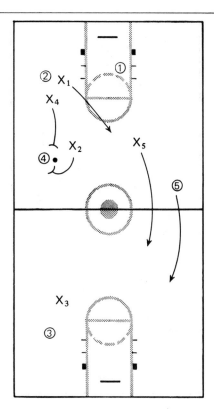

Fig. 10.28 *2 is able to pass to 4. X_4 joins X_2 in a double-team. X_1 cuts to the top of the circle to prevent a pass to 1. This leaves 2 open, but should the ball be returned to her, the players resume the same positions held previously. X_5 continues to play the intercepting angle to 5, while X_3 does the same to 3.*

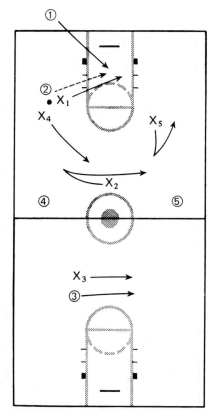

Fig. 10.29 *If 2 cannot pass to 4 but is able to return a pass to 1, X_1 and X_5 must move quickly to double-team her as rapidly as possible. X_4 moves up to cover the middle while X_2 moves over to play the intercepting angle to 5. As 3 cuts to the ball side, so does X_3.*

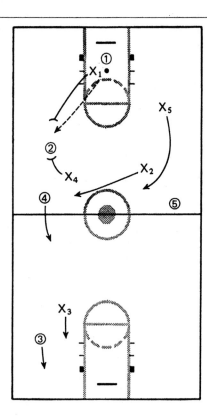

Fig. 10.30 *Player 1 anticipates the double-team approaching and returns the ball quickly to 2. The defensive players reverse their actions to cover the intercepting angles. X_1 returns with X_4 to double-team 2. X_2, X_5 and X_3 recover as shown.*

Fig. 10.31 *If 2 is able to pass to 4, the defensive players move to the same relative positions they had when 4 was double-teamed previously (Fig. 10.28). X_1 must be ready to return to either 1 or 2 in case 4 passes back. If this should occur, the players resume the positions previously described (Fig. 10.30).*

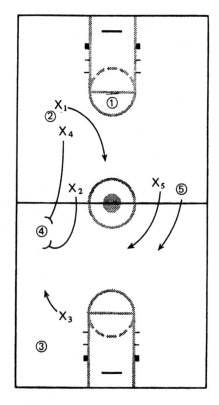

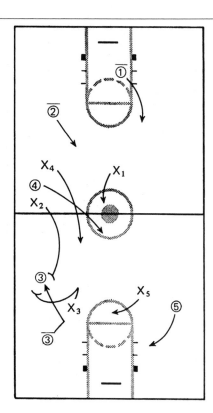

Fig. 10.32 *After 4 gets the ball in Fig. 10.28, she is able to pass to 3. X_2 helps X_3 double-team 3. X_4 cuts to the ball side of 4, while X_1 is ready if a pass is returned to 2 or 1. X_5 covers the passing lane to 5.*

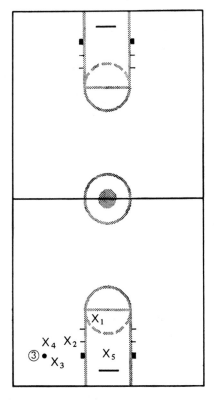

Fig. 10.33 *Position of the Players When the Ball Moves in to the Defense's Left Corner. X_2 fronts any player in the medium post area. X_1's position is adjusted according to where the opponents are positioned.*

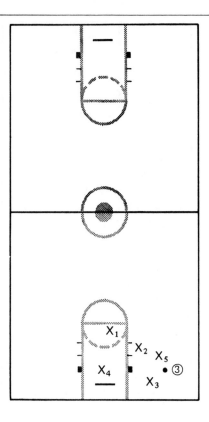

Fig. 10.34 *Position of the Players When the Ball Is in the Defense's Right Corner. X_2 fronts any player in her area and X_1 adjusts her position according to the position of the opponents. When the ball is successfully advanced downcourt, the defense has the option of continuing with the press or reverting to a normal zone defense.*

Drills for Full Court Presses

1. Two teams in position for the ball to be in-bounded to the defender's left of the basket. The initial pass is made in-bounds on signal from the instructor. The defenders move accordingly. A subsequent pass is made on another signal, and the defenders react accordingly. Attack players must remain stationary at this stage so that the defenders can gain knowledge of intercepting angles. Later, as they acquire this ability, the attack players are permitted to move wherever they choose but must continue to pass on signal. At first also, the instructor designates where the next pass is made; later, the players use their own discretion.

2. Two teams. The team that is practicing the pressing defense possesses the ball in their frontcourt. Any player may shoot, and when the goal is made the team moves quickly into their pressing alignment before the ball can be in-bounded. The instructor must watch carefully to see that the offensive team rebounds properly. Players have a tendency to shoot and run to their position in the press. They must first rebound before they can move to their pressing positions.

HALF-COURT PRESSES

If a team does not have the personnel to employ a full court press, it may be able to use a half-court press successfully. Periodically, it may also prove valuable as a surprise tactic if a team does not have confidence in using it throughout a game. It has obvious use when a team is behind in score.

Numerous half-court zone pressure defenses can be established. The most popular ones are the two-two-one, one-two-one-one, one-one-two-one, one-three-one, and the two-three. For the odd front

zones the front line starts one step across the division line; but for the even front zones, the front line starts on the defensive side of the division line. It should be noted that all of the zones resemble one another after the initial pass.

When using any of the half-court presses, there are basically three places where traps are set: (1) the corners of the court at the center line; (2) the areas opposite the foul lines at the sideline; and (3) the corners of the court at the baseline.

Certain principles apply to all half-court presses. The point player must position herself between the

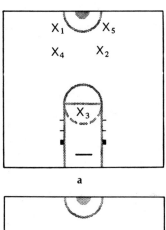

Fig. 10.35 *Two-Two-One Half-Court Press.*

ball and the midpoint of the free throw line. Players involved in a trap must cut off the sideline. They must not foul as they harass the ball handler. The offside wing player should be on a line between the ball and the offside corner.

The Two-Two-One Half-Court Press

Player qualifications for the various positions are the same as those described for the full court press. Since the defense is much stronger to the defender's left than to the right, every effort should be made to influence the ball in this direction or reverse the positions of the front and wing lines. As the ball moves to the right wing position, player X_1 (a guard) is in the lane after X_5 had dropped back from her double-teaming duties near the division line. When the ball goes into the right corner, X_5 drops down into the lane about 6 ft. in front of the basket to afford better protection against taller opponents under the basket and for better rebounding strength.

The positions of the players as the ball moves around the perimeter of the zone are shown in Fig. 10.35.

The One-Two-One-One Half-Court Press

Player qualifications for the various positions are the same as those described for the full court press. Fig. 10.36a–k show the movements of the players, and Fig. 10.37a–g show the positions of players as the ball moves around the perimeter of the zone.

a

Fig. 10.36 *One-Two-One-One Half-Court Press.*

b

c

d

e

Fig. 10.36 *continued.*

f

g

h

i

Fig. 10.36 *continued.*

j

k

Fig. 10.37 *One-Two-One-One Half-Court Press*

The One-One-Two-One Half-Court Press

Of the two guards, X_2 should be the quicker and better skilled defensive player. She has considerably more territory to cover than does the other guard. Of the two forwards, X_4 should be the better defensive player if the ball is to be influenced toward her side of the court.

The positions of the players as the ball moves around the perimeter of the zone are shown in Fig. 10.38.

The One-Three-One Half-Court Press

Player X_1 must be quick as she has a large area to cover. The back player, X_2, may be a guard or forward; she must be quick as she must cover from corner to corner. The three players in the middle should have good height. It is difficult to play this defense effectively with short players across the middle. X_4 should be the better defensive player if the ball is to be influenced toward her direction.

The positions of the players as the ball moves around the perimeter of the zone are shown in Fig. 10.39a–e.

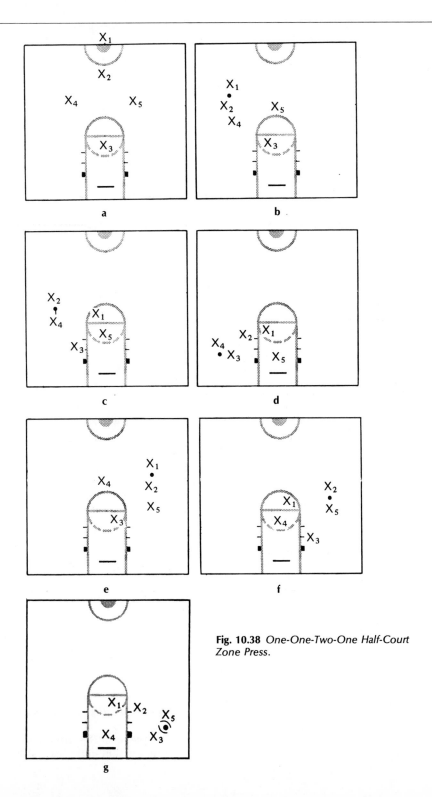

Fig. 10.38 *One-One-Two-One Half-Court Zone Press.*

Fig. 10.39 *One-Three-One Half-Court Zone Press.*

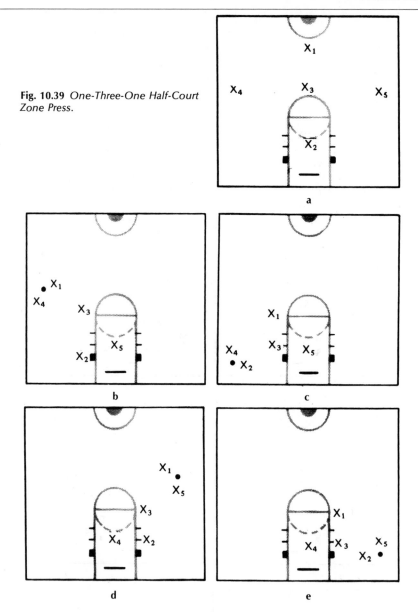

The Two-Three Half-Court Press

The guard assigned to the X_2 position should be the quickest defender. Because both forwards and the pivot cover a great deal of area with this press, all must be agile. The player assigned to the X_5 position should be the best rebounder. Player X_5 must also sprint under the basket when the ball moves from the right wing to the right corner position so that the team does not give away a great height advantage under the basket.

The positions of players as the ball moves around the perimeter of the zone are shown in Fig. 10.40.

Drills for Half-Court Presses

The drills used for zone defenses can be adapted for instruction in the half-court pressure defenses.

Fig. 10.40 *Two-Three Half-Court Press.*

OFFENSE AGAINST A PRESSING DEFENSE

Both teacher/coach and players must understand why an opposing team chooses to use a pressing defense. The common reason is to disconcert the attacking team, cause them to lose their poise, and force them to make a ball handling error. Basically, this is done by overplaying those players close to the ball and trying to double-team the player with the ball. Players should recognize that this is a very weak defense since one player should always be free if the opponents are trapping the ball handler. Therefore, after a team passes the ball through the double-team, it has a player advantage and should be able to maneuver quickly for an easy shot. If a

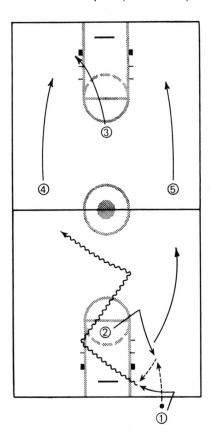

Fig. 10.41 *Against a Man-to-Man Press. 1, the best ball handler, in-bounds the ball. 2, the other guard, fakes and receives the pass. 2 returns the ball to 1 and clears toward the sideline to allow 1 as much space as needed to dribble downcourt.*

team lacks poise or experience against a press however, it may be in for a long afternoon! Through practice, players learn to attack the press — rather than being attacked by it!

Because a press takes time to set up, it can be beaten immediately by a quick pass in-bounds. (Presses are organized after a score has been made.) Although this is true, there is a difference of opinion among coaches as to which player should in-bound the ball. There are those who believe that it is absolutely essential to in-bound the ball as rapidly as possible. Therefore, the player closest to the ball retrieves the ball and passes it in-bounds. Other coaches believe that this may be dangerous because the player who in-bounds the ball may not be a good ball handler and may cause an intercepted pass. These coaches believe that the best ball handler should always put the ball in play even though the pass in may be delayed temporarily as she moves behind the endline. This is caused because the best ball handler is usually playing in the position of guard and may be 20–30 ft. from the endline at the time the goal is scored. The choice of which player is to in-bound the ball must be left to the discretion of the teacher/coach.

It is important that the players stay scattered against any type of pressing defense. They should avoid weaves, any type of lateral crosses, and lateral screens which bring the defenders close and aid them in trapping. There should be extensive player movement to cause the defense to adjust their positions. Pass and cut techniques are helpful in beating the press. Competitive teams should practice against both man-to-man and zone presses so that they become acclimated to the various moves and can attack the press with ease and confidence.

Offense Against a Man-to-Man Press

The primary means of advancing the ball downcourt against a man-to-man press is to give the ball to the best dribbler and let her go one-on-one against her opponent. The rest of the players clear the backcourt to allow the dribbler to use the entire backcourt area to elude her opponent.

When in-bounding the ball, a team generally tries to rely on only one player to receive the pass. Fig. 10.41 shows typical positioning of players for the in-bounds pass. If this is not successful, a team sends another player into the backcourt. (Positioning is shown in Fig. 10.42.) If the in-bounds passer is the best ball handler, the receiver returns a pass to her so that she may dribble downcourt.

If a team does not have an exceptional dribbler to advance the ball, a forward or center who is

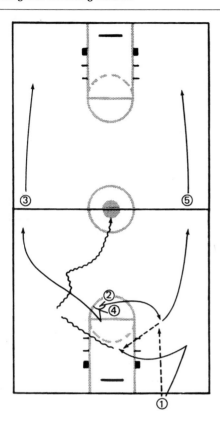

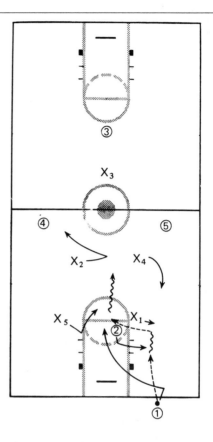

Fig. 10.42 *Offense Against a Man-to-Man Press When 1 Has Difficulty In-bounding the Ball. Player 2 fakes and cuts off 4 to receive the pass. 2 returns it to 1, and both 2 and 4 clear to allow 1 to dribble down court.*

Fig. 10.43 *Dribbling to Beat a Trap Against a Two-Two-One Zone Press. 1 passes to 2, and 1 cuts up the middle. 2 commences to dribble to draw defenders X_1 and X_4 for the trap. Before they can set it, 2 returns a pass to 1 who drives between X_5 and X_1 before they can double-team.*

guarded by a weak opponent may be given the responsibility of dribbling the ball into the frontcourt. Other techniques used against a man-to-man press include the use of short passes in which the receiver moves toward the ball. Pass and cut tactics are effective. Occasionally a long pass into the frontcourt may be successful, but the passer must be completely aware of the position of all opponents and be certain that her pass will be successful.

Offense Against a Zone Press

All zone presses are predicated on employing a double-team. All zone presses deploy one player deep and have two players involved in a trap, leaving the two remaining defenders to cover three of-

fensive players. As a result, an attacking team should take measures so that trapping and zoning tactics by the defense will be unsuccessful. Since traps are easier to set at a sideline or in a corner (because the sideline serves as another defender) the attack should try to advance the ball down the middle of the court. Before a trap is about to be set the ball handler should split the two defenders by dribbling between them (Fig. 10.43) or pass to a teammate cutting behind the trappers (Fig. 10.44). This method continues to advance the ball up the court and provides the offense with a player advantage.

When playing against a zone press, an attacking team should also always have a trailer behind the

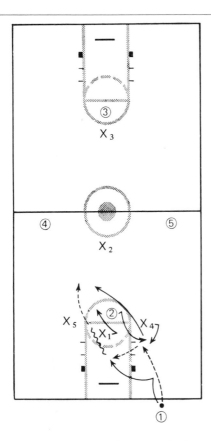

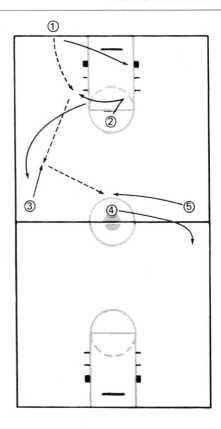

Fig. 10.44 *Passing to Beat a Trap Against a One-Two-One-One Zone Press. 1 passes in to 2, and 2 returns the pass to 1. 1 dribbles toward the trap as 2 cuts behind X_1 to receive the pass from 1.*

Fig. 10.45 *Pattern Offense Used Against Any Type of Zone Press. Player 2 fakes and cuts for the pass. 3 cuts for the next pass as 1 cuts behind 2 toward the opposite sideline. After 2 passes to 3, 2 cuts to fill the outside lane. 5 cuts to the middle for the subsequent pass as 4 clears to the sideline. The lanes are now filled for a fast break.*

ball handler. The defenders guard the areas in front of the ball and cannot defend well against a trailer. Therefore, the trailer serves as a safety valve and should be free when needed for a pass.

In planning an attack against a zone press, screening techniques should be used. It is also wise to dribble only when necessary or for some predetermined reason. After a player is forced to pick up the ball following a dribble, she is far easier to trap. Therefore, a pass receiver should attempt to pass immediately upon receiving the ball or plan a controlled dribble to draw two defenders so that a pass to a teammate allows her to escape a trap and advance beyond the front line of the defense. These are the two keys to success in beating a zone press.

The zone press should be attacked at its weakest point. Basically this is in the middle of the court.

Also, players are freest after the defense has moved to establish a trap. As this occurs the ball handler must recognize where her teammates will be and find a free player to whom she can pass. She must always face her frontcourt so that she can see the action of both her teammates and the opponents; but, she should understand that she will have a trailer to whom she may pass if no one in front of her is really free.

Players should practice against the most common zone press defenses employed in their region so that they can "attack" the press rather than go on the defensive. It is better to plan to move toward a

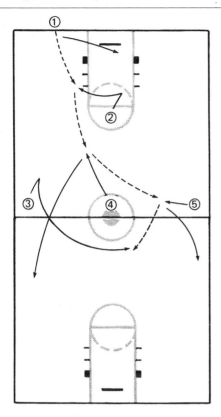

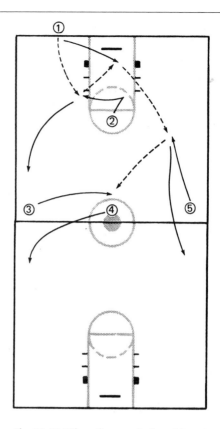

Fig. 10.46 *If 3 is not open, 2 looks for 4 to be free in the middle. 2 passes to 4, who passes to the weak side 5. 3 cuts to the middle and 4 fills the wing position.*

Fig. 10.47 *When the pass to 3 or 4 is not open, 2 passes to 1 who has remained behind 2. 5 cuts for the next pass, 3 cuts to the middle for a pass, and 4 fills the other wing.*

trap and pass off before it is set than to move in an uncontrolled manner and either throw the ball away or cause a tie ball when the trap occurs. Most coaches agree, however, that they would prefer to have a tie ball rather than a poorly thrown pass that ends up in an easy score for the opponents. If the attacking team can pass the ball beyond the front line of the zone press once, they are in an excellent position to move further downcourt with a player advantage. If it results in several easy scores, the opponents will soon resort to a different means of defense.

Different offenses have been designed to use against zone presses. An example of a pattern that utilizes five mobile players, all of whom are capable of ball handling is shown in Figs. 10.45 to 10.47.

If one player is less mobile and/or not a good ball handler, a different alignment of players is necessary. Examples are shown in subsequent diagrams.

Drills

The same practice techniques used to develop skill in operating against either a man-to-man or zone defense should be utilized in learning an attack against a press. The development of this attack takes considerable practice time and patience on behalf of both player and coach.

Some coaches profess to attach an odd front zone (one-two-one-one) by sending the in-bounder to the same side as the ball. With the front player and the ball side wing involved in the trap, a pass back to the in-bounder should be open, if the ball cannot be advanced downcourt. Against an even front zone (two-two-one), the in-bounder may be sent to the side opposite from the ball. The in-bounder should be free for a pass if necessary, as the weak side wing defender moves to cover the middle area.

Figs. 10.48–10.50 identify potential passes against an odd front zone.

Figs. 10.51–10.53 identify potential passes against an even front zone.

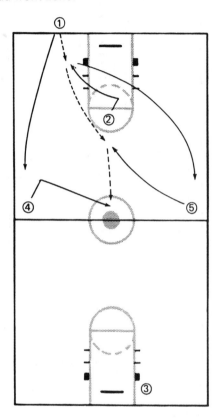

Fig. 10.48 *Pattern Against an Odd Front Zone Press. 2 fakes and cuts for a pass from 1. 2 immediately turns and passes to 5 cutting to the middle. 1 and 2 fill the lanes on the fast break. 3 goes to the side opposite the inbounded ball.*

Fig. 10.49 *Player 2 was unable to pass to 5, so 2 passes to 1 who quickly dribbles beyond the attempted trap on 2. 1 passes to 5 who dribbles down the middle of the court for the player advantage.*

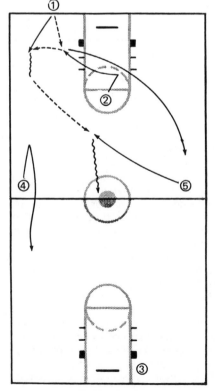

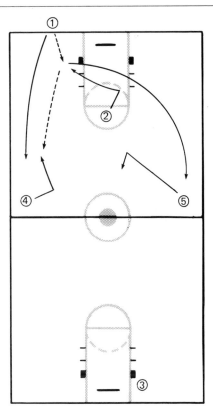

Fig. 10.50 *Player 2 passes to 4 who passes to either 1 or 5 to break the press.*

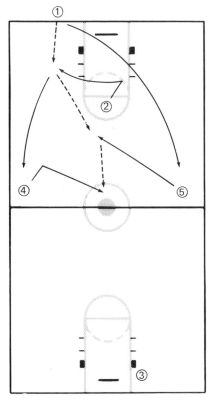

Fig. 10.51 *Pattern Against an Even Front Zone. After 1 passes to 2, she cuts to the side opposite the ball. 2 passes to 5 in the middle and 5 passes to 4. 1 and 2 fill the wings.*

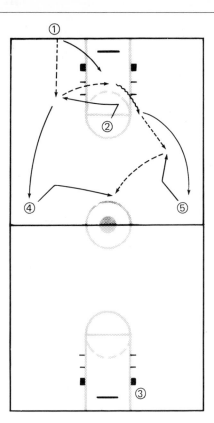

Fig. 10.52 *Player 2 is unable to pass to 4 or 5. 2 passes back to 1 who dribbles if necessary before passing to 5. 5 immediately turns to pass to 4, and the fast break develops with 2 and 1 on the wings.*

Fig. 10.53 *Player 1 passes to 2 who passes to 4, then to 5, 1 and 2 fill the wings.*

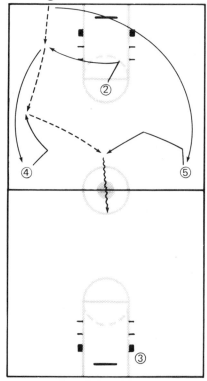

4

Special Situations

11

The Stall Game

The purpose of a stall offense is to change the pace of the offense, to maintain possession of the ball for a longer period of time than normal, and to protect or increase a lead already gained. In high school competition where Federation rules are used there is no 30-second clock and a team may "freeze" the ball for as long as it desires. Because the freeze style offense is generally devised to consume one, two, or more minutes, it cannot be employed in AIAW games due to the 30-second clock rule. The following paragraphs will discuss the stall offense. Those teams which wish to freeze the ball can utilize the same principles, but extend them indefinitely.

There are times when a stall offense may seem desirable either very briefly or through a series of offensive opportunities. For example, the team that has gained possession of the ball within the last 30 seconds of each quarter may desire to maintain possession as long as possible, to acquire the "last shot," thus precluding the opponents from gaining another offensive opportunity.

When a team has a slim lead near the end of the game, it may wish to abandon the fast break style of play it used and adopt a more controlled style of offense. This accomplishes two purposes.

1. It consumes more time, thus forcing the opponents who are behind in score to gamble somewhat more. This, in turn, opens scoring opportunities for the offense.
2. A controlled style of play keeps ball handling errors at a minimum and fewer turnovers should result.

During the game, there may be times when it seems desirable just to change the pace of the offense. By consuming close to 30 seconds on each possession, a team develops discipline in its offense and recognizes that it has the poise and capacity for controlling the ball as long as the rules permit. Psychologically, this may also affect the defensive team adversely and cause them to take unnecessary chances or become a little careless or sluggish in meeting a control pattern.

BASIC PRINCIPLES TO USE WITH A STALL

In selecting an offense to use to stall, a teacher/coach may choose to use the basic pattern that has proved most effective during the contest, or a special offense may be devised. In either case the offense should be constructed so that a ball handler cannot be trapped at a boundary line or in a corner. The ball should stay in the central portion of the court as much as possible so that double-teaming is less likely and so that the ball may be passed in all directions. Crossing in front of or behind a player with the ball should be avoided so that the opponents may not double-team. Crossing is still appropriate for players without the ball, however.

Players should eliminate all dribbling or keep it to a minimum unless a spread offense is used in which it is difficult to double-team. The ball should be passed constantly so that there is extensive ball movement and little chance for double-teaming.

Occasionally, an exceptional dribbler can consume a great deal of time, but even then there is difficulty in preventing a double-team unless she has excellent timing and good peripheral vision so that she can entice a double-team and pass off to a free player. Often, however, the dribbler is forced to turn her back to the basket and cannot see her teammates before she is trapped by two opponents. If a dribbler is about to be tied or called for a jump, she can call time-out so that her team is sure to maintain possession of the ball. (Some time-outs should always be saved for the last few minutes of a contest.)

Cross-court passes should be avoided. These are long and high and easily intercepted. During a stall, all players should be encouraged to go to meet the ball, even more so than usual. Actually, the offensive pattern used should force the players to cut toward the ball so that there are fewer chances for interceptions by the defense.

When a stall is to be followed for a series of possessions, the best ball handlers should be in the game. This may mean that a third ball handler replaces one of the forwards. This may be done only, however, if a great height disparity is not created when the offensive team goes on defense.

Only sure shots should be attempted during a stall offense. The offensive team should continue to make scoring thrusts, but take only those shots that are of a high percentage nature. If the offensive team fails to look for scoring opportunities while they run the clock, the defense can afford to take more chances in an effort to get an interception. As the opponents press, the offensive team can look for backdoor cuts. Other options should be devised from the basic pattern so that an advantage can be taken of any defensive carelessness.

When a team starts to use a stall offense, it may also begin to press the opponents when they secure the ball as a surprise tactic. This tends to delay the opponents from getting the ball downcourt, which in turn consumes more time. Often it is also a psychological barrier to the team behind in score, since they recognize they must hurry and are being slowed in their own backcourt. They also may be surprised by the tactic at this time and make careless passes that result in easy baskets for the team leading in score.

One more consideration should be given when a team is using the stall during the last few minutes of the game. Because the opponents are likely to guard closely under these circumstances, they also are likely to commit more fouls. For this reason the offensive team should have good free throw shooters on the court at this time.

STALL PATTERNS

There are several stall patterns. Fig. 11.1 shows one that is commonly used. The reader will note that the players remain spread throughout the pattern, that no player crosses another one with the ball, that the ball is always passed from the middle of the court, and that the lane area is kept open for cuts on options. This is a simple pattern to learn and can be used effectively.

At the University of Iowa, Ralph Miller used a stall offense with a high double post around which the other players cut. Fig. 11.2 shows this pattern. Two players cut around one of the posts, while only one player cuts around the other one. Timing of the cut around the post is an important part of this pattern, as receivers are always moving to meet the pass. Passes may be made to other players who become free momentarily for a shot.

The four corner offense popularized by Dean Smith has been used by a number of teams. The alignment of players is shown in Fig. 11.3. An alternate alignment has two players out front and three back with one at the foul line. If a team has an exceptional dribbler, it may choose the three-player front since it enables the dribbler to drive down the lane and pass off, if necessary.

When using the four corner offense, the dribbler must penetrate toward the free throw area. She wants to split two defenders who harrass her. The other offensive players at the center line maintain their positions near the sideline unless a passing lane to them is not open, in which case they must move to an open area on the court. Before a trap

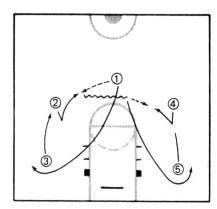

Fig. 11.1 *Stall Pattern. 1 passes to 2 and cuts to the corner. 2 dribbles, passes to 4, and cuts to the corner. The pattern continues as 3 replaces 2 and 5 replaces 4.*

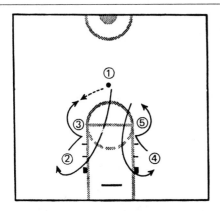

Fig. 11.2 *Miller's Stall. 2 fakes and cuts around 3 to receive a pass from 1. 1 cuts down to replace 2. 4 times her cut so that she is moving toward the ball to receive a pass from 2. The pattern continues, with 1 and 2 interchanging positions and 4 staying on her side of the court.*

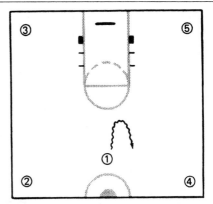

Fig. 11.3 *Four Corner Offense. Player 1 penetrates as much as possible. Before she is trapped, she passes to 2 or 4 who moves into the middle and continues to penetrate. 1 replaces her in the corner. 1 may also pass to 3 or 5 who should pass out to 1, 2, or 4.*

can be set, the dribbler must pass off to one of her teammates. That player must penetrate, but will pass the ball to the best dribbler as soon as possible.

If additional help is needed, the ball may be passed to one of the players at the baseline corner. That player must cut to meet the pass and then pass out front again to continue the stall. Rather than make a long pass, it is desirable to dribble to shorten the length of the pass.

In high school competition the stall can be continued indefinitely. In college play the offensive thrust should be started at about 8 seconds. Having stalled for that period of time, the team should then try to score before the 30 seconds expire. If a back defender moves out to stop the dribbler, the baseline corner players can cut high and go backdoor for a pass as shown in Fig. 11.4.

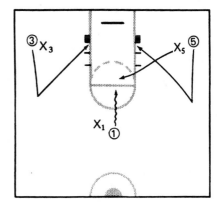

Fig. 11.4 *If X_5 moves out to help, 5 cuts high and goes backdoor.*

DEFENSE AGAINST THE STALL

When the stall is employed at the end of the quarter for a last shot or for a change of pace, the defensive team is wise to continue to use its normal defense. There is no need at this time to press the opponents. Instead, the defensive team should sag off their opponents slightly and cut off the passing lanes into the free throw lane and other high percentage shooting areas. At this time the defensive team must remain patient and force the offensive team to come to them. They desire to prevent a

short shot and force a long shot. However, they must remain alert and not become lackadaisical in their defense or the offense will make a premature scoring effort at the defensive weakness. During the last 12–15 seconds that the offensive team has before they must shoot, the defense should tighten up slightly and press the opponents more in an effort to force them to take a shot beyond the range from which they would like. Or, the defense should force them to take an off-balanced shot, a shot from an undesirable spot on the court, or cause a weak shooter to make the attempt.

When a team is behind in score and time seems to be running out, they must employ a pressing defense, if not full court, at least half-court. At this stage they can ill afford to sit back and wait for the opponents to consume close to 30 seconds before shooting. If they have any hope for winning, they must get the ball. As they operate their press, however, they must be careful not to allow an easy shot. Nevertheless, if it comes down to the last possession before time expires and they are behind by one or two points, they must take chances to get the ball. It makes little difference whether a team loses by two or four points.

High school teams that are behind in score must initiate action within 10 seconds. The defensive team, therefore, cannot sag off. They must make an attempt to get the ball.

LAST SHOT

In the closing seconds of a quarter (other than the fourth quarter) a team may delay their shot so that they do not allow the opponents another offensive opportunity. Usually a team attempts to maneuver for its last shot with approximately 8 seconds remaining. This gives the team time to pass the ball to the desired shooter, allow her to attempt her shot, and provide time for a rebound shot if the original attempt is unsuccessful. Yet it does not allow time for the opponents to recover the rebound and pass it downcourt for an unrushed shot for goal.

In making an attempt for the last shot in any of the first three quarters, a team generally does not call a time-out to decide what action should be taken. Instead, a specific maneuver is predetermined, or a signal for a play is given as the ball is advanced downcourt. The play may have been successful previously, or may have been devised specifically for this situation. A team may also choose to spread four of its players wide and give the ball to the best one-on-one player and let her maneuver in the last few seconds for a shot.

LAST SHOT IN THE GAME

Concern over the last shot in the game occurs when the game is tied or when the team in possession of the ball is behind by one, two, or three points. If the game is tied, the offensive team wants to run down the clock to the last few seconds so that it obtains

the last shot. If a team is behind by more than three points during the last seconds of the game it must take and make shots very soon after it acquires possession of the ball. Then it must press and regain the ball so that it may score quickly again. Basically the same tactic must be used when a team is behind by three points, as a defensive team should never foul under these conditions to provide the opportunity for a three-point play.

Before attempting the last shot in the final quarter, a team usually calls a time-out and establishes exactly what tactic should be followed. In this way all players should be aware of their exact responsibilities, including rebounding. Since the ball is put in play from out-of-bounds, a specific play may be devised for use at this time, or common out-of-bounds tactics may be used to get the ball to the desired shooter. If a specific play is not to be used, a primary shooter should be designated and the player who receives the ball in-bounds should try to get the ball to her. If she is guarded too closely, the ball should be passed to the secondary shooter who also was designated during the time-out. One of these two players should attempt the last shot. If both are so well guarded that the ball cannot be passed to either of them, then some other player must make an attempt preferably with at least 5 seconds remaining so that a rebound attempt may be made if the shot is unsuccessful.

Defense Against the Last Shot in the Game

The team that is ahead in the last minute or two can afford to sag off their opponents slightly and cut off the desirable passing lanes. If they are ahead by four points or more, they should encourage the outside shot — particularly by players who have not demonstrated much success. Good outside shooters should be guarded more closely. The defensive team encourages numerous passes by the offense so that more time is consumed.

If the defensive team is ahead by only three points, it continues to encourage the opponents to consume as much time as possible. Great defensive care should be exercised so that the opponents do not secure an easy shot. They should attempt to score quickly, but the defense should not be flustered and foul when they attempt a shot even if it appears to be an easy field goal. They do not want to give the opponents a chance for a three-point play. It is better by far to allow the easy basket, get the ball out-of-bounds, and then control it for the rest of the game. This way they win by one point. This is far smarter than to risk a tie game.

If the defensive team is ahead by two points, the players know they can do no worse than a tie unless of course, they foul a player in the act of shooting. They must not do this! Again it is better to allow the easy basket causing a tie game than to foul a player in the act of shooting. If she makes the shot she can win the game with a free throw. Although the team must think DON'T FOUL, they must also force the opponents to work hard for a desirable shot. The defensive team should be able to ascertain those players likely be designated as shooters. Although they do not wish to leave any opponent open for an easy shot, they can direct more of their attention to the more likely shooters and the spots from which they like to shoot.

If the defensive team is ahead by one point or the game is tied, they should recognize that the game is about over if the opponents score. As the players take their positions for the in-bounds pass, the defenders should press their opponents slightly to force the in-bounds pass to go backwards. Under no circumstances should they allow the ball to be passed toward the basket. By forcing the pass backward, time is consumed before another pass can be made forward into shooting position. The player guarding the player who passes the ball in-bounds must retreat quickly so that a pass and cut maneuver is not possible. Players on the near side should guard their opponents tight and on the ball side. Teammates on the far side can sag or float to clutter the free throw lane. The defense must make it difficult for the opponents to shoot and force them to take an undesirable shot. Again the defense cannot afford to foul!

DRILLS FOR THE STALL GAME

Offensively, AIAW teams should learn whatever pattern they intend to use in this situation and then practice it frequently with a 30-second clock operating. They must become aware that 30 seconds is a long time when they are controlling the ball. (For high school play the clock should be set for increasing periods of time. For example, a team should learn to stall for 30 seconds. When this is mastered, the clock may be set for 1, 2, 3, 4 or 5 minutes.) By frequent practice with opponents pressing, they can gain the poise necessary to use a controlled offense. At the proper time the offensive thrust should be made to allow time for rebounding efforts. During practice sessions, various individuals should be assigned as the primary or secondary shooter so that it can be ascertained who is most successful under stress.

While one group is practicing offensive measures for the last seconds, the defensive team can simultaneously acquire poise in the way in which they meet the offensive tactics. They must learn to recognize when it is better to allow an unmolested shot rather than risking a foul and possibly the game. They must also become aware of when to sag and when to guard closely.

The following drills may be used to practice offensive and defensive techniques:

1. Five seconds remain; the score is tied with the ball out-of-bounds at midcourt.
2. One team leads by 2 points with 2 minutes to play.
3. One team leads by 10 points with 10 minutes to play.

12

Jump Ball, Out-of-Bounds, Free Throws

Several situations will be covered in this chapter, and each will be treated from both the offensive and defensive points of view. Included within this discussion are jump ball, out-of-bounds, and free throw situations.

JUMP BALL

Although jump balls may not play a major role in determining the winner of a game, thoughtful and intelligent play is necessary for a team to win their share of the taps. A jump ball situation occurs approximately ten times during a game — four of them occurring at the start of periods.

Regardless of whether a team believes it will win or lose the tap, thoughtful consideration should be given by the jumper and those players positioned around the circle to ensure that some member of her team will acquire the ball. No team should ever assume that they will win the tap and take no measures to assure that they will; similarly, no team should ever assume that they will lose the tap and take no measures to prevent the opponents from gaining it.

Possession of the ball is the most important factor. Elaborate plays emanating from a jump situation are helpful only if the team gets the ball. Every

effort should be made to obtain possession of the ball. Lacking this success on any tip, a team must not allow their opponents to score from the tip.

Technique for the Jumper

A right-handed jumper should turn her right side to her opponent, with feet in a forward-backward stride parallel to the jumping line and toes pointed toward the sideline. Her right foot should be forward and the stride no wider than her shoulders. Ankles, knees, and hips should be flexed. The degree depends upon her leg strength. A more flexed position allows her to exert force over a greater distance and permits her to jump higher, but also requires more strength to accomplish the greater work (raising her body a greater distance). Thus, the degree of flexion depends upon the individual's leg strength. Weight should be evenly balanced over her two feet so that the force can be exerted directly upward. The right hand should swing forward and upward as her legs extend. The jump should be timed so that, at the peak of the jump, the ball may be contacted with the arm in an extended position. To acquire the timing for this action, players should practice jumping and have various people tossing the ball. The height of tosses differs, and jumpers must make the necessary timing adjustments. All players should practice jumping against players of different heights. Lack of height is no excuse for not practicing jump ball plays.

When contacting the ball on the tap, jumpers must direct it to a teammate. Simply contacting it is not sufficient! Prior to taking their position in the circle for the jump, each jumper should check the positions of her teammates. She looks to see if her own opponent is covered when her opponent is not one of the jumpers, and she checks for defensive balance in case the tap is lost. She also determines which teammate is in the freest position to receive the tap. The jumper may signal her teammates to notify them to whom she will attempt to tap the ball. This allows them to screen opponents near the receiver so that the player can obtain the tap. Specific plays may also be designated. In all instances the tap should be directed away from the side of the defender (Fig. 12.1). The receiver should be ready for the tap and, upon receiving it, protect the ball if she is closely guarded.

It should also be apparent to the jumper that it is easier to tap the ball accurately in certain directions. In Fig. 12.1, player X_3 can tap the ball with greatest accuracy to either player X_1 or X_4, but with less ease to player X_2, as she is not completely within the visual field of the jumper and the jumper must abduct her shoulder to tap the ball in this direction. Since player X_5 is behind the jumper, she is outside the jumper's vision and is, therefore, the least likely player to receive the tap.

Depending upon the situation and abilities of the players, different formations may be used during a jump. Fig. 12.1 shows a box formation by one team. Fig. 12.2 shows a diamond, and Fig. 12.3

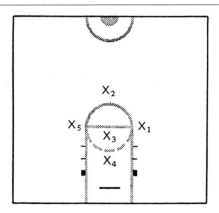

Fig. 12.2 *Diamond Formation.*

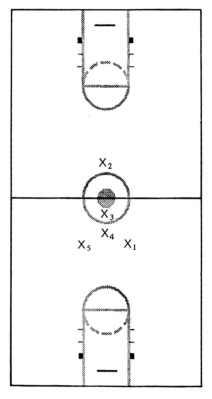

Fig. 12.3 *Y Formation.*

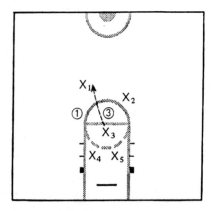

Fig 12.1 *Box Formation. Player X_3 is shown tapping the ball to player X_1 and away from Player 1.*

shows a Y formation that is used for a defensive position only. A formation may be used for a specific purpose, although players should discern that the configuration may be changed when the rules allow players to move as soon as the ball is tossed by the official.

It is wise to assign players to a specific position in a formation. This eliminates the last second shuffling by players to assure that all places in the formation are covered. Each player takes the same position around the circle every time. If a different player is involved in the jump, the former jumper replaces the new jumper in her assigned position at the circle. This method tends to eliminate confusion during a game. When competing against different opponents, it may be desirable to change the assigned positions for that particular game in order to take advantage of the weaknesses of particular opponents; but, the same positions are assumed by all players throughout the game.

Team Tactics on Jump Balls

Teamwork is just as important on jump balls as at any other time during the game. When a jump ball is called by an official, all players should immediately and carefully size up the situation. They should ascertain whether they will win or lose the jump, or if it is a "toss up." They should also consider whether the jump is taken in the center circle or at the offensive or defensive end. When taking the jump in the defensive end, greater precautions are taken, regardless of whether a team believes it should secure the jump.

A team should make every effort to get in position for the jump ball first because the opposing team usually lines up in the same formation. A team should also try to position themselves so that there is an open spot into which the ball can be tapped. This means that two teammates would like no opponent between them. This advantageous position is not always possible since the opposing team is allowed alternate spots around the circle.

Tactics When a Team Should Win the Tap

In this situation a team should not become complacent and allow the opponents (who have a height or jumping disadvantage) to outmaneuver them and acquire the tap. The jumper must try to determine if the opponents are taking their positions in such a manner that they may move to double-team or cover an otherwise free player. The jumper should

tap to the player most likely to be freest after the opponents have moved because it is extremely important that a team obtain possession of the tap when they have an apparent advantage. This is not always easy to ascertain. In certain positions on the court, players can assist a teammate in becoming free by screening the opponents. Figs. 12.4 and 12.5 show screens set at the center circle. (*Note:* The screeners move to the outside of the circle to establish their screen so that they can move sooner [when the ball is tossed, if allowed by the rules].) This also permits them to move into the defender's cutting lane, which is not possible if the screeners cut into the circle.

Either the diamond or box formation may be used if the jump is taken at the offensive end of the court. A diamond formation is shown in Fig. 12.6. Player 4 is a dangerous scorer and the opponents

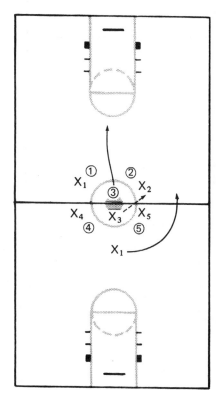

Fig. 12.4 *Expect to Win the Tap — Tap to Front Court. Player X_3 taps to the open space for X_1 and X_3 cuts down the middle for a 4 on 3 situation. Player 1 or 2 should have dropped back to prevent this play.*

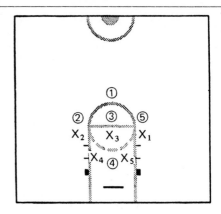

Fig. 12.6 *Expect to Win the Tap — Offensive End. Player 4 is a dangerous scorer and is double-teamed. Other offensive players are covered goal side by a defender. Player 1 is free at the top of the circle in the least dangerous position to shoot. Player X_3 should tap the ball between players X_2 and X_4 unless another move has been pre-arranged.*

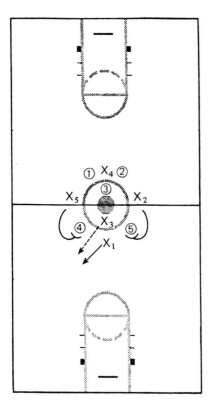

Fig. 12.5 *Expect to Win the Tap — Tap to Backcourt. If the opponents take measures to prevent the tap from going to X_4, then X_3 can tap the ball into the backcourt for X_1 as players X_5 and X_2 screen. If 1 or 2 move back to the top of the circle and their teammates reposition, a screen should not be necessary to free X_1.*

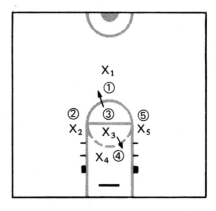

Fig. 12.7 *Expect to Win the Tap — Offensive End. Player 4 is free on her right side. The tap may be made there, but 3 and 4 should be aware of any movement by X_5, who may slide down to help X_4. If this occurs and 4 receives the tap, she should immediately pass to 5, who will be free. If player 3 anticipates the move of X_5, she may tap back between 1 and 2. This is the safest tactic.*

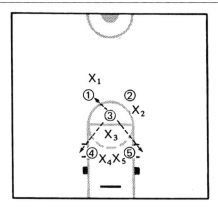

Fig. 12.8 *Expect to Win the Tap — Offensive End. Using a box formation and the defending team responding with the same, 3 should be able to tap to 4 or back to 1.*

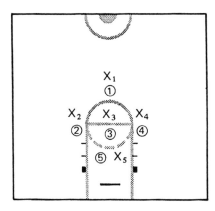

Fig. 12.9 *Expect to Win — Defensive End. Player 3 must tap accurately to 1 or 2. A poor tap may result in an easy score for the opponents.*

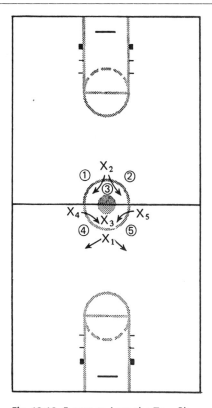

Fig. 12.10 *Expect to Lose the Tap. Player X_1 lines up three feet off the circle and is ready to retreat quickly in either direction, depending on the direction of the tap. As the ball is tapped, players X_4 and X_5 move inside the circle to intercept a tap to 4 or 5 or deflect it backward to X_1. Player X_2 is ready to move to cover either 1 or 2, but is particularly aware of 2 because it is easier for 3 to tap in her direction.*

have double-teamed her. This is rather common procedure with this formation. The tap should go back to 1. If the defense takes their positions as shown in Fig. 12.7, the tap may go to either 4 or 1. If both teams line up in a box formation, possibilities for the tap are shown in Fig. 12.8.

If the jump is taken at the defensive end, the team must take defensive precautions in case of a poor tap or an unexpected successful tap by the opposing jumper. The position of the players is shown in Fig. 12.9. Player 3 must tap accurately to player 1 or preferably, player 2.

Tactics When a Team May Lose the Tap

In this situation a team should never concede the tap to the opposing team. They must take measures to prevent them from receiving the tap or at least force them to tap the ball backward. By thoughtful positioning the team may deceive their opponents into thinking a player is open; but may have a player move to the open position and other players rotate to cover the players most likely to receive a tap. Fig. 12.10 shows the team expecting to lose the tap in a diamond formation and the moves of the players. Fig. 12.11 and 12.12 show the team expecting to lose

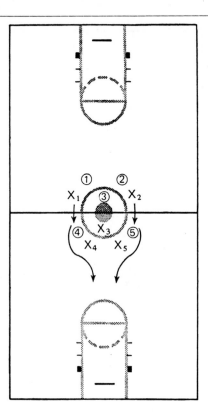

Fig. 12.11 *Expect to Lose the Tap. Players X_1 and X_2 leave their opponents as soon as possible to help double-team 4 and 5. If the ball is not intercepted, playes X_1 and X_2 retreat and meet their opponents as they move into the frontcourt.*

Fig. 12.12 *Expect to Lose the Tap. Player X_5 retreats to be in a defensive position in case the attack gets the ball. The other defensive players rotate counterclockwise to attempt to intercept or deflect the tap. Note that X_2 moves to the outside, while the others go in to the circle. This is necessary because she has a greater distance to cover; by taking this route she may move as soon as the official tosses the ball when the rules permit. Note: if the rules disallow movement until the ball is tapped, X_2 should step back off the circle so she can start her move when the ball is tossed and time her movement on to the circle when the ball is tapped.*

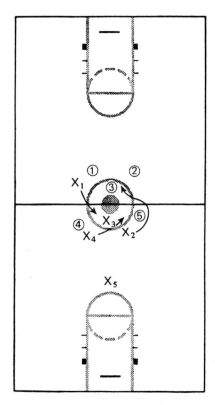

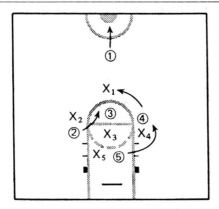

Fig. 12.13 *Expect to Lose — Offensive End. Player X_3 has a height advantage on player 3. Player X_3 usually is reluctant to tap the ball backward in this position. Therefore, 5 may leave her position as soon as possible and move up to cover X_4. Meanwhile 4 has moved up near X_1. When the ball is tapped, 2 moves in to the circle to cut off the tap in that direction. Player 1 retreats to prevent the long tap.*

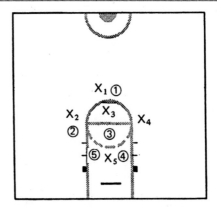

Fig. 12.14 *Expect to Lose — Defensive End. Player X_5 is considered to be a dangerous scorer and is double-teamed. Player 2 is goal side of her opponent. If the tap goes to X_4, 4 moves back to guard her own player.*

the tap in a box formation. Fig 12.11 shows how a team may double-team the likely receivers. Fig. 12.12 shows a more daring tactic.

If the jump is taken at the offensive end of the court and the attacking team expects to lose the tap, Fig. 12.13 shows possible tactics for use.

When the jump is taken at the defensive end and a team expects to lose the tap, certain measures may be taken. Figs. 12.14 and 12.15 demonstrate these tactics.

Defensively, a team should listen for numbers, names, or other signals identifying passing lanes.

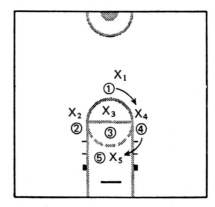

Fig. 12.15 *Expect to Lose — Defensive End. As the ball is tossed, players 4 and 1 rotate clockwise. If the ball is secured by X_1 or X_4, 1 and 4 return to guarding their respective opponents.*

Drills for Jump Ball Situations

1. Groups of three (all approximately the same height). One player tosses the ball while the other two practice jumping and tapping the ball to a predetermined target. Rotate.

2. Two teams. Tactics should be practiced for situations when it appears as though a team will win a tap or lose a tap at each of the three restraining circles.

OUT-OF-BOUNDS SITUATIONS

During the course of a game, the ball will be put in play from the defensive endline and from the sideline at both the defensive and offensive ends of the court. Different formations and tactics are used for in-bounding the ball in each of these situations. Under most circumstances special measures need not be taken to in-bound the ball in the defensive end from either the endline or sideline. Only when the opponents exert pressure is there potential danger. Methods of combating pressure (or applying it) are dealt with elsewhere in the text. Nevertheless, the in-bounder must always look for a lurking defender before passing to a teammate. An interception here usually results in a score. Receivers must always cut to meet the pass and use faking techniques if necessary.

If pressure does occur on a sideline play, the pass is usually made backward to a player who cuts quickly in that direction.

SIDELINE OUT-OF-BOUNDS SITUATIONS

When in-bounding the ball from the sideline in the offensive end of the court, a team generally uses quick cuts or screens to free a player. In any case a good passer should be assigned to put the ball in play. Some teams assign their best passer to in-bound the ball, while others assign either a forward or a guard — depending upon the spot from which the ball is put in play. The teacher/coach must determine which choice is more suitable for her player personnel. Regardless of which system is selected,

the same player or her substitute should always put the ball in play. While moving into position the in-bounder should analyze the positioning of the defense and allow her teammates time to move into the desired positions. Meanwhile her teammates hustle to get into position.

Several formations can be used to confuse the opponents and vary the out-of-bounds maneuvers. These are shown in Figs. 12.16 to 12.19. The box formation is probably the most popular because it lends itself to more options. The vertical and parallel formations are more commonly used at the endline. Nevertheless they may be used occasionally with success from a sideline position. However, definite precautions must be devised when utilizing the vertical formation from a sideline because of the obvious defensive dangers involved.

When installing any of the formations, the teacher/coach may exchange the positions of individual players if desired. The pivot is usually assigned a position near the basket in either the box or diamond formation. Her position is obvious in the diamond formation, but the pivot may be placed either on the ball side or the far side in the box formation. Figs. 12.20 to 12.23 show her on the near side, while Figs. 12.24 to 12.26 show her on the far side.

The player putting the ball in play should take her position about 3 ft. from the sideline. This allows her enough space to step forward or to move slightly without committing a line violation. She gives a signal of some kind to initiate the moves of her teammates. The signal is usually given by slapping the ball or calling the name of a play.

The plays devised for use from out-of-bounds should be simple. They should all look similar with

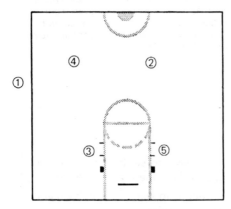

Fig. 12.16 *Out-of-Bounds — Box Formation.*

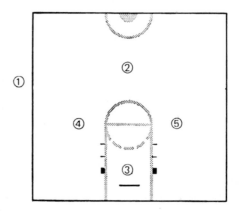

Fig. 12.17 *Out-of-Bounds — Diamond Formation.*

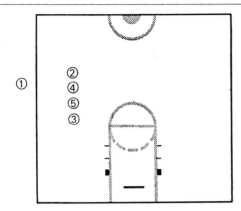

Fig. 12.18 *Out-of-Bounds — Vertical Formation.*

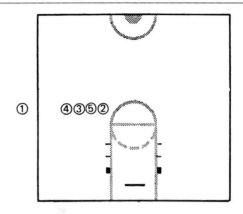

Fig. 12.19 *Out-of-Bounds — Parallel Formation.*

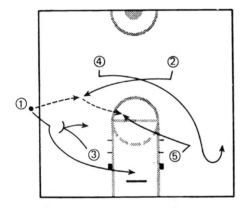

Fig. 12.20 *Out-of-Bounds. On signal, 4 fakes and screens for 2, who fakes and cuts for the pass from 1. 3 moves up to screen for 1 as 5 cuts for a pass from 2. 1 cuts off the screen and 3 rolls. 5 has the option of shooting or passing to 1 or 3. 1, 3, and 5 have rebounding responsibilities.*

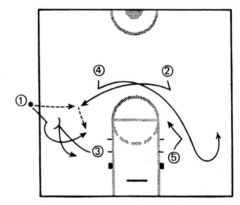

Fig. 12.21 *Out-of-Bounds. The moves start as in Fig. 12.20. 1 passes to 2. 3 cuts to screen for 1. 1 fakes and cuts to receive the pass from 2. 3 rolls or cuts, and 5 clears to the free throw line. 1 can drive, shoot, or pass to 3, 5, or 4.*

Fig. 12.22 *Out-of-Bounds. 4 fakes and cuts back to receive the pass from 1. 3 fakes as 5 cuts for a pass from 4. 2 fakes and cuts down the lane for a pass from 5. 3, 2, and 5 rebound.*

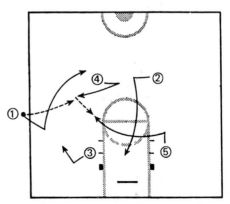

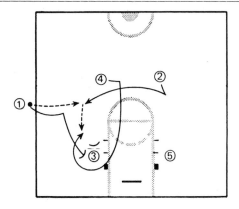

Fig. 12.23 *Out-of-Bounds. 4 fakes and 2 cuts off her to receive a pass from 1. 4 cuts down the lane and behind the double screen formed by 3 and 1. 2 passes to 4, who may shoot or use any of the double screen options. 3, 4, and 5 rebound.*

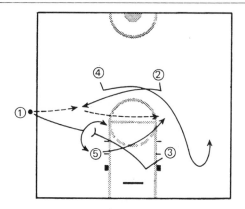

Fig. 12.24 *Out-of-Bounds. 4 moves over and screens for 2. 2 cuts for the pass from 1. 5 cuts and 3 cuts. 2 passes to 5 as 1 cuts either side of 3. 5 may shoot, pass to 1 or 3 who rolls.*

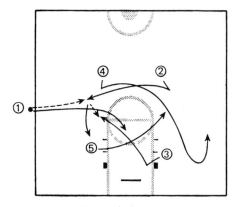

Fig. 12.25 *Out-of-Bounds. 4 and 2 make their usual moves. 3 cuts after 5 to receive the pass from 2. 2 cuts around 3 followed by 1. All of the options on a scissor play are available.*

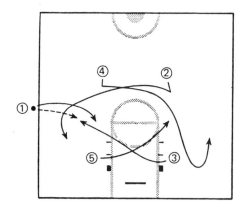

Fig. 12.26 *Out-of-Bounds. 4 and 2 make their usual moves. 1 fakes to 2. 5 and 3 make their usual moves, and 1 passes to 3. 2 and 1 cut around 3 and the scissor options are available.*

one or two changes so that the defense must make different adjustments. Figs. 12.20 to 12.26 provide some examples of tactics that can be used from the sideline.

Defense Against a Sideline Out-of-Bounds Play

Whenever the opposing team is ready to put the ball in play from the sideline the defending team takes measures to force them to pass the ball backward or away from the offensive basket. The defender guarding the in-bound player should stand on a diagonal between her opponent and the basket. She should never stand directly opposite her, for she is extremely vulnerable to a pass-and-cut tactic. Fig. 12.27 shows both the correct and incorrect methods of guarding the out-of-bounds player. The other defenders exert pressure on the basket side to encourage the pass backward. These tactics are particularly important when the ball is being put in play in the defensive team's backcourt. The defense

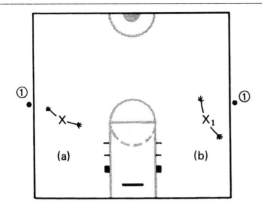

Fig. 12.27 *Player X_1 stands between her opponent and the basket with her arms extended toward her opponent and the basket. As soon as the ball is inbounded, she takes a few steps back toward the basket to prevent a pass and cut maneuver (a). Poor defensive position by X_1 allowing her opponent to cut for the basket (b).*

should be particularly aware of the possibility of a return pass to the out-of-bounds player, and cut off the passing lane to her. As soon as the ball is put in play, the in-bounder's opponent steps back toward the basket and then applies pressure on the in-bounder.

When the opponents are behind in score in the last few seconds of the game and are in-bounding the ball from the sideline in the frontcourt, the defense desires to force them to pass backward toward the division line or into their backcourt. Therefore, the player guarding the in-bounder plays between her and the basket, and the other defenders guard their opponent closely on the basket side to force the pass backward. Once the ball is inbounded, players should guard their opponent closely, not allowing a free shot. If a team has not used a press during the game and is competent in executing it, the new defense may surprise the opponents and delay them in attempting a shot. Otherwise the standard defense employed by a team should be used. Every effort must be made, however, to prevent the opponents from obtaining an unguarded or unchallenged shot. Players within 15 ft. of the basket should be guarded extremely close so that it is difficult to pass in to them. If the opposing team has one or more weak shooters, it may be desirable to allow them to receive passes freely and encourage them to shoot anywhere beyond their range.

Basically, there are four things the defense is trying to prevent:

1. any unchallenged shot.
2. any player receiving the ball within 15 ft. of the basket.
3. a layup shot or offensive rebound shot.
4. a foul against a player in the act of shooting, which may result in a three-point play.

ENDLINE OUT-OF-BOUNDS SITUATIONS

Any of the formations shown previously may be used at the endline although some adjustments are made. In the box formation the outside players generally are opposite the foul line while the other two players are closer to the first hash mark. A similar situation occurs in the diamond formation with all players adjusting slightly goalward. This is probably the least used formation at the endline. The vertical formation is used with players lined behind the free throw line or close to the basket along the lane line. For the parallel formation players line up along the free throw line. Under the basket the coach may wish to use her best passer as the inbounder or she may prefer to use a taller player with good passing skills.

Suggestions for plays are shown in Figs. 12.28 to 12.31.

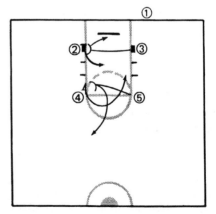

Fig. 12.28 *Out-of-Bounds. Players 3 and 5 screen and roll; players 2 and 4 cut to the open spaces. Player 5 rolls back to the foul line for defensive purposes.*

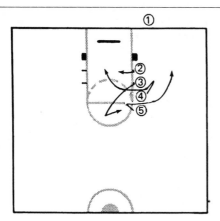

Fig. 12.29 *Out-of-Bounds. Player 1 looks for 2 for a lob pass and 4 and 5 on a cut. Player 3 moves to the foul line.*

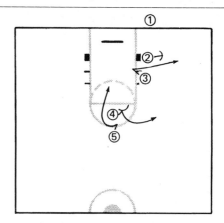

Fig. 12.30 *Out-of-Bounds — Vertical Formation Variation. Players 2 and 4 screen for cuts by 3 and 5.*

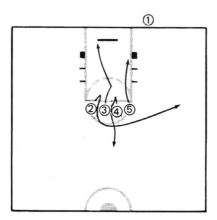

Fig. 12.31 *Out-of-Bounds. Player 1 looks for 3 and 5 on their cuts and 2 for a safety pass if the lane is clogged. Player 4 drops back.*

Defense Against Endline Out-of-Bounds Plays

All defensive players should have one foot in the lane to prevent a pass into the lane. The opponent of the passer must force the ball to the corner, disallowing a pass into the lane. Cutters should be blocked and attention should be given to players who are rolling after a screen. A lob pass to a post should be disallowed. The passer often is the recipient of a return pass so her opponent must be alert to this possibility.

When the opponents are behind in score in the last few seconds of the game and are putting the ball in play from the endline in their backcourt, the defenders must prevent a long pass downcourt. They must closely guard players in the midcourt and frontcourt area and allow a player to remain free near the in-bounder. They encourage the short pass and then double-team the player, taking all precautions to prevent fouling. A coach may prefer not to double-team in which case pressure is placed on the ball and other defenders force their opponent away from the basket. The pivot defender must not

---

Drills for Out-of-Bounds Plays

1. One team in position for a designated play. Practice without defense and give particular attention to the timing of the cuts. Alternate sides and substitute players into different positions.

2. Same as drill 1, but add defensive players. Instruct the defenders how they should play.

3. Same as drill 1; after several plays have been introduced only place players on the court in normal playing position and call an out-of-bounds play. Let players react, move to the proper position, and execute the play.

4. Scrimmage. At any time during the scrimmage the coach designates the out-of-bounds play to be run.

---

be lured away from the lane area so that she remains in position to intimidate any opponent trying to shoot from that position and maintains good rebounding position. The defenders must try to force an opponent to shoot off-balanced and out of good shooting range.

FREE THROW SITUATIONS

When a team is awarded a free throw, both teams must have at least two players line up along the lane lines, although all of the players may line up if this seems desirable. The defensive team should place its two strongest rebounders in the spaces nearest the basket. The best rebounder should be on the same side as the best rebounder from the offensive team. If the defensive team has a distinct height disadvantage, it may choose to have two other players line up also. This alignment is shown in Fig. 12.32. The team's third best rebounder lines up on the same side where the height disparity exists. With defensive players on both sides of the taller opponent, some of the advantage she has should be overcome by reducing the space in which she can maneuver.

If the defensive team believes that it can control the rebound without double-teaming one player, it may line up as shown in Fig. 12.33. This provides for a defensive player in the corner on each side and as a rebounder obtains the ball, she can immediately turn to the outside and make her outlet pass. If one of the offensive players should shun her rebounding responsibilities and move to press one of the defender's in the corner, the corner player should notify her teammate that she is covered so that a pass will not be made in her direction.

If the defensive team is certain that it will obtain the rebound, or if an extremely accurate free throw shooter is at the line, it may choose to line up in a manner to start a fast break very quickly and, as a result, place a great deal of pressure on the team taking the free throw. This alignment and a modification of it are shown in Figs. 12.34 and 12.35. The latter is a dangerous formation if there is a chance of losing the ball, for it should automatically give the opposing team a player advantage. The team must be certain that it will obtain the rebound and also that accurate passes can be made to get the ball

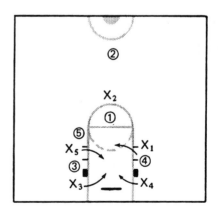

Fig. 12.32 *Free Throw Situation. Player 3 has a height advantage, so X_3 and X_5 attempt to reduce her rebounding effectiveness. Player X_1 moves in to the middle of the lane to prevent a rebound or tip from going to 1. As X_3 or X_4 obtains the rebound, X_2 cuts to the near side for the outlet pass. Player 2 is in a safety position.*

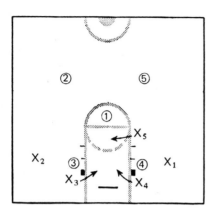

Fig. 12.33 *Alternate Method of Lining Up for a Free Throw.*

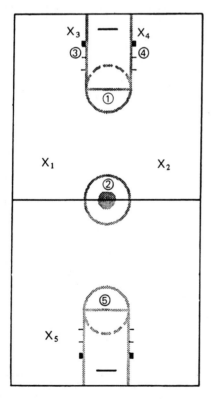

Fig. 12.34 *Free Throw. Defensive positioning to start a fast break.*

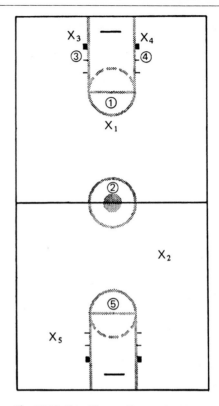

Fig. 12.35 *Free Throw. Extremely aggressive position of the defensive team to start a fast break.*

into the frontcourt. On the other hand, use of either of these formations causes the opponents to think about defense before the free throw is even attempted. This may psychologically affect the free throw shooter in particular, causing her to lose concentration and miss the free throw. The offensive rebounders may also be more concerned with going back on defense than attempting to maneuver for a missed free throw.

Rebounding Techniques by the Defensive Team

The two defenders closest to the basket stand as close to the lane space mark as possible. When the free throw shooter is ready, the defenders raise their arms partially overhead and lean in toward the center of the lane. (Their arms may not be extended into the adjacent lane space in front of an opponent.) After the ball has been released, each defender takes a step with her outside foot diagonally backward and into the lane in an effort to block out the offensive rebounder. The step should be so timed that the foot strikes the floor at the same time as the ball hits the rim or the backboard. The player assigned to block out the free throw shooter pivots on her inside foot and steps out with her outside foot so that she is parallel to the endline and in front of the shooter. The defender may have to take a shuffle step in order to get into the middle of the lane. The footwork is shown in Fig. 12.36.

Rebounding Techniques by the Offensive Team

The best rebounders are assigned to the second lane spaces. The best rebounder attempts to move to the side opposite the best defensive rebounder. As the ball is in the air during the shot, the offensive players time their moves so that they may take the first step into the lane with their inside foot and land in the lane at the time the ball hits the backboard or

rim. A second step is taken into the lane, and they may need to use a shuffle step to acquire a position beside the defensive player with another step, placing one leg in front of the defender. These moves are also shown in Fig. 12.36. If the offensive player can obtain the rebound, she should try to catch it and go back up with her shot. Since the area is congested, this is not likely to occur very often. Her next choice should be to tip the ball into the basket. If this is not possible, she may try to tap the ball back over the head of the defender to her teammate at the free throw line or to a teammate who is positioned deeper (Fig. 12.33). If unable to catch or tap the ball, she should try to harass the rebounder at least momentarily to prevent a quick outlet pass to start a fast break.

If the defenders tend to slide into the middle of the lane to keep the offensive rebounders blocked out, the offensive player may choose an alternate method of gaining the rebound. She may fake into the lane with her outside foot, push hard off it, and

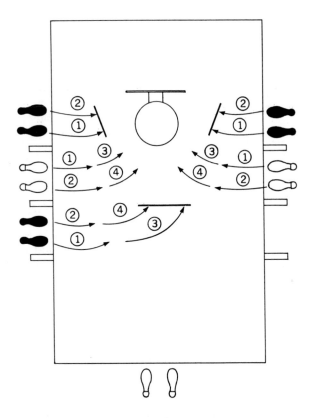

Fig. 12.36 *Basic Footwork for Both Teams in Trying to Obtain a Rebound Following a Free Throw.*

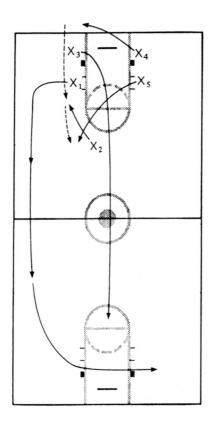

Fig. 12.37 *Fast Break After a Free Throw. Player X_4 quickly recovers the ball. X_1 clears to the side line and cuts downcourt. X_3 clears down the middle of the lane. X_4 passes in to X_2, who passes to X_5 who has cut off X_3. Player X_5 may pass to X_1 or X_3, or work one-on-one if a pass is not open to either of them. If X_1 does not receive a pass, she clears to the opposite side to allow X_5 more space in which to maneuver.*

step with her inside foot behind the defensive player. The offensive player continues moving toward the outside to get in front of the defensive player. From this position she may be able to deflect the ball if she is unable to catch it.

This move is selected prior to any action taken by a defensive player because the initial step is taken with a different foot. Since a defender almost automatically moves into the lane in the manner previously described, this technique may be effective occasionally. The player must be quick in her move however, or the ball will rebound before she can reach it.

Fast Break Options by the Defensive Team

The defensive team may attempt a fast break after a successful or an unsuccessful free throw. Because the defensive rebounders have the inside position, they should acquire the rebound if the shot is missed. The rebounder turns toward the outside and executes her outlet pass as quickly as possible. If the defenders are lined up as shown in Fig. 12.32, player X_2 cuts toward the ball side for the pass. Player X_1 cuts up the middle, and X_5 fills the lane on the right. If defenders are situated in the corners, the rebounder passes to the near side player. If the defenders have only two defenders lined up along the lane (Figs. 12.34 and 12.35), the rebounder passes to the near side player at the division line. Obvious fast break opportunities develop from this situation. The player who receives the pass dribbles down the center as the other potential receiver cuts down the unoccupied lane. With two players in the frontcourt (Fig. 12.35), it may be possible to pass the ball to one of them quickly for a two-on-one situation to develop.

When the free throw is successful, one player should always recover the ball, run out-of-bounds with it, and in-bound it as fast as possible. The player on the side opposite from where the ball is to be in-bounded should be the player assigned to this task, since she is facing the ball on the side from which it will be in-bounded and can race more quickly into position. Fig. 12.37 shows one possibility for a fast break. Others may be devised.

5

Teaching and Coaching

13

Teaching Beginners

Teaching beginning players any team sport is a challenging and demanding task — and basketball is no exception! Like field hockey, lacrosse, and soccer, basketball is difficult to teach (and learn) because the ball moves almost constantly, and the players must adjust not only to the moves of their teammates but also to those of their opponents. This means that players must make continual adjustments during even a very elementary maneuver. They must acquire not only an understanding of the way in which tactics are performed, but also the skill to execute them properly. All of this takes time, practice, and patience!

PROBLEMS OF BEGINNERS

If one were to observe beginning players in the early stages of learning the game, certain incompetencies would be clearly evident regardless of the players' ages or grade levels.

1. No organization for play. Players are grouped near the ball or under the basket. When the opponents obtain possession of the ball, a long pass downcourt usually accounts for a goal.
2. Players on offense stand (often because they do not know where to move or when to move), often very close together, which cuts off the passing lanes.
3. Ineffective dribbling — frequent dribbling, often while standing still without benefit of forward or lateral movement. Beginners often develop "bouncitis," the act of bouncing the

ball each time it is received. This is a most difficult habit to break later and one that should never be developed.
4. Poor passing is usually the result of not pivoting to look to see if a teammate is free. Often an unorthodox pass is used because the player has not pivoted to face her teammate. Passes may be made automatically in a predetermined direction regardless of whether the teammate is free. Passes are made to players standing still, with a resultant interception by an alert defensive player. Passes lacking "zip" are usually intercepted.
5. Players have little confidence in their ability to score. As a result most players always consider passing as the primary choice of action. Those who desire to shoot often are inaccurate because the ball is released from a very low height (waist or shoulder level). Frequently, these players are off-balance.
6. Defensively, players maintain poor position. Their weight is too high and too far forward. They generally fail to take a step back from their opponent after the ball is passed, and thus cannot stay in a proper defensive position as the opponents cuts.
7. Defensive players often lack judgment in trying for an interception. Therefore, when they miss the interception their opponent is free to dribble toward the goal.
8. Defensive players often guard too closely and make every effort to get their hands on the ball. This generally brings their weight on to their toes and often causes them to move to the side of their opponent when she pivots. Thus, the opponent is left free to drive or cut toward the basket after she passes.

321

These problems are witnessed most frequently. The problems that are known to exist for beginning players must be curtailed, if not eliminated, as rapidly as possible. This requires careful planning and critical analysis of individual skills throughout the learning process. The teacher must understand and recognize correct performance so that she may lead each student through a natural progression and assist her in realizing her own potential.

It is advisable to help students learn a few skills well rather than many skills ineffectively. Therefore, considerable attention should be devoted to drills of a gamelike nature in order that skills and elementary tactics are overlearned so that they may be applied and executed properly under conditions of duress in a game.

It seems questionable that a great variety of drills is necessary to motivate the students. Looking through a book of drills and coming up with one that looks "interesting" is an antiquated concept. It makes far more sense to ascertain what the students need to learn to apply in the game, and then construct a drill that will accomplish that purpose. If a player in a guard position has difficulty in passing a chest pass to her teammate in a guard position, practicing a chest pass in a shuttle formation will not help this player! Instead, place the two players on line with one another and, facing the basket, encourage them to pivot toward one another before passing! The shuttle formation would help a guard pass to a wing and vice versa, but why not have the two players in their proper position on the court with the guard passing to the wing, then cutting for the basket to receive a return pass, thus learning to pass and cut. This is one of the elementary offensive tactics! In this way, proper passing techniques are acquired and a useful game tactic is learned as well.

CLASS ORGANIZATION

As a teacher observes her class, she is likely to become aware that she does not have a very homogeneous group. She is likely to have some students who have never used a basketball, others who may have played with one occasionally, and other students who have played frequently with brothers or other friends. In this case, the teacher cannot teach at one level and keep all of the students interested and motivated, but must prepare her lessons to treat groups at different levels of achievement. In this day and age, no one can any longer advocate teaching to the "average" student! One must be concerned with helping each student achieve her maximum potential.

In order to meet the needs of all the students in her class, the teacher may choose (at times with suggestions from the students) either of two techniques. She may prepare entirely different lessons for the various skill levels, or she may have all students practicing the same skills or tactics but at different levels of execution. Probably she will use both techniques.

When practicing any skill or tactic it is desirable to establish goals toward which the students may work. For example, in shooting layups the goal for inexperienced players might be three successful shots out of ten; for those with some experience, five out of ten; and for those who have had even greater experience, seven out of ten. These goals may be adjusted upward or downward, depending upon the students' ability. The goal selected, however, should be attainable by the majority within that group. Later, the success level for each group may be increased so that it continues to be motivating. Or, rather than establishing group goals, let each student establish her own goal.

Throughout the entire learning process, but particularly during the early learning stages, it is important to have the class working in small groups. A ball for every two players is desirable. A ratio of one ball to more than four players is impractical from a learning point of view. Students are unable to secure sufficient practice with an inadequate supply of balls. Basketballs, however, may be supplemented with soccer balls, volleyballs, and playground balls although students using these supplementary balls should be allowed to exchange frequently with students using basketballs.

The small group technique can be used even with large classes. For practicing individual skills, players can take those positions on the court they choose to play; and, with proper directions, they can work individually or in pairs on the skills required for that particular position. For example, basic faking techniques can be learned by all, and then each player can apply what she has learned effectively to her own position. Wings can practice faking toward the endline and cutting out to receive a pass from a guard, or faking out and cutting across the lane for a pass from the other wing or pivot. Guards can practice faking right and cutting left or vice versa, or faking to the side and cutting for the basket. A pivot can fake to the side and cut out to the free throw line, or fake out and cut across the lane. These are specific moves that can be used in a game and seem more appropriate than spending considerable time on moves that will not be used, except in a drill.

From the previous discussion, it would seem obvious that the author encourages students to choose a position — wing, guard, or pivot — early during the unit after the characteristics and qualifications for each position have been discussed. Basketball is too complicated a game to expect any student, let alone a beginner, to become proficient in the moves necessary for every (or several) position(s) on the court. It is impossible and unrealistic to request such competency from any player. Opportunity, however, should be provided for students to change positions if the one that was originally selected does not prove satisfying. Players should be encouraged to make such changes early in the unit.

In addition to practicing individual skills in small groups, it is also advisable to introduce and practice elementary team tactics in small groups. Practicing with two offensive players against two defensive players provides all players with the opportunity to react to the movement of the ball and facilitates learning. Acquiring skill in passing, receiving, faking, changing direction, starting and stopping, and defensive skills all are enhanced by this method. Becoming familiar with the pass-and-cut technique, setting screens, and the defense for these is also facilitated by working in small groups. Extensive practice can be gained by this method, as all players in the group are involved in every move. Later the players must have the opportunity to attempt their newly acquired skills with other team members. In some instances, it may be desirable to wean beginning players slowly from a two-player team to the regulation five-player team. This may be accomplished by adding only one player to form a team of three (usually two guards and one forward); or, that stage may be omitted by adding two players to form teams of four (two guards and two forwards). Finally, another player can be added to form a team of five.

While working in groups of four the court size can be modified so that many groups can be practicing at the same time. It is not always necessary for small groups to have access to a basket, so a court may be divided into four parts, accommodating sixteen players simultaneously. If the gymnasium is lined for two courts, thirty-two players may be involved at the same time. With players working in groups of eight — four per team — additional space is necessary. It is necessary to provide a wider area in which the players may operate; otherwise negative transfer is introduced as the players practice in a very cramped space. The length of the space in which students practice is not as important as the width. 18–20 ft. in length is ample for beginners to practice, but if four players per team are

practicing, the minimum regulation width (42 ft.) is needed for proper learning.

When court space and/or number of baskets is limited, adjustments can be made. Tape can be used to mark extra keyholes if additional space of this kind is needed. These are particularly useful when teaching a pattern offense or zone defense. Each team (or most of them) may practice the necessary movements without waiting for a "turn." If there are not enough baskets for all groups, players can go through the offensive pattern of making shots at a nonexistent basket. The pattern or moves involved can be inculcated so that players understand the concepts. Teams should be rotated to baskets frequently.

While utilizing the small group technique, it seems advantageous to retain the same groups for every class period with minor changes made as necessary. Each group can be assigned to a specific area, and little time is wasted at the beginning of the class period for organizational purposes. This procedure not only facilitates class organization, but also improves learning. Students have the opportunity to play with the same individuals for a period of time and can become acquainted with the type of cuts they prefer, the speed with which they move, and their defensive and offensive strengths and weaknesses. In this way they do not have to readjust to new teammates daily.

When players are learning specific offensive or defensive tactics, they may change their role in any of several ways.

1. One team may be designated as the offensive team for a designated length of time. At the end of that time interval the teams exchange responsibilities for a similar period of time.
2. The role may change each time the defensive team gains possession of the ball.
3. A modified game of baseball may be played in which one team is on offense (at bat) until the defensive team gets three outs — turnover, interception, or rebound. Play a designated number of innings. The score is the number of baskets made.

Some teachers using the second method also request that the change take place after each field goal. (Some smart players will miss a shot purposely so that they may remain on offense!) Other teachers allow the scoring teams to continue on offense (make it, keep it). All methods of exchange have merit, but the first one is preferred during the beginning stages; the others are preferable during the later stages.

As indicated previously, all players in the class

need not practice the same skill or tactic. As a matter of fact, there may be as many different activities in progress as there are groups. The primary consideration is that the task be relevant and that it be based on previously learned material. There are times when the students should be given the prerogative of selecting their own activity, at least for a portion of the period if not all of it. Some will select individual skills to improve, while others may be more interested in either offensive or defensive team play. As a result, in some areas of the gymnasium, one may observe players working individually or in groups of two, three, four, six, eight, or ten. Some may be playing half-court while others are playing full court. During this time the teacher can move freely to all groups and provide whatever assistance is necessary.

When players have attained a level of achievement sufficient to enjoy and have success in a game with four or five players per team, it is wise to teach them a very basic pattern to follow for their moves. If this is not done, all players tend to congregate under the basket. The pattern simply gives them direction. It helps them to know where and when to cut so that all players do not end up in the same place at the same time. It helps by letting them know their responsibilities at a specific time. Generally, a pattern encourages the use of all players in the ball movement. Otherwise one or two more skilled or knowledgeable players may dominate play.

Rules should be taught concurrently as skills or tactics are learned. Players can become familiar with traveling violations when they are learning to start, stop, change direction, and receive passes. Dribbling violations are introduced as players learn how to dribble. Lecture, discussion, or demonstration of rules without immediate application is unprofitable.

OFFENSE VERSUS DEFENSE

Teaching defense in any team game is considered easier than teaching offense by most experts. The timing of moves is important but not quite as vital; the coordination of action with teammates is less crucial; and, of course, they are not involved with the ball. For these reasons one generally attempts to develop offensive tactics first. Defensive measures are then taught to counteract the offense, and the cycle is repeated many times over.

Depending upon the tactic being taught, it may be desirable initially to allow the attack players to attempt the maneuver without hindrance by any de-

fensive players. Once the concept is gained, one defensive player may be added. Assuming that only two attack players are involved, the defensive player is assigned to guard the player with the ball — she is not permitted at this stage to try to defend against both attack players. Later, a second defender is added. This progression might be used in learning the pass-and-cut tactic, for example.

For teaching other offensive tactics (screens, scissor), the defensive players should be passive initially and follow the stipulated method of guarding (stay man-to-man; play switching man-to-man, etc.) so that the offense can gain confidence in the tactic and the timing involved. Then the defense can be instructed to defend as usual, but the manner should be designated again. After the offense begins to have some degree of success with their newly acquired skills, then time should be devoted to the defense and the means of counteracting the offensive moves. When this has been learned, new options should be learned by the attack and the process is repeated. Both attack and defense players must be sympathetic with one another, as they are trying to learn new tactics. Each should help one another by using the techniques that will make the opposite group successful. By progressing slowly and competently from one stage to the next, both skill and confidence will be acquired.

MAN-TO-MAN VERSUS ZONE DEFENSE

Almost all authorities agree that man-to-man defense should be learned prior to zone defense. Although a player's primary responsibility in a zone is to defend an area, once a player enters that area her actions are predicated on her ability to use individual defensive techniques according to whether the player has the ball or is moving to receive it. The basis for all defense must be man-to-man defense, and students who are not given the opportunity to become proficient in its use will never become skillful zone defenders.

There is also another very practical reason for teaching man-to-man defense first: beginning defensive players often "lose" their opponents and allow them to become free near the basket. Since team defense has not been introduced at this time, the player should be free for a pass and a relatively easy shot. This gives the offensive team some sense of accomplishment and achievement, and encourages more players to try shooting. Beginning players find it very difficult to penetrate a zone defense. When they get the ball by one defender, another one moves into position. For this reason it is hard for beginners to acquire as many close shots and they often become discouraged. Teaching man-to-man defense first seems to provide a better balance between attack and defense.

Man-to-man defense should be taught first to all players, except possibly those who may never have instruction in basketball again. These players include seniors in high school who elect basketball for the first time or students in college. Often their purpose in choosing the activity is simply to learn something about the sport so that they might enjoy it to a greater extent in intramurals or a park league. These students can acquire success more quickly with a zone defense and, because of this, may enjoy defense to a greater extent. Nevertheless, it may not be as satisfying to play against because of the inability to penetrate it consistently.

TEACHING AIDS

Various aids may be used for beginning players to help them acquire skill more quickly, or to help them with their understanding of the game and specific tactics. Some are included below, but the reader is encouraged to devise others to meet the needs in her own situation.

1. Use junior size balls with young children — junior high school age or younger. Lower the height of the baskets and decrease the size of the playing area for youngsters.
2. Use wall surfaces to allow students to increase the crispness and accuracy of their passes.
3. If glass backboards are not available, place markings on the backboard to identify a point of aim for layups or other shots.
4. Through discussion, help students to recognize that shooting is nothing more than accurate passing. Show them that two balls will fit in the basket at the same time, thus demonstrating that there is space for error and that there is more than one entry into the basket.
5. Place tape or another substance on the floor to show the angle of a cut from a specific position or a designated pattern to follow. This is extremely helpful when first teaching the layup shot, as players tend to make the angle of approach to the basket much wider than desired.
6. Footprints can be placed on the floor (rugs with rubber backing or footprints drawn on the floor) to help students follow the desired

cutting path or to help them to learn to change direction.
7. A percussion instrument may be used to help students acquire the rhythm of a two-step stop. The same technique can be used in teaching the footwork for a layup shot.
8. Limit the number of bounces a player may take within a designated distance. Encourage players to cover distance with each bounce.
9. Groups of four or five may be formed to aid players in cutting and timing their move for a cut. Players are positioned informally on approximately one-half the court. Player 1 starts with the ball and passes to 2 as she cuts. Player 3 times her move and cuts for the next pass. This continues with the last player passing to 1 to repeat the process. Only the receiver of the pass cuts, and at first she should cut in a direction that makes passing easy. Later, she may cut anywhere so that a pivot may be required of the ball handler before she can pass to the cutter. If desirable, players may be positioned in their normal playing positions and make their cuts accordingly.
10. When players are practicing in small groups and without benefit of a basket, targets may be placed on the walls to give students playing offense an objective to hit. It also provides defensive players with a target so that they can refer to it for maintaining good defensive position. If targets on walls are impractical, wastebaskets, boxes, or other objects may be placed behind the playing space (far enough back so they are not hazardous) to serve the same purpose. Both offensive and defensive skills can be learned by using this technique. A game such as "Keep Away" teaches only rules and offensive skills, and for this reason its use seems questionable when additional skills can be learned by other means.
11. If players tend to be slow in passing, they may be instructed to "pass on the whistle." Each time a player receives a pass, the teacher whistles to signal time for the next pass. The speed with which the whistle is sounded should depend on the players' skill level. The purpose is to hasten the speed with which they look for a receiver and execute the pass.
12. A magnetic board is a valuable tool for demonstrating player positions and moves for numerous offensive and defensive situations. It generally is more useful than a blackboard for showing concepts concerning player movement, since students can see more readily the new positions of players without interference of numerous chalk lines.

13. Use of films, loop films, and film strips can be valuable in demonstrating various skills or offensive and defensive maneuvers. Video tape is an excellent tool for reviewing skills or game action by players so that they can become aware of their strengths and deficiencies. Observing college and professional games on television can also be a learning experience, particularly in demonstrating skill techniques. It also has some value in showing team offense or team defense, although this is limited to the court coverage visible to the viewer. The "instant replay" has provided the viewer with a new dimension in witnessing superior play.

14. Evaluative measures should be used throughout the unit. This may be done by means of progression charts, incidence charts, rating scales, and other devices. Students should recognize the progress they have made throughout a unit. They should also be aware of areas in which they have weaknesses so that they may be motivated to improve them.

TEACHING PROGRESSION

It is unrealistic to propose a teaching progression for any activity, because each situation is unique and demands a progression that is suitable for the students involved. Each class varies in age, skill level, and previous student experience, among other factors. The choice of activities also depends on the individual teacher's beliefs with regard to those aspects of play she considers most essential. There are probably no two circumstances under which the same unit would be taught identically to different groups. Therefore, it is with considerable hesitation that the following units are presented as guidelines for those teachers who would like some assistance in structuring a sequential progression.

The activities in the units are merely listed. Drills and the progression for teaching each skill or tactic are presented in the chapter in which each is described. During the development of each unit, considerable attention is devoted to one-half court play. More time should be devoted to the one-half court method of practice than use of the full court. Other than the fun of participating in a regulation type game, little is gained by advancing the ball from the defensive court to the frontcourt. Furthermore, twice as many players can be accommodated on one court by playing halfcourt. Periodically, in all units the players should experience the true game form. And, probably the amount of time devoted to this should increase as the players become more competent.

An attempt has been made to formulate six units — each based on previously learned materials. The starting point for teaching any class should be based on where the students are at the current time. In many instances the starting point should not be at the beginning of one of the units, but part way through it. Learning may continue into the following unit. In one class, it is entirely possible that some students will be learning activities suggested in Unit I while others may be practicing those in Units III or IV.

No attempt has been made to identify the units' length. The units' length will vary according to the students involved and also on the level of achievement desired. It is relatively safe to assay each of these units, however, and anticipate that a unit of more than ten or twelve lessons is necessary to complete it. Longer units must be prepared for students to gain a reasonable degree of competency in an activity.

Unit I

1. Chest and overhead passes. Practice catching.
2. Two-step stop. Rules on traveling.
3. Pivot, with emphasis on facing the player to whom the pass is made. Review the rules on traveling related to the pivot foot.
4. Passing to a moving receiver, with emphasis on 1–3 (Unit I).
5. Dribbling. Rules related to number of bounces, changing hands, and "carrying" the ball, with emphasis on using the dribble only to gain distance or to draw a defender.
6. Play two-on-two using half court and a target as a goal. Rules on boundaries, putting ball in play, with emphasis on defensive players choosing one opponent and staying with her (X_1 guards 1 when 1 is on offense; player 1 guards X_1 when X_1 is on offense).
7. Individual defense. Position when guarding a player with the ball and guarding one without the ball. Introduce the fact that there may be no body contact (no need to distinguish between fouls at this stage — award ball out-of-bounds rather than taking free throws).
8. Play two-on-two, with emphasis on individual defense — players sliding and correct position.
9. Layup shot, with emphasis on footwork and releasing ball high overhead.

10. Two-on-two, with emphasis on shooting lay-ups whenever free. Rules on scoring.
11. Starts and changing direction.
12. Pass and cut by attack players.
13. Two-on-two, with emphasis on pass and cut and shooting layups. Keep score.
14. Defense for pass and cut.
15. Two-on-two, with emphasis on defense positioning for pass and cut.
16. Feints.
17. Three-on-three half court. Feint before each pass. Feint before shooting if necessary. Emphasize that one player must always be back — all may not cut under the basket; if one player cuts under the basket and does not receive the ball, she clears back out to her position and does not stay under the basket. Use pass and cut. Defensive players pivot toward the outside when they obtain a rebound and pass toward the side line — never across the basket.
18. Short one-hand shots. Practice within 6–8 ft. of the basket. This is the area from which they will shoot — no point shooting from 15–20 ft. at this stage.
19. Three-on-three, emphasizing Nos. 16–18 (Unit I).
20. Four-on-four (use of three-on-three may be omitted if desired and go immediately to four-on-four). Two groups of two may combine to form a team of four players. Emphasize all of the above points (not in the same lesson though) as they practice. Use a simple weave pattern (Fig. 13.1) so that players know when and where to cut. Let them formulate their own options from the pattern, but insist that at least one player is back for defensive balance.
21. Continue using four-on-four, with emphasis on whatever tactics need improvement.
22. Five-on-five. Use the same pattern and add the pivot player moving independently trying to acquire position for a pass. Rule on 3 seconds in the key.
23. Play full court. Rules, strategy, and positioning for center jump. As players pair off, they guard each other (X_1 guards 1 when 1 is on offense; player 1 guards X_1 when X_1 is on offense). Players stay on the same side of the court for offense and defense (a player on defense in the right wing position becomes the offensive right wing). Allow no defensive player to interfere with play until the ball crosses the division line. The best ball handler is instructed to dribble the ball downcourt, while the other players move to the opposite end of the court and get into position. Shoot free throws after fouls are called. Study rules for free throws and scoring.

Throughout Unit I, time is taken periodically and when necessary to review previously learned skills or tactics. Progress in the unit may be interrupted at any time to assure that overlearning is acquired.

Unit II

1. Players review passing, catching, feinting, individual defense, shooting layups and other short shots, stops, starts, changes of direction, and pass and cut. Review the pattern used previously when playing four-on-four and five-on-five, with emphasis on performance improvement in all skills. Distance from the basket should be increased for shooting.
2. Jump shot; emphasis on release and when to use.
3. Putting the ball in play from out-of-bounds. Guard in-bounds the ball in the backcourt and either a guard or a wing in-bounds it in the frontcourt. Emphasis is placed on the positioning of players on the court and the timing of their cuts so that all players do not cut to the same place at the same time; use an elementary play.
4. Lateral screens. Players practice in a two-on-two situation. Two guards or a point guard and wing practice together, and a post and wing practice together. Defensive players are instructed to play man-to-man. No switching.
5. Five-on-five, with emphasis on lateral screens intermixed with pass and cut. As a screen is

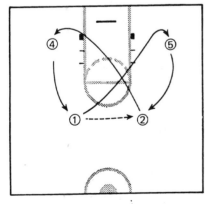

Fig. 13.1 *Four-Player Weave. 1 passes to 2 and cuts for the corner. 4 replaces 1 and receives the pass from 2. 2 cuts to the corner and 5 replaces her. Continue.*

set, other players clear the area to allow space for the drive.

6. Defense against the lateral screen. Players go over the top. Practice two-on-two.
7. Five-on-five, with emphasis on both the offense and defense with lateral screens. Sagging and floating by defenders.
8. Defensive players are instructed to start their moves too soon, and the attack cuts away from the screen. Practice two-on-two.
9. Five-on-five, with emphasis on attack cutting away from the screen whenever the defense moves too soon. Emphasis is on correct moves by all.
10. Screen switch. Defenders switch players as a screen is set. Two-on-two.
11. Screen and roll or cut. As the defense switches, the attack player passes to the one who is rolling or cutting. Defensive players are instructed to switch. Practice two-on-two.
12. Five-on-five. Defensive players are instructed to switch on all screens. Emphasis is on correct timing and moves by the attack.
13. Two-on-two. Defensive players are instructed to either stay man-to-man or switch — their choice. The attack adjusts to the actions of the defenders.
14. Five-on-five. Same emphasis as 12 above.
15. Three-player lateral screens if time permits.

Review basic skills throughout as necessary. Allow time for improving shooting techniques, and warm up with one-on-one moves at the beginning of the period. Allow students to incorporate pass-and-cut techniques with the screens. Let them use their own initiative, and insist that at least one player is back for defensive balance.

Unit III

1. Review previously learned skills, with emphasis on passing, cutting, individual defense, shooting, and lateral screens. Practice one-on-one, two-on-two, and five-on-five.
2. Inside screen variations and defense against it. Practice two-on-two (two guards or point guard and wing). Pivot players can work in another area on pivot moves and defense.
3. Five-on-five. Emphasis is on use of inside screen variation. Fake a lateral screen and use a inside screen variation, or fake the inside screen variation and move for a lateral screen.
4. Five-on-five. Encourage players to use all screens and offensive tactics learned to date.
5. Inside screens. Two-on-two.

6. Defense against inside screens.
7. Five-on-five. Emphasis is on inside screens and use of all types of screens. Attack must adjust to actions of defense. Defense changes tactics to confuse the offense.
8. Play full court as desired. Allow the defensive players to defend in the back court if they desire. Guards bring the ball downcourt and use screens if necessary.

Unit IV

1. Improve competency in passing, fakes, shooting, screens, and defense. Play five-on-five, improving positioning and timing of moves on offense.
2. Blocking out on rebounds defensively; offensive rebounding.
3. Five-on-five, incorporating 2 (Unit IV).
4. Scissor maneuver. Two guards or wing and point guard and the post. Three-on-three while the wings practice shooting in another area. Defensive players are instructed to stay man-to-man.
5. Five-on-five, using scissor tactics whenever possible. Forwards are instructed to clear the area and move to the top of the key as the scissor starts.
6. Three-on-three, with emphasis on defensive moves against the scissor.
7. Five-on-five, with emphasis on both attack and defense.
8. Three-on-three with the post, one guard, and one wing; repeat 5–8 (Unit IV).
9. Three-on-three. Two guards or wing and point guard and the pivot. Defensive players are instructed to switch. As the attack sees that the scissor does not work as well, both attack players cut to the same side. Defenders continue to switch.
10. Five-on-five. Defenders are instructed to change their tactics at their discretion — stay man-to-man or switch. Attack players use the scissor and adjust to the defense's action.
11. Three-on-three. The pivot, one guard, and one forward. Repeat 9 and 10 above.
12. Five-on-five. Players utilize all of the tactics and skills they know, and work to improve competency.

During Unit IV, allow time for shooting and practicing one-on-one. Provide time for full court play and administering free throws. Differentiate between pushing, charging, and blocking.

Unit V

1. Improve skills and tactics learned to date.
2. Introduce the hook shot for those who are ready.
3. Fast break.
4. Defense against the fast break.
5. Five-on-five full court, with emphasis on fast breaking whenever possible.
6. Five-on-five incorporating screens, pass and cut, and scissor maneuvers. Defensive players improve in defensive positioning for man-to-man and switching when necessary.
7. Two-one-two zone (or any other zone desired).

8. One-three-one offensive alignment utilizing tactics already known.
9. Five-on-five, both half and full court. Improve competency in all areas. Rules related to fouls.

Unit VI

1. Improve skills and tactics learned to date.
2. One-three-one zone (or other).
3. Two-three offensive alignment as used previously.
4. Allow the teams to choose their own offensive and defensive alignments. Let them test their choices against the opponent's choice. Five-on-five both half and full court.

14

Coaching

Coaching well-skilled players is not unlike teaching beginning players. The primary difference is that the players start at a higher level of skill and understanding. The same techniques used with beginners are continued in developing greater proficiency with higher skilled players. Drills for improving individual competencies and drills for two-, three-, and four-player tactics are used frequently. Scrimmaging or playing half court are also common means of improving teamwork.

While working with highly skilled athletes, a coach must remind herself (if necessary) that the educational benefits which accrue from competition are the primary purpose of an athletic program. The experiences provided for the athlete should be educationally sound and should supplement other educational experiences provided by the institution. The benefits to the individual athlete should remain uppermost in the mind of the coach as she makes any decisions bearing on the player's welfare. The coach must recognize that the purpose of the interscholastic or intercollegiate program is not for promoting her own self-vested interests or for the notoriety that a successful program brings to a school.

QUALITIES OF A COACH

Other than technical knowledge of a particular sport, the characteristics of well-qualified coaches are similar. Since they are working so closely with youth for extended periods of time, the selection of

a coach by the administration should be given careful consideration. Coaches must exemplify the highest ideals of anyone in the teaching profession.

With the increasing number of schools continuing or embarking on varsity programs for girls and women, there is an essential need for more qualified coaches. The demands on a coach are great in terms of time, energy, organization, planning, and emotional pressures involved with winning and losing. Coaching is a very time consuming job! One must derive satisfaction from working with youth for the job is not rewarding economically!

High school coaches have the difficult task of teaching players the fundamentals of the game. This often takes considerable time and patience, but the reward is great when one sees young players performing techniques properly. Many college coaches can attest to the fine job that is being done at the secondary level as players are entering the college ranks with far better basic skills than just a few years ago. This can be attributed to both better prepared coaches and a larger number of players who now have the opportunity to participate in an interscholastic program.

Anyone who has coached high school girls recognizes their high motivation. Those who participate in the program do so because they want to, and many hope that they can qualify for a college scholarship. Players recognize that the competitive program is demanding upon their time but they also know or learn the satisfaction that comes with doing one's best. Those who choose to compete usually are sincerely interested in playing and becoming better players. No coach could ask for more!

It will be interesting to see if this same attitude persists at the college level as more players become recipients of scholarships. Most athletes at this level continue to be as keen as their high school counterparts, but it will be interesting to see whether increased opportunities at lower levels change the aspirations and attitudes of the college athlete.

Respect

The coach can gain her players' respect by demonstrating her knowledge of the game. Depth of knowledge in terms of correction of errors, rules, and their interpretation, and strategy of an offensive and defensive nature are necessary. She must not only possess this knowledge, but must also help the players gain an understanding of these aspects and become proficient in applying them during game play.

She must treat all players with equal respect. She cannot afford to show favoritism to any player or group of players. To avoid giving the impression that she is closer to some players than others, she must give equal attention to all. Praise and criticism should be given to all — in the proper manner and at the proper time.

Plans for each practice should be drawn carefully, with time allotments established so that no time is wasted. Managers should be notified before practice of any drills that require special equipment so that this can be readied in advance.

Attitude

The coach's attitude is often reflected in both mannerisms and language. Each should be exemplary. Dress should be appropriate. The coach must demand that the players follow a similar code. Boisterous talking or laughter or other means of drawing attention is inappropriate.

Emotional Control

The coach must learn to keep complete control over her emotions. In any conversation or discussion with players, she should remain calm and keep her voice in its normal tone. Under the stress of a game situation, emotional coaches may have more difficulty in keeping their "cool." Generally when a coach displays her emotions, players on her team exhibit the same type of action. Players question officials' decisions; begin to pull opponents off-balance on tie balls; and retaliate against good play by elbowing, pushing, or other more subtle means.

None of these actions should be condoned or permitted.

The coach is the key influence in the conduct of players and spectators toward officials. Any questioning of calls by officials should be done quietly and during a time out. There should be no outbursts against an official while the game is in progress. If the coach can conduct herself in a quiet orderly manner, players and spectators will usually follow a similar behavior pattern.

Guidance

The coach is in an excellent position to guide her players in making numerous judgments. In order to aid players in this fashion the coach must have an open door policy, and players must believe that the coach is interested in their welfare. The coach must demonstrate faith in their actions and an understanding of their problems.

Throughout the season the coach should be concerned about the scholastic standing of the players. If a player's academic work is suffering because of the rigors of a season's schedule, the coach should help guide the player to drop basketball so that her academic average does not decline. Tutorial help for students having trouble in a particular subject area may help. Players should be encouraged to make up their work for missed classes *before* they leave for away contests or tournament play so that it does not accumulate.

LEGAL LIABILITY

Since the mid-sixties there has been an increasing number of law suits brought against coaches, particularly on the two coasts. The suit often names the head coach, assistant coaches, and school district officials as the defendants. Although negligence is the most common charge, individual rights and teacher incompetency are also causes for litigation. Banning a player from competing because of smoking or drinking when they are of legal age may be cause for a suit.

It is absolutely imperative that medical examinations be given to players before they are permitted to practice or compete. Without medical clearance there is no doubt about the coach's negligence. The wise coach will also obtain medical clearance following any injury or lengthy illness.

Medical assistance should be available for every practice session and contest. Medical authorities connected with the school should be contacted to develop the best plan to implement this assistance.

Certified athletic trainers are a great asset to any school system. Coaches are prudent to possess a valid first aid certificate.

Waiver forms signed by parents alledgedly negating responsibility of the school for injuries have no weight in court since a parent cannot sign away the "rights of a minor."

Coaches who leave the gymnasium to answer the telephone, talk with salespeople, visit with a parent, or obtain additional equipment are negligent if an accident occurs in their absence. Coaches also place themselves in a tenuous position if they use private cars to transport teams.

Coaches with insufficient training in a particular sport are particularly vulnerable. In small schools and colleges coaches may be appointed because of the scarcity of qualified personnel. If they fail to follow reasonable progression in presenting techniques or encourage players of different maturation levels to compete against one another, an injury may be sustained for which the coach is liable. Playing freshmen against seniors if their physical maturation is dissimilar should be avoided. Playing girls against boys may present similar problems.

In many instances the coach is granted immunity from prosecution due to employment by a state agency. Nevertheless, it would seem prudent for every coach to obtain liability insurance. Courts have ruled that the teacher or coach owes the student a higher standard of care than that expected by the general public. The courts have also established that minors are not responsible for their own actions. It behooves coaches to learn of particular statutes in their own state that have implications for the coaching profession.

INSERVICE TRAINING

For the benefit of players each coach has a responsibility to continually upgrade her knowledge of the game. There are many instances of players at the local, regional, and national levels who have great potential for stardom, but who never attain that status due to inadequate coaching. There were several athletes who demonstrated great promise at a trial for a United States team; but when they returned two years later for another trial they had improved only slightly in basic fundamentals. Whether their coach failed to understand the proper techniques; whether the coach failed to demand proper execution when the player was a "star"; or whether the player herself lacked the mental or physical discipline to achieve her potential may be conjectural. Nevertheless, the onus for players acquiring fun-

damentals is placed on the shoulders of the coach. It is for that reason that every coach should avail herself (himself) of opportunities for improvement.

Coaches should attend as many clinics as possible. Even if only one new concept is learned, the clinic is worthwhile. There are different philosophies on many aspects of the game, e.g., forcing opponents to the inside or toward the sideline, and faceguarding or opening to the ball on a backdoor cut. Hearing different points of view allows a coach to determine which technique works best with her own overall philosophy.

Talking to other coaches, both male and female, about fundamentals as well as specific strategy under different circumstances is also helpful. Subscribing to periodicals dealing with basketball, observing good coaches during practices, observing well-coached teams either at the local or district level or at regional tournaments, and watching college teams in the immediate area (for high school coaches) provide clues for success.

SCHOLARSHIPS AND RECRUITMENT

Coaches at both the high school and college levels have a responsibility for knowing the current regulations concerning college recruitment and scholarships. Ignorance of these regulations is no excuse for violations. College coaches should become completely familiar with the regulations appearing in the annual Handbook and should ask their voting representative in AIAW (NJCAA) to distribute copies of updated regulations that are distributed from the national office periodically during the year. High school coaches can obtain the same information from their state high school association as the same materials are sent to them.

High School Coaches

Players who have the academic ability and interest to attend college should be encouraged to do so. High school coaches have a responsibility to help the individual player select an institution that will best meet her needs. It is a mistake to channel all players to one institution or to different institutions that the coach knows little about other than it is a big time athletic institution.

The high school coach can obtain academic information about a school's offerings through the counseling and guidance department in the school or by contacting the institution in question. Beyond academic information about an institution, the high school coach should become familiar with the philosophy and aptitude of the college's coach. For a highly skilled player the single most important factor in the tutelege and improvement of her skill is the ability of the coach to help the player achieve her potential. All other factors are secondary. In order to become familiar with the basketball program at colleges in the immediate area, a high school coach should make every effort to attend college games. It is only through this means that the coach can evaluate the ability of the coach and the quality of the program. Once this is done the high school coach can provide the student with information about the college coach's "coaching personality," the level of intensity of competition, the apparent knowledge of the game by the college players, and the attitude of the players and coach, among other things. In this way the high school player will be better prepared to select an institution that meets her needs and desires.

It is important that high school coaches give an honest appraisal of the ability of players. College coaches want a true evaluation of a player's skills as well as her desire and coachability. College coaches are "turned off" by high school coaches who build up their players beyond their native abilities. Once again it is for this reason that college teams should be observed so that valid evaluations can be made.

It is also imperative that high school coaches completely understand the regulations of the state high school association. The answers to questions about restrictions on players attending basketball camps, college auditions, participation in all-star games, participation with or against college players on teams outside of school teams, visits to college campuses, etc. should be known.

Knowledge of AIAW (or NJCAA) regulations on recruiting and scholarships is most important. The high school player must be counseled so that she does not violate any regulations that will jeopardize her college career. She must also be sufficiently familiar with the college regulations so that she knows when she is being illegally recruited and the possible consequences if she attends the institution committing the infractions.

Junior College Coaches

These coaches must know regulations for recruiting high school athletes and the regulations of AIAW so that they may counsel those students desirous of completing four years of higher education. They must be particularly informed about those regula-

tions dealing with recruitment and eligibility of students who complete a program at a junior college.

University/ College Coaches

There is no excuse for college coaches to violate any of the regulations of AIAW or NJCAA. Current information is sent to athletic directors and voting representatives, if not directly to basketball coaches. Information is accessible, and coaches have the responsibility for knowing and abiding by current regulations.

Although no organization can legislate individual's ethical practices, hopefully those coaches who have "laundered monies" to illegally recruit will soon find that it is difficult to constitute a schedule. Opposing institutions can simply opt not to schedule the institution in question.

College coaches should also provide high school coaches and potential recruits with an honest evaluation of their program. Deciding what institution to attend is one of the most important decisions that a teenager must make, and college personnel should provide the student with valid information that will help the student make the correct choice.

PROMOTION

It is important that coaches become involved with the promotion of their program. This way they can gain student support and recognition of the program as well as parental and community support.

The coach should be available for interviews by any of the local media and should make players available for interviews at appropriate times. The coach must be willing to supply background information on each player if a press guide has not been prepared.

Posters displayed in school and in stores in the community and wallet-size cards distributed to interested people are a means for publicizing the game schedule. Some schools have had success in sponsoring a promotional affair before the season starts at which time players are introduced and an intrasquad game is played. The purpose of the event is to rekindle interest in basketball and demonstrate the talent and the style of play to be used during the season.

In a college setting the Sports Information Director (SID) can be invaluable in tabulating the statistics during the season and writing the copy to be sent to the media. Since they have the major responsibility for promotion, the coach should work closely with the SID office. Printing the schedules, posters, game programs, tournament programs, press releases, press guides, game and seasonal statistics, and league statistics all come under their jurisdiction. It is important that the working relationship between the coach and the SID remain at a high level.

ROLE OF ASSISTANT COACHES

Those schools that have one or more assistant coaches are indeed fortunate. Greater individual attention can be given to players, and expertise of assistant coaches which augments the head coach's can be utilized to good advantage. The responsibilities given to assistant coaches will vary according to their experience, knowledge, and dependability; often they are responsible for a particular facet of the game such as ball handling skills, shooting, or the entire offense or defense.

Because the coaches must work closely together, often in pressure situations, it is important that they respect one another. It is also important that the head coach take the time to outline fully the responsibilities of the assistant coach. The assistant coach must become completely indoctrinated in the philosophy, system of play, the offenses and defenses, and the strategy employed by the head coach under varying circumstances. In this way the assistant coach can be of greater help during practice sessions and can offer meaningful suggestions during game situations.

The assistant coach must always recognize that the position is subordinate to the head coach's. Accordingly the assistant coach must adhere to the responsibilities assigned by the head coach and not exceed them. Suggestions must be made in an appropriate manner and at an appropriate time.

Having at least two coaches also provides the players with a choice of coaches to whom they can best relate. This is important so that lines of communication remain open with all players. However, the assistant coach must remain professional in all discussions with players. When discussing player performance or strategy, the assistant coach must always say "We believe. . . ." The players must believe there is solidarity of views among the coaches. But saying "I think. . . ," even if inadvertently, gives the impression that the coaches disagree. An assistant coach who publicly second guesses the head coach is worse than no coach at all!

PREPARATIONS DURING THE OFF-SEASON

Budget

A tentative budget should be prepared to give a detailed account of anticipated income and expenses for the season. It should be itemized by category and designed in accordance with the budget policy of the department or institution.

Income provided by the institution should be listed separately from income anticipated from other sources — clinics, workshops, gate receipts, concessions, guarantees, etc.

Anticipated expenses might fall under the following categories:

1. Equipment — backboards, goals, electric scoring-time devices
   a. Purchase.
   b. Repair.
2. Supplies — basketballs, scorebook, timer's clock, timer's horn (if electric device not available), air pump, etc.
3. Laundry — practice gear, uniforms and warmup suits (if provided)
4. Travel
   a. Transportation — bus, car, air; number of miles per vehicle and cost per mile.
   b. Lodging — number in group, number per room, cost per room, number of nights.
   c. Meals — number in group, allowance per meal, number of meals.
5. Officials — number of games, cost per official.
6. Entry fees — for tournaments.
7. Home game — rental fees, labor, sodas, other.
8. Miscellaneous — rule book, other.
9. Contingency — regional, national tournaments (college level).

Care of Equipment

Leather basketballs should be cleaned and a leather conditioner applied. They should be partially deflated and stored in a cool, dry place. Rubber basketballs should be washed, partially deflated, and stored with the leather basketballs.

Practice gear, uniforms and warmup suits should be repaired, washed, or cleaned, folded or hung on hangers, and stored in plastic bags in a cool, dry area.

Other items used during the season should be

cleaned, repaired, and stored in an appropriate place. New equipment or uniforms should be marked and stored.

Facilities

At least a year in advance facilities for practices and games should be scheduled for the following season. When both men's and women's teams share the same facility, it should be scheduled on an alternate basis. The women use the gymnasium early one week while the men practice later. The following week the two teams exchange practice times. Other equitable arrangements can be made.

Scheduling

The formulation of a schedule should be done carefully. An effort should be made to schedule teams that traditionally are comparable in skill or slightly better. Little is gained by either team when one wins by twenty points or more. In order for a team to continue to improve, it must meet competent opponents who challenge their skills and knowledge.

When arranging a schedule, the coach should view the talent for the following year and determine how strong the team should be. If it appears that the team will be inexperienced, it may be wise to schedule the easiest opponents first so that the team has time to mature before meeting more difficult opponents. If the team is composed of veteran players it may be wiser to schedule a few games against difficult opponents first so that the players are challenged early in the season and see the need for continued learning. Games against traditional opponents should be scheduled near the end of the season.

Games scheduled at home and away should be equally spaced throughout the schedule. Each season a similar number of games should be scheduled at home and away; if possible, distances for travel each year should be comparable. (It may be difficult for an administrator to understand why the budget requires considerably more money one year than another year with no apparent additional benefits.) In all cases, travel should be held to a minimum. Travel is tiring and takes time. Games that require students to miss classes should be few in number. Long trips should be scheduled on weekends when travel will not interfere with classes.

Some games may be scheduled over the telephone, but game contracts should be issued for all contests. The site, time, number of games, color of uniforms, responsibility for furnishing officials and guarantees should be included.

An information sheet may be prepared to forward to visiting coaches to give them additional information. This might include directions to the site of the game, parking facilities for cars or buses, entrance for players, restaurants in the area with types of food and average price, motel and/or dormitory accommodations and prices.

When the scheduling has been completed for the following season, copies should be prepared and forwarded to the proper authorities, opponents, and distributed to other interested parties.

Special events should be scheduled such as Parents Night, Alumnae Night, and High School Night. Half-time entertainment can be arranged.

Officials

Following the completion of the schedule, arrangements should be made to secure the most qualified officials. Engaging a competent official is an asset to a highly skilled team. Games officiated by less competent officials often become rough and induce injuries as a result.

It is recommended that women officials be secured whenever possible. Nevertheless, only qualified and certified officials should be hired. Officials who are not certified to call a particular set of rules should not be hired. Rules differ and it is unfortunate when an official applies another organization's rules. If the official is certified by the governing body, this situation should not occur.

Travel

Tentative travel arrangements should be made for all away games. This includes reserving cars or buses and making reservations when overnight accommodations are required.

File on Opposing Teams

A file on each opponent may be made and supplemented annually. The file should contain general information on the site and facility and specific information on team play. Basically it should include:

1. General information
    a. Directions to the playing site.
    b. Parking facilities for cars and buses.
    c. Motels and cost per room; any special accommodations.

   d. Restaurants — type of food served and average cost.
   e. Dressing facilities and meeting room.
   f. Playing facility — court size, type of backboard, space around court, ceiling height.
   g. Opponents' uniform color.
2. Characteristics of team
   a. Individual characteristics
      1) Name, number, and class of each player
      2) Is she right- or left-handed?
      3) Does she dribble in both directions? Does she favor one side?
      4) What are her pet moves?
      5) Is she a playmaker?
      6) What type of shots does she attempt? From where does she like to shoot?
      7) Is she a good defensive player?
      8) Does she rebound offensively or defensively?
      9) Is she a good ball handler? Does she have poise? Can she be pressed?
      10) Other?
   b. Team offense
      1) Do they fast break? Who is the ball handler? How is it started? How do they tend to finish it?
      2) What is their offensive alignment?
      3) Who do they attempt to free for shots? How is this done?
      4) Where is the pivot positioned? How is she used? What are her assets? Weaknesses?
      5) What alignments are used on out-of-bounds? Jump balls? What are the pet plays?
      6) Can they be pressed?
      7) Who is the weakest player? Strongest player?
   c. Team defense
      1) Do they play man-to-man? Switching? Are they tight or loose?
      2) What kind of a zone do they use? How far is it extended?
      3) Do they press? Where? Man-to-man or zone?
      4) Are they susceptible to fakes?
      5) How do they rebound?
      6) Who is the weakest player? Strongest player?

A file of this nature reminds a coach of the strengths and weaknesses and general pattern of play for each opponent. Although it is based on a previous season, basic team tactics are not often changed drastically from year to year unless a new coach is appointed. Comments can be added as new information is gained; information that no longer is correct is deleted. Names of players who graduated or who are no longer members of the squad are eliminated, and names and information about new players are added when they become known.

Notes of this nature are not as valuable as a current scouting report, but few women have the time and/or budget to permit them to scout even a portion of their rivals. If more complete or current information is desired, it may be possible to have alumnae or former players who live near the school in question scout one or more of their games. If this can be arranged, they should be given a scouting sheet so that they know the specific information desired. One word of caution must be raised about reports by nontrained friends. Often they fail to depict exactly what formation and moves the players are following. Wrong information about a team is probably worse than no information at all. To have prepared for one type of offense or defense and have the opponents play something entirely different is psychologically deflating to players.

Preparation of Player Handbooks

Some coaches find it helpful to devise a "play book" for their players for their review and digestion. Often given to players in the Fall, it rekindles their interest and establishes a good mental set to start the new season. Because players have time to become mentally prepared, it takes less practice time for learning positioning or patterns. All of this can be learned beforehand. Usually a handbook of this nature contains the following information:

1. An introduction by the coach stating her philosophy and expectations for the season.
2. Game schedule — indicating time of game, home or away, and whether one or two games (varsity and junior varsity) will be played.
3. Preseason conditioning suggestions.
4. Date and time for first practice; practice schedule throughout the season.
5. Offensive alignments, patterns, plays, options.
6. Defensive alignments; zones, press.
7. Special plays.

The coach should make some provision for checking the handbooks out to players at the beginning of the season and having them returned at the conclusion of the season so that revisions may be made. The handbook should also be turned in by any player who drops from the squad during the course of the season. Care must be taken to guard the security of the information within the handbook. No coach wants the plays to be public information.

Miscellaneous Arrangements

Well in advance of the start of the season, arrangements should be made with the school doctor (or health service) for medical examinations of the athletes prior to the first day of practice.

Health insurance should be checked annually to ascertain whether players are covered by a school policy or should be advised to secure their own insurance. It should be noted that recent court litigation in some states has declared illegal the purchase of insurance for athletes by public funds.

High school coaches should arrange for accessibility of a school nurse or school doctor during practice periods and home games. If the medical staff has other responsibilities at the time, arrangements should be made for contacting one of them or an alternate in case of an emergency. The coach should be certain that she has access to a nonpay telephone with emergency numbers listed near it. The coach should have immediate access to the name of the parents, their address, telephone number (business and home), and the family physician in case of emergency.

At the college level, the coach should check the hours that the student health service is open and make arrangements for emergencies at other times. The coach also should have access to a nonpay telephone with emergency numbers listed nearby. The athletic trainer should be notified of the practice and game schedule.

College coaches would also be wise to send the Dean of Women (or supervisor of dormitories) a schedule for the season and a list of all players and their dormitory. If, due to an emergency, players will be out beyond scheduled hours, house mothers can be notified easily. The coach should also check on special arrangements that may be made for players who miss the scheduled meal hour because of practices or games. In some instances it is possible to make arrangements for box lunches or meals to be served later or earlier than usual. The coach should also check the policy regarding the housing of opposing teams. In some situations this is considerably cheaper than motels; in other instances it is more expensive.

The method for dispensing uniforms should be determined. Provision should be made for recording the number of each item issued to a player so that the responsibility for its return is placed on each player.

PREPARATIONS DURING THE SEASON

As all coaches are aware once practices start, the season becomes very busy. Teaching classes and preparing for daily practices and games take a considerable amount of time. Good organization is a necessity at this time.

First Day of Practice

Either the first day of practice or some time earlier, a meeting is called for all prospective candidates. At this time the coach welcomes the candidates and reveals expectations for the season. Rules are discussed concerning tardiness, absences, dress code, etc. This should eliminate problems that could develop during the season. When regulations are publicized at the start of the season, they generally are accepted by the group. When imposed later, they are assumed to be directed toward a particular individual or group and resentment may develop.

In addition the coach may remind players of the importance of proper conditioning. If the meeting is held during preseason, comments may be made on how "conditioned" players should be by the first day of practice and suggestions may be offered for attaining this level. The date to start a weight training and/or running program may be set.

Players should be encouraged to retain or improve their grade point averages during the season, and to request help as soon as they encounter any difficulty. Players may be reminded that their education is the most important factor and that basketball is secondary. They may also be reminded of the current eligibility rules.

The importance of punctuality should be stressed. It should also be made clear that the coach expects 100 percent effort on the part of all players and that the season should bring a great deal of fun and satisfaction. However, these do not develop as a result of clowning or horseplay during practice. A team that practices in this manner is likely to play in this manner. Above all the coach should make it known (and demonstrate it thereafter) that teamwork is the most important factor in any team's success. Players must be selfless and undertake any role that will help improve the play of the team.

Players should be reminded of the importance of immediate care to any injury and the damage that may result from unattended blisters, cuts, floor burns, sprains, etc. The availability of medical staff and a trainer should be cited.

Careful attention should be given to the method of selecting the squad. Players should know on what basis selection will be made, the number of cuts that will be made, the dates for each of those cuts, the general conduct of practices until that time, and the number of candidates who ultimately will comprise the squad.

Managers

One of the most valuable assets to a coach is dependable, resourceful, and loyal managers. They can be responsible for numerous items that ease the coach's load. Depending upon the number of responsibilities assigned the managers, the coach may choose to have one or more managers. It seems desirable to have at least two to carry out all of the responsibilities, but some coaches may not see a need for this number; others will desire more.

It is recommended that each manager be assigned specific duties for daily practice sessions, home games, and away games. These assignments may be made by the coach or by mutual agreement of the managers involved. Below is a list of responsibilities that may be assigned to managers.

Practices

1. A list of equipment is compiled and checked off daily as it is taken to the gym. The list should include a designated number of balls; pinnies, preferably the color of the uniform of the next opponent; timing devices; score sheets; shot charts; other devices for collecting data; water bottles; and a first aid kit if a trainer is not on duty.
2. Other equipment or materials are taken to the gymnasium on specific occasions as designated by the coach.
3. During practice, balls not in use are collected and placed in bags or other receptacles. Data are collected, and other duties are performed as requested.
4. Towels are made available during practices and for showers after practice.
5. All equipment is counted and returned to the equipment room. Items left by players are collected.

Home Games

1. The gymnasium is prepared for the game (if the custodians are not responsible for this). The scoring table with at least five chairs is readied. Chairs (or benches) are set out for both teams on either side of the scoring table. Timing devices are checked.
2. Uniforms are dispensed (if not assigned for the entire season).

3. Equipment is taken to the gym: a designated number of practice balls, a game ball, scorebook, timing devices, shot charts, other charts, first aid or training kit.
4. The visiting team is greeted as it arrives, and is escorted to the dressing room. When ready, these players are taken to the gymnasium.
5. The officials are greeted upon their arrival and shown to their dressing room.
6. Refreshments are prepared.
7. Towels are made available for both teams.
8. A manager may serve as a scorer, timer, 30-second clock operator, or statistician.
9. Balls are collected after pregame and half-time practice; all equipment is counted and returned after completion of the game.
10. Uniforms are collected.
11. Refreshments are served.

Away Games

1. Uniforms are dispensed.
2. Equipment is collected for travel: a designated number of practice balls (if not provided by the home team), scorebook, timing device, shot chart, other charts, water bottles, first aid or training kit.
3. A manager may serve as a timer, scorer, or statistician.
4. Practice balls are collected after pregame and half-time practice (if team's own balls are used).
5. Equipment is counted and collected after the game and returned to the gymnasium upon return.
6. Uniforms are collected.

Miscellaneous

1. Balls are cleaned and inflated periodically.
2. A card file of information on each player is prepared. Data collected might include name, address (dormitory), telephone, parents names, parents address, parents business and home telephone, family physician, uniform number, locker assigned, lock combination (in high school it is usually owned by the school), and other desired information which may be useful if an emergency occurs.

If dependable managers are secured, they relieve the coach of attending to all of these items and save the coach considerable time. It makes little difference who is selected to serve as managers, as long as they have the desirable qualities. Those selected may be players who were cut from the squad, students with a physical disability which prohibits them from participating otherwise, or interested students who would simply like to have some part in the athletic program.

Team Selection

A sufficient length of time should be devoted to tryouts so that a careful analysis can be made of the strengths and weaknesses of all candidates. The time that is necessary varies with the group, but two to three weeks should be ample for making wise judgments. Longer than that seriously cuts in to the amount of practice time for the squad prior to their first game, and less time probably does not give all candidates a fair chance for observation.

During tryouts it seems desirable to use specific drills that utilize all basic skills involved in the game. By observing players performing in small groups, the coach can analyze their ability in performing individual skills and their potential for improvement. Drills should include passing, stopping, pivoting, faking, shooting, individual defense, blocking out, and rebounding.

Scrimmages should also be a vital part of the tryout program. During the tryout period each player should play with and against players who are better than she, poorer than she, and players who are of equal ability. This may be done by formulating teams to compete in a round robin tournament each day. On different occasions every player should be assigned to play on a relatively strong team, a weak team, and an average team. Thus each player has an opportunity to demonstrate her skill against all levels of ability. The coach is also able to see how well she can adjust to playing with different individuals. And, perhaps more enlightening, the coach can see each player's mental attitude under various conditions.

The coach also should be concerned about each player's coordination, speed, quickness, reflexes, enthusiasm, coachability, aggressiveness, jumping ability and desire.

Since a basketball team is comprised of individuals who play various positions, each with their own qualifications, the coach must determine prior to tryouts exactly what talent is needed. How many players are desired on the squad? Will there be one team or two teams? Twelve to eighteen players generally comprise a squad. The squad must be balanced with a sufficient number of players able to play post, guard, wing, and corner.

While observing players during tryouts (as well as during the season), it is wise to use data-collect-

ing devices in order to appraise the players as objectively as possible. These may be in the form of Shot Charts, in which shooting range, types of shots, location of most shots, and accuracy can be detected; Incidence Charts, which identify the number of assists, rebounds, turnovers, fouls, violations, tie balls, and interceptions gained; and other devices favored by the coach. Reference to performance records eliminates the halo effect and provides a more vivid picture of the attributes and deficiencies of individual players. The coach may then compare abilities of individual players and determine which players will complement the others to the greatest degree.

Conditioning

One of the most important facets in any sports program is that of proper conditioning. A team that is unable to run at top speed throughout the game will not win championships. In addition physicians support the theory that 60 percent of all injuries incurred in basketball are the result of improper conditioning — both physical and mental. This means that not only must cardiovascular and muscular endurance be increased, but also that the player must be mentally prepared for practice and game situations.

To attain top physical condition a player must continue to increase her workload until the desired level is achieved. Continued activity will maintain that level. The workload can be increased basically in either of two ways:

1. increase the extent or amount of work.
2. increase the intensity of the work (the amount done in a given time).

Related specifically to basketball, periods for half-court play or scrimmaging are increased throughout the early practice sessions. With unconditioned players it may be wise to start with five-minute playing periods. This is increased to eight-, ten-, twelve-, fifteen-, and twenty-minute periods with rest periods shorter and less frequent. To increase the intensity of the activity, the same time period may be used but the workload within that time period may be increased. For example, early in the season, drills in a practice session may be alternated so that there is one that requires considerable running, followed by one that is less demanding. As endurance increases, running is included in all drills.

To improve cardiovascular endurance, the legs must be involved in the activity. Jumping, hopping, running, and sliding are the usual activities chosen for basketball players. Some coaches suggest that their players undertake a preseason conditioning program, while others wait for practices to start. Although each coach usually has pet drills for conditioning her players, some suggestions follow:

Preseason

1. Group. Sprints. Run a designated number of 440's in a specified time alternated with rest periods.
2. Group. Cross-country running. Designate a distance to be run and the maximum time allowed. As time goes on increase the distance and the time allowed.
3. Weight training. Prescribe a program for strength development for each player. Supervise the program carefully. Devise a circuit with the available equipment.
4. Players run up and down stairs at the gymnasium, in the dormitory, or at the football stadium. Increase the length of time in which the task is continued, or increase the number of stairs climbed in the same time period.
5. Harvard step test variation. A bench 16–18 in. high is needed. The player steps up on to the bench with one foot, then steps up with the other foot to an erect position; she steps down with the lead foot and steps down with the other foot to the starting position. The player may change her lead foot, if desired. This is continued as long as possible; increase the number of cycles periodically. Or, the player may complete a designated number of cycles in a specific time period; increase the number of cycles within that time period periodically.

In Season

1. Jumping in place. The player takes ten short jumps followed by ten high jumps. Continue. During the short jumps the player's feet just rise above the surface by a few inches. During the high jumps, the player jumps as high as possible on each jump. The number of cycles must be increased periodically.
2. Individually or as a group. Sprints. The player starts at one endline and sprints to the opposite endline, then jogs back to her starting position. Continue. Increase the number of cycles.
3. Individually or as a group. The player assumes a proper defensive position at one endline. She maintains that position as she slides to the other end, turns, and slides back to the starting position without rising to a standing position. Increase the number of cycles.

4. All players line up along the endline or sideline and move around the court counterclockwise. As they come to a sideline, they sprint to the other end; across the endlines they slide with their hands touching the floor. Increase the time performed or the number of cycles.
5. All players line up along the endline or sideline and move around the court counterclockwise. They run, slide, hop on one foot, hop on the other foot, or hop on both feet (not for very long; balance is lost) on signal from the coach. During this drill, the run may be a jog rather than a sprint. The players should touch the floor with their hands whenever they are sliding. Increase the time or the number of cycles.
6. Russian layup. Preferably no more than twelve players. Two lines are formed for layups at the end baskets. One ball is in play at each basket as layups are taken from the right side (or left side) at both ends. Players move to both ends of the court. They move from the shooting line at one end, to the rebounding line at the same end, to the shooting line at the *opposite* end, to the rebounding line at the opposite end, and back to the shooting line from which they started. This cycle is continued. With only twelve players involved, it should force the players to run continually if, after shooting, they run out to the division line before falling into the rebound line. If more players are added to the drill, players run in place while waiting to shoot or rebound. The drill is continued as long as possible. Increase the time periodically.
7. Russian layup variation. Proceed as described above, but continue until a designated number of layups have been made consecutively — fifteen, twenty, twenty-five, or fifty. Count layups at both ends of the court. Increase the number of consecutive layups periodically.
8. Suicides. Start at the endline; run to the free throw line and back; run to the center line and back; run to the far free throw line and back; run to the far endline and back. Complete in 30 seconds. Adjust the time as necessary.

Injuries

Early in the season two of the most common injuries that occur are blisters and shin splints. Blisters usually can be prevented early in the season by wearing two pairs of wool socks and by using a commercial skin toughener. Cotton socks do not provide the same type of cushion as woolen socks. Shin splints are an inflamation of the muscle between the shin and the foot and usually occur due to unaccustomed activity on a hard surface. Early season running on grassy surfaces should be encouraged for those who have had little activity recently. Running on a hard surface track is little better than the gymnasium floor. Prevention of this injury is considerably easier than the treatment.

Injuries to the ankle, knee, and fingers are also common in basketball. All of these can be treated immediately by elevating the extremity and applying pressure and ice. The limb is elevated to decrease arterial flow and increase venous flow. Pressure is applied to decrease arterial flow (it also decreases venous flow), and the ice is applied to keep swelling at a minimum. If ice is to be applied for a long period, a thin towel should be placed over the skin surface. Ice is applied on top of the towel to prevent possible frostbite. In all cases following any type of an injury the player should be referred to the school nurse or doctor or to the health center. No player should be permitted to resume practice following a serious injury until a medical release is given.

The scope of this book does not permit a full discussion of injuries and their treatment, but a coach should become prepared in this area through appropriate courses or workshops.

Practice Sessions

During the early part of the season, emphasis should be placed on the improvement of individual skills. Later, emphasis should be changed to improving teamwork, although individual improvement should not be neglected.

It is during this early practice period that the coach should prepare the team with a basic offense and variations, a secondary offense, a primary and secondary defense, a pressing defense, and plays for special situations. If enough time is not allowed, only a portion of these may be learned prior to the start of the season. Once the season starts, there may not be time to learn many more of them. If a team is inexperienced, it may be desirable to learn only one offense and one defense so that the players can learn to execute them well. One offense with good execution is better than two offenses with poor execution.

Throughout the season ample time should be devoted to shooting practice. Players need time in which to develop new shots, improve on known shots and increase their shooting range. Players should be encouraged to develop new moves prior to shooting. They must practice shooting without an opponent and against defense so that they develop confidence in their ability.

Time should also be devoted to the improvement of other individual skills, as needed. As a matter of fact, a list of activities for the start of practice can be posted at the entrance to the gymnasium. For example, two pivot players may be assigned to work on pivot moves and defense against the pivot; another player may work on shooting quickly from the corner; two others on blocking out and rebounding; another player may work on shooting quickly from the corner; two others on blocking out and rebounding; another on free throw shooting; four others to work on two player moves and the defense against it; another player on guarding a dribbler, etc. At this stage, some portion of the practice should be individualized.

During the early stages of the season, the coach needs to learn which combination of players consistently brings the best results. The coach also should assay which offense provides the greatest number of shots and the shooting accuracy attained from each. This usually indicates which offense frees players to the greatest degree and allows them unhurried shots from a distance within their shooting range. For example:

Alignment	Time Played	Opponents's Defense	Number of Possessions	FGA	FGM	%
Fast break	—	—	5	4	3	75
2–3	8	M-M tight	13	11	6	55
1–3–1	8	M-M tight	10	9	4	44

In order to assess data such as this accurately, the same defense must be used against each of the offensive alignments and each must be played for the same length of time. The above data were gathered from two quarters of full court scrimmage. In this situation the fast break resulted in the highest shooting percentage as one would expect. The two-three alignment produced a higher shooting accuracy and more goals scored than the one-three-one alignment. Data may be collected for half-court play under gamelike conditions, which would produce considerably more possessions and shooting opportunities — but no fast break attempts.

To make these data more useful, the coach should try various combinations working together under the same conditions. Also, defensive changes should be made to learn if results differ under these conditions. For example, these offensive alignments should be used against a loose man-to-man defense and against one or more zones.

Up to the time when games are played, the activities scheduled for the daily practice session may increase in intensity until players have attained the desirable level of conditioning. This means that attention should be given to longer periods of continuous play than normal (fifteen to twenty minutes) in scrimmages of a half-court nature or full court. (For high school students or players not in good condition, the time allotment should be adjusted.) Once the season starts and games are played once or twice a week, less full court scrimmaging may be desirable except for those who do not play in these contests. These players should engage in a full court scrimmage at the practice following the game. For the other players the workout may be moderate in intensity unless a weekend has interceded; in this case, a more strenuous session may be planned. Prior to all games, activities should be scheduled that are relatively light and not exhausting.

Publicity

Arrangements should be made to have a team photograph taken after the squad has been selected. Players often wish to purchase copies, and a copy should be kept in the coach's files for reference at a later date. The photograph can also be used for publicity purposes to accompany articles in the school or community newspaper, for bulletin board display, for use in the school yearbook, among others.

News releases should be prepared throughout the season for the school and local papers. Names of veteran players returning to tryout and a resume of the preceding season provide interesting reading when notification of this year's tryouts is given. This may be followed up by an announcement of the candidates who made the squad. Later highlights and results of each game should be submitted.

PREPARATION FOR TRAVEL

Attention to detail is necessary so that trips are uninterrupted by delay due to incomplete directions, improper or incomplete motel accommodations, or poor service.

Arrangements for Travel and Meals

Communication is made with the motel to verify or alter the tentative arrangements previously made. Arrival and departure time should be stated as well as any special accommodations that are desired. A list of the players and their room assignment can be forwarded so that keys for each room may be placed in an envelope and ready for distribution on arrival. This eliminates a large group from congregating in the lobby and permits players to settle in their rooms more quickly.

Restaurants should be alerted to an arrival time so that they may be prepared to serve a large group. They should also be notified if one large table to accommodate all players is desired. If a special menu is desired, the management should be informed so that the food may be prepared and served more quickly. This information also permits them to have sufficient waitresses on duty to assure good service to all diners.

Itinerary and Trip Directions

A complete itinerary for each trip should be formulated. It should include the time and place of departure, mode of transportation, name(s) of the driver(s), destination, estimated time of arrival, time of game, motel, restaurant(s) listed for different meals, time of departure, and anticipated return arrival time. A telephone number for the host school and the name of the home team coach should be included. A copy of the itinerary should be given to the athletic director and other administrators as desired. A copy may also be given to each player, particularly if the trip extends for more than one day. Additional copies should be available for parents and other interested parties.

When more than one vehicle is used, travel directions should be given *in writing* to each driver. The information should include maximum speed limit, routes to follow, in-town directions for turns on specific streets to reach the gymnasium, estimated time of arrival, parking accommodations, procedures for vehicle breakdowns and additional fuel, and a name and telephone number to call in case of emergency. If stops are to be made en route, the location of each and approximate arrival time should be noted. If an overnight stay is involved, directions to and from the motel to the gymnasium should be included. Each driver should also receive a copy of the itinerary.

Player Conduct

At the practice prior to departure on the first trip each year it is wise for the coach to review the dress code and conduct that she expects during the trip. Briefly, this discussion might include such items as

1. wearing apparel to and from the game.
2. the need for promptness at all times.
3. the desire to bring respect to themselves as well as to the institution.
4. their actions should not differentiate them from any other group representing the school.
5. they are the guests of the school (and a motel as well) which has invited them and their action should reflect this; they should care for their property as though it were their own and not "borrow" souvenirs.
6. their actions following the game should be the same whether they win or lose.

Departure and Arrival at Destination

Each player is given the responsibility for taking her own uniform. The coach makes a final check to be sure the managers have all necessary equipment, data sheets, and first aid or training kit. Before departure the coach counts the number of players in the vehicles to determine whether all are accounted for. The same procedure is followed before departing from the host school.

A team should arrive at their destination in time for players to become mentally prepared to play the game. There should be ample time for them to dress, have a team meeting, and warm up before the contest is scheduled to begin. If a game is scheduled in the afternoon following classes, the players should be warned against eating pregame snacks. If an early evening contest is scheduled, a light meal may be ingested during early afternoon; no meal should be eaten within four hours of game time. If desired, a meal or snack may be enjoyed following the game.

If a team is participating in a tournament, it is desirable for them to follow a normal routine as much as possible. This means that they should arise at a near normal hour and have breakfast together. If they are scheduled for an afternoon game, breakfast should be ingested four hours before game time and then the players should return to their room for rest until time to leave for the gymnasium. If they are scheduled for an evening contest, they may be placed on their own during the remaining portion of the morning. However, they must always be with at least one other player. By early afternoon they should be in their rooms resting. The pregame meal should be eaten four hours before game time.

PREPARATION FOR A GAME

The coach should prepare the team to meet any eventuality during practice sessions prior to the first game of the season. They should be prepared:

1. to face various zone defenses.
2. to deal with pressing defenses and man-to-man defenses; also to deal with different offensive alignments.
3. to put the ball in play from out-of-bounds against various defenses and to defend against various offensive alignments chosen by the opponents.
4. for jump ball situations at each of the restraining circles under conditions when they may win or lose the tap.
5. to follow a specific plan of action if they are ahead or behind, or if the score is tied in the last few minutes of the game.
6. to use warm-up drills with which they are familiar so that they may proceed in an organized fashion.

In order for the team to demonstrate poise and confidence in all of these, they must have practiced each of them many times under gamelike conditions.

Two or three practice sessions before the first game is scheduled, the team should experience a regulation intrasquad game in which uniforms are worn, regular warm-up procedures are followed, and officials conduct the game using all regulation procedures. At this time the coach can identify the weaknesses under game conditions and conduct additional practice sessions for correction before the initial game. With high school players in particular, the coach is able to ascertain whether all players can follow correct substitution procedures. She can also check to see if the designated players look at the bench for signals for a specific offensive maneuver or a change in tactic. Players also can demonstrate their understanding of the responsibility for calling time-outs.

After each game is played the coach analyzes what areas appear to be the weakest and takes measures to correct or improve them as much as possible before the next contest. If possible, practices should be conducted in surroundings similar to those in which the next game will be played. If it is an away game and the court is much smaller than the home team court, it may be wise to place chairs or other objects on the court to reduce it to a similar size. If possible, lighting and other conditions should be made similar.

What Type of Defense Should the Team Play?

Every team should be able to play a strong man-to-man defense. Regardless of what type of defense is chosen, when an opponent has the ball a defender must guard her with man-to-man techniques. Even though a team might opt to play a zone as their basic defense, it should be by choice rather than necessity!

Actually a team should be able to play both man-to-man and zone defense well. There are times when tactics dictate playing zone and other times when a team should play man-to-man. A team able to do both has greater flexibility in coping with their opponents' strengths.

It is also desirable that a team be able to play one or more types of presses, preferably half court and full court. A press is helpful against a team that has poor ball handlers or that likes to advance the ball slowly downcourt. A press is also mandatory if a team is behind in score with only a short time remaining to play. By utilizing a press, a team learns the principles upon which the press is based and can better understand how to break opponents' presses.

Some suggestions follow on ways to combat opponents' strengths.

Opponents Are Tall; Your Team Is Shorter. The size differential often can be hidden to a greater degree when a shorter team plays zone. The best rebounders can be placed in the most advantageous positions; whereas if the defensive team plays man-to-man the best rebounders can be drawn to the perimeter and out of rebounding range. By changing the zone defense periodically the passing lanes

change and the offensive team may be confused temporarily.

If your team is a good defensive squad, you might play a half-court pressure man-to-man defense with a great deal of pressure on the ball and players one pass away from the ball. The defense should be able to cause turnovers by forcing bad passes.

If your team is quicker than the opponents and better conditioned, you can offset the height advantage by pressing full court, by using either a man-to-man or zone press. By utilizing your quickness on defense and your speed in executing the fast breaks you reduce the effectiveness of the tall player to a minimum.

Opponents Build Their Offense Around a High Scoring Post Player. Your team has the option of playing a tight zone to prevent the post from receiving the ball, and should she receive a pass, the zone collapses on the post to make scoring difficult. This tactic then encourages other less skilled players to shoot and the defensive team can rebound and start their own offensive thrust.

Another alternative is to play a sagging or collapsing man-to-man defense where the post is overplayed and extreme pressure is placed on the ball. If the post receives a pass, the defenders collapse in the lane to make maneuvering by the post difficult. Both of these tactics leave outside players free, which is the premise of this defensive adaptation.

Opponents Possess Outstanding Outside Shooters. Although most coaches agree that a team cannot win through outside shooting only, there are times when an opposing team does rely primarily on outside shooting, particularly if they are much shorter than the defenders. If they are having success and hold a tangible lead in score, the defensive team is forced to make some type of adjustment. If they are playing a zone, they must spread it wider to place more pressure on the shooters or go to a man-to-man defense. If the outside shooters do not drive well, the defender can rush at the pass receiver to cause harassment on the shot or encourage a drive. The choice to be made is dependent on the defender's speed and ability to cover the opponents man-to-man. Another alternative is to play tight defense on the rest of the opponents, keep them off the boards, disallow any easy baskets, and acknowledge that the high scorers will hit their average, more or less.

Opponents Prefer to Advance the Ball Slowly from Backcourt to Frontcourt. The defensive team should press them full court either man-to-man or zone. If the opponent's ball handlers are weak also, the man-to-man press will cause the most difficulty. Use of trapping techniques with either the man-to-man or zone press will add greater harassment for the opponents. If the opponents have an exceptional ball handler, man-to-man pressure techniques will be fruitful only if trapping techniques are utilized.

Opponents Are Poor Ball Handlers. Use of the same tactics as described above with emphasis on man-to-man pressure defense with trapping. Place extensive pressure on the opponents in the backcourt and overplay opponents without the ball and play tight on the ball handler. Poor passes should result in many steals and easy baskets.

Opponents Have Only One Scoring Threat. One means of combatting this player's contribution is to play her man-to-man with the other four players in a box or diamond zone. This tactic is often referred to as a zone with chaser. It can be effective. The players involved in the zone must allow the man-to-man coverage when the chaser moves through the zone. This technique is effective against a player in the post area or on the periphery. One disadvantage of the tactic is the special preparation that is necessary to use it for a game unless the team utilizes the defense throughout the season. It takes time for players to learn the coverage in a four-player zone and the coach must determine whether the time for preparation will produce a corresponding result.

Opponents Like to Drive Through the Lane. Against a team that cannot shoot well from the periphery, the defensive team can play zone and sag on the driving players. This should greatly reduce their effectiveness. Against a team that has outside shooters, the defense may overplay to the inside and force the dribbler toward the sideline while playing man-to-man. If this tactic is used, the team must be prepared to help on the baseline side.

Another alternative is to play a help-and-recover type of man-to-man defense in which two defenders help stop any driving attempt by the attack. As soon as the dribbler picks up her dribble and the original defender recovers, the helping player recovers onto her own opponent.

Opponents Have a Limited Shooting Range. The defensive team again has a choice of man-to-man tactics or zone. If employing man-to-man tactics, the defenders can pressure their opponent once she moves into shooting range, but they should not be pulled out beyond their opponent's shooting range. Often a team with poor outside shooters will spread the defense to open gaps and allow the drive for the shot in the lane. Defenders should not be lured into this coup. A zone defense also provides excellent coverage against this type of offensive team.

Opponents Fast Break as Often as Possible. The fast break must be stopped, and this may be accomplished in one of three ways. First, pressure may be placed on the rebounder so that the pass to the outlet is delayed, if only temporarily. If this maneuver is successful, the offense loses a second or two, which allows the defenders time to recover to the backcourt. The defensive team may also place pressure on the outlet pass. This may be done by either covering the outlet receiver or a defender's moving into the normal passing lane to the outlet. The third tactic is to send two players back on defense whenever a shot is taken. Of course, a combination of all of these tactics will produce the best results.

What Type of an Offense Should the Team Play?

The basic question the coach must answer is whether the team should play a fast break offense, free lance offense, pattern offense, or combination of these. A team can fast break successfully only if it has strong rebounders, good speed, and good ball handlers. Without these skills a team is likely to lose more points attempting fast breaks than it will gain from them. If a team has players with these attributes, it may attempt to fast break on every possession. The fast break then becomes its primary offense.

Many teams have players who prefer the pattern style of offense. By moving in a predetermined fashion, players can learn the basic options of the offense and need adjust only to the way in which the opponents defend that pattern. This system is organized, and can free players at specified places on the floor. It is an offense that can be completely controlled.

An alternative is a free lance system in which the coach can apply certain rules. The motion offense was developed on this system. Fundamentally players have certain options for movement, but they are at liberty to utilize any one they wish. There is no such thing as a predetermined cut; as a matter of fact most coaches utilizing this system would not allow players to execute the same maneuver repeatedly. This system of play can be utilized to greatest advantage by teams with a basic knowledge of screening and cutting techniques, and with individuals who understand court spacing, timing of cuts, and using teammates well when picks are set.

The use of a complete free lance system without any rules is proposed infrequently; it is not recommended. Experienced players can effectively use this system, but they, too, profit from a more organized approach.

The coach may choose to fast break when the opportunity arises. If a fast break does not materialize, a pattern offense may be used as the primary offense with a motion offense as a secondary offense. In this way a coach can utilize various talents possessed by different individuals.

Once the coach decides which type of offense best suits the abilities of the team members, she can design a specific offense to exploit the talents of the outstanding offensive players. It is possible to accomplish this purpose through either a pattern offense or free lance type offense with rules.

High Scoring Post Player. Every effort should be made to get the ball to the post. The team might utilize the free lance style with players concentrating on screening for the post although this tactic cannot be used exclusively. In a pattern offense a double post system may be used with one post serving primarily as a screener to free the other post. A pattern offense could be designed with a corner player who is an effective shooter so that her opponent cannot sag against the lane and help out on the post. Considerable movement on the periphery precludes defensive players from simply sagging into the lane.

Exceptional Passer. When a team possesses an outstanding ball handler and passer, it may choose to play with a point guard offense. With a point offense it is common to play with two wings and two posts or with two wings, one post and one corner player. In order to use this system, the point guard must be a leader and a "take charge" type of player. She must be able to dribble with ease in both directions and pass to her left or right with equal skill. She knows that a poor pass will most likely result in an opponent's score. The use of a point guard allows a team to attack from more varied positions on the court.

An Exceptional Player Other than a Post Player. The offensive team should exploit the talents of this player as much as possible by getting the ball to her.

Against a zone the team will position this player in a seam of the zone so that she will be free to receive a pass. Against a man-to-man defense the offensive team should use screens away from the ball to free her for a pass or screens on the ball when the outstanding player has the ball. The team can also have their better player screen for a ball handler when the opponents use a switching defense. This would free the better player on her roll or cut.

The Offensive Team Is Quick and Has Good Ball Handlers. The team should use a fast break offense to take advantage of its speed. This is particularly true if the team is shorter than most of the opponents which it plays. This is the premise on which many Asiatic teams base their offense. They get the ball downcourt as quickly as possible. If they can initiate a fast break and reach scoring range before the taller defenders can recover, they have a better chance of scoring.

The Opponents Play an Aggressive Type of Man-to-Man Defense. The offensive team may counteract this tactic by cutting backdoor whenever the overplay is exerted. In addition an offense based on screens off the ball will effectively free players for a pass. The offensive team can also structure their offense so that it is spread to lure the opponents out and provide greater space for drives as well as space to free players off screens.

The Offensive Team Has a Height Advantage. Against a shorter defensive team a double post may be used either in a high-low configuration or in a double low post, depending upon the talents of the two post players. If this tactic does not seem to be feasible because of the lack of a second low post, the offensive team can use a flash post. This player could be a wing, corner player, or second guard in a two-guard offense. The offensive team using this tactic should try to get the ball to the flash pivot and allow her to go one-on-one against her opponent with the other players clearing the area.

The Opponents Have One or More Weak Defensive Players or a Player in Foul Trouble. The offensive team should exploit the poor defenders. If the defenders are playing man-to-man, the opposing coach will assign the poor defensive players to defend against the weaker players on the offensive team. The offensive team should maneuver so that the weak defenders must cope with screens and/or their opponent with the ball. If these poorer offensive players are not sufficiently capable to exploit the defenders then there is little point trying to establish an offense in this manner. If this is the case the offensive team should establish their offense to cause the poor defenders to get caught on a screen; hopefully the defense will switch, causing the poorer players to guard the better offensive players. Another alternative is for the better offensive players to drive at their opponents knowing that they will receive little help from the weak defenders.

If the opponents are playing zone, the weak defenders should be isolated so that they are forced to go one-on-one against a better player. The attack may also overload their zone, which should produce a free player for a desirable shot. In any event the offense should be geared toward providing shots in the areas of the poorest defenders, but only if these areas are also a strength of the attack. Too often a team tries to take advantage of a poor player by changing their offense; this often plays right into the hands of the defensive team.

When the opponents have a player in foul trouble, the offensive team can feed players in her area of the zone or give the ball to her opponent in a man-to-man defense. The defender is likely to play conservatively so that she does not foul. She is not likely to play aggressively off the ball; nor is she likely to play tight against a driving player or a shooter. However, the same caution needs to be exercised here as above; the offensive team does not want to alter its offense significantly. It must do whatever it does best.

The Offensive Team Trails in Score with a Short Time to Play. Should a team trail by ten points (for example) it must start to press sooner than if a team only trails by three or four points. The coach must decide at what point a press must be initiated to allow the team to tie the score or go ahead. By using a press a team hopes to score several easy baskets quickly. If successful, it often changes the momentum of the game. By practicing with a lead and when trailing, a team can gain confidence in its ability to overcome a lead and to hold a lead.

When a team trails in score late in the game it must be aggressive and try for steals; it can no longer attempt to play a team even. If the defensive team is not in the one-and-one situation, it can be more aggressive but should not commit careless fouls. The team must play tight defense and not allow any easy field goals. On offense the team cannot play deliberately and consume a great deal of time; nor can they run downcourt and take poor shots. They must shoot quickly, but they also must take good shots and stress offensive rebounding.

Game Plan

In addition the coach should establish a game plan of measures to take against the upcoming opponent. This should be based on known information about the opponents' play. If the coach has no information about the opponent the team must be prepared to do whatever it does best and anticipate as much as possible what the opponents might do.

Once the coach has established a game plan, it should be discussed with the players. During the next few practice sessions players practice the execution of the game plan. Usually the second team is asked to play the defense the opponents play so that the starters and substitutes can gain experience opposing it. Similarly, the second team is taught the opponents' offense as much as possible so that the defense can become prepared. If any idiosyncrasies or pet moves of opposing individual players are known, the second team players try to emulate them so that the starters and substitutes become familiar with them.

GAME PROCEDURES

Players should report approximately one hour or more before the game is scheduled to start. Players who need taping should report earlier. This provides players with ample time to get dressed, be taped, and ready for a team meeting approximately thirty to forty-five minutes before game time.

Team Meeting

During the team meeting the coach reviews with the squad the game plan for the day. The coach points out specifically how each player must contain her opponent. The team defense is also outlined: how to stop their fast break; what measures are to be taken against their ball handler; how to play the post player; whether or not the team will press, etc. Offensive tactics are reviewed including under what conditions they are to fast break; who should bring the ball downcourt; what offensive alignment they are to start with and which options are likely to be most successful; and the strategy for the tap at the start of the game. The coach may desire to diagram on a blackboard alignments and/or options for review for the players.

Time is provided for questions. The starting lineup is announced, warm-up procedures are reviewed and the team goes on the court approximately twenty minutes before game time.

Pregame Warm-up

Players should move onto the court in an organized fashion. They usually move from the squad meeting to the gymnasium and trot out onto the court led by their captain or someone appointed as captain for the day. This system gives them a feeling of *espirit de corps* and should replace the unorganized system of players moving onto the court when they are ready.

The purpose of the warm-up period is to provide the players with time to capture the feel of the ball and gain the rhythm of their shots and timing for passes and cutting. It may also serve to intimidate the opponents if a team moves from one drill to another crisply and executes each with proficiency.

Often the warm-up is started by running a simple layup drill. This is followed by several other drills before players informally practice the shots they are most likely to use in the game. All players should shoot free throws as well. While players are shooting, there should be a ball for every two players. When more than six balls are used, however, it becomes somewhat difficult. Most coaches prefer to have those players who are most likely to see action enjoy most of the shooting time. All players may shoot for a designated length of time and then those players who will not see much action may return to the bench or stand near the division line and observe both teams shooting. Those players who are shooting usually pair off, and one player takes several shots before giving the ball to her partner.

Many coaches prefer to end the pregame session with the shooting activity. Others prefer to return to some kind of team drill or playing three-on-three or five-on-five utilizing a team offense. Often coaches interrupt drills to return to the dressing room for last minute instructions.

Examples of common warm-up drills are shown in Figs. 14.1 to 14.3.

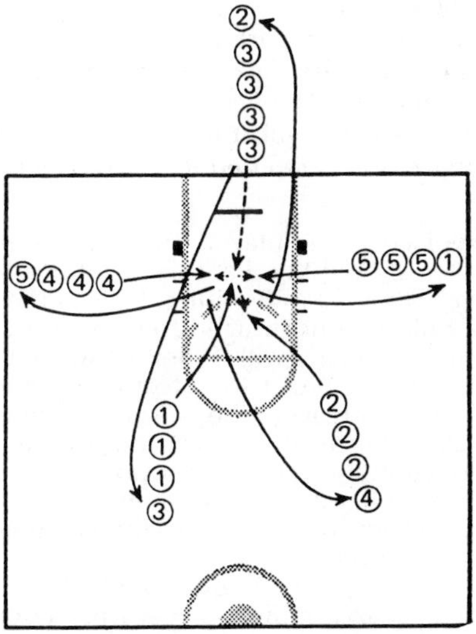

Substitutions

In almost every instance a coach discovers that there are five players, who overall, are better than the rest of the squad. These five players should be named to the starting line-up for a game. Conceivably the top five individual players may not bring the best team results. If each player is a "star" and unwilling to assist teammates, the coach might wish to look at players with lesser talent who will contrib-

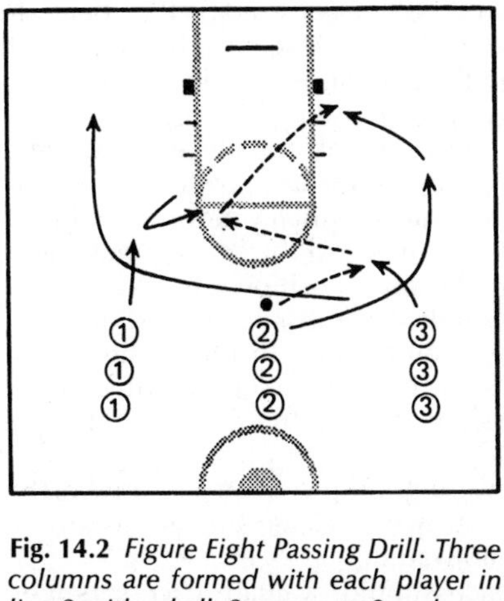

Fig. 14.1 *Passing Drill. Players start in columns as shown. Player 3 starts with the ball and passes to 1 who passes to 5 to 4 to 2 and to 3 and the pattern is repeated. The cuts are timed so that each player may hand off the pass to the next cutter. After passing, each player goes to the right and end of the line to which she passed. The drill can be modified so that players in line 2 shoot and 3 recovers the rebound before starting a new sequence.*

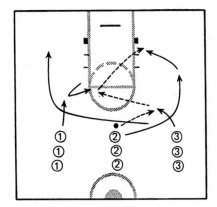

Fig. 14.2 *Figure Eight Passing Drill. Three columns are formed with each player in line 2 with a ball. 2 passes to 3 and goes behind 3. 3 passes to 1 and goes behind 1. 1 passes to 2 and goes behind her. 2 shoots. No dribbling is allowed.*

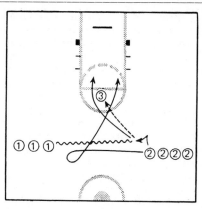

Fig. 14.3 *Pivot and Shooting Drill. Players line up in a shuttle formation as shown with one or two pivot players alternating at the high pivot position. Two balls are used. Player 1 dribbles across as player 2 cuts to the opposite side. Both players pivot (on the inside foot) and 1 passes to 3. 1 cuts around 3, followed by 2. 3 hands off to either one for a layup. As the ball is rebounded, the next players start.*

ute to a greater degree to the team effort. The five players who contribute to the end result in the best fashion should be the starters.

It is unusual, except in an all-star situation, for a coach to have too many stars. More often the coach has to analyze the strengths and weaknesses of each player and determine the ones who together possess the capabilities desired by the coach. In a lineup at any one time there must be players who have ball handling ability, shooting ability, defensive ability, and rebounding strength. It is rare for all players to possess all abilities equally well.

There may be instances when a team has four players who are obviously more skilled than any of the other members of the squad. That team may be weak at the post position (for example) with no player demonstrating skills that are far superior to the other contenders. In this instance the coach should start the player who had outstanding practice sessions during the week or the post who played the best in the preceding game. Coaches must reward good play with starting berths and/or extensive play if so-called substitutes are to remain highly motivated.

A coach should evaluate each member of the team in all aspects of the game so that when specific situations arise the coach can substitute a player with the talents needed at that particular time. When it is necessary to clear the defensive boards,

the coach can substitute a good rebounder. When defensive ability is needed to stop a hot shooter, the coach should know who to substitute. When speed is needed, a quick player can be inserted. When a threat is needed against a tight zone, an outside shooter is substituted. Identification of players by their specific talents and substitution of those players at the appropriate times should bring good results and should also ensure good unity and morale on the team. In this way every player knows that she can contribute in some way.

The substitutes who usually see action sit close to the coach so that the coach can convey any necessary information to them. Players least likely to see action sit near the end of the bench. While the game is in progress the substitutes cheer their teammates and shout words of encouragement. Substitutes should watch particularly the player for whom they may substitute and her opponent. Often the substitute can detect a flaw in the opponent's skill and relay that information to her teammate. Also, by watching the opponent she should be better prepared to defend against her when she enters the game.

For the greatest part of the game the coach should play the five players who are performing the best on that particular evening. Nevertheless, there will be times when substitution is necessary. The following reasons are cited for substituting:

1. Replace a tired player. The coach and substitutes should keep a wary eye for any player who appears to be tiring. Players themselves should be encouraged to signal for a substitute and many will if they know they will be reinserted into the contest after a brief rest.
2. Replace a player who is not playing with her usual vim or ability. The player may not be concentrating completely on the game or she may be having an "off" night. Often temporarily removing her from the game will have the desired effect.
3. Remove a player in foul trouble. It is common practice to remove a player who acquires two quick fouls. Often the third one follows very shortly. If a player is charged with her second foul near the end of the first half, the coach may remove her so that she does not acquire a third foul before the end of the first half. When a player is charged with her fourth foul, she often is removed to save her for the final few minutes of play. At times this practice has merit, but if a player is forced to sit on the bench for a long period of time before re-entering the game, she may be "cooled" off — both physically and mentally — and not perform up to capacity.

4. Remove a player who begins to "hot dog" ineffectively.
5. Put aggressive players into action. If a team has fallen behind in score and appears to be playing somewhat sluggishly, the insertion of an aggressive player may bring them out of their doldrums and "fire" them up.
6. Insert players with special abilities. If a team wants to be sure to recover a rebound, good jumpers may be inserted. Good ball handlers may be inserted when the team wants to control the ball as long as possible. A player who is particularly good defensively may be inserted to defend against a high scoring opponent.
7. Remove one or more of the best players midway in the second half so they will be rested for crucial action near the end of the game.
8. Remove a player a few minutes before the end of a period or before a planned time-out to provide added rest time.
9. Allow players who often see little game action to gain some playing experience. Insertion of players when a team has gained a good lead should be made extremely judiciously. Once momentum is lost, it is sometimes difficult to regain. Therefore, when a team has moved to a rather large lead in the first half it may be wise to only substitute for one or two players at most. In the second half, when it appears as though a large enough lead has been attained, starters should be replaced by others. Not only does it give the substitutes game experience which may prove beneficial in years to come, but it also helps to improve team morale.

In order to substitute wisely the coach must also know the temperament of the players and how they react under different circumstances. For example, some may play far better in a game situation than any time in practice. Sometimes the roar of the crowd encourages a player to play a little harder and a little better. Other players may react the opposite and play considerably better when there is not a large audience. Some players seem to be at their best when they enter the game as a substitute rather than as a starter. Some players react favorably to the home crowd cheers while others may perform better away from home and their friends in the audience. Some players play better when they start a game; others play equally well as a starter or coming off the bench.

Team Time-outs

Since there are a limited number of time-outs permitted in a game, they should be used judiciously

and for a particular purpose. Usually only the captain or another designated player is permitted to call a time out other than those that the coach signals. Some coaches do not allow their players the freedom of calling a time-out at all and permit only those that are signaled from the bench.

At least two time-outs should be saved for use late in the game, if they are needed. Before calling any time-out, the coach should check the official game clock to be certain that there is enough time left in the period to warrant taking a time-out. Time-outs are usually taken to:

1. slow the momentum the opponents have gained, particularly if they have scored five or six consecutive points.
2. change strategy on offense or defense.
3. run a specific offensive play.
4. rest or make a substitution.
5. prevent a tie ball from occurring when a player is double-teamed (called by the player involved).

When a time-out is called the players gather near the bench. Some coaches prefer to have them remain standing while others let them sit down. Whichever system is used, the substitutes gather behind the players and all are quiet. The coach allows the players to catch their breath for a few seconds as a manager distributes towels and water. Instructions are then given.

When a time-out is called by the opposing team a coach may institute a change in defensive tactics or alter the offensive alignment so that instructions given to the opposing team may be counteracted.

Intermissions Between Quarters (High School)

The team gathers at the bench in a fashion similar to team time-outs. Players are permitted to rest 15–30 seconds before instructions are given. Comments are made relative to individual and team play. For example, they may be instructed to change to a two-three offense or to go into a two-one-two zone and start a press after their first score. The first out-of-bounds play and the moves on the jump ball also are determined. During the intermission, players are supplied with towels and water.

Half-Time Procedures

The home team should make provisions for both teams to meet in separate rooms that are suitable for rest, discussion, and instruction. These rooms should be close to the gymnasium and equipped with a blackboard.

During half-time intermission, the players should be allowed to rest for two or three minutes. Injuries should be checked as towels and water are distributed. During the time that the players are resting, the statistics are summarized and the coach studies the data from those and the scorebook. The coach quickly reviews the strengths and weaknesses, and makes suggestions for improvement. They are informed of any changes that should be made in the offensive or defensive strategy. The number of fouls each has committed and the number of fouls charged to each opponent is reviewed. Comments are made to individuals, the starting line-up is given, and the players are permitted time to warm-up for a few minutes.

Although the length of the intermission at half-time is considerably longer than a time-out, time is a premium and the coach must be prepared to use it to the greatest advantage.

Postgame Procedures

Immediately following the game the captain thanks the officials, and all players return to the dressing room for showers. The two coaches meet to offer condolences or congratulations as the case may be and thank the officials before leaving for the dressing room and their respective teams. If the team has won, the coach may offer her congratulations and, if necessary, quiet their enthusiasm. If the team has lost, the coach should be sympathetic. In either case congratulations should be offered to those players who played well. Particular attention should be given to those who play a subordinate role and do not normally receive the acclaim given to the high scorers and "flashy" ball handlers.

TEAM STATISTICS

Accurately recorded team statistics reveal vital information that a coach and players can use to analyze individual strengths and weaknesses. The information is not easy to collect, and only individuals who are dependable and give attention to detail should be appointed to these positions. In universities the SID (Sports Information Director) is responsible for the basic statistics. If additional data is desired, managers or other individuals may be trained to record data. In a high school, parents, faculty, or managers may be trained to record the statistics.

Most coaches collect data on field goal attempts, field goals made, field goal percentage, free throws attempted, free throws made, free throw percentage, rebounds, assists, turnovers, steals, and fouls. Some also record minutes played. Fig. 14.4 can be used to collect all of this data. A similar sheet is used to record the opponents' statistics. It is apparent that this form requires considerable attention to record data accurately, particularly if one individual is recording data for both teams. If recorders are less experienced it may be wise to utilize several forms with different individuals recording on each. A separate rebound chart is shown in Fig. 14.5.

Fig. 14.4 allows the recorder to tally the items indicated. The recorder must locate the number (or name) of the player and then place the tally mark in the appropriate place. When using this sheet, it is wise to place the players in alphabetical order, numerical order, or list the starting five players followed by the substitutes who are most likely to see action. Whatever system is selected, it should be followed all season to make the recording easier.

Fig. 14.6 provides shooting charts for each half and a place to record the number of the player involved. A recorder may find it easier to record a number in the appropriate spot rather than searching for a name. At the end of each half the chart has to be collated to ascertain the contribution of each player. On this chart substitutions are also recorded. The number of the substitute, the number of the player for whom she is substituting, the time of the substitution and the score are all recorded. This chart identifies the total time each athlete plays and the relative degree of her contribution when the score at her entrance and exit are taken into account.

The information collected may then be consolidated on a box score sheet similar to Fig. 14.7. Cumulative statistics can then be obtained as shown in Fig. 14.8. This chart shows among other items, total rebounds and average per game, number of personal fouls and times disqualified, assists, total points and point average per game, and the player's highest point production in any one game. Turnovers and steals may also be added. The chart also provides a running account of the scores of every game and the won-lost record.

Information that can be gleaned from these statistics is useful. In relation to field goal shooting, the coach can learn who is shooting and who is not and to what extent each player is successful. If minutes played are recorded, the coach can learn point production per minute which may be a better indication of a player's shooting habits. Similar infor-

SCORE AT HALF: CMSU ________ FINAL SCORE: CMSU ________

DATE: ________ CMSU vs. ________ at ________ Opp. ________ Opp. ________

TEAM STATISTICS FOR: ________

TEAM REB
1 2 3 4 5 6 7 8
9 10 11 12 13 14

Name & No.	Field Goals....Made – Attempted	%	Free Throws....Made – Attempted	%	TP		Indiv. Rebounds	Assists	Turnover	Steals	Fouls
	1 2 3 4 5 6 7 8 9 10 11 12 13 14 15 16 17 18 1 2 3 4 5 6 7 8 9 10 11 12 13 14 15 16 17 18		1 2 3 4 5 6 7 8 9 10 11 12 13 14 1 2 3 4 5 6 7 8 9 10 11 12 13 14			O D	1 2 3 4 5 6 7 8 1 2 3 4 5 6 7 8	1 2 3 4 5 6 7 8 9 10	1 2 3 4 5 6 7 8	1 2 3 4 5	1 2 3 4 5
	1 2 3 4 5 6 7 8 9 10 11 12 13 14 15 16 17 18 1 2 3 4 5 6 7 8 9 10 11 12 13 14 15 16 17 18		1 2 3 4 5 6 7 8 9 10 11 12 13 14 1 2 3 4 5 6 7 8 9 10 11 12 13 14			O D	1 2 3 4 5 6 7 8 1 2 3 4 5 6 7 8	1 2 3 4 5 6 7 8 9 10	1 2 3 4 5 6 7 8	1 2 3 4 5	1 2 3 4 5
	1 2 3 4 5 6 7 8 9 10 11 12 13 14 15 16 17 18 1 2 3 4 5 6 7 8 9 10 11 12 13 14 15 16 17 18		1 2 3 4 5 6 7 8 9 10 11 12 13 14 1 2 3 4 5 6 7 8 9 10 11 12 13 14			O D	1 2 3 4 5 6 7 8 1 2 3 4 5 6 7 8	1 2 3 4 5 6 7 8 9 10	1 2 3 4 5 6 7 8	1 2 3 4 5	1 2 3 4 5
	1 2 3 4 5 6 7 8 9 10 11 12 13 14 15 16 17 18 1 2 3 4 5 6 7 8 9 10 11 12 13 14 15 16 17 18		1 2 3 4 5 6 7 8 9 10 11 12 13 14 1 2 3 4 5 6 7 8 9 10 11 12 13 14			O D	1 2 3 4 5 6 7 8 1 2 3 4 5 6 7 8	1 2 3 4 5 6 7 8 9 10	1 2 3 4 5 6 7 8	1 2 3 4 5	1 2 3 4 5
	1 2 3 4 5 6 7 8 9 10 11 12 13 14 15 16 17 18 1 2 3 4 5 6 7 8 9 10 11 12 13 14 15 16 17 18		1 2 3 4 5 6 7 8 9 10 11 12 13 14 1 2 3 4 5 6 7 8 9 10 11 12 13 14			O D	1 2 3 4 5 6 7 8 1 2 3 4 5 6 7 8	1 2 3 4 5 6 7 8 9 10	1 2 3 4 5 6 7 8	1 2 3 4 5	1 2 3 4 5
	1 2 3 4 5 6 7 8 9 10 11 12 13 14 15 16 17 18 1 2 3 4 5 6 7 8 9 10 11 12 13 14 15 16 17 18		1 2 3 4 5 6 7 8 9 10 11 12 13 14 1 2 3 4 5 6 7 8 9 10 11 12 13 14			O D	1 2 3 4 5 6 7 8 1 2 3 4 5 6 7 8	1 2 3 4 5 6 7 8 9 10	1 2 3 4 5 6 7 8	1 2 3 4 5	1 2 3 4 5
	1 2 3 4 5 6 7 8 9 10 11 12 13 14 15 16 17 18 1 2 3 4 5 6 7 8 9 10 11 12 13 14 15 16 17 18		1 2 3 4 5 6 7 8 9 10 11 12 13 14 1 2 3 4 5 6 7 8 9 10 11 12 13 14			O D	1 2 3 4 5 6 7 8 1 2 3 4 5 6 7 8	1 2 3 4 5 6 7 8 9 10	1 2 3 4 5 6 7 8	1 2 3 4 5	1 2 3 4 5
	1 2 3 4 5 6 7 8 9 10 11 12 13 14 15 16 17 18 1 2 3 4 5 6 7 8 9 10 11 12 13 14 15 16 17 18		1 2 3 4 5 6 7 8 9 10 11 12 13 14 1 2 3 4 5 6 7 8 9 10 11 12 13 14			O D	1 2 3 4 5 6 7 8 1 2 3 4 5 6 7 8	1 2 3 4 5 6 7 8 9 10	1 2 3 4 5 6 7 8	1 2 3 4 5	1 2 3 4 5
	1 2 3 4 5 6 7 8 9 10 11 12 13 14 15 16 17 18 1 2 3 4 5 6 7 8 9 10 11 12 13 14 15 16 17 18		1 2 3 4 5 6 7 8 9 10 11 12 13 14 1 2 3 4 5 6 7 8 9 10 11 12 13 14			O D	1 2 3 4 5 6 7 8 1 2 3 4 5 6 7 8	1 2 3 4 5 6 7 8 9 10	1 2 3 4 5 6 7 8	1 2 3 4 5	1 2 3 4 5
	1 2 3 4 5 6 7 8 9 10 11 12 13 14 15 16 17 18 1 2 3 4 5 6 7 8 9 10 11 12 13 14 15 16 17 18		1 2 3 4 5 6 7 8 9 10 11 12 13 14 1 2 3 4 5 6 7 8 9 10 11 12 13 14			O D	1 2 3 4 5 6 7 8 1 2 3 4 5 6 7 8	1 2 3 4 5 6 7 8 9 10	1 2 3 4 5 6 7 8	1 2 3 4 5	1 2 3 4 5
	1 2 3 4 5 6 7 8 9 10 11 12 13 14 15 16 17 18 1 2 3 4 5 6 7 8 9 10 11 12 13 14 15 16 17 18		1 2 3 4 5 6 7 8 9 10 11 12 13 14 1 2 3 4 5 6 7 8 9 10 11 12 13 14			O D	1 2 3 4 5 6 7 8 1 2 3 4 5 6 7 8	1 2 3 4 5 6 7 8 9 10	1 2 3 4 5 6 7 8	1 2 3 4 5	1 2 3 4 5
	1 2 3 4 5 6 7 8 9 10 11 12 13 14 15 16 17 18 1 2 3 4 5 6 7 8 9 10 11 12 13 14 15 16 17 18		1 2 3 4 5 6 7 8 9 10 11 12 13 14 1 2 3 4 5 6 7 8 9 10 11 12 13 14			O D	1 2 3 4 5 6 7 8 1 2 3 4 5 6 7 8	1 2 3 4 5 6 7 8 9 10	1 2 3 4 5 6 7 8	1 2 3 4 5	1 2 3 4 5
	1 2 3 4 5 6 7 8 9 10 11 12 13 14 15 16 17 18 1 2 3 4 5 6 7 8 9 10 11 12 13 14 15 16 17 18		1 2 3 4 5 6 7 8 9 10 11 12 13 14 1 2 3 4 5 6 7 8 9 10 11 12 13 14			O D	1 2 3 4 5 6 7 8 1 2 3 4 5 6 7 8	1 2 3 4 5 6 7 8 9 10	1 2 3 4 5 6 7 8	1 2 3 4 5	1 2 3 4 5
TOTALS											

Fig. 14.4 *Statistic Chart.*

REBOUND CHART

Team A vs. Team B At: Team A Date: Feb. 18

Name	No.	Offensive				T	Defensive				T	TT	Name	No.	Offensive				T	Defensive				T	TT
		1	2	3	4		1	2	3	4					1	2	3	4		1	2	3	4		
Brown	33	//	/		/	4	/	//	/	///	7	11	Jones	21											
Smith	24	//	/	/		4		/	//	/	4	8	Martin	32											
Propst	55	/		/		2		/			1	3	Lyon	43											
Pohlman	12	/		/		2	/		/		2	4	Young	52											
Towle	14		/			1						1	Hunt	34											
McNally	23												Black	15											
Team		/		/		2		/	/	/	3	5	Team												
Team Total		5	3	3	4	15	2	5	5	5	17	32	Team Total												
First Half		8				15	7				17	32	First Half												
Second Half			7					10					Second Half												

Fig. 14.5 *Rebound Chart.*

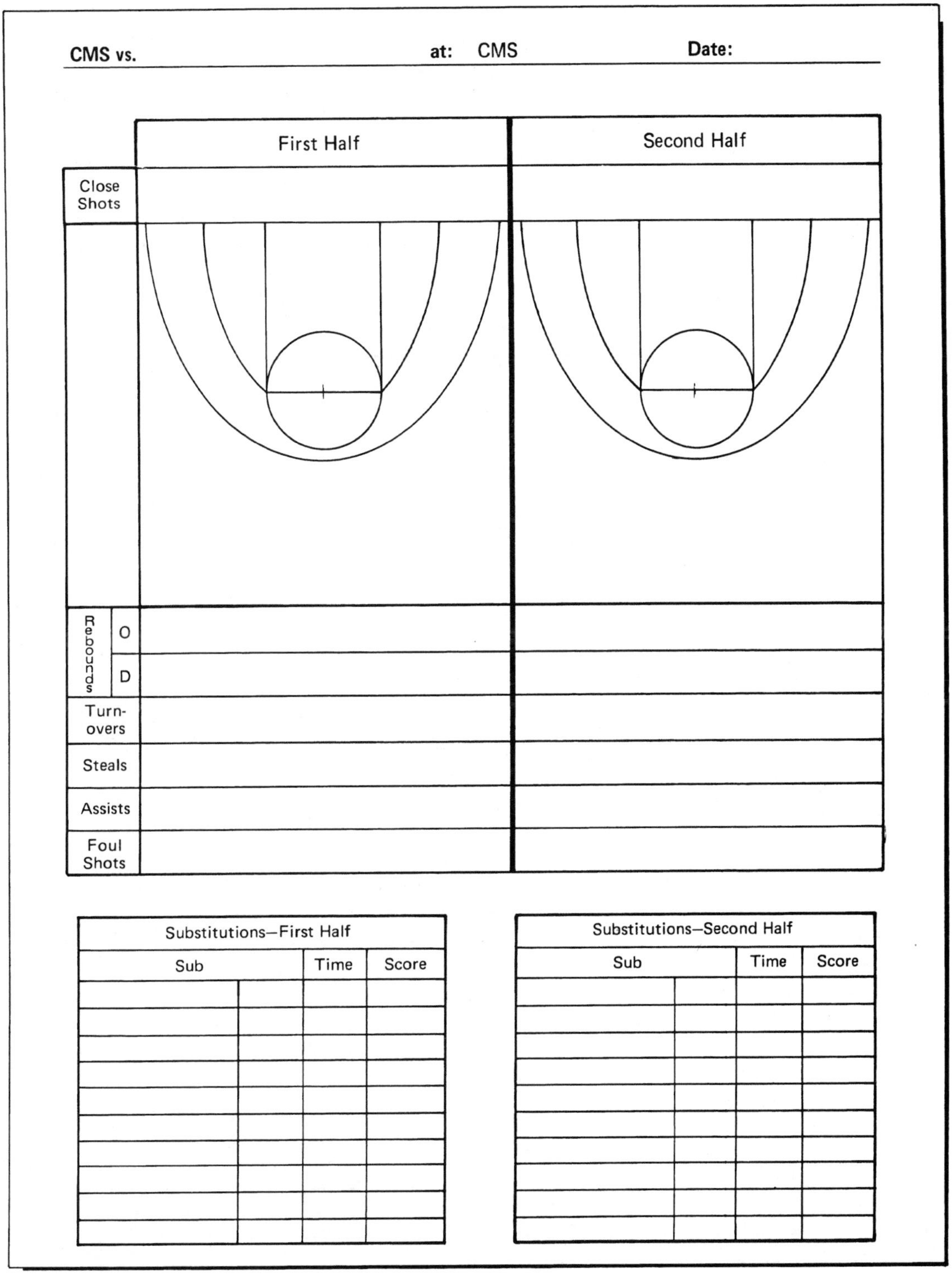

Fig. 14.6 *Shooting Chart.*

BASKETBALL BOX SCORE

CMSU	Field Goals		Free Throws		Re-bounds	Ass'ts	Per. Fouls	Total Points	Turn-overs	Steals
	Made	Att'd.	Made	Att'd.						
Kathy Anderson	6	13	1	1	6	1	4	13	2	2
Marilyn Carlson	8	13	1	1	8	2	2	17	7	1
Candy Rangler	5	11	0	0	15	1	2	10	6	0
Joyce Elder	0	4	0	0	2	3	3	0	2	2
Kathy Hargrave	2	6	0	0	1	2	1	4	3	2
Debbie Easley	3	7	0	0	3	0	1	6	2	3
Reta McCartney	0	1	0	0	0	0	0	0	0	0
Denise Toney	2	2	6	9	4	1	3	10	2	1
Linda Scott	0	1	0	0	0	0	2	0	0	1
TOTALS	26	58	8	11	39	10	18	60	24	12

PERCENTAGES: FGs: 1st H __49.1%__ 2nd H __36.6%__ Game __44.8%__   Shots Missed __25__

FTs: 1st H __80.0%__ 2nd H __66.6%__ Game __72.7%__   Team Rebounds __6__

ISU	Field Goals		Free Throws		Re-bounds	Ass'ts	Per. Fouls	Total Points	Turn-overs	Rec.
	Made	Att'd.	Made	Att'd.						
Pat Simpson	4	11	3	4	8	0	4	11	2	3
Cathy Lyon	8	21	1	1	1	0	3	17	2	2
Sue Mitchell	3	12	0	0	4	0	3	6	4	3
Beth Lerner	4	8	0	2	10	0	2	8	6	3
Joan Goodrich	2	6	0	0	1	0	1	4	3	0
Sue Perkins	1	1	0	0	1	0	0	2	1	1
Laurie Reese	1	2	0	3	4	0	3	2	1	0
Lydia Johnston	0	0	2	2	0	0	0	2	0	0
Barb Ruby	1	3	2	2	0	0	1	4	0	1
TOTALS	24	64	8	14	29	0	17	56	19	13

PERCENTAGES: FGs: 1st H __33.3%__ 2nd H __41.2%__ Game __37.5%__   Shots Missed __46__

FTs: 1st H __75.0%__ 2nd H __33.3%__ Game __57.1%__   Team Rebounds __7__

Officials _____

Attendance __7500__

Date __1-29-79__

SCORE BY PERIODS	1	2	3	4	OT	OT	FINAL
CMSU	34	26					60
ISU	25	31					56

Fig. 14.7 *Box Score.*

356

(Final)

1976–77 Central Missouri State University Jennies
Cumulative Basketball Statistics Through 29 Games

Name	G	FGM-FGA	FG%	FTM-FTA	FT%	REB-AVG	PF-D	A	PTS-AVG	HG
Kathy Anderson	29	174–375	46.4	70–125	56.0	206–7.1	98–4	20	418–14.4	35
Marilyn Carlson	29	170–365	46.6	61–107	57.0	230–7.9	82–4	67	401–13.8	28
Candy Rangler	29	179–338	52.9	42–66	63.6	311–10.7	99–9	18	400–13.8	29
Joyce Elder	29	109–257	42.4	34–60	56.7	106–3.6	66–1	35	252–8.7	20
Denise Toney	29	57–123	46.3	63–108	58.3	104–3.6	82–2	15	177–6.1	16
Kathy Hargrave	28	52–142	36.6	25–34	73.5	29–1.0	37	30	129–4.6	17
Debbie Easley	29	49–147	33.3	22–32	68.7	60–2.	36	20	120–4.1	14
Reta McCartney	29	33–81	40.1	18–31	58.1	43–1.5	31	3	84–2.9	10
Ellie Kunkel	16	14–34	41.2	3–5	60.0	16–1.0	10	7	31–1.9	6
Linda Scott	26	17–58	29.3	12–27	44.4	33–1.3	32–1	25	46–1.8	6
Sheryl Burgener	13	6–22	27.3	1–6	16.6	8–0.6	12	3	13–1.0	5
Christy Lewis	13	5–16	31.2	1–3	33.3	9–0.7	6	2	11–0.8	2
**Reiko Schroff	2	0–0	00.0	2–2	100.0	0–0.0	0	0	2–1.0	2
CMSU TOTALS	29	863–1958	44.1	354–606	58.4	1155–39.8	591–21	245	2080–71.7	97
OPP TOTALS	22	527–1466	35.9	244–422	57.8	730–33.1	426–11	99	1298–59.0	83

Date	Opponent	Score	W—L	Leading Scorer		Leading Rebounder	
*12-6-76	Simpson College	93–70	1–0	Anderson	35	Anderson 13	
12-8-76	Tarkio College	44–66	1–1	Carlson	15	Carlson 8	
12-10-76	Southeast Missouri	97–42	2–1	Anderson	17	Rangler 12	
12-11-76	U. of Tenn.-Martin	78–64	3–1	Elder	20	Carlson 11	
#*12-17-76	Stephen F. Austin	58–67	3–2	Rangler/Anderson	10	Rangler 11	
#*12-17-76	E. Kentucky Univ.	78–69	4–2	Rangler	28	Rangler 11	
#*12-18-76	Clemson U. (SC)	86–76	5–2	Anderson	27	Rangler 11	
#*12-18-76	Kentucky University	67–74	5–3	Anderson	18	Rangler 11	
1-7-77	Grand View College	76–42	6–3	Anderson	22	Anderson/Carlson 7	
***1-12-77	Southwest Missouri	65–56	7–3	Carlson	28	Carlson 16	
1-14-77	SIU-Carbondale	56–42	8–3	Rangler	23	Rangler 9	
1-16-77	St. Louis Univ.	81–48	9–3	Anderson	15	Rangler 20	
1-18-77	U. of MO.-St. Louis	80–48	10–3	Anderson	24	Rangler 16	
1-21-77	Northeast Missouri	69–58	11–3	Anderson	18	Anderson/Carlson 7	
1-26-77	Northwest Missouri	63–56	12–3	Anderson	16	Rangler 13	
1-29-77	Iowa State Univ.	60–56	13–3	Carlson	17	Rangler 15	
@2-4-77	E. Kentucky Univ.	81–83	13–4	Carlson/Rangler	19	Rangler 8	
@2-5-77	U. of Northern Iowa	66–62	14–4	Anderson	13	Anderson/Carlson 7	
@2-5-77	U. of Indiana	57–41	15—4	Carlson/Rangler	15	Carlson 14	
2-8-77	U. of MO.-Columbia	73–63	16–4	Rangler	22	Rangler 19	
2-12-77	U. of Kansas	70–68 (OT)	17–4	Rangler	22	Rangler 19	
2-14-77	Kansas State Univ.	76–61	17–5	Anderson	23	Rangler 10	
***2-19-77	Wichita State Univ.	65–56	18–5	Carlson	14	Rangler 11	
2-21-77	Emporia-K.S.C.	71–54	19–5	Rangler	18	Rangler 15	
##2-25-77	Southwest Missouri	67–52	20–5	Carlson	19	Carlson 13	
##2-26-77	U. of MO.-Columbia	91–88 (OT)	21–5	Rangler	24	Carlson 12	
@@3-10-77	St. Cloud State U.	66–53	22–5	Carlson/Rangler	16	Rangler 11	
@@3-11-77	U. of MO. Columbia	71–69	22–6	Rangler	29	Rangler 17	
@@3-12-77	U. of Neb. Omaha	81–77 (OT)	23–6	Rangler	19	Rangler 13	

#Mississippi University for Women Tournament
@Illinois State University Invitational Tournament for Women
##AIAW Missouri Women's Basketball Tournament
@@AIAW Region Six Large College Basketball Tournament
*Opponent Statistics Not Available **No Longer On Team
***Assist Statistics Not Available

Fig. 14.8 *Accumulative Statistics.*

mation is available for free throw shooting.

In reviewing the rebound data on the box score and cumulative statistics, the coach can evaluate team strength by ascertaining whether the team has outrebounded the opponents. Also, individual strength on the defensive and offensive boards can be evaluated. Collectively, a team should attempt to pull down 40 percent of its total rebounds on the offensive boards. This figure includes team rebounds as well. (A separate place to record team rebounds should appear on any rebounding chart.) Because a rebound must be recorded for every missed shot, any time a player cannot be credited with a rebound, a team must. This includes the following situations:

1. a violation is called after a free throw is attempted.
2. a foul is called after a field goal is attempted.
3. either a free throw or field goal goes out-of-bounds before it is touched by any player.
4. a shot is blocked and goes out-of-bounds (if it remains in play, whoever recovers it is credited with the rebound).
5. a team gains possession of the ball after a tap on a held ball that results from a rebound.

Assists are awarded to players who pass the ball directly to a player who shoots and scores. Should the player precede her shot with a dribble, no assist is awarded. A team that has few assists recorded relies on individual moves with the ball (one-on-one tactics) to score. A team with a high number of assists possesses one or more players who are excellent passers.

A turnover is charged against any offensive player who commits a violation or an offensive foul before her team attempts a field goal on that possession. Players who commit a large number of turnovers need more practice in basic skills. The coach must recognize that the ball handlers on the team are likely to have more turnovers because they handle the ball considerably more than their teammates. Nevertheless, a ball handler who commits many turnovers needs to be replaced!

Shot Chart

Coaches who wish to know where shots are attempted use what is commonly called a Shot Chart. Shots attempted at the basket to the charter's left are recorded on the left side of the diagram. The number of each player who attempts a field goal is recorded where the shot is attempted; if successful,

a circle is placed around the number. If the coach desires additional information about the type of shot taken and how it was derived, other symbols may be used. In this way it can be determined how many shots resulted from a fast break and drives and whether the shot was a layup, tip-in, hook, or jump shot.

Fig. 14.9 shows only a portion of the entire shot chart. Preferably on one sheet, there should be four diagrams for recording data for each quarter. Following the second diagram, in addition to the totals for that quarter, space should also be provided for totals for the first half. This should also be included following the fourth quarter for totals for the second half only, and an additional line for totals for the entire game. For college games only two diagrams are needed but some coaches prefer to use four diagrams and divide each half into quarters for each in recording and analyzing. An alternative is to use a multicolored pen to identify each ten minute segment in a different color.

In a game that is likely to be a high scoring affair or that may result in many layups, it is wise to record those shots at the end line so that the diagram does not become cluttered and numbers indistinguishable. This is absolutely necessary if the type of shot is also recorded because of the additional space it requires.

The Shot Chart shows that Team A attempted thirteen shots and made six. They made three out of five layups and attempted six other shots within 15 ft. of the basket and made three of them. Two long set shots were missed. They had two fast break attempts and scored on both of them. In one instance, player No. 3 stopped to shoot a jump shot. Player No. 5 had the only jump shot she attempted, blocked. The team attempted no hook shots or tip-ins. Players 5 and 12 were both fouled on attempted shots. Both made the shots, and No. 12 converted hers into a three-point play.

In analyzing the data, the team was successful in penetrating the opponent's defense for many shots within good shooting range. They should continue to maneuver in the same manner, and players 12 and 3 should be discouraged from any further attempts at long shots and encouraged to pass the ball into better scoring position. In viewing this chart, the opponents must change their defense so that they do not allow the extensive penetration into the lane. Since one opponent has not attempted any shots, they should loosen their defense against her and allow that defensive player to help her teammates when necessary.

Team B attempted ten shots and was successful

SHOT CHART

First Quarter _Team A_ vs. _Team B_ At: _Team B_ Date: _Feb. 8_

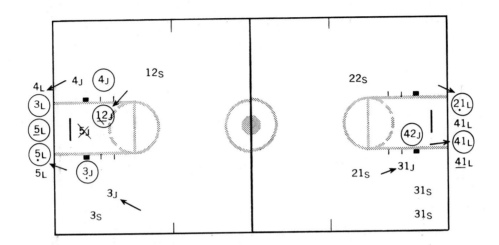

FGA _13_ FGM _6_ % _46_

Offense Used _2-3_

Opponent's Defense _M-M_

FGA _10_ FGM _3_ % _30_

Offense Used _2-3_

Opponent's Defense _2-1-2 zone_

H	hook shot
J	jump shot
L	layup
S	set shot
T	tip-in
←	drive
•	shot completing a fast break
✕	blocked shot
4	shot missed
④	shot made
—	fouled
+	fouled; made the free throw

Fig. 14.9 _Shot Chart._

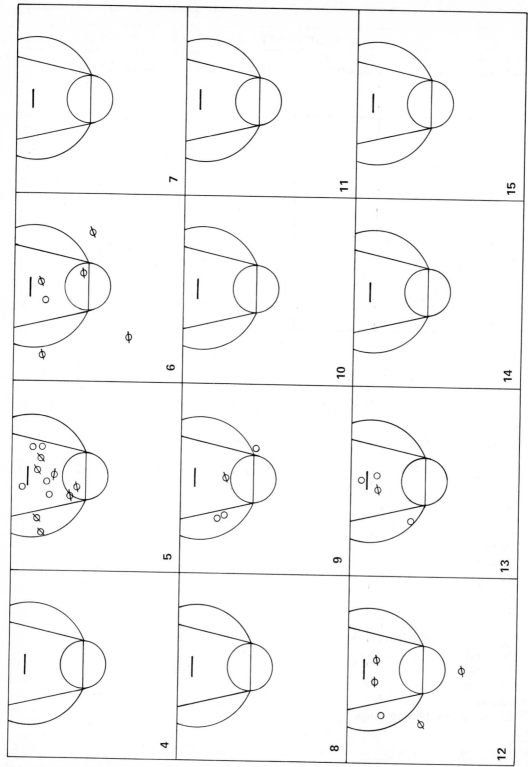

Fig. 14.10 *International Shot Chart*

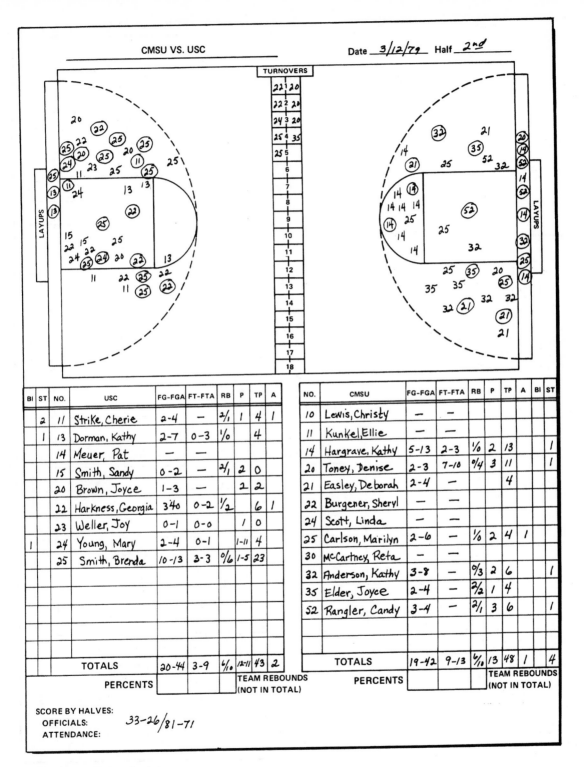

CMSU VS. USC   Date 3/12/79 Half 2nd

TURNOVERS

BI	ST	NO.	USC	FG-FGA	FT-FTA	RB	P	TP	A
	2	11	Strike, Cherie	2-4	—	2/1	1	4	1
	1	13	Dorman, Kathy	2-7	0-3	1/0		4	
		14	Meuer, Pat	—	—				
		15	Smith, Sandy	0-2	—	2/1	2	0	
		20	Brown, Joyce	1-3	—			2	2
		22	Harkness, Georgia	3-40	0-2	1/2		6	1
		23	Weller, Joy	0-1	0-0		1	0	
	1	24	Young, Mary	2-4	0-1		1-11	4	
		25	Smith, Brenda	10-13	3-3	0/6	1-5	23	
			TOTALS	20-44	3-9	6/0	12-11	43	2
			PERCENTS				**TEAM REBOUNDS** (NOT IN TOTAL)		

NO.	CMSU	FG-FGA	FT-FTA	RB	P	TP	A	BI	ST
10	Lewis, Christy	—	—						
11	Kunkel, Ellie	—	—						
14	Hargrave, Kathy	5-13	2-3	1/0	2	13			1
20	Toney, Denise	2-3	7-10	0/4	3	11			1
21	Easley, Deborah	2-4	—			4			
22	Burgener, Sheryl	—	—						
24	Scott, Linda	—	—						
25	Carlson, Marilyn	2-6	—	1/0	2	4	1		
30	McCartney, Reta	—	—						
32	Anderson, Kathy	3-8	—	0/3	2	6			1
35	Elder, Joyce	2-4	—	2/1	1	4			
52	Rangler, Candy	3-4	—	2/1	3	6			1
	TOTALS	19-42	9-13	6/0	13	48	1		4
	PERCENTS				**TEAM REBOUNDS** (NOT IN TOTAL)				

SCORE BY HALVES:
OFFICIALS: 33-26/81-71
ATTENDANCE:

Fig. 14.11 *Half Time Statistics.*

ABBREVIATED HALFTIME BOX   Date _____ 1-29-79 _____

Crowd _____

	CMSU		ISU	
Halftime Score	34		25	
Field Goals Attempted	28		27	
Field Goals Made	15		11	
Field Goal Percentage	53.6%		40.7%	
Free Throws Attempted	5		4	
Free Throws Made	4		3	
Free Throws Percentage	80%		75%	
Rebounds (Total Individual)	18 + 1		12	
Individual Scoring Leaders	Kathy Anderson	7	Cathy Lyon	9
	Marilyn Carlson	8		
	Candy Rangler	6		
Individual Rebounds Leaders	Candy Rangler	10	Pat Simpson	5
Players With Three or More Personal Fouls			Pat Simpson	3

Additional Information _____

_____

_____

_____

_____

_____

Fig. 14.12 *Half Time Totals.*

362

CMSU vs. ISU   *January 29, 1979*

Time	CMSU	ISU	Score
			0–0
19:34	Carlson Foul		0–2
19:24		Simpson Jump	2–2
19:03	Anderson Jump		2–4
18:10		Goodrich Jump	4–4
17:51	Carlson Jump		4–4
17:33		Mitchell Foul	4–4
17:22	Elder Foul		4–4
17:06		Simpson Foul	4–4
16:41	Hargrave Foul		4–4
16:39		Simpson Foul	6–4
16:31	Carlson Layup		6–6
16:00		Goodrich Jump	8–6
15:42	Rangler Jump		8–8
15:30		Goodrich Jump	10–8
15:10	Rangler Jump		12–8
14:48	Hargrave Jump		12–10
14:23		Lyon Jump	12–10
13:35	Elder Foul		12–12
13:20		Lerner Layup	12–12
11:47	Anderson Foul		12–14
11:31		Lyon Jump	12–14
10:59		Mitchell Foul	12–14
10:31		Lyon Foul	14–14
10:06	Toney Jump		15–14
10:06	Toney Makes 1 of 1	Lerner Foul	17–14
09:37	Anderson Jump	Simpson Foul	18–14
09:37	Anderson Makes 1 of 1		18–14
09:34		Time Out	18–16
09:22		Lyon Jump	20–16
09:10	Anderson Jump		20–19
08:47	Scott Foul	Lyon Makes 1 of 1/Jump	22–19
07:44	Carlson Jump		22–21
07:19		Mitchell Jump	24–21
06:47	Easley Jump		24–23
06:27		Perkins Jump	26–23
05:42	Toney Layup		26–23
05:35		Time Out	28–23
05:18	Toney Makes 2 of 2	Goodrich Foul	30–23
05:19	Rangler Jump		30–23
04:01	Carlson Foul	Lerner Misses 1 of 1	30–23
02:53	Toney Misses 1 of 1	Lyon Foul	32–23
01:20	Carlson Jump		34–23
00:54	Anderson Layup		34–25
00:01	Rangler Foul	Johnston Makes 2 of 2	

Fig. 14.13 *Play by Play.*

on only three of them. All three were from close range — one, a result of a fast break and the other a hook shot by No. 42. They attempted four long shots and were not successful on any of them. Player No. 41 was fouled on one of her attempted layup shots. All players attempted a shot, but only three scored and no one scored more than one field goal. There were no tip-in attempts.

Team B was successful on two out of three of their driving attempts, so they should attempt to score in this fashion more often. They must adjust their offense so that they can secure better percentage shots. They must also attempt to score more from the left side unless that defender is particularly strong and the right side defender is weak. Team A should continue to use the same defensive tactics, but should question why more shots have been taken from the right side than the left side. Nevertheless, they should not extend their defense to the right until player No. 31 or others begin to score.

At the end of each period the coach makes a similar analysis before offering suggestions to the players. At the end of the game the data should be totaled so that there is an individual record for each player by game and totals for the season. This analysis should include the type of shot attempted (if desired), whether the shot was successful or not, from what range, the number of shots that were blocked, the times she was fouled, and the number of three-point plays that resulted (if desired).

An example of a shot chart used in some international play is shown in Fig. 14.10. It contains twelve sections with each player's number listed in the lower left-hand corner. This sheet was used in the first half of a game. Another sheet is needed for the second half. As can be seen, only players numbered 5, 6, 9, 12, and 13 attempted shots. A circle represents an attempted field goal; a circle with a dash shows a successful attempt. This chart with the width of the international lanes can be adopted for United States play.

Statistics for Each Half of the Contest

Figs. 14.11 and 14.12 show examples of data for each half of a game. The information is self-explanatory. The coach must decide what information is desired and develop a suitable form to accumulate the data.

OFFENSIVE EFFICIENCY RATING (OER)

A system for determining offensive efficiency was developed by Paul Keller. By using his system a coach can learn how many points are scored on every possession. Theoretically two points can be scored on each possession, but realistically less than that actually is scored. Offensive rebounding and few turnovers contribute to a good OER.

PLAY-BY-PLAY RECORD

It is possible to record a play-by-play of the game while it is in progress. This record shows the score at any given time; the number of times the game is tied; the number of times the lead changes; the length of time a team goes without scoring; the length of time a team goes without scoring a field goal; or the length of time a team holds the opposition scoreless. Through analyzing a number of these charts a coach may learn which players tend to be clutch shooters.

Through use of the chart, a coach can recall, following a game, the exact sequence of events. Often this information is hard to recall, especially in close contests. Fig. 14.13 shows a sample of a play-by-play record as actually typed while the game was in progress.

In international competition outside the United States this tabulation is used on international score sheets to record the scoring. The basic difference is that the exact time is not recorded for scoring, only the minute in which the scoring occurred. The conventional score sheet as known in the United States is not used elsewhere in the world.

POSTSEASON PROCEDURES

The first thing a coach probably wants to do at the end of the season is to emit a large sigh and then enjoy the first weekend at home in several months! After that the coach should check to see that accumulated statistics are compiled, records are recorded, and equipment is checked in, cleaned, and properly stored.

Often a team enjoys scheduling a banquet, picnic, supper, or other get-together to complete their season. This should be encouraged.

Glossary

Alive. A term used to denote an offensive player who has not yet dribbled.

Assist. Credit awarded a player who passes to a teammate if the pass results in an immediate score.

Attack. Offense. An act by which a team attempts to score.

Attack Players. Players on the team in possession of the ball who are attempting to score.

Backcourt. That half of a court which a team defends; that half of the court which the opponents attack.

Backcourt Players. Players who play in the guard position; may be two guards in a double-guard offense or a point guard.

Backdoor Cut (play). A reverse cut — one in which a player cuts behind her defender in an attempt to become free to receive a pass.

Ball Control. That type of offensive system in which a team moves slowly downcourt and passes carefully until an opportunity arises for a high percentage shot; it is the opposite of a fast break style of play.

Blast. An offensive maneuver in which a player (usually a guard) cuts hard for the basket, often when the post player has the ball.

Blocking Out. A tactic employed by the defensive team to keep the offensive players behind them and prevent them from gaining good rebounding position.

Corner. That area of the court that is approximately 5 ft. in from the intersection of the endline and each of the sidelines at both ends of the court.

Corner Player. A player who is positioned in the corner.

Cover a Passing Lane. A tactic used by a defensive player in which she plays in front of her opponent or at an intercepting angle between her opponent and the passer.

Cross Block. A tactic in which a defender first moves over to guard a free opponent who is prepared to shoot and then blocks her out from the rebound. Meanwhile the defensive player assigned to guard the free opponent moves over to block out her teammate's opponent.

Cut. An offensive technique in which a player runs to a clear space on the court either to get free for a pass or to clear a space for a teammate.

Deep Rebound Position. The position taken by one of the defenders at the top of the circle when a shot is attempted.

Defense. The act by which a team attempts to prevent the opponents from scoring.

Defensive Balance. A tactic used by the offensive team while in their frontcourt. One or more players are assigned to be in the free throw area or at the top of the circle in a position to defend if the opponents gain possession of the ball.

Defensive Players. Players on the team which does not have possession of the ball.

Defensive Team. The team that is not in possession of the ball.

365

Double Cut. A scissor maneuver involving a post player with the ball and two players cutting off the post.

Double-Team. An act by a defensive team in which two players guard one opponent; utilized extensively when employing a zone press.

Drive. A tactic used by an offensive player in which she dribbles toward the basket.

Far Side Corner. The corner player on the side away from the ball.

Far Side Forward. The forward on the side away from the ball.

Far Side Guard. The guard on the side away from the ball.

Far Side Wing. The wing on the side away from the ball.

Fast Break. An act by the offensive team to move rapidly from their backcourt to their frontcourt in an attempt to gain a player advantage — particularly, in a two-on-one or three-on-two situation.

Five-on-Five. Five attack players maneuvering against five defensive players.

Float. Floating — a defensive tactic in which a player moves laterally toward the basket when an opponent is two passes away from the player with the ball.

Four-on-Four. Four attack players maneuvering against four defensive players.

Free Lance. A type of offense in which players are given freedom in their moves to take advantage of defensive weaknesses.

Front. Fronting — a defensive tactic in which a player (often a pivot defender) is between her opponent and the ball in an effort to prevent her opponent from receiving a pass.

Frontcourt. The half of the court that contains the goal for which a team is shooting.

Give and Go. Pass and cut. An offensive play in which a player passes to a teammate and cuts for the basket.

Hedge. A tactic used by a defensive player to help a teammate who is screened. It is executed by taking a step toward the side of the driving opponent to force her to go wide around the screen and allow the screened defender time to regain good defensive positioning; the player hedging then returns to guarding her own opponent.

Help and Recover. Hedge. A defensive tactic in which a player steps out to help a teammate who

temporarily has lost good position against her opponent and then recovers against her own player.

High Post. A player who positions herself 15 ft. or more from the basket with her back to the basket for the primary purpose of passing to cutters.

In-bounder. The player who puts the ball in play from out-of-bounds.

Inside Screen. An offensive tactic in which a player cuts to a position between a teammate and her opponent. The player may stop in front of her teammate or continue running beyond her teammate.

Lateral Cross. A term usually applied to two guards moving laterally. The guard on the right side of the court moves to the left side, and the guard on the left side moves to the right side. They usually cross close together with an inside or back screen or inside screen variation. The term may also be applied to the point guard and wing who move in the same manner.

Lateral Screen. Side Screen. A maneuver in which an offensive player sets a screen to the side of an opponent.

Low Post. A player who maneuvers through the free throw lane or positions herself outside the lane within 9 ft. of the basket for the primary purpose of scoring; when outside the lane she stands with her back to the basket.

Medium Post. A player who cuts through the free throw lane or positions herself to the side of the lane 9–15 ft. from the basket. She has her back to the basket and attempts to score or pass off from this position.

Middle Rebound Position. The position taken by a member of the defensive team near the free throw line to secure a long rebound away from the basket.

Near Side Corner. The corner player on the side on which the ball is being played.

Near Side Forward. The forward on the side on which the ball is being played.

Near Side Guard. The guard on the side on which the ball is being played.

Near Side Wing. The wing player on the side on which the ball is being played.

Offense. The act by which a team attempts to score.

Offensive Players. Players on the team in possession of the ball who are trying to score.

One-on-One. One attack player maneuvering against one defensive player.

Open Stance. A position taken by a defensive player in which she places her inside foot back so that she is partially facing the ball.

Outlet Pass. The initial pass made following a rebound usually toward one of the sidelines.

Outside Screen. An offensive tactic in which a player cuts to a position basket side of a teammate and her opponent. In this position the player may stop or continue running beyond.

Overplay. A term used to describe defensive position against a player with the ball or against a player one pass away from the ball. When used against a player without the ball, the defender steps up into the passing lane and encourages her opponent to go backdoor. Against a ball handler the defender forces her opponent to go in a predetermined direction. The defender plays either with one foot opposite the midline of her opponent and the other foot to the side, or she plays with one foot opposite one foot of her opponent and the other foot to the side.

Pass and Cut. An offensive tactic in which a player passes to a teammate and cuts for a return pass. The player may make a front or backdoor cut.

Passing Game. An offense popularized in the 1970s based on screens away from the ball. It is primarily a free lance system guided by certain rules for movement.

Passing Lane. The term used to denote the path through which the ball must go; usually used to refer to the direct path between the passer and a receiver.

Penetrate. A term used to indicate the need for the attack to get the ball within the area covered by a zone defense; passing or driving into the lane area. Sometimes used in reference to man-to-man defense.

Percentage Shot. A shot, taken near the goal, which has a good chance of being successful. Shots taken closer to the basket have a higher percentage of success.

Perimeter. A term usually used in connection with the position of the defensive players; it is the area outside (away from the basket) all of the defenders.

Pivot. Post. A player who maneuvers close to the basket, usually through the free throw lane or just outside of it, for the purpose of shooting or passing to cutters; also, a means of turning while keeping one foot stationary.

Point Guard. A player who plays in the point position; used when a team uses a single guard in their offense.

Point Position. That area on the court that is roughly 5 sq ft. located just outside the top of the restraining circle at each end of the court.

Post. Pivot. A player who maneuvers close to the basket, usually through the free throw lane or just outside of it, for the purpose of shooting or passing to cutters.

Press. A defensive tactic attempted to force the opponents to make errors. It may be executed using man-to-man or zone defense and can be applied full, three-quarter court, or half court; it often involves double-teaming tactics.

Pressing Defense. Tight defense. An aggressive defense in which the defenders overplay their opponents. It may involve a single player, several players, or a whole team. It may be used full court or in the defensive end only. If played by the whole team, it usually involves double-teaming and some zone principles.

Rear Screen. An offensive tactic in which a player cuts away from the basket to an open space and stands while a teammate drives or cuts around her.

Reverse Cut. A backdoor cut. A player cuts behind her defender in an attempt to become free to receive a pass.

Roll. An offensive technique in which a player pivots and cuts for the basket after having set a screen. The roll is an effective technique when the opponents play a switching man-to-man defense.

Run and Jump. A switching defense in which a nearby defender moves out to surprise a dribbler and continues to defend against her. The dribbler's former defender switches to defend against a free opponent.

Sag. Sagging — a defensive tactic in which a player drops back toward the basket and away from her opponent.

Sagging Defense. A tactic in which defensive players slide away from their opponent back toward the basket. This tactic may be used by an entire team when the opponents are beyond shooting distance, or it may be used by weak side players to permit them to see the ball and their opponent at the same time, and to be in a position to help against a lob or backdoor cut.

Scissors. Double cut. A maneuver involving a post player with the ball and two players cutting off the post.

Screen. An offensive technique designed to temporarily delay the progress of an opponent or to force her to move in a path other than that which she desires.

Side Screen. Lateral Screen. A maneuver in which an offensive player sets a screen to the side of an opponent.

Strong Side. A term used to refer to a portion of the offensive alignment. It refers to the side of the court in which there are three or more offensive players; it does not refer to the position of the ball or the abilities of the players involved.

Three-on-Three. Three attack players maneuvering against three defensive players.

Tight Defense. Pressing defense. An aggressive defense in which the defenders play close to their opponents and usually cover the direct passing lane. It may involve a single player, several players, or a whole team; it may be used full court or in the defensive end only. If played by the whole team, it usually involves double-teaming and some zone principles.

Top of the Circle. That area outside the restraining circle at each end of the court, approximately 21–25 ft. from the basket.

Trap. A defensive tactic in which two players double-team an opponent. Often used when the double-team takes place near a sideline or in the corner.

Turnover. An act by the offensive team in which they lose possession of the ball before they can attempt a shot; caused by a violation, interception, or poor pass.

Two-on-Two. Two attack players maneuvering against two defensive players.

Weak Side. A term used to refer to a portion of the offensive alignment. It refers to the side of the court in which only two offensive players are positioned. It does not refer at all to the position of the ball or the abilities of the players involved.

Weave. An offensive tactic in which three or five (usually three) players dribble and hand the ball off in a figure eight pattern.

Wing. Position — a term used to denote a place on the court approximately 10 ft. on each side of the free throw line and opposite it.

Zone. A method used by the defense in which they guard from the goal outward. Players are responsible for a particular area on the court rather than a specific player.

Index